THE TREE OF GERNIKA

THE TREE
OF GERNIKA

A Field Study of Modern War

G. L. STEER

With a new introduction by
Nicholas Rankin

faber and faber

This edition first published in 2009
by Faber and Faber Ltd
Bloomsbury House, 74–77 Great Russell Street
London WC1B 3DA

Printed by CPI Antony Rowe, Eastbourne

A CIP record for this book is available from the British Library

ISBN 978-0-571-25513-9

INTRODUCTION

Nicholas Rankin

George Lowther Steer raced through his life, packing eight books and four wars into his final decade, and died abruptly at the age of thirty-five when he crashed an overloaded jeep in wartime Bengal on Christmas Day 1944. By then he was a lieutenant colonel in the Intelligence Corps of the British Army, commanding the Indian Field Broadcasting Units he had founded for the Special Operations Executive. His armed propaganda squads worked at close quarters in Burma, megaphoning music and messages to Japanese soldiers in their bunkers, trying to get them to surrender, and they also moved among the local villagers, setting up markets and networks, doing 'hearts and minds' work. The impact of the crash tore the watch he habitually wore off Steer's wrist. When his Indian soldiers found it near his body, they read the inscription on its back: 'TO STEER FROM EUZKADI' – to Steer from the autonomous Basque Republic.

To understand why the Basque people gave Steer that gold watch, and why seven decades later their descendants erected a bronze bust of the young foreigner in the very heart of their homeland, take the advice that the American war correspondent Martha Gellhorn gave her mentor Eleanor Roosevelt early in 1938:

> You must read a book by a man named Steer: it is called the Tree of Gernika. It is about the fight of the Basques – he's the London Times man – and no better book has come out of the war and he says well all the things I have tried to say to you the times I saw you, after Spain. It is beautifully written and true, and few books are like that, and fewer still that deal with war. Please get it.

'The war' was the Spanish Civil War, which started in July 1936 when General Francisco Franco led a right-wing insurrection against the left-wing government of the Republic of Spain, and did not end until April 1939. As the country fractured and crazed along many dividing lines, the Republic offered greater autonomy to Spain's regions in return for their military support against Franco's rebels. The two richest industrial areas in the north-west and north-east, the Basque country and Catalonia, went for the deal. People in both areas spoke their own language, enjoyed their own distinctive cultural traditions, and nursed dreams of Basque or Catalan nationhood. General Franco's rebels, however, claiming to speak for the greater nationalism of one unified Spain, hated any devolution from central control and, summoning military aid from foreign powers like Nazi Germany and Fascist Italy, determined to destroy the 'Red separatists'.

G. L. Steer, not long returned from the Italo-Abyssinian war, reported some of this early fighting in north-west Spain for *The Times*, and slowly got drawn deeper into the lives of the beret-wearing Basque people. *The Tree of Gernika* tells how Euzkadi, the democratic republic that the Basques created in their green homeland by the Bay of Biscay, fought for freedom and decency in an atrocious civil war. After a year of struggle, blockaded by sea, bombed from the air, fighting against overwhelming odds in their own hills, the Basques in the end lost to Franco's forces – but they lost honourably, without resorting to murder, torture and treachery.

Steer was a twenty-seven-year-old reporter, then freelancing for *The Times*, when he wrote the most important dispatch of his life, alerting the whole world to the destruction from the air of the town that Basques spell Gernika and Spaniards Guernica. His story, run by both *The Times* and the *New York Times* (which put it on its front page) on Wednesday 28 April 1937, described how a fleet of German aircraft dumped high-explosive blast-bombs and thousands of thermite incendiary bombs on Gernika, the undefended small town whose oak-tree symbolised Basque liberties and democracy, while German fighter planes swooped low to machine-gun its fleeing civilians.

Now the twentieth century's greatest painter enters the story. Reading about this atrocity in the newspapers and seeing stark photos of the burning town at night, Pablo Picasso in Paris began painting his huge black and white canvas *Guernica*. Meanwhile, the strong public reaction to the bombing of civilians forced a change in the hands-off policy of the British government, which subsequently allowed 4,000 Basque children to find refuge, and new lives, in the United Kingdom.

The Tree of Gernika, subtitled *A Field Study of Modern War*, was first published by Hodder & Stoughton in January 1938, a few months after the Basques were defeated by Franco's forces, with many imprisoned and thousands more forced into exile. In his scholarly study *The Royal Navy and the Siege of Bilbao* (CUP, 1979), the diplomatist and naval historian Sir James Cable recognised Steer's book as 'a work of passionate engagement, a vivid, moving, exciting justification of Basque nationalism, a shrewd, if slanted, analysis of the circumstances and causes of their defeat, an urgent warning to his own countrymen of the wrath to come.' For Cable, 'the special value of [Steer's] account . . . resides in its very bias.'

'It goes without saying', George Orwell opened his *Time and Tide* review of *The Tree of Gernika* in February 1938, 'that everyone who writes of the Spanish war writes as a partisan.' But then there is really no such thing as objective war reporting. 'In a war, you must hate somebody or love somebody', the Hungarian war photographer Robert Capa once said, 'you must have a position or you cannot stand what goes on.' (Quoted in John G. Morris, *Get the Picture: A Personal History of Photojournalism*, Chicago, 2002.) In her biography *Martha Gellhorn* (Chatto & Windus, 2003), Caroline Moorehead suggests that the murderous violence of the Spanish Civil War made Gellhorn question 'all that objectivity shit.' Her first-ever dispatch from a war zone was about the citizens of Madrid trying to live their daily lives under erratic and brutal shelling; for Gellhorn, the pity and terror of such events made 'objectivity' inhuman.

The Tree of Gernika is a masterpiece of narrative history and eyewitness reporting by someone close to the key events, for Steer was granted unrivalled access by the Basque government. Why did Steer get on so well with the Basques? For one thing, they were 'not very Continental', not the dodgy and over-excitable foreigners that what he called 'the bonehead Englishman' traditionally despised. It is as well to deal with such racial stereotypes from the start because Steer calls the Basques a 'race' in the very first sentence of the introduction to *The Tree of Gernika*. Although educated at Winchester and

Oxford, Steer was born and spent his childhood in South Africa where people thought in terms of 'races'. A creature of his age, Steer generalises and typifies, writing of 'the Basques' and 'the Basque' because cultural difference is the crux of his story. In chapters II and III of *The Tree of Gernika* (deliberately *not* spelled 'Guernica', to assert local rights) Steer explained that Basque nationalism and Basque democracy were based on 'the Basque's' sense of exceptionalism: 'his ancient language, with its unrelated roots in the pre-history of Europe, his customs of land tenure and local government, his melancholy songs and Homeric sports, his simplicity against the cunningness of Spain.'

What Steer finds in Basquedom is a version of Britishness. Here is another 'profoundly nautical' people who have gone out into the world on boats to trade, and who, Steer stresses, were the first to establish the principle of the freedom of the seas in a maritime treaty with Edward III of England in 1351. These commercial links developed with the nineteenth-century industrial revolution that transformed Bilbao. It was British skilled workers, imported for the mining, steel and shipyard sectors, who first introduced soccer into the Basque country and founded Athletic Club Bilbao around 1898. (Under the regime of General Franco, the football team had to change its name to the Spanish *Atlético de Bilbao*, but later they reverted to traditional English spelling.)

When Steer met the autonomous Basque president José Antonio Aguirre for the first time (see Chapter X), and began to establish the kind of close, valuable relationship he had had with Emperor Haile Selassie in Ethiopia, the reporter noticed the president's 'chesty walk', a relic of his time as former inside-right for Athletic Bilbao. He also found 'something rather sporting' about Aguirre's humanitarian attitude to the war. Not for the Basque president the murderous ruthlessness of the Spanish, neither 'military Fascism from without' nor 'proletarian pressure from within'. Steer reckoned that 'the Basque fought against both extremes ... for tolerance and free discussion, gentleness and equality.'

> [Aguirre] was captain of a soccer team again, and even if they lost they were going to obey the whistle and the rules. No biting; no hacking; no tripping. Not very Continental, in fact. And the Basques were not. As one went out into the drizzle

again, it looked a bit like Liverpool, with the shops shut, and the Irish away at Blackpool and the Protestants decently staying at home and keeping the King's Peace.

The standard narrative of the foreigner in the Spanish Civil War is one of disillusionment. Idealistic lad joins up hopefully, finds war is beastly and foul, is wounded or retires upset. Steer's book is not really like that. Unlike most of those siding with the Spanish Republic, he is not naturally a man of the left, but being a mild Anglican, neither is he a dupe of the Catholic right. Steer is an intellectual who enjoyed reading George Herbert in the trenches, but he is not neutral or pacifist. He likes or accepts war. He sometimes finds being shelled – and he was under fire scores of times – hilariously funny. At other times war is like being in a nightmarish jackdaw's garden, 'full of hard, sharp things that reflect light and of the wretched dead worms and grubs and broken insects that serve him for fodder.'

Though sometimes cynical, Steer is never callous: the descriptions of civilians after bombings, the young men who are maimed in the line, the last battalions going up the slopes of their duty into the dark, the silent wounded in the night-time ship awaiting evacuation, all draw from him tender prose. Not all is good: the mixture of overwriting and sarcasm at Durango is less successful, and he might have reconsidered the tone of this early section if he had not had the pressure of writing in wartime. It is possible he never saw galleys or proofs; there are quite a few literals, typos and small mistakes (e.g. it was Marcel not Albert Junod of the Red Cross). Despite this, his gift for sketching character and scene in a few words is marvellous, and his imagery and prose rhythms often masterly. Well-read and cogent, Steer can command many styles. He is not just a hack tapping out staccato news, but a real writer who shows tantalising glimpses of the great novelist he might have become had he lived longer. And his liking and admiration for the Basques shines through the last paragraphs of the book's noble ending.

In many ways, *The Tree of Gernika* is an argument with Great Britain at a time when the Conservative governments of Stanley Baldwin and then Neville Chamberlain were anxious to appease Nazi Germany and Fascist Italy. While the democracies like Britain and France rigorously upheld a policy of non-intervention in Spain, the opposing dictatorships smilingly pretended to comply while in fact deliberately evading it. Early in April 1937, the British Cabinet forbade British cargo ships from going into besieged Bilbao because, they claimed, Franco's naval blockade was effective, and the sea-ways mined. In Bilbao, Steer discovered this was not true; the blockade was mostly bluff, the mines were cleared, and the Basque capital was on the brink of starvation without foreign food ships. Steer considered the British stoppage of trade was tantamount to intervention in the Spanish Civil War on Franco's side. His reports in *The Times* pressed the point, and behind the scenes Steer was also covertly lobbying key Members of Parliament to get the naval policy changed so that basic food-stuffs could get through. Recent research in the correspondence of the Labour MP (and future Nobel Peace Prize-winner) Philip Noel-Baker shows how active Steer was in the Basque cause.[*] British official humbug should never stop a committed reporter from doing his job, Steer explains in Chapter XVI:

> I take to myself the credit that I, before anyone else, exposed the fake in the blockade and recovered the truth. A journalist is not a simple purveyor of news, whether sensational or controversial, or well-written, or merely funny. He is a historian of every day's events, and he has a duty to his public. If he is kept from his public, he must use other methods; for as a historian in little, he belongs to the most honourable profession in the world, and as a historian must be filled with the most passionate and most critical attachment to the truth, so must the journalist, with the great power that he wields, see that the truth prevails. I did not rest until I had torn this falsehood to pieces.

Perhaps the British should have been doing more to support the democratic Basques, not just for the historic reason that in the First World War Basque ships had dodged German submarines to bring much-needed iron ore to British steel-makers, but

---

[*] See Chapter 2, 'Journalism at War: George Lowther Steer, Guernica and the Resistance to Fascist Aggression' in Tom Buchanan, *The Impact of the Spanish Civil War on Britain* (Sussex Academic Press, 2007); and Chapter 8, 'The Sentimental Adventurer: George Steer and the Quest for Lost Causes' in Paul Preston, *We Saw Spain Die: Foreign Correspondents in the Spanish Civil War* (Constable, 2008).

because helping the Basques in the present served Britain's strategic interest as Europe re-armed. Before the civil war, about a third of the 2.7 million tons of iron ore exported from Spain came to Britain to supplement the UK's own low-grade resources. In May 1937, the *Economist* magazine gave its materialist reading of the Spanish conflict:

> If General Franco is victorious, Italy and Germany will obviously obtain access to much needed supplies of strategic minerals for their drive towards self-sufficiency in the face of exchange difficulties. New reserves of iron ore would greatly benefit the enlarged German and Italian iron and steel industries, which are both suffering from a shortage of supplies.

On 27 June 1937, speaking at Würzburg, Adolf Hitler openly confirmed this: 'Germany needs to import iron ore. That is why we want a Nationalist Government in Spain, so that we may be able to buy Spanish ore.' This was why Nazi Germany and Fascist Italy sent up to 100,000 soldiers, sailors and airmen to help General Franco's insurgency against the elected government (in addition to the 20,000 Portuguese and 75,000 Moroccan volunteers that Franco employed). Those forces were loaned on credit, to be paid back in the minerals necessary to manufacture even more vehicles and weaponry for future fascist *blitzkrieg*.

Thanks to Steer, the *Legion Kondor*'s bombing of Gernika on 26 April 1937 became the best-known *aktion* of the German military intervention in Spain. Because he had been tracking the experimental weapons and tactics employed by the Luftwaffe pilots flying for the Nationalists, Steer could report in *The Times* their massive use of 1 kg thermite incendiary bombs, setting the place ablaze. Because he was close to the Basques, Steer could also explain why the destructive attack on 'the village which was the centre of their national feeling' mattered so much. Steer describes again the dramatic events of that day vividly in Chapter XX of *The Tree of Gernika*:

> We tried to enter, but the streets were a royal carpet of live coals; blocks of wreckage slithered and crashed from the houses, and from their sides that were still erect the polished heat struck at our cheeks and eyes. There were people, they

said, to be saved there: there were the frameworks of dozens of cars. But nothing could be done, and we put our hands in our pockets and wondered why on earth the world was so mad and warfare become so easy.

Steer draws some morals from the air-raid in chapters XXI and XXII, suggesting that the news affected British public opinion strongly because it evoked memories of the Great War of 1914–18, when German aircraft had first bombed British cities, and also suggested dreadful future possibilities: '[t]he blotting out of Hull, for instance . . . Or the end of Portsmouth.' He also points out that the destruction of Gernika led to 'horrible and inconsistent lying' by the radio and press on the Nationalist side, who dishonestly denied any bombing from aircraft and accused 'Basque incendiarists' of destroying their town with dynamite and petrol.

> All these statements were denied by hundreds of real eye-witnesses with whom we spoke . . . Not only myself; but the correspondents of *Reuter*, the *Star*, the *Daily Express*, and *Ce Soir* of Paris. They told the same story: if there had been a tale of 'Red destruction' to tell, they would have been the first to cry out. For they were peasants with politics more of the Right than the Left, and they had lost all their property in the fire.
>
> We saw the great bomb-holes in the plaza, the churches, the school, round the hospital – all of us with our own eyes. They were not there when I passed through Gernika the day before. We picked up unexploded German incendiary bombs and bomb-splinters, and saw people dead of bomb wounds and machine-gun bullets. There was no sign of petrol.[†]

In the introduction to *The Tree of Gernika*, Steer explains why he uses the words 'we' and 'our' when referring to the Basques in his narrative:

> I do this because I came to know the Basque militia well, and

[†] See the still magisterial *Guernica! Guernica! A Study of Journalism, Diplomacy, Propaganda and History* (California, 1977) by Herbert R. Southworth, for the fullest ramifications of truth and lies.

because it was a usual journalistic method, when I was in Spain, to refer in such language to the side on which one was working. It is not to be inferred from my use of these terms that I participated in any way in the struggle.

The last sentence is economical with the truth. We can adduce from page 353 that Steer not only picked up a rifle but stood on the cobbles by the bridge firing it up at the diving planes. He was certainly in the thick of the action when he tagged along in the field with the forty-nine-year-old Frenchman he mostly calls 'Colonel Jaureghuy' but whose real name, 'Monnier', he lets slip by accident during a description of the last conference at the Carlton Hotel on page 324, and which no one caught in the proofs.

Robert Monnier was a hero of the First World War, a born leader who served with the elite Chasseurs Alpins. He was wounded four times, with two palms and four stars on his *croix de guerre*. In the early 1930s he got in touch with one of his former colonels, now a general on the Conseil Supérieur de la Guerre, who in turn put Monnier in touch with the Army Staff's Deuxième Bureau for military intelligence and military missions abroad. Soon after Franco's uprising in July 1936, Monnier was at work in the Spanish Basque country under the cover of a war correspondent, sending secret reports back to Paris. After the bombing of Guernica, Monnier became President Aguirre's military adviser, with the tacit approval of Paris.‡ Steer befriended Monnier at the Torrontegui Hotel in Bilbao; later they shared a flat at 60, Gran Via, nearer the Presidencia. What Steer cannot really reveal in *The Tree of Gernika* is how much Monnier was running the show, taking command in the line, rallying the Basque militias with good soldiers like Pablo Beldarrain and Colonel Putz, and shooting his way out of trouble if need be with his broom-handle Model F Astra machine-pistol made in Gernika.

It is very clear from *The Tree of Gernika* that, often with Monnier and sometimes without him, George Steer was deliberately putting himself in harm's way. He says in the

‡   See Colonel Yves Jouin, 'Le Commandant Robert Monnier, héros de la guerre 1914–1918, organisateur de la résistance éthiopienne', *Revue Historique de l'Armée*, Numero 4, 1971, pp. 38–49.

introduction that other journalists were given the same facilities to get to the front. '[T]hat they did not use them is no fault of theirs, for they had more to lose than I in the firing-line.' This oblique sentence needs unpicking. It really means: 'Other journalists chose not to risk their lives at the front because they had other people who did not want to lose them.' This is a clue to the secret story behind this remarkable book.

When George Steer returned from the Italo-Abyssinian war, weeks before the Spanish Civil War broke out, he was newly married to a beautiful and brilliant journalist, Margarita de Herrero y Hassett, whose father was Spanish and mother English. *The Times* sent Steer down to the Franco-Spanish frontier to cover the initial fighting in the Basque country, as described in his book's first chapter. After the fall of San Sebastian to Franco's forces on 14 September 1936, Steer left the staff of *The Times* and crossed the frontier into Nationalist Spain, where he completed his book about the Italian invasion of Ethiopia. At some point, late in 1936 or early in 1937, the Nationalists expelled him from their territory; possibly because Italian Intelligence read and objected to Steer's *Caesar in Abyssinia.*

The leaving was the making of him. Back in Hendaye, where the British Embassy had been evacuated from Madrid, he charmed British diplomats and managed to arrange passage on a British warship to the edge of Basque territorial waters off Bilbao, getting himself into the besieged enclave of Euzkadi for six days in late January 1937 (he describes this in Chapter IX).

It was at this point that news came from England that his wife Margarita, by then heavily pregnant, was dangerously ill. The Basque government laid on a fast trawler to get him to Bayonne, and settled his abandoned hotel-bill. Steer got back to England at the end of January to find that his wife and unborn child had both died at the London Clinic. The funeral was delayed and Margarita's body embalmed, to allow George's mother (who had never seen the daughter-in-law who married her only child) time to get there by sea from South Africa. Grief-stricken, George Steer visited Margarita's dead body every day for many weeks. Then more bad news came: many of the young Ethiopians he had known and loved in Addis Ababa had been massacred in the savage Italian reprisals after a failed assassination attempt on the Viceroy, Marshal Graziani.

Steer took his wife's body south to be buried in Biarritz, then immediately crossed back into the Basque country in early April 1937, a few days after General Mola launched his assault on Euzkadi by bombing Durango, massacring many civilians. Steer's grief and shock as he plunged back into reporting-work during April, May and June 1937 can only be imagined. But perhaps his suffering also made him empathise with the sorrows of other people at war; *The Tree of Gernika* shows a tender heart as well as a clever mind. Death had seized his wife and unborn child, and nearly maddened him. That helps to explain why he was so careless of his own life among the dangers of the line. It is also why this extraordinary book, the greatest account of the Spanish Civil War never (until now) to be reprinted in English, carries the dedication 'TO MARGARITA, SNATCHED AWAY'.

TO

MARGARITA

SNATCHED AWAY

LIST OF ILLUSTRATIONS

MAPS

THE TREE OF GERNIKA:

A Field Study of Modern War

INTRODUCTION

THE BASQUES, whose suppression is the subject of this book, are a religious, deep-drinking, non-swearing race who live on the mountainous south-eastern shores of the Bay of Biscay. They are profoundly nautical; they swing and fish in the Bay without ever feeling sea-sick. The principle of the freedom of the seas was first established by them, in a maritime treaty with Edward III of England in 1351.

Their provinces of Vizcaya, Guipuzcoa are among the richest and are by far the most progressive of Spain. Spain? There are a few things which the patient Basque will not tolerate, and one is the suggestion that he is Spanish. For him, Iberian is the safer term: it nearly conveys the idea of that antiquity and Peninsular twilight in which the Basque finds his source. Very cold, rock-bound, in scored glacial valleys, far away, pre-Mediterranean, among stones. *Unlike every other Western European people, he has never passed through the feudal stage.* He has always owned his land, and he has never known a landless class, either slave or villein. He has always been a member of a full democracy, in which every man has voted. To him therefore the class war, the idea of aggressive capitalism or an aggressive proletariat is meaningless. His civilisation is too old to understand the clash of motive due to a feudalism through which it has never passed. So old it is, that the words for knife, and plough, and axe are still derived from the Basque root aiz, meaning stone: so fixed is the Basque in his land, that his surnames still mean Hillside, and Warm Valley, and Appletree, and New Plum, and Rock and Fast River. His language and

11

his people, like his democratic classless laws, rise in some mist mountain unknown to the expeditionary stunting of our new science. And why should the modern world, with all its interest engaged on Aryans and non-Aryans and the evident supremacy of Romans over blacks, trouble to explore so small and strange a cradle-load of civilisation? What has the Basque to do with progress?

Nothing of value, clearly. In the modern world he stands only for freedom between the classes, camaraderie and truthfulness, humanity under war conditions, unwillingness to fight for any extreme and violent doctrine; self-reliance, stubbornness, straightforwardness and simplicity, dislike of propaganda on his own behalf, and an open-eyed guilelessness in face of the enemy's. He is naturally orderly, fitting into no fancy scheme of order. A big, handsome man, he is not aware of his own strength and beauty.

None of these qualities are valid in the twentieth century, and the worst of these is freedom. For which the Basque fought—and lost. He fought against great odds. And though it is more fashionable now to court the other side, I think that the common man—when he reads this story— will see, mapped out in pine-clad green mountains between Otxandiano and Bilbao, Irun and San Sebastian, the battle-ground in grand prototype of his own fight for liberty. He may hope, as I do, that it will be more successful; but he can scarcely expect that it will be more honourable.

Like the common man, the Basque fought against both extremes. He did not wish to be regimented either way. He was perfectly happy, and he wanted to be left alone. The modern forces of systemisation, the senseless slogans and salutes and party disciplines attacked him on either side. He tried to shake himself free of them.

His centre of resistance in this struggle was his great difference of type from the people who were attacking and undermining him: his ancient language, with its unrelated roots in the pre-history of Europe, his customs of land tenure and local government, his melancholy songs and Homeric sports, his simplicity against the cunningness of Spain.

The Basques are industrious, and the Spanish are idle.

The Basques are all yeomen, and the Spanish would all be gentlemen. To the Spanish Basques are "brutos" and "bestias," and to the Basques the Spanish are intriguers, twisters and political parasites, who live on the products of other people's industry, and somehow evade payment before bankruptcy. These local differences were the visible fighting points for the Basques; but, in reality, the Spanish attack upon the Basques represented something less parochial and customary. It came in the guise of military Fascism from without, and proletarian pressure from within. In either way it was an attack upon Basque liberties, and the Basque organism resisted until it broke down.

In this war the Basque fought for tolerance and free discussion, gentleness and equality. This book shows how he lost. His was a very human tragedy the destruction of man by a system, of spirit by routine.

I was able to watch the Basques at war during four periods: August to September, 1936, when I was on the Franco-Spanish frontier; January, 1937, when I was in Bilbao; during the last ferocious offensive of Mola in the months of April, May and June, with which this book largely deals; and in August, 1937, just before they were tricked into surrender. These were the months when foreign ideas and their instruments were brought to bear on the Basques most intensely, finally destroying them.

Through the year in which the Basques existed as a semi-independent people, one can trace the development of the forces arrayed against them—from their beginning in a class and regional Spanish rising, to their end in a Fascist military dictatorship. For in their enemies, too, the moderate and natural were slowly being extinguished: their enemies, who first came against them in August all gay in red berets, with flowers in their rifles from the upland province of Navarre, now crawled slowly forward under the air fleet of Germany and Italy, before the fire of the artillery of Germany and Italy, and with Italian troops to right and left. An international staff drove them forward, and in their centre, lost in the battle of the systems, were the last few brigades of Navarre—steel-helmeted now from some foreign factory.

The vast majority of the things that I write about in

this book were seen by me. In August and September, as the book shows, I had a very intimate window on the war: an umpire's view. During the last great offensive, from April to June, the Basque authorities in Bilbao permitted me absolute freedom of movement and manœuvre within their territory. I could go without hindrance or escort to any part of the front at any time. Other journalists were given the same facilities: that they did not use them as much as I did is no fault of theirs, for they had more to lose than I in the firing line.

Throughout the latter part of this narrative, since it is on the whole first-hand, I use the words "we" and "our" in reference to the Basques. I do this because I came to know the Basque militia well, and because it was a usual journalistic method, when I was in Spain, to refer in such language to the side on which one was working. It is not to be inferred from my use of these terms that I participated in any way in the struggle. Nor that by my sympathy with the Basque people, crushed like many of us between the two extremes, I was unable to detect their failings, the often rheumatical movements of their armies, their stubbornness and occasional unwillingness to co-operate, their extraordinary inability to organise their rearguard in a way fit to meet the psychological shocks of war. This book is, on the other hand, full of a Lower Criticism of the most objectionable Oxford kind. It will, perhaps, be banned by the Basques when they get back to Bilbao.

But I do not think they will go so far against me. They always faced free criticism, and echoed the laugh against themselves. That is why I liked them, and regret their untimely eclipse, and look forward to a resurrection of Europe's oldest, more honest, democracy.

I

IN THE NORTH OF SPAIN something like stability had reigned since the revolt began.

The Basque provinces of Guipuzcoa (capital San Sebastian) and Vizcaya (capital Bilbao) had declared for the Government, which promised Basque autonomy: the dream of all this fishing race in the blue swagger berets and the striped blue trousers was to restore the ancient Basque republic—classless, gruff and moneyed—under the leaves of the tribal oak at Gernika. Catholics to a man —not to a woman only as in other parts of Spain—they nevertheless prized their freedom from the class-ridden, over-rhetorical tradition of Castile so highly that they were willing to make terms with agnostic Madrid. The Statute! That was the divine end of their coalitions. The Statute; the Basque tongue, as crumpled and old yet evergreen as their oak; their own free peasant life; their own taxes and dues: they wanted little more, and nothing so deeply.

At first all went easily. In Vizcaya and its great port Bilbao there was no resistance to the Republic. In San Sebastian revolt, ill improvised, taken aback by the suddenness of Mola's rising, was soon crushed.

Yet how little stood between the revolt and triumph in San Sebastian.

Do you know San Sebastian in summer, under the Republic? It used to be, when the Habsburg-Bourbons ruled Spain, the smartest resort of the peninsula. The richest families of Spain built villas at Zarauz. Alfonso XIII, after a short stay at Santander, would spend August and September at his summer palace of Miramar above the sweeping Concha, whose bright sands

15

were covered by the tent-shelters and the striped parasols of hundreds of the middle class. These, their eyes drowsily bent upon the level ocean accented *aigu* or *grave* by the white wind-stepped verticals of a hundred yachts, swelled as smooth as Biscay with the contemplative pleasure of summer, when all Europe, that has the means to, rests.

True, Primo de Rivera had closed down upon the gambling tables, and to play your games or enjoy a night club you had to cross to the French side. But the simpler vegetative amusements kept many Spaniards at San Sebastian: fêtes at the Club Nautico, dancing in the silken evening on the square at Zarauz, where the fishermen had called the aristocracy *tu* from childhood and danced beside them, drawn by the glitter of such beautiful features, forms and movements. For the Spanish aristocracy, with its many faults, was elegant above all others.

The Republic succeeded to the inheritance of San Sebastian; Alcalá de Zamora, timid President, came down to summer at Miramar in the safe company of seven hundred *guardias de asalto*. The bourgeois Republican element in its festivities prevailed more and more in the capital of Guipuzcoa. The Concha was crowded: less tents, more cheaply-slippered feet in circulation. At the Perla more dancing and more beauty contests: Miss Avila, Miss Santander, Miss Dax, Miss Biarritz were acclaimed in turn by competitive Republican blondes with bathing dresses cut lower and voices cast a trifle more raucous than before. The municipal authorities installed drastic loud-speakers around the beach, even above the Ambassadors' select cove behind the prison (in whose waters, on clear halcyon days, the prison drains could be seen emerging). Alternately, the loud-speakers blasted dance music and riveted advertisements into the democratic consciousness. Bathing belles shrieked with excitement as the new cold water of the sea reached danger point about their groins. The remarkable noise was echoed from the skies, where small planes frenzied across San Sebastian beach, dropping coloured advertisements, and rarely one of the local macintoshes as a gift. Children and grown men, yelling in unison, scrambled and strangled each other for these precious parcels. The

quieter Monarchist presidents of the Aero Club and the
Club Nautico were replaced by Basques more loudly based
upon the régime.

To be short, San Sebastian in summer became grandly
vulgar; the row was appalling, and taste was indus-
triously democratic. Girls dressed up as their favourite
film stars, the fluffier the sweeter. Children were continually lost on the beach, but their parents enjoyed to the
full the opportunity to bawl their names and descriptions
down the loud-speakers.

The Basques were glad: it brought San Sebastian up to
date, made it the *plage* of the classes released, enriched
and suddenly confronted with Need of a Holiday by the
revolution of 1931. The partisans of the old Court still
came to the coast, for they could not abandon their
properties there: but the Basques, who are tough and
uncompromising creatures, regarded these less rich, still
titled, still beautiful people as effete. It was the nice noisy
people who were going to give them their Estatuto.

They went on broad-shoulderedly beating about their
pelota courts, drinking their rough wine and sweating it
off in exercise, hoping that the Estatuto would arrive one
day, dropped from the sky like the parcels containing
their gift macintoshes.

When Calvo Sotelo was murdered in vengeance by the
police agents of the Republic, his friends—there were
many of them quietly resting by the sea—attended a
memorial service for him at San Sebastian. It was broken
up by the police.

When Mola proclaimed the rebellion in Pampluna, the
commander of the garrison at the Loyola barracks outside
San Sebastian also collected his officers and proclaimed
martial law. He made an extraordinarily Spanish muddle
of it. For, first of all, he warned the Civil Governor of
the step which he proposed to take, and the Civil Governor
armed the civilian population in defence of the Government.

Many adherents of the Right were lying low in San
Sebastian, and joined the conspirators at the Maria Cristina
Hotel—smartest in San Sebastian—and their old Club
Nautico and the Casino, under arms. But not enough
to defend these scattered buildings.

If the soldiers had had more courage and come out

into the open street, they could have taken San Sebastian the first day of the revolt. In spite of their arms everybody panicked; nobody except the extremists organised: the Basques, for all their contempt of Castile, are slower-witted people. White flags were up everywhere. All the holiday-makers were sure—not only now, but for days afterwards—that other rebels stood in thousands on the hills.

Unlike Queipo de Llano in Seville, the leaders of the San Sebastian revolt took no advantage of the public dismay. They sat in their buildings wondering what next to do.

The white flags, since no one seemed to care for them, were shamefacedly removed. The public became aggressive. A paper called the *Frente Popular* was founded, and a committee of the coalition which it represented took over the management of San Sebastian, loud-speakers and all. Every radio voice sternly ordered the rebels to yield. Barricades replaced the white flags.

It was a matter of days to starve the people out of the Maria Cristina and the Club Nautico. The advertisement plane, naturally prone to untruth, flew over the Loyola barracks pamphleteering again: "You will all be spared if you surrender." On July 30th, Colonel Carrasco and twenty other officers who had led the revolt in the Loyola barracks, and who had surrendered, were spared . . . further indignities by being propped against a wall and shot.

That's what comes of confining yourself to barracks.

The Frente Popular in San Sebastian had now recovered its nerve, and began its house-to-house search for suspects. Arms were handed out to the townsmen whom it thought reliable. Country Basques, like the people of the village Azpeitia in the hills to the south, were not yet trusted. The basis of the militia was definitely urban and prole-tarian, not Basque Nationalist, and it is to that that I attribute its failure in Guipuzcoa.

Of course, there was no noise of failure now. Elated, they seized all the smart cars of the visiting aristocracy, painted them hugely U. H. P. (for Unidos Hermanos Proletarianos), and flagged them to party choice—red for

Socialists or Communists, black-red for Anarchists, the pretty scarlet and apple-green cross of Basque Nationalism. In these new toys they raced hither and yon. It was a grand holiday now for all classes, except the Castilian Rights.

Very few of them took the rebellion seriously, even when the water supply of San Sebastian was cut off in the Pampluna hills.

Very few of them knew not only what modern warfare was—that did not matter: they were never to experience it—but what ordinary in-fighting with the rifle and machine-gun could be like in their own hills; they had to be taught even to fire rifles. For them life was a pro-longed warm afternoon in Hyde Park without the moral censorship of the London policeman. Lovers in overall-uniform littered all the trenches. Preventatives, so long excluded by the Church from the armoury of the poor, were now to be found on every militia man. Eugenics were suddenly promoted to first place among the branches of proletarian military science.

It was illuminating to watch how the films had moulded their technique: the dear old Westerns, not your effete class close-ups. While the forage cap with tassel at the peak was the more natural military cap of Spain, a slouch hat was more highly prized, for it looked more devil-may-care. Even when they had to fight in the open they stuck to their flaming red bandanas, and battled with cigarettes in their mouths. Canadianas, however, were the most popular combative clothing in Guipuzcoa.

A Canadiana is the kind of jacket, woolly and checked, that a Western cowboy is supposed by Spaniards to wear when corralling cattle and doing desperate things to the sheriff's daughter. The leading Frente Popular officers all wore Canadianas.

Revolvers, as the most dramatic and most useless of all weapons, dangled from all ranks.

The Committee of San Sebastian, which quickly made contact with the Committee of Irun, tried to reduce this new holiday mass to military order.

It seems to have been realised from the first that inva-sion of the next province, Navarre, could not be attempted.

Guipuzcoa must stand on the defensive, and await the onset of Navarre.

A brother's war: that was to be the way Guipuzcoa and Navarre would fight. A brother's war, fought as affectionately as the war between Cain and Abel. For the Navarrese are also Basque.

I suppose it must be because they face landward, towards Castile, not seaward at the fish that the Navarrese have abandoned their Basque speech and, bar stubbornness, their Basque ways. But the difference between the two brother races is so astounding that the reason seems a wretched excuse to give. Navarre peasantry not only have no regional ambitions to be achieved by the passing of an Estatuto; they positively loathe anybody, like their brother Guipuzcoans, who have.

As fanatically as the Guipuzcoan and Vizcayan Basques desire a Federal Spain, the Navarrese will never be satisfied until the Peninsula becomes again the centralised absolute monarchy that it was under the Catholic kings. The friend of the maritime provinces, the Frente Popular Government, was Navarre's select devil.

Enthusiastically Catholic, their Requeté formations had assumed not only the pressed scarlet beret of Carlism: on their hearts, pinned perhaps with tinsel saints and itself a poor flag of flimsy paper, they carried what they loved most—the Bleeding Heart of Jesus. To them Madrid and all its friends were anti-Christ; hideous Republican materialism. They hated, every man of them, the very idea of secular education: the teachers sent to instruct their children by Madrid were monstrous agents to be rooted out. Even women teachers were shot, or marched about Pampluna with shaven heads. For the intelligent people that they were, the extremism of their single passion takes the foreigners' breath. They were served by a clergy which, for Spain, was not ill-educated nor naturally ill-lit in the mind. These, with long purple tassels hanging from their berets, fought beside them against their brother priests of Guipuzcoa, who stood with the Sacrament next the fallen militiamen ready to console him and flight his escape from the fratricidal earth. Or, if they were captured, these priests, by either side, they were shot as traitors. Alas, poor Yorick!

Initiative opened and remained with the Navarre Carlists. It was they who acclaimed Mola on the day of revolt in Navarre, and before evening provided him with thousands of picked men, and shook the square of Pampluna with their marching song. The Carlist clubs had long been ready for a last defence of Iberian Catholicism: their men, specially chosen for physique, military capacity, political dependability, even moral purity, were fully equipped, and answered the signal in a few hours. Soon they were hammering pieces of sheet-iron into place to make armoured cars out of lorries and chars-a-bancs — strange weapons for such uncompromising Traditionalists.

They were far better war material than the city militia of San Sebastian and Irun. They were better organised, armed and led; they were more numerous. They were despatched in two main columns against the province of Guipuzcoa, one along the Vera road aiming at the Bidasoa frontier and Irun, the other in the Vitoria highway to San Sebastian. Flowers of summer drooped from their hot rifles as they drove away in lorries through the larches, up the valleys of the rapid mountain rivers.

They had to support on either side, east and west, the single infiltration which the rebels had been able to maintain in Guipuzcoa: Beorlegui's few hundred Carlist volunteers who held the mountain village of Oyarzun from the very beginning of the revolt.

Oyarzun is a small collection of Basque houses surrounded by maize fields, which lies only two miles south of mid-point on the road between Irun and San Sebastian. Roads from each town led to it, but no roads from the south. Beorlegui, therefore, depended for supplies upon mule transport, which struggled scattering stones from the mountain pathways of Three Crowns — their high route back into Navarre. Despite this initial weakness of his position, Beorlegui was never seriously threatened in Oyarzun.

I do not know whether to attribute it more to the rank inefficiency of the militia, or to the brilliant play that Beorlegui made of his opportunities; but the holding of Oyarzun meant the conquest of Guipuzcoa.

Beorlegui dispersed his seven hundred men on the two roads north-west and north-east of Oyarzun. They kept up a continual fire, and moved with alarming speed from point to point; and so Oyarzun, which the Frente Popular assumed must be held by several thousand men, was never attacked by them. At any time they could have taken Oyarzun in a day.

War, which most people think heroic or fearful, is made up of incidents like Oyarzun—opportunities lost by one side, exploited to the maximum by the other, and often cardinal to the main objective. Every war can be described as a series of colossal idiocies culminating in defeat, and if wars were always lost by the militarists it would be worth while debunking them on that model.

Instead of attacking Oyarzun the Frente Popular trained fortress guns upon the village.

The Basque coast from San Sebastian to Irun is sprinkled with forts built after the Carlist wars: Urgull and Ulia at the capital. San Marcos farther out, and the fortress of Nuestra Señora de Guadalupe between Irun and the sea. The old-fashioned 155 mm. guns of the last two now concentrated on Oyarzun. We used to enjoy the sight of Nuestra Señora performing from the Hotel Eskualduna in Hendaye Plage across the roadstead, where the placid Fuenterrabians fished.

Nuestra Señora was an undoubted nest of cannon. A fearful explosion from the ridge was followed by a heavy cloud of Scotch mist, which spread opaquely over Guadalupe mountain. I have never seen guns expel Djinns so large. The Frente Popular officer, who directed them, had to wait for the weather to clear away before he fired the next shot.

Victor Schiff, of the *Daily Herald*, I remember, interviewed this scientist. He found a learned-looking man, stoop-shouldered and thin as Professor Piccard, putting him in mind rather of a notary than an artillery expert. And I dare say a notary he was, and for all Beorlegui cared about it he was firing dud parchment bonds, for, though they smashed up Oyarzun, they did no damage to his soldiers. The old Morocco colonel, heavy and searfaced in dirty overalls, with his battered glasses and his stick, soon taught the levies not to worry about a mere bombardment from antique coast guns. They pounded away at an empty village.

Thus it was at the beginning of August. From Hendaye, across the bay formed by the International mouth of the Bidasoa, one could see in the lovely summer weather, first, the fishermen in row boats fishing. Behind them the pinch-backed mountain Jaizquibel which ran level with the coast and above it, between Fuenterrabia and Pasajes, the port of San Sebastian. Fuenterrabia, a sprinkle of holiday villas, a heavy brown convent-castle upon the strand on the near end of Jaizquibel, the memorial cross of Nuestra Señora, and her occasional mist representing action. To the south of all this, and bound to France by two railway bridges and a road bridge, lay Irun, with its big railway yards, its wood mills and its chocolate factory, now bossed by a Frente Popular committee. Along the southern foot of Jaizquibel ran the road and railway to the other Frente Popular centre, San Sebastian.

South of the road a ridge of hills protected Irun from the land side. These hills began at Puntza on the Bidasoa, a little beyond the Spanish frontier village of Behobia. Dressing in pine along the crest, they spread out through Zubelzu to the central vantage of San Marcial, where a whitewashed hermitage, with a tall tiled tower, stood up to spy inland in the sea of the dark woods. Then the slopes tumbled down to Oyarzun, which was protected from Irun by another hill planted thick with pines.

Behind Oyarzun, the village always invisible at the back of its pine hill fence, rose the majestic Peña d'Aya, or mountain of the Three Crowns, 2,500 feet high. Its three rugged heads were yet luxuriantly green, and reflected the heat into deep Pyrenean valleys. Through glasses at this time we could see a small encampment near the easterly peak, and noiseless petty plumes of smoke showed that from somewhere it was being shelled.

This was the support camp of Beorlegui.

Along the frontier, east of all these inland heights and forest ledges, ran the River Bidasoa, in fields of maize which now were ripening and rustling like half-burnt paper; a narrow, shallow stream. On the Spanish side at every two hundred metres sprouted a small red brick douanier's shelter, in front of which stood—or, in more frequent indolence, lay stretched—a Spanish frontier guard, performing upon a cigar. Behind this unconvincing barrier, and beyond the infinitely more wakeful maize, ran the small-gauge railway track, and the road which led via Enderlaza and Vera to hostile Pampluna. Both followed the glancing stream into the Pyrenees, where it ceased to be the frontier; and thence their course need not worry us, for it was through Carlist territory which never saw the war.

On the French side of the frontier everybody is letting out glasses and telescopes and advantageous rooms. Crowds are gathering on every hill, and experts in public strategy are preaching their own version of the Sermon on the Mount. The French love no news better than a war, and here before their eyes it is going to unfold itself, with running commentary for two francs from anybody who has done his military service and knows the names of the mountains opposite the Spanish sun.

At Enderlaza, on the boundary between Guipuzcoa and Navarre, the Frente Popular blew up the bridge which carried the Pampluna road to the other side of the Bidasoa, and from Erlaitz, a small ruined fort of the Carlist wars which stood near two miles on a hill-top down river, they peppered the gap in Carlist communications with two small cannon. Here were the beginnings of a nice little war. At this period, however, the lunch hour and the siesta were observed between twelve and five-thirty p.m., and night attacks were considered by both sides cowardly and mean.

By a sudden breach of this convention, which I can only attribute to a stroke of genius, the ridge of Pikoketa—next to Erlaitz—was occupied by the Carlists in the dark hours of August 10th to 11th. At the same time their second column poured into Tolosa, south of San Sebastian, where the Frente Popular line two miles outside the city, after withstanding three daylight attacks, was surprised and pierced. These two successes were the elements that set the Basque front into motion and braced the females behind the binoculars on the French side for something more like a bull-fight.

Larrañaga, the energetic young Communist who was San Sebastian's War Commissar, raced into Tolosa just in time to haul his militiamen out. The boys in the red berets poured in through the gap, their amateur cavalry first. A San Sebastian armoured car, which careered through Tolosa without knowing that it has been lost, was turned to red pulp inside with a bomb.

The Carlist commander walked to the Alcalde's house, where he found the remains of the meal which the Frente Popular officers had been eating. About one hundred prisoners were taken, but I doubt whether they were long kept waiting. On the 12th, the Carlists had occupied Villabona four miles farther north. The general offensive on Irun—San Sebastian seems to have been timed with the arrival of new aviation material from abroad, which Radio Castilla (Burgos) not only boasted, but Mola now used to bomb Pasajes.

At sea, too, the rebels were preparing to take the initiative. The cruiser *Almirante Cervera* (7,850 tons, eight 6-inch guns) moved eastward from Gijon, which it had been ineffectually bombarding. The battleship *España* (15,452 tons, eight 12-inch guns), the cruiser *Canarias* (10,000 tons, eight 8-inch guns), and the small destroyer *Velasco* (three 4-inch) got up a head of steam in the naval harbour of El Ferrol.

Now came the testing time for San Sebastian. On the 13th, five of the new Italian planes bombed the town: off the Concha, in the calm translucent sea, lay the low two funnels of the "pirate ship," as the San Sebastian radio shrieked. Her needle guns were trained across the painted ocean upon Fort Urgull, whose old pieces replied by covering the *Almirante Cervera* from their height on a rocky forehead of land at the end of the Concha's semi-circle. The *Almirante Cervera's* ultimatum expired at midnight: if San Sebastian did not yield to the land forces, she was going to be blown to bits.

The answer was that prisoners of the families holidaying at San Sebastian would be executed if the town were attacked. *Almirante Cervera* thought again.

On the 14th up came *España* and *Velasco*, to begin the ultimatum game again, while leaflets from rebel planes ordered immediate surrender. So Lieutenant Ortega, the Carabinero who governed San Sebastian, threatened to shoot five prisoners for every person killed by bombardment from air or sea. Everybody laughed at this war of counter-threat except the prisoners.

It had become a strange town, the holiday resort of San Sebastian. Water was rationed at the fire hydrants in the street, and half the shops were shut. Everybody was nervous in the hotels behind the Concha (on whose beach, however, everybody still optimistically shrieked and paddled). Daily there were new arrests, but those who were left behind still listened without concealment to the rebel Burgos radio. The prisoners of the Right were taken to the Casino: in Irun, as a precaution against bombardment, they were put in the cellars of Fort Nuestra Señora de Guadalupe.

Pressure on Irun was increased by the sudden encircle-ment and capture of Erlaitz with its two guns on the 15th. Erlaitz had been doomed since the fall of Pikoketa: the interval had been used by the Carlists upon an ingenious scheme.

I have said that the road to Irun was cut—and very nicely cut—by the destruction of the bridge at Enderlaza. But that did not baffle the Carlist command. They tore up the railway for two or three miles south of Enderlaza, where it ran on the same side of the river Bidasoa as the road north of Enderlaza. Near Vera the railway could be joined from the road the other side of the Bidasoa by a perfectly undamaged bridge, which, as it was, connected the road with a country station. All they had to do was to roll the dismantled permanent way, and it became a rough road, corrugated but serviceable to their lorry traffic. A long tunnel provided ideal cover for shell-dumps (for the Frente Popular in San Sebastian had three old planes who sometimes bombed the Bidasoa valley).

In Irun they were much alarmed by the loss of Erlaitz, which straightened out the rebel right between Oyarzun and the Bidasoa. The planes, with scarlet bands across their wings, beat up the mist-laden Bidasoa valley in the evening to bomb—and hit French Biriatou with three or four light explosives. *Attraction!* The proprietor of the house charges two sous to spot the hole in his roof.

An armoured train, vamped up from an engine and a powerful little loose box used in happier days for taking bulls to bull-fights, was driven up the Pampluna line from Irun; in red letters upon the engine was "U. H. P."

The first engine driver commissioned to conduct the People's Toy Special said "No," so he was pushed into the cellars of Guadalupe. The second thought that engine driving would indeed be more comfortable, so off he blazed up the Bidasoa, fired his two machine-guns at the startled Carlists, and before they retorted came back to rest at Gastinaldia, a little village opposite French Biriatou and in front of the Puntza, where he was toasted as a hero. But I think the first engine driver was also a bit of a lad. When they brought him out for execution he kicked the chief of the firing squad in the stomach, vaulted a wall, swam across to France, and gave an interview to the *Temps* which struck everyone as commendably impartial.

It was now that the Frente Popular in Irun decided to abandon a policy of scrapping in the hills; at which the Navarrese beat them every day. The French and Belgian instructors who had been sent over the International bridge by the French Communist party began to construct a defensive line within the range of Guadalupe forts. The square Carabinero post below the Puntza, at the edge of the river Bidasoa, became a block-house. Thence each day we saw the line progressing through sand-bagged redoubts over the Puntza, under the pine trees on Zubelzu crest, across the valley gap where a rough road led up from Enderlaza to San Marcial. San Marcial was strengthened with artillery, and from the mountain in front of San Marcial the line led down to the Oyarzun trenches, built earlier in the struggle.

French and Belgians instructed the pupil militia in machine-gunnery, and a few odd cannon were hauled out of somewhere.

August 15th was the Feast of the Assumption: a great holiday and fiesta in France as well as Spain. Broad bourgeois crowds of French stolidity massed before the International Bridge at Hendaye and up the river: in Tolosa the Requetés brandished their rifles as they danced through the streets with little children, angel-winged in silver, to the strains of a military band. Thus did the French and the Spanish celebrate one of Catholicism's high festivals—in the contemplation and preparation of war, sweetened by the little ones dressed up as unavenging messengers of grace.

Tolosa and Erlaitz were now the advanced headquarters of either wing for the attack on Guipuzcoa. When the pageant was over the Carlists left for the front. They took Andoain six miles south of San Sebastian.

One would have imagined that by now the offensive on San Sebastian and Irun would have been ordered on land and sea, and in the air. But, as a matter of fact, it was only ordered on the sea, whence it was hoped, perhaps, to destroy the coast fortresses which, laboriously swivelled round by their amateur crews, now threw their 6-inch shells beyond the Frente Popular line inland. On August 13th it will be remembered, the ultimatum of *Almirante Cervera* expired; on August 14th the somewhat repetitive ultimata of *Almirante Cervera, España* and *Velasco* expired again. The game of expiring could hardly go on for ever. It gives some measure of the time-table of this war that by the morning of August 17th, *España* and *Almirante Cervera* were not only determined, but ready to shoot.

Their offensive opened with full intensity when the coast haze was off the waters, at nine a.m. precisely. I looked from my balcony over the sweet blue sea at Hendaye: five miles out stood a long grey form, whose stiff funnel seemed to stilt it against the pale horizon. The *España* stood still. Two points of flame lit with a horizontal startlingness along her shallow side. Long after, the thunder of the double detonation: the hotel shook its windows together like a discreet dinner gong. Everybody's head popped out. A deep boom! boom! and two great thickets of smoke rose round the fort of Guadalupe.

At the same time *Almirante Cervera* opened fire on the forts and the Concha of San Sebastian. I could hear the dull detonation of its guns through the long careful pauses of the *España* off the point opposite.

Almirante Cervera fired twenty rounds into the city before midday. Siesta. She fired thirty rounds, now she had the range more prettily, before four o'clock in the afternoon. Her objectives were the forts of Mount Urgull, San Marcos, Manpas and Choritoquieta. English people who went through the bombardment say that the population showed the greatest *sang-froid*: the women still queued in the streets for water, and went about their daily shopping on the Frente Popular chits, statuesque, hatless women of Spain.

At four, *Almirante Cervera* joined *España* opposite Guadalupe. *España* had been pounding Guadalupe without cease, but with long silences for the correction of aim. The Fort was now a forest of smoke to left and right, and shells sometimes slipped over the ridge into the pretty gardens just above Fuenterrabia. All the fishing boats had fled, and the deserted bay shook in obedience to thin pencil points of flame. Till seven they attacked the Fort, steaming steadily backwards and forth. It is astounding that they had not silenced it by evening, when they turned westward and home, the low sun swallowing in its spread furnace the mathematical fierce flickers of their artillery.

Guadalupe must have taken quite eighty shells. As night fell it dropped two of its own on ruined Oyarzun.

Next day *Almirante Cervera* opened on Guadalupe, *España* on the curved Concha of San Sebastian. *Almirante Cervera's* guns alone were less impressive: where *España* had made our windows a dinner gong, with *Almirante Cervera* they simply rustled; would take no trouble. Guadalupe replied, 6-inch for 6-inch; and the Calvary above the Fort —commemorating Our Lady for miles around—split from each in a welter of unsubstantial yellow dust. In the afternoon *Almirante Cervera* sheered off to San Sebastian, where *España* at her aloof and solemn distance from the shore had been firing her heavy shells all over the town.

España that day discharged quite eighty rounds of 12-inch into the hapless town. The sirens sounded, and this day there weren't any queues; the older people went down into the cellars. Only the children, the swarming children of Spain, played on in the streets. In the cellars even agnostics became religious and discovered a rosary to draw between the fingers. Mary, Mother of God . . . crash goes a shell through two storeys of the Maternity Hospital. Lips move to Our Father . . . another knocks the front off a rich man's house in the Concha. In the Calle San Martin a woman is killed in a basement, for 12-inch shells dig deep. The thunderbolts scatter into the Avenida de Francia, the Calle Ronda near the Railway Station. They drop on Urgull, who barks a sharp reply. As *Almirante*

Cervera carelessly steamed into line with *España* that afternoon, Urgull struck her in the side.

She made off west, and at eight-thirty she was outside Gijon, which now, except for the Simanca barracks, had fallen to the Asturians. Listing heavily to port, and showing a hole above the water-line she fired a few random shells into Gijon, then wirelessed El Ferrol that she was returning for repairs. I did not see her again for a long time.

In San Sebastian they counted their dead. Two girls of twenty-one and twenty-two, a woman of fifty, and an old man of seventy: thirty-eight wounded. So they executed eight prisoners, I believe without trial, as well as an infantry captain and four officers of Carabineros after court-martial. They had promised to execute: the war of menace and fulfilment had to drag its broken-backed way along, in Guipuzcoa no less than in the rest of Spain.

Next day, the 19th, the *España* shelled San Sebastian again, but the population had recovered from its funk. It is doubtful whether these naval bombardments were of any value: they silenced no forts, and the demoralisation that they caused was only temporary. The land forces did not even take advantage of the embarrassment of Guadalupe and San Sebastian to launch their general offensive. They were still waiting for reinforcements of men and artillery to fill the centre, and in their determination to be careful missed a golden opportunity.

On the 20th Guadalupe and the forts of the capital were firing inland again, and the navy's work devolved upon the rebel air force, which from now on bombed Irun and San Sebastian without the intermission of a day, and with increasingly heavy loads.

They also began to bomb San Marcial from Italian Caproni 101 monoplanes. On the hills to the south, in bracken and pine, the crests were picked out now with the red-yellow-red of Old Spain. Each new position was marked with a gay little flag from the age of romantic war, and on the centre of each was a picture of the Virgin. The divine, emotionless eyes looked out on the folded mountains of Guipuzcoa, where war was almost invisible, yet everywhere. A few strands of barbed wire; a new brown mark upon a hill, where they have laid sand-bags for a machine-gun redoubt. But no man to be seen: how cruelly unlike the wars for which flags were invented, when smart lads and boastful veterans stood in scarlet ranks upon the neat incline, and the officer bowed like a gentleman with his absurd request: *"Que Messieurs les Anglais tirent les premiers."*

Opposite Biriatou the Frente Popular are excavating the railway for a last minute mine. They have blown up the road behind it already. Their armoured train is two hundred yards back in Gastinaldia village, a few white-washed houses in plane trees whose roots drink from the Bidasoa. All day echoes the exchange of machine-guns in the valley beyond Gastinaldia, where the Spanish moun-tains slope and tumble into the overlord Peña d'Aya. And next morning on the little hill across the river, where an apple orchard sprinkles the near skyline, in the very crook of the Bidasoa's arm, I can see with the naked eye red berets in movement, only six hundred yards from the Frente Popular defensive line.

From the 23rd to the 25th the cruiser *Canarias* shelled San Sebastian and Guadalupe without killing anybody. One-hundred-pound bombs were dropped on Irun station, where dynamite experts were arriving from the Asturias, and Anarchists from Barcelona. These last came in by small parties through France and Hendaye: the French police kept their passage as quiet as possible: arms were issued to them when they reached Irun. In the quiet one could hear the coming of the storm. We went up to a little restaurant that let rooms at Biriatou, where from a ledge under vines in the French hills one could see both sides filling in.

Behind the apple-crowned hill, where the upper Bidasoa turned sharp east into Spain and the hill hid the road from the Frente Popular, Beorlegui's men had hauled up a battery of artillery; it lay next the road, camouflaged with branches of the gay-green plane tree. Lorries were at rest further up the road and hundreds of soldiers in blankets crouched in this dead ground to take their food at evening. In the valley the enemy were very close, and echoes of random shots ran full melancholy circle of the bowl of the hills. Smoke from the small lonely farmhouses between had become extinct.

Deserters reported the arrival of a battalion of the Foreign Legion at Erlaitz. Pembroke Stephens saw them at Oyarzun: they were Beorlegui's old Moroccan battalion, picked assault troops seven hundred strong. Most of them were Spaniards, with a few Germans.

They told Stephens that they had been flown across the Straits of Gibraltar in fifteen of the great convertible commercial-trooper-bomber planes turned out by Junkers: flown by German pilots. Each plane carried twenty-five men. They had fought at Badajoz.

It became very tense in Irun. Six-inch guns were planted in Fuenterrabia, low down near the water. Lighter artillery were limbered into position on a farm between Behobia and the Puntza. The high sand-bag barricade at the Carabinero post on the flank of Puntza was manned. The toy armoured train stood two hundred yards forward, in Gastinaldia, with steam up under the plane trees. The wounded Frente Popular militiaman stopped potting at white pigeons on the thick red-tiled roofs of Gastinaldia village: was taken to the rear.

The storm broke at six next morning, Wednesday, August 26th. It began upon equal terms in numbers, about three thousand men a side, but with artillery, rifle and automatic fire power greatly to the advantage of the rebels.

* * * * * *

It was a night of desultory firing: but at six the machine-guns started in earnest across the Bidasoa, and we jumped out of our beds. For the rebels they spoke from the apple-crowned hill and their conversation was with Gastinaldia village: thence, rather more feebly, the Frente Popular guns replied. Three hundred yards of bracken and a gentle fold in the ground separated the fighting men.

On the road below Apple Hill I suddenly heard the low grind of tracks. River mist covered the road with a loose net of invisibility: in dim outline, moving very slowly behind it, rolled a light tank with a turret, from which came the steady stammer of another machine-gun. Cautiously, stopping and measuring its distance from the armoured train, it pattered its bullets on the resistant plating. Very gradually it moved up to the gap in the road: one by

FRANCO'S TERCIO BEFORE IRUN:
SEPTEMBER 2ND, 1936.
[Photo: *The Times*.

GOVERNMENT MILITIA BEFORE IRUN:
SEPTEMBER 2ND, 1936.

one, six armoured cars crept behind it. All scrawled in sweeping letters of white chalk *Viva España!*

Picture the scene, the sun just risen, the mist still rising. The river at our feet one hundred and fifty yards away: beyond it trembles with a flimsy stiffness a narrow field of maize, alternating with strips of open fallow. Beyond the maize, the straight little railway and the road running hand in hand across the front scene. Behind and above them, Apple Hill, and just beyond Apple Hill the back hangings of the stage, a magnificent curtain daubed pine-green, grey for the rock of the Spanish mountains, water-blue for the Spanish sky, gaining colour every minute under the new dazzling limelight of the southern sun. The mist scatters, the searching light scribbles the battle in full outline; a thousand rifles settle into staccato song. It is clear day.

To the right, the driver of the armoured train is machine-gunning from behind sand-bags on Gastinaldia platform. To the left, round the soft curve of Apple Hill, concealed in the maize, comes the first platoon of Fascist infantry. Only the yellow tips bend stiffly and shake their dry scalps as they pass. In the middle the tank stops, firing furiously, before the road gap.

The mine behind does not explode. Its electrical apparatus has been cut by a daring Carlist raid in the night. A young man runs from behind the tank into the hedge at the left of the road. With a white flag he signals the little castle off the road, to a safe passage into the field and back again. It tilts upwards. Others in sombre cowls, steel helmets dulled deep grey-green, pushed the tank behind. Up she goes, skirts the gap, tumbles down again. Very, very slowly she moves upon Gastinaldia.

It takes an hour and a half. There is a lot of stumbling backwards and forwards in war. Tank faced up to small armoured train; which was to turn first? . . .

At seven-thirty the engine driver jumped into his engine, when the duel was at only one hundred yards distance. With great dignity, as if it were the only gentlemanly thing to do, he pulled into retirement. The tank pondered a little, then drove forward into Gastinaldia and shot the dust off the ponderous red tiles and the white plaster off the bullet-bitten walls: to no one's harm. The village was abandoned.

Infantry moved up through the maize, in stealthy groups, at the river-side. It shivered and parted. Out came a section in blue and khaki overalls, in scarlet berets, forage caps and steel helmets, clattering rifles, bayonets, machine-guns, grenades, blankets, pots, pans and aluminium cups. Plunging out of the maize they ambled head down and heavy over the fallow strip, fell flat as dead men behind the next sowing of maize. They fired all the time. Then, as the other sections came up, staggered up again and forward. At eight, they scattered grenades in the last crackling yellow patch before Gastinaldia: balls of white smoke, furry cobwebs hung around the maize heads. Then they rushed the village.

The young man in a beret who carried the red-yellow-red flag fell flat by the first house, grasping his stomach. He tried to rise, then fell again. A few others tumbled to a hidden machine-gun in the T-wood of young pines on the hill to the right, behind Gastinaldia: on whose crest the Frente Popular redoubts now stood in full sunshine, square, neat and challenging. I counted eight positions break into fire upon the fallen village. A few grenades were thrown by Carlists here, and in one house they hauled away a roof cover to snipe on the block-house down river.

Their officer, a tall young man, bareheaded, shouted orders: we could hear every syllable above the gun fire. His men, crouched waiting behind walls, cried "Viva España" and "Mañana a San Sebastian."

The whole Frente Popular line began serious shooting. Every machine-gun sprang to quarrelsome life: one could hear the antiphony of light and heavy in the whole battle choir. Heavy artillery of the rebels began to drop high explosive in the sapling beds on Zubelzu, below the ridge and the redoubts. Brown mushrooms of smoke and earth opened out and clammied the sky above them. The Frente Popular replied with lighter pieces and shocking ammunition, which fell but often did not burst, between Apple Hill and Gastinaldia.

Two of the red-winged planes from San Sebastian tried to bomb the village station, the armoured cars still jammed behind the unmended gap, the savage artillery in the elbow of the Bidasoa. Over San Marcial and Irun again the

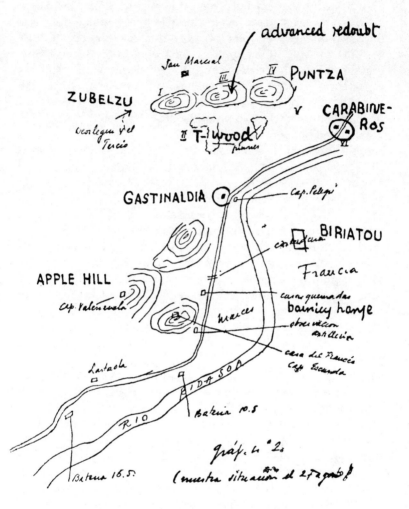

MAP BY INSURGENT OFFICER OF FIGHTING BEFORE BIRIATOU,
AUGUST 27TH, 1937

Capronis glittered, scattering bombs and leaflets, YIELD. Aviation did not yet impress me.

And so it went on until nine that night. After Gastinaldia no progress was made against the Frente Popular defences. But platoon after platoon of rebel infantry poured through the maize into Gastinaldia, and deployed through the bracken along the base of Zubelzu slope. Great squares of larches thickly intertwined spread in diagonal to the top, and the purple brown fern of the mountain side and its folded mule tracks also promised skilful cover.

What had happened elsewhere?

From Biriatou I could see little puffs of brown, distant shell-explosions, on the mountains behind Apple Hill screening the Peña d'Aya. This was Guadalupe shooting at Beorlegui's artillery, which for its part did not shoot at San Marcial, his objective, because Beorlegui was afraid of hitting France. Instead it fired upon the left of his front, on the sector facing Oyarzun, where a violent battle raged.

Beorlugei directed everything from Erlaitz. That day his maximum advance, in the centre valley leading up to San Marcial, was a mile and a half. He had hoped to attack San Marcial in front and from the left flank, but the legionaires whom he used on the left went wide of their mark: it took several hours to fill out the line and adjust the error.

As night fell the dead and wounded were taken to the base, heads downward, on a mule. Shallow trenches were dug in front of Zubelzu. The Irun command claimed that they had killed two hundred in front of their line, which had not been pierced. I suppose we shall never know how big the casualties were, for in this war only the Foreign Legion kept a list of dead and wounded—and kept it secret. Certainly the losses of Beorlegui's men were far greater than those of Irun: on the opening day of the battle for Irun not one of the redoubts was hit by his artillery.

Two advanced posts, Gastinaldia on the Bidasoa and a hill on the extreme left had fallen to the rebels.

* * * * * *

Next day the fight continued with rather diminished intensity. The usual aerial bombardments by the rebels on the pine-woods of San Marcial, on Irun, and by the Frente Popular on the rebel artillery. Beorlegui's men made some progress through cover at the farther end of Zubelzu ridge, where it hung in pine-mantled calm over the valley to San Marcial: but a frontal attack on Puntza at the nearer end, without preparation of artillery, led to several casualties. At midday bugles sounded the cease fire and the wounded were brought down on litters.

One could see that Beorlegui's aim was still to pinch the Frente Popular line from front and flank, just where it curved in front of San Marcial. At its most sensitive point. But though he had a superiority of artillery, he had not yet enough to break through.

He now sent to Pampluna and to Burgos for more. Meanwhile the Frente Popular guns in front of Behobia laid down shell after shell along the Bidasoa. After midday the firing died down: at Biriatou now one smelt the acrid smell of battle, began to see the spreading tins and litter of war.

Deserters described the mixed force that was attacking San Marcial in the mountain angle: the left wing of Beorlegui's army; 550 Legionaries, 450 Carlistas, 440 Guardia Civil, 400 Falangistas (Fascists), with officers nearly 2,000 in all. It was a nice cross-section, representative even as to proportions, of the forces supporting the rebellion in Spain. First Franco's own army, the spearhead, rushed from front to front, ready for all desperate work: then the Navarrese, the deep regional enthusiasm behind the movement; the Guardia Civil, symbol of law and order, of a rather unthinking Spanish dignity, a self-respectful and solid conservatism; last, the new Fascists, a queer organ of the class war clamped rather artificially on to Spanish life, gathering thousands of adherents, few of whom were fit to fight. The love of a *fiesta* drew many of the lower classes into their ranks, in the Castilian country towns, Burgos and Palencia, Valladolid and Salamanca. Any social scrap iron was enlisted by the leaders of the Falange Española: it kept thoughtless people quiet marching them round in blue shirts to a blaring band, and the tougher specimens could be drafted into the trenches.

* * * * * *

Friday, the third day of the attack, Beorlegui continued his pressure on the angle of San Marcial, despite losses to his legionaries. It was very hot. They were very tired: dispirited. But he was determined to get the most out of them. The Fuenterrabia artillery turned its attention entirely to them, leaving the Gastinaldia-Puntza front to the Behobia guns.

Gastinaldia itself was heavily shelled, and the two tanks and the armoured cars covered with summer greenery were forced out of the stuffy little village, now smoke-laden. They withdrew down the sultry valley just as their infantry on the slope which rose steeply up the redoubt of Puntza were driven back again. The third frontal attack on Puntza had failed: the rebel artillery, though only a thousand yards from their target, had not yet found and pulverised it.

Men in blue overalls could be seen running down, in cover of the pines. A machine-gun was withdrawn. Everyone was fidgeting for cover.

In the valley bottom, where bracken grew spongy and thick against the sallowing grass of Apple Hill, they had deepened and lengthened and parapeted the trenches. The rebels were digging in.

So had the rebels dug in on the furthest crest of Zubelzu. There during the night, spangling the black silhouette of the pines with blue points of light and dully piercing the country quiet with the solemn burst of bombs and mortars, they had established themselves inside the Frente Popular line. They bore a day of vicious counter-attack; fighting was thirsty and ungrateful under the mountain sun.

To counter this threat, the Frente Popular improvised two more shallow redoubts on the middle of Zubelzu.

As night fell on the scene, the heavy black spread of mountains was enflamed at point after point where pine-belts pulsated red under the incendiary shells of Fuenter-rabia. Irregular splashes of hot red mottled the sad immovable horizon. Just across the river, which glinted the summer stars in less barbarous, less human outline, a farmhouse struck from Behobia threw to Heaven tormented scarves of fire. They were still digging and talking in the shadows fretted backwards and forwards by its rising flicker, when at eleven that night, the whole of Zubelzu burst into the sparkling geometry of battle under a cool clear moon.

It raged for four hours. A night battle in forest is a magnificent sight to see. The unpleasant details of war are sponged away by night. No tired men, no wounded in sweat, no dead lying heavy on the dry uncomfortable grass. You are saved the view of the broken ammunition cases, the discarded tins and piled filth of the temporary camp. Quickly trowelled trenches do not gash the fern-banks and the roads and fields are not pitted with ugly irregular shell holes under a pall of dust. War is idealised into a symphony of blue and yellow lights against a dull background of explosions: bullets and shells take the part of strings and portentous wind in an untiring orchestra.

It is ethereal, war by night. Over there, where Zubelzu woods look in profile up to Erlaitz, the dark forest glitters with thousand upon thousand tinsel flashes, level spurts of fairy flame that illumine the tree boles like stiff upright threads. At the centre of Zubelzu, where a sable dome of hill cuts the light and starry night sky, tinsel sparkles back. Between, mortars discharge like red reflecting ornaments and their shells explode like candles lighting yellow. Tinsel, hangings, candles, glitter, the dark background: what is this but a giant Christmas tree alight, now hiding, now revealing from its foliage the decorations of our childhood, surfaces that catch and splinter fire into its prettiest particles, scarlets and electric blues and golden rays too fragile to be touched.

Charming illusion to me, who sit wrapped in pyjamas and in an infant wonder, gazing across the river that spins under the moon. And I hear the harmless crackle of this tinfoil game, like hangings that rub with metallic sharp-ness against the branches of the shaken Christmas tree when presents are cut down; and the louder explosions — those are crackers pulled round the festive candles of Zubelzu.

No killing and maiming, thirst, hunger and pain to be picked out through curious field-glasses. Only the pretti-ness of war, under the moon and against the sober foil of mountain and pinewood.

The Legion lost many bold men that night, but they pressed the Frente Popular back to within two hundred

yards of San Marcial. Before Saturday dawn they had
dug in: painful detail reappeared.

* * * * * *

Saturday and Sunday were quiet days, the fourth and
fifth of the attack on Irun. What a slow thing is war—in
broad daylight. Beorlegui straightened out his line from
Zubelzu down the slope to Gastinaldia and tried to penetrate the line to the right of San Marcial, but he was again
beaten back. He took his tanks off the Gastinaldia road
and sent them up the frontal track to San Marcial; an
Italian officer there was astonished at their capacity for
mountain-climbing.

Gradually, the artillery was being assembled from the
back areas of rebel Spain. They and urban panic were
to do for Irun, and for the whole of Guipuzcoa. Panic
first.

At the week-end, rebel planes dropped leaflets saying
that Irun, if she did not give in, would be bombed from the
air and shelled from land and sea. I am told, but have
not been able to verify, that the same threat was made
against San Sebastian. The effect of this propaganda was
astonishing.

The flood over the International Bridge at Hendaye
began at about ten on Sunday evening. By midnight
1,500 women and children had crossed the bridge from
Fuenterrabia, where the Alcalde had ordered the evacuation. Later during the night 2,000 crossed from Fuenterrabia and Irun, which had contracted the sudden fear;
and at eight on Monday morning there was still a large
clamouring crowd at the bridge waiting their turn to
present permits and pass the barrier. All, including some
disguised sympathisers of the Right or loyal servants of
those already escaped, were dressed as poorly as possible
and carried red favours to catch the sympathy of the
frontier guards. (An idle and sedentary race of men, who
spend their long span of life in *al fresco* arm-chairs, disposed
in the celebrated Spanish formation of the *tertulia* or Conversational Circle, issuing tobacco smoke from their nostrils
in centripetal monotony. But to-day they were quite
foredone with work.)

Motor coaches cramming as many as fifty at a time came in throughout the day from San Sebastian. Others walked over the hills behind the firing line. Those who were lucky enough to crowd into the cars—which seated thirty—reported that light was entirely cut off in private houses and hotels of San Sebastian, and that women queued in the streets now for milk as well as water. Fish had not been sold for a month because of the rebel warships, who arrested all fishing-boats. Food of every kind was scarce and the daily arrests continued, filling the Casino and the battered Club Nautico with partisans of the Centre and the Right.

Though the continual bombardment from the air and the renewed attacks from the sea were getting on everybody's nerves, they could see no inclination to yield. New militia were being enrolled, even from the young men of the suspect classes.

There was the same show of defiance that Monday in Irun, when its colours were given to a new militia unit, the Thaelmann group, in token of its determination to fight to the finish.

In the afternoon the number of refugees had risen to 5,000. For the most part they were women and children, or old men; but it was the beginning of the rout at Irun.

They carried their babies in their arms, other children clung to their black skirts or their hands, very frightened. Hardly any had money: they were the people, the real people. Many were crying. With them came their baggage, all that they could save; and it was their men who carried their baggage, and that was the beginning of the rout at Irun.

Baggage: first their clothes, old, neat and well-washed, like the clothes of all Spaniards. In bundles tied with rope, or pathetic crumpled suit-cases made of brown stuff like carton, cheap muck for the poor. Then their few animals were driven over, if they came from a farm: their iron bedsteads and their bed-clothes. Their few pictures: the men ran back into Irun to bring this and that piece of precious cheap furniture. One could see that it was the beginning of the rout at Irun.

The militia which defended Irun were fed and supplied by a system based on the home. It was their wives and mothers and sisters who cooked their meals: it was these

and their girls who kept up their *morale*, who made them
fight hard. The militia had sprung into being with the
rebellion: it stood to reason that its organisers could not,
in these brief forty days, construct out of nothing a perfect
commissariat as well as an efficient fighting force. They
had to take many things for granted. The Spanish home
was one of them.

From now on the men defending San Marcial were not
only poorly fed: the foreigners, the French and Belgian
political enthusiasts who stuck it out in the front line, were
not once relieved. Many young men of Irun, I know,
fought to the end. But just as many remained in Irun to
superintend the migration of their families, and their girls,
and the children, whom Spaniards love so dearly: to save
from the coming wreck the savings of a humble life-time,
the carefully gathered objects, few but dear to them, which
since their birth had made their home. They did not run
away, perhaps, but they were busy in the rear-guard.

Their whole war organisation, a young structure and
perilously balanced, tottered now from the base up. That
evening, rather wildly, *España* carried out its promise and
shelled Fuenterrabia. South of San Sebastian, when all
eyes were turned towards the frontier, by a dawn surprise
the rebels took Mount Buruntia, the last natural barrier
between them and the capital of Guipuzcoa.

All day the roads to Irun from the south shook to the
progress of heavy artillery, summoned by Beorlegui to blow
the Frente Popular out of their last redoubts on the ridge.
The sixth day ended.

When it was dark the enemies from their front line
shouted or sang abuse at each other. The Navarrese
Catholics were "priests' bastards"; the Frente Popular
were "Marxist canaille." They also called each other
"cowards": to-morrow we were going to see what confirmed liars both parties were.

At seven o'clock on Tuesday morning, a lovely clear day,
five rebel aeroplanes flew over Irun and dropped thirty
100-pound bombs, only two of which did not explode.
Three old men, a child, and two officials of the Republican
Centre, which they hit fair and square, were reported
killed. Previous bombardments had concentrated on the

station: this was general, to destroy and damage and to terrify the population. Irun was yellowed over in the sickly smoke. It drifted to sea.

On the way back the planes bombed San Marcial and set a large pine-wood in front of it on fire. This was the signal for the most bitter and determined offensive on the Government line Zubelzu-Puntza that we had seen, and for the heaviest artillery bombardment of the Civil War until Madrid stood its siege.

Immediately a battery of 155 mms. (6-inch), brought up by the rebels during the night to the angle of the Bidasoa, opened fire over Apple Hill upon the centre of Zubelzu. On Puntza and down the steep shoulder of the ridge to the Carabineros' house, the shells of another 155 mm. battery fell in shattering mathematical line. A third battery farther inland dropped upon western Zubelzu. Three more concentrated upon San Marcial itself. Altogether fifty guns broke out upon the silent sunny ridge: so the rebels told Pembroke Stephens, and I believe it to be the truth.

High explosive was used. Beorlegui wanted to blow those redoubts to kingdom come and to split in a hundred red sopping pieces every machine-gunner in them. The rugged old man had, at last, the means.

Four shells at a time dropped regularly and four brown clouds rose on central Zubelzu. Four on Puntza. A thickening fog of smoke behind the pines at Zubelzu's end showed where shell after shell battered San Marcial.

The shooting was good. Very quickly the shells narrowed the margin of error, leapt nearer the target, tumbled waterspouts of the hillside earth on the sparkling machine-guns, which jerked to rapid fire from each still neat redoubt, just under the skyline.

As the guns grew more accurate I saw two at least of the Frente Popular redoubts evacuated. In particular, they quit the most advanced and largest redoubt on Puntza, which jutting over T-wood had fought back many frontal attacks during the past week, and driven the hardy Carlists down the slopes to Gastinaldia. The last man to leave, very leisurely he was, carried a red flag. It must have annoyed. As he quit, a shell with a perfect direction seemed to blow the inside of the redoubt to pieces.

On the central point of Zubelzu, under the pines, a heavy battle with trench mortars and later with grenades raged between the front-line trenches, here only two hundred yards from San Marcial.

The guns ceased. The redoubts seemed empty. Infantry, covered by machine-guns which were pushed half-way up the steep of Puntza, were thrown into the attack across Zubelzu, three-quarters of the way up the mountain-side. They took cover in the red bracken which furred the slope, working rapidly round towards the river and the vacant redoubts. On the turf they ran in open order with, it seemed, machine rifles. They were too late.

As the barrage finished the militia crept back, along shallow communication trenches, to their damaged redoubts. None of us saw them return. But from the centre of Zubelzu they enfiladed the little fluttering figures in khaki and blue against the bracken, and the zip of the bullets from the advanced redoubt on Puntza drove back one of their supporting M.G.'s. The rebel infantry took refuge in a thick fir-wood. But they had gained ground.

They had made good all the slope this side of the pine crest to almost the middle of Zubelzu, and they had covered their winnings by the capture of the whole eastern Zubelzu ridge.

Across the slope, sheltered by hedges, their attack headquarters' wing moved up, with a huge red-yellow-red flag at the head and a mule-train laden with two mountain guns behind. A small white farmhouse near the summit was occupied, the flag suspended from the window: in an hour smoke curled out of the chimney for the officers' midday meal.

The mules picked their way down the hill, past seven trim yellow haycocks, sheltered in the valley, to Gastinaldia. The next rebel assault was on their extreme right, by the road which led along the Bidasoa valley through Gastinaldia at our feet. Its objective was the Carabineros' house at the corner down river.

Suddenly round the corner of the Pampluna road came four armoured cars and drove into Gastinaldia village. There, slowing down, they began to fire—they were home-made armoured cars from Navarre, an unusual variety. Sometimes through their surprising slits rifles protruded;

sometimes the rifles were impulsively withdrawn and replaced by machine-guns. At one hundred yards from the
Carabineros' house they stopped, turned left to offer a
broadside, and went on to permanent duty with their
automatic weapons.

Their two batteries behind Apple Hill simultaneously
opened on Puntza and the shelving ridge to the river. It
was perfect shooting, precision repeated again and again.
The advanced redoubt on Puntza was penetrated five times;
its sand-bags scattered in pieces over the hill. It is impossible that any of the militia who recovered it survived.
Later explosions blew up corpses into the air before our
eyes.

At the Carabineros' house, where the shells could not
reach, the defenders stood their ground with the coolest
courage. The armoured cars poured hail into their sand-
bags and ripped the massive plaster front of the house to
pieces. Soon the top sand-bags were all shorn away.
Not a shell from their own side came to their help, for the
Irun artillery had been cowed for ever: only the shells
of the enemy could be seen, blasting the steep shoulder of
Puntza above their heads, shooting dust into the river
below them.

I watched them through glasses at one hundred yard's
range, at this bottle-neck of the river which they held.
They were calmly firing, cleaning their rifles, and firing
again from the chairs on which they sat smoking. Defiant
red bandana handkerchiefs showed their heads and necks.
They did not turn a hair, fought the armoured cars behind
their riddled sand-bags for an hour. The cars withdrew,
their ammunition spent. Jeers and abuse rose from the
Carabineros' post.

During the afternoon the advanced redoubt on Puntza,
twice destroyed, was reoccupied a second time by the
militia.

At about five-thirty the third artillery barrage of the
day was laid down on Zubelzu and Puntza. The advanced
redoubt, now unrecognisable, showing no sand-bags but a
crazy pile of earth and logs, was once more blown into the
sky. A Government stretcher party came up to the post
and took two bodies, then stumbled away. A shell blew
the last of them into insignificant pieces on the horizon.

The other redoubts were not hit, and fought back a half attempt of the infantry to advance. A little shrapnel came over from Fuenterrabia to help the hard-pressed militia.

At eight in the evening they re-entered the advanced redoubt for the third time. Five more shells dropped in the dusk around the redoubt, which had taken forty-seven since seven o'clock that morning. Perhaps the little garrison were killed again; but at nine that evening the minute flashes of a machine-gun in the dark showed that Puntza was still entirely Frente Popular. They must have lost dozens of men; they held firm.

But at the angle in front of San Marcial, Beorlegui had now deeply penetrated their defences. Three-fifths of the slopes were his. He rested that night, after the most wearing day of the war.

Morning of Wednesday, the eighth day of the attack, came without clouds to disclose a position much as before. But the Frente Popular line across the saddle of Zubelzu and the high knoll of Puntza looked uneasy. Men sniped down into the near woods at awkward angles. The redoubts had been repaired, not thoroughly. Small tumbled squares of branch and sacking, dusty and pock-marked, they did not look as if they could stand more bombardment. But the morning passed quietly. Only short neuralgic bursts of the machine-guns in the muffled pines.

It was very hot at midday. A staff car, all glitter, passed up the road from Enderlaza to the rebel artillery at the road-side. The black beetle body twitched close to the ground round corner after corner: stopped by the camouflaged guns and the ammunition dugouts. As its dust steadied and dissolved in clear air, the reflective river caught the scene—black car, grey guns, under the fluttering plane trees and against the rich green of Apple Hill. Reflective river, contemplative sky. From rocks two hundred feet up I watched. Ammunition poured out of the ground at a quick command.

At twelve-thirty three guns in front of Fort Erlaitz, over there in the mountains, dropped shells on Zubelzu. A battery at the junction of the Pampluna-San Marcial and the direct Pampluna-Irun road followed. The battery at

the angle of the Bidasoa below me took up the same terrible
tune. Firing high explosive and shrapnel, they raked the
ridge from where the pinewood ended to the advanced
redoubt on Puntza, a distance of about four hundred yards.
From left to right, from right to left they played. They
blew the advanced redoubt to heaven for the fifth time in
two successive days, and they shattered another position
behind thin maize on the saddle of Zubelzu. The ridge
was scarred and lacerated with war: brown gashes jetted
a blood of sand and the skin of Puntza was punctured again
and again.

The infantry, after their lesson of yesterday, were close
enough.

At one-twenty, over two hundred shells had battered
Zubelzu-Puntza ridge. Out of near thickets of young pines
and fern the infantry moved up, heralded by four men
throwing grenades, to the advanced position on Puntza.
It was empty. They entered the redoubt walking in a
trail, and over the bloody refuse there an officer raised the
flag of the monarchy. Italian journalists by my side cried
"*Viva España*," and the Legionary reserves in Gastinaldia
below broke out into a marching song of the regiment.
Mules with mountain guns pattered forward.

Two platoons of rebel infantry burst out of rusty beds
of bracken under Zubelzu saddle, to the left. Throwing
bombs, the sunlight flanking their bayonets, they entered
the sunniest position of the Frente Popular. The ridge of
Zubelzu, its squat haystacks and its small farm-houses in
grey ashes, was now entirely in their hands, and the flags
moved forward like pins on your home-fought wars upon
the map.

The artillery, which fired this afternoon at a rate which
I had never seen before in Spain, turned again with a roar
upon the extreme right, the eastern shoulder of Puntza,
where a position on a lower peak still held out, hanging
high above the Carabineros' house and the Bidasoa. After
twenty minutes of bitter fighting the monarchist flag stood
on the redoubt at three o'clock. The battle went on at a
speed that took one's breath away: the Frente Popular
line was crumpling up before one's eyes.

Last came the turn of the Carabineros' post at the river's
edge, below the steep. It held out stubbornly for two

more hours, attacked by two machine-guns in front, one machine-gun from the fallen redoubt above, which covered the flank of their sand-bags. And finally they were encircled behind from over Puntza. Men crept down their old communication trenches, shallow ditches, to snipe them subtly.

The armoured train was sent away at four, being too valuable to lose. The defenders, thirty or forty men, squeezed into the sand-bags in front to avoid the flanking fire, and blazed straight ahead of them at the hidden enemy in Gastinaldia until the barrels were steaming from the barricade. Others manned every bullet-gnawed window in the house. At five the four armoured cars, beaten back yesterday, came up to the fight again and finished it.

Three hundred men in steel helmets with grenades and rifles followed them, trotting in bunches, shouting *"Viva España"* and cheering. The bullets flattened and skidded on the armoured cars in hundreds as they moved up. The cars drove up square to the sand-bag barricade and swivelled their guns into the defence. Dynamite sped from the touch of the red cigarette: the infantry flung their grenades over the sand-bags, and the block-house was a hell of smoke, cries and explosions.

Fifteen minutes' hand-to-hand, round the sand-bags and about the house: the most desperate defence on the Irun line was overcome, and the survivors ran from the reddened road or jumped from the windows to roll into the river. Scrambling back under the cruel sweep of the bullets, many of them made their way into the maize behind the block-house, others lay dead. Fighting went on inside the house for half an hour: those who were caught within would not surrender. Three cars behind the post turned Irun-wards that flew the red flag burst into flames with bullets through their petrol tanks. Men in the maize crept away on their stomachs, across the rich green runnels that irrigated the fields of Behobia, grateful for this smoke and for these thick dangling tresses, stiff military stalks and impenetrable leaves of the corn. The machine-guns on the crest fired steadily into the fields, wounding some.

That day all the old men and women and children of Behobia ran across their little bridge, by the green Island of Pheasants where Louis XIV once sought a wife, into French Behobie. In Behobie everything was shuttered up, bullets sang and caressed the walls, the French women and children cowered in shelter. The whole French bank was sprayed with the rebels' fire.

On San Marcial, now, they concentrated all their artillery.

At seven that evening a few survivors deafened and bleeding from the barrage, crept down the supply road that yesterday had still seen the lorries pass up from Irun to the white convent. Its high tower, which fringed in pines dominated Irun and Fuenterrabia like a warning finger, was no longer Irun's. Night fell. The whole line had fallen to the enemy.

The Frente Popular had promised them heavy street fighting in Irun. Even now one knew as one saw the men crouch in the maize, firing back at some desperate target, at no target at all, at the accursed ridge treacherously fondled by the summer twilight: even now one knew that their bruised moral was past the reach of medicine. As long as they could they fought heroically. It was an unequal battle that laid bare Irun, won by the side with the artillery. Against the remorseless salvos of Beorlegui's trained batteries the Frente Popular sent back precisely ten shells, five of which did not explode and none of which did harm.

Now that it was too late, in the dark, the guns of Fuenterrabia sent a few more shells into San Marcial hill.

Towards midday of Thursday the rebels moved up their artillery along the Bidasoa. Lighter field-pieces were hauled into the rich sun on Puntza ridge. About twenty lorries and half a dozen staff cars passed to and fro. By four-thirty in the afternoon the people of Biriatou, agape on their hill on the French side, watched over 1,500 new troops, material for the direct assault on Irun, pass beneath them. All sorts of uniforms were there, for the army attacking Irun was one of the most heterogenous in the world —regular army, Tercio, Carabineros, Guardia Civil, Guardia de Asalto, Requetés and Falangists and Renovacion Española, of the monarchist fraction.

One thousand deployed to the left at midday, over the steep slope of Zubelzu to San Marcial: how quiet it was after the battle! At four-thirty, two hundred of the rest were standing ready around the old advanced redoubt above T-wood on Puntza, listening to a speech from their commander, while the Frente Popular raggedly shelled the country in front of them. The rest gathered at the battered Carabinero post on the Bidasoa, with their four armoured cars and a field gun. They were immediately ordered forward.

The ground, which is level meadow land planted with maize between the railway and the river all the way to Behobia and rises gently to the smooth seaward slopes of Puntza and Zubelzu, had been combed throughout the night by patrols. These had occupied some of the scattered farmhouses where Behobia tailed out into country. During the morning there had been much monotonous sharp-shooting at the village boundary, where all was shuttered up and no chimneys smoked, and in the maize. Shells on San Marcial for a while inspirited the Behobia Militia, who included two women and several boys in blazers.

Many had fled in panic across the bridge the night before. Those who stayed took turns at the machine-guns, while their friends came over for drinks and a short rest in a bullet-spattered bar in French Behobie. Fine handsome men, some of them; their drinks finished, back they went to the machine-gun, with a friendly salute to the French gendarmes.

Or they helped to save things forgotten in yesterday's panic. Beds, sewing machines, dazed poultry, baffled pigs, finally two magnificent marble barber's chairs with the shaving paper still unrolling from the back like carnival streamers were trolled across the bridge.

That afternoon they fought back the rebel advance along the road, and the rebel machine-guns which, at long distance, pattered on their roofs. The armoured cars were kept back by *dinamiteros* hidden in the maize. Two machine-guns of the Frente Popular did their best from the Spanish Quarantine Office at the frontier bridge-head, and from behind an old stone wall at the river-side. By sunset no progress had been made along the road, but the rebels had descended San Marcial and were encircling Behobia.

A match factory burned from end to end that night beside the Bidasoa. In the weird, unsteady half light the militia of Behobia, nervy and cold again, could be seen one by one slinking into France. It was drizzling; the world shivered. One by one in the shadows, till two hundred had handed their weapons to the French guard.

At two that morning a devastating fire was poured into the village from all sides. The armoured train—wretched little toy—moved back to Irun. The machine-gunners at the bridge-head stood their ground until their drums were finished. At four, nineteen fled into France; the twentieth lay dead. The troops of Beorlegui occupied Behobia, hoisted the red and yellow flag at the bridge, gravely bowed to the French.

Between four and dawn, militia posts on the way to Irun were surrounded and their occupants killed. One or two hastily dug trenches on the Irun road were cleared; so was the debris of the match factory, which barred the way of the armoured cars. It was all very expeditiously done; resistance was feeble.

A chance shot set the dynamite workshop near Irun station ablaze with a mighty explosion.

Panic must have been struck into the Government Committee at Irun by this sound . . . by the fall of Behobia . . . by the return of the armoured train . . . by the break-down of their entire defensive organisation, the utter hopelessness of their task. Their followers say that the members of the committee who ruled Irun were the first to quit—at four in the morning. Only the foreigners and the Anarchist leaders remained. A traditional Spanish fraction of the Left showed traditional Spanish stubbornness.

Irun went stark, staring mad.

It started before dawn. The militia began to bolt across the International Bridge between Irun and Hendaye, where road and railway cross the Bidasoa on three separate structures. First they were few, then they came in hundreds. Road or railway bridge, it was the same to them; over both flew the bullets of the terrible rebels, terribly near Irun.

Some ran, most crept and crawled. They were an abject spectacle. They said that they had no ammunition left, no leaders: they were bitter about their leaders. All their limber came over with them—the dear old beds

and wardrobes, the dear old pigs and poultry. Through
the day two thousand crossed the bridges. Cars still
painted in the party colours of the Left shot over into
France; returned to Spain in reverse, so afraid were
their drivers of the risks of turning in Irun. Mattresses
were laid out in the mud.

Hendaye was packed. Those who wished to continue
fighting—five hundred men—were grouped at the station
for a special train which was to take them to Barcelona.
Those who had had enough—three-quarters of this demoralised wreck—were sent by car and lorry to camps
at Pau, Bordeaux, Angoulême and Poitiers. But they
had not changed their political views. They drove through
the town with clenched fists, flourishing red ribbons,
perched on enormous bundles.

As they burst through the bridges, a company of French
troops was sent to aid the struggling gendarmerie. Arms
had to be taken away and dumped, directions given.

Throughout the morning the evacuation of a different
class went on from Fuenterrabia. Many holiday-makers of
the Centre and the Right, caught and half-imprisoned
there after the suppression of the military revolt at San
Sebastian, were escaping across the Bidasoa in fishing
boats. Even some of the hostages in Guadalupe escaped
that day. And though Larrañaga, the War Commissar
from San Sebastian, threatened with his revolver the
Militia who would fight no more in Fuenterrabia, he could
not stop them from embarking also. The fishermen of
Fuenterrabia, a generous race, manned their smacks and
rowing boats free of charge to ferry the mixed refugees
of all parties over to France. In Hendaye could be seen,
sitting on briny trunks in rough clothes, tieless, hatless
and unwashed, anybody from a stubble-chin Spanish
marquess downwards. A few days of suffering had blurred
many of the outer distinctions of class.

Heart-broken fathers and mothers ran through all the
hotels of Hendaye. "Can you tell me what has happened
in Guadalupe? Have they killed them? My son is
there. Have you news?"

Meanwhile the Anarchists, under the black-red flag,
had taken charge of the whole of Irun, Fuenterrabia, and
the Guadalupe promontory. A few determined foreign

Communists set up a machine-gun post at the International Bridge, which fired towards Behobia.

First, the Anarchists destroyed two pieces of artillery for which they could find no more ammunition, and then they fired a few shells through the rest at random. They dynamited and shattered the houses where the army of Beorlegui was threatening to enter Irun. They burned most of the cars in the garages, and with the petrol that was left they lit houses at all the entrances to Irun. They circled the town with flames. Then they turned to the centre.

They lit the gambling club, the Paris Hotel, the chocolate factory, the station, the whole Paseo de Colón, and many other streets in the centre of the town. They poured petrol over this roof and that. Forty-odd cars were brought over safe and sound from the Customs; but shots were sent by the Anarchists through the petrol tanks of those left in the streets, and they burst into flames. The whole day, from sunrise to sunset, they poured benzine and threw dynamite over the little town of Irun, which once housed sixteen thousand Spaniards.

As the sun of the tenth day set, Irun, a fair understudy, took its place in the sky. Irun was burning sulky red at a hundred points that stifled the dark. Along the Avenida de Francia, where the cars were candles in a row, long flags of flame flickered now all the way to Irun; there a ravenous and pulsing furnace swallowed up their individual life, obliterated their frailer, more sensitive, and volatile existences in universal Fire. It covered the night horizon with itself: its smoke billowed upward to soot out the stars. Against it one could sometimes see moving darkly the tormented and violent people who created it.

On Saturday morning Beorlegui occupied the town with a regiment of mixed infantry, four armoured cars and two companies of the Tercio. The rest of his force lay outside the town, which was still burning: its main streets were now a cracked and smoky shell, squeezing from its crevices cinders and intolerable heat. Nearly all the factories had been burnt, and the hotels and a part of the station. Here five men held out, and were dispatched with grenades. Two or three cars rushing through the town were shot at until they stopped or went up in flames. A few prisoners were taken, and shot. A few old women, to the surprise of all, were found to be still peacefully residing in burning Irun. Since this was Basque territory, the churches had been spared.

The men who escaped over the bridge at the finish, about midday, were mentally prostrated. They beat their heads with their fists, chewed the stuff of their overcoats, wept bitterly without respite. Two had terrible stomach wounds.

It was midday when the armoured cars came down to the Customs House at the bridge, and drove out the last machine-gun post of Irun. Two of its little crew were caught by the biting bullets in the girders of the railway bridge, half-way to safety, and turned convulsively over the permanent way, spouting blood and slowly dying. The victors dragged them back; they died on the road as the monarchist flag was hoisted over their poor empty munition box and their scattered shells, and the Navarrese covered their faces and danced in a cere-monious circle to celebrate their conquest of an outlet to the sea.

These men who stuck their ground were both foreigners. I have the Communist Party unemployment insurance card of one, a young lad from France.

It was Beorlegui's hard-won victory; his day. His stubborn, ruthless and persistent spirit had seen the matter through from the beginning, when he kept the Carlists steady under gun fire at Oyarzun. He made mistakes, particularly in the first days of the assault on San Marcial, when he attacked without artillery preparation. But he was a fine and fearless soldier: to him alone the conquest of Guipuzcoa was due.

As he watched the final battle at the bridge, a bullet from that French boy's machine-gun struck Beorlegui in the calf. He made light of it, went back to Vera to have it dressed, returned to lead his troops to San Sebastian, the next step. He was dead within a month, for the wound gangrened.

I wonder what was his conversation with the young Frenchman when they met to compare notes and their mutilations in the other world? Under the labels, I dare

say, they had much in common. The mother tongue
of both was courage.

The first news that we had of Guadalupe and its
prisoners that afternoon was from a small rowing boat
seen off Hendaye at seven-thirty. It was manned by four
men, who held up its solitary oar with handkerchiefs tied
to the end, as signals of distress. A wind was blowing up
from the Gascony Gulf, and the sea was short and choppy
in the twilight; the boat soon tipped over. Twenty
minutes later a solitary swimmer came ashore, exhausted.
The others were picked up in the surf-singing dark by a
Basque fisherman. They were all hostages from Guadalupe.

Meanwhile at Hendaye Point, where a spit of sand
narrows the Bidasoa mouth, a different crew could be
studied across the river, under a noisy northerly gale that
fretted and thrashed the fishing quay. The last defenders
of Fuenterrabia were burning all the cars they could lay
their hands on, or driving them light-heartedly off the
quayside into the cold and clamorous surf. Thrilling
contrast: the icy wind and waters, the cars red-hot,
wallowing devils. A small trawler lay off shore, bumping
up and down; it filled up gradually with the wild-haired
militia, with three women and two boys. A man plunged
into the river near the rowing boat which was attending
the trawler. He dined with me that evening in Hendaye.
He was Señor Casadevante, a young Spaniard, son of a
member of the Diputacion (County Council) of San Sebastian, and he had been imprisoned in Guadalupe since
the middle of August.

He said that there were over two hundred people there,
thirteen of whom had been shot.

They were kept in the cellars of the fort, which were
unlit and which surrounded a small courtyard where
the prisoners were not allowed to take exercise. They
were fed fairly regularly, but there were no sanitary arrangements.

At the beginning of the week, when Fuenterrabia was
evacuated, there were five escapes from prison, among them
Señor Manuel Blanco, the individualistic railwayman, who
had shown a certain unwillingness to drive the Government
armoured train into action. The four others were shot.

There were no further shootings until Friday, said Casadevante, although the prisoners were frequently assembled in the courtyard and threatened. On Friday, the morning that Irun panicked, their guardians fled. Only slowly they realised that the prison was no longer held, and a few daring spirits got out. While the rest were working out a plan of escape, C.N.T. lorries arrived. The Frente Popular committee had thrown up the sponge and the extremists were succeeding them.

The C.N.T. men called up their prisoners, and from the roll selected the names of Honorio Maura and Jaoquin Beunza. Maura was a Deputy and a leader of the Renovacion Española, the Monarchist group in the Cortes; he came of a famous political family, for his father, Antonio Maura, led the Conservative Party under the Monarchy, and his brother Miguel was the first Minister of the Interior under the Republic. Maura also wrote comedies and was political correspondent of the *A.B.C.* Beunza was a Deputy and leader of the Basque Traditionalists, a small fraction of the Right opposed to the Basque Nationalists.

The two men were led out and a machine-gun was heard. Their bodies were rifled and thrown into the shell-holes left by the rebel cruisers *España* and *Almirante Cervera*.

During Friday afternoon and evening the C.N.T. seemed to be losing grip and the F.A.I., the central Spanish Anarchist organisation, took over the guard of the prison from them. They called up the prisoners again and made a punitive choice.

Leopoldo Matos, who had been a Minister under Antonio Maura and under General Berenguer; Felix Churruca, an engineer; Miguel Ayesteran, the priest of Fuenterrabia; Saez, of the Guardia Municipal of Irun; Galarza, a captain of night-watchmen; the Marqués de Elosegui and the Conde de Llobregat, a retired officer who had been A.D.C. to the Prince of the Asturias—these were led out, and the machine-gun was heard again. The prisoners were called up a third time, asked if they had said their prayers, told to face the wall . . . the guards laughed, and sent them back to the cells again.

Friday night was a night of fear for them, spent upon their knees. Next morning they saw the kites skirting the prison on flat wings, then diving suddenly at the corpses.

The same tricks were played on them again . . . nobody was shot.

They wondered what was to happen to them, when at five that afternoon they suddenly saw that their guards, whose heads only had been visible to them above the cellar windows, had disappeared. All except one, who beckoned to them to come out. They ran through the zig-zag passages of the prison and through holes knocked by shells into the open air. Then divided, for they were sniped at as soon as they were seen. The last Anarchists were leaving Fuenterrabia below.

Four of the hostages took a boat, others sheltered in fishermen's cottages. Casadevante ran down to the Fuenterrabia quay and dived in wearing his shirt and beret. The tangle of currents caught him and drifted him dangerously near a steamer where the Anarchists were embarking under arms. A fisherman in a rowing-boat picked him up and advised him to lie in the bottom with his beret over his face, as if drowned. The calm old man then pulled over to France in the company of the Anarchist steamer, chatting amiably with them about his aristocratic "corpse."

That evening the bells of the brown convent in Fuenter-rabia, by the massive ruined walls of Charles V's castle, played a cheerful tune in the tenor: and as the sun was sinking they ran up the red-yellow-red of old Spain. It was the fugitives of Guadalupe who occupied the village. Next morning, in a hysteria of cheering and song, they welcomed the military and were shouldered high.

Why spin out the story? The fall of Irun led to the immediate fall of San Sebastian, to which Larrañaga now retired.

The one thing that the Basque Nationalists of San Sebastian would not tolerate was the burning of their city: they took arms against the Anarchists, a small faction, and with the women of San Sebastian demanded the surrender of the city without a fight.

Thirty thousand left for Bilbao: they were terrified of the Moors—of whom I saw none yet on this front. In their frantic hurry they did not open; they simply sawed off in a solid block the *coffres forts* of the banks of San Sebastian, shoved them on to a lorry and drove them to Bilbao.

Beorlegui's men entered San Sebastian without a shot fired. The old colonel reviewed his troops from a window, seated in a chair, then withdrew to die.

The new Frente Popular line lay between Eibar, the arms factory and the sea: just behind the provincial boundary of Vizcaya. All Guipuzcoa, with its splendid access to the sea, fell to the rebels. The position was not to alter materially for six months.

Every effort was now concentrated on Madrid, because Franco ordered it, and because Bilbao under a government of moderates had at last found the means to defend herself.

II

SAN SEBASTIAN is now behind us. The good families of
the Right are now going back to collect and tabulate their
property there, and to see that a certain number of people
swing for the temerity of defending the Republic against
the glorious *Movimiento Nacional Salvador*. Their hand fell
with particular severity on members of the Basque
Nationalist Party—on those, in fact, who had seen that San
Sebastian was evacuated with decency and order, and
therefore had left them some small proportion of their
worldly goods to enjoy, and unburnt houses to live in.

A Council of War sat on these—after the Falange Espanola
had done a certain amount of murder without trial, *pistolero*
style. Among those executed in better form were seventeen
priests of Basque Nationalist sympathies. A military
governor plastered the town with notices telling everybody
to be quiet because there were spies about. The use of
the Basque language was first frowned upon, then by
proclamation forbidden. The beggars returned to the
pavements, and the upper classes and bootblacks, at
different altitudes, to the cafés. There was much permanent beflagging of buildings in the main streets, and a
lot of Basque grousing in the alleys.

Moral standards were slightly improved to satisfy the
Catholic Church. Women now bathed in short skirts and
the population were not allowed to walk off the beach
and into the town in dressing-gowns or bathing dresses
covered by a towel-burnous. This second move gratified
the upper classes, who noted that San Sebastian looked
less populous and better dressed than ever since the
foundation of the Republic.

But let us leave San Sebastian behind us, and chase the

Basque bourgeoisie, the Socialists, and the Anarchists of Pasajes to Bilbao, the greatest city of the Basques and third industrial centre of Spain. And see what they have been doing since the rebellion started on June 19th.

* * * * * *

Bilbao is the Basque heart. To understand the Basques one must know something of the history of Bilbao.

She lies some fourteen kilometres up the trench of the River Nervion, which is navigable all the way. Steep hills escort the river on either side: on the east they shelter the wealthier suburbs of Las Arenas and Algorta, on the west the heavy industry and the massed metal of the iron mines that have made Bilbao richer, for her size, than any other city in Spain. Pines have clothed these hills for the last forty years.

Before, another tree flourished in Vizcaya—the oak. And it is upon the value of this tree and the iron and ships which it helped to produce that the early prosperity of Bilbao was founded.

Bilbao built many ships for the Invincible Armada and the trade with the New World. Her mariners have always been famous since the days of the Vizcayan Juan de la Cosa, Columbus's great sea captain, and of Elkano the Basque navigator who brought Magellan's fleet round the world, and the discovery of the Newfoundland cod fisheries by the Basque deep-sea fleet.

Wood and iron: economic organisation. John Evelyn in his "Sylvae" (1664) writes in Chapter XXXII, paragraph 12:

> "The King of *Spain* has neer *Bilbao* sixteen times as many acres of *Copse-wood* as are fit to be cut for *coal* in one year; so that when 'tis ready to be *fell'd*, an Officer first marks such as are like to prove *Ship-timber*, which are let stand, as so many *sacred* and *dedicate* Trees. But by these means the iron-works are plentifully supplied in the same place, without at all diminishing the stock of *Timber*. Then, in *Biscay* again, every *proprietor*, and other, plants *three* for *one* which he cuts down; and the *Law* obliging them is most severely executed. There indeed

are few or no *Copses*; but all are *Pollards*; and the very *lopping* (I am assur'd) does furnish the *iron-works* with sufficient to support them."

Copsewood is no longer fuel for iron, nor timber material for ships. But the iron mines and ship-building were still the industry of Bilbao, and the forests were conserved with the same care. Economy and statistics still guided the calculation of the hard-headed Basque, even of the young enthusiasts who were soon to rule Vizcaya.

With the era of economic liberalism in the 1880's, Bilbao had risen to new heights. Her shipping had developed until it took first place in Spain. Her capital spread into every other Spanish enterprise, electricity, phosphates, roads, railways, explosives, the new iron mines of the Riff.

She had always enjoyed close commercial relations with England, across the Cantabrian Sea; and she borrowed now many of her social and political ideas from England. Perhaps it is truer to say that something familiar in the English system made her re-examine her own traditions and rediscover her own democratic basis.

In the eighties and nineties the massive square-block classical buildings of commercial Bilbao were raised — the banks, which extended a financial control all over Spain, the insurance and savings businesses, the shipping companies, iron corporations, the municipality, the clubs. The whole New Town to the west of the Nervion was rebuilt in this plutocratic and colossal idiom; but a quickly advancing age and grime, the work of the Bilbao drizzle, gave Bilbao the benign Unitarian appearance of a smaller Liverpool.

The clubs were furnished in heavy wood, spreading bronze chandeliers, powerful staircases, and thick deep leather sofas and chairs; their interiors remained subfusc, like decent English clubs. The boys of the rich and even of modest families were often educated in Great Britain.

Soccer became the sport of the bourgeoisie, and nine or ten of the Spanish national team were regularly Basques.

But throughout the weaving of this industrial middle class on the English pattern there ran a master thread typically Basque, found nowhere else in the world. This thread was coloured dark blue, the colour of his beret which all classes wore, and which was the symbol of Basque social equality.

Basques detest titles. To them everybody is plain mister, and for preference they address perfect strangers by their surnames without the prefix. They dislike the elegance of Castilian manners and the elaboration of Castilian grades. In Bilbao there were great differences of wealth, but none of class were admitted. The Bilbao millionaires tried to keep to themselves by affecting Monarchism; but even their ranks were split by the all-pervading social theory that all honest men were equal, and that in a country so moral and well-ordered as the Basque everybody could be rated honest.

The theory was based on the fact that the Basques were at heart peasants, and passionately devoted to the soil. They were not a full bourgeoisie, and never would be such in either the English or the Continental sense of the word: they were an industrial race rooted to the land, individual small-holders interested financially in the city. The ideal even of the working-class in the mines (so far as it was Basque) was to save a little money and return to the land or its acreless counterpart, the sea. But many of the miners were cheap labour imported from abroad from Galicia, Murcia, the Asturias; the Basques, brought up to a family life on independent farm holdings, did not like to tie himself too much to industry and draw a small wage, even if he was afraid that he might be thrust off the land; he had a higher standard of living than those who drifted to the town to join the proletariat.

For this reason he was resistant and insensitive to socialist reasoning and his feeling permeated even the poorly paid labour in the Basque factories and mines. They did not become extremist, as labour was driven to become in other parts of the Iberian peninsula. In Bilbao there was, until the refugees poured in during the war from Pasajes and the Austurias, no Anarchist or Communist organisation worth the name. The Socialist Union, the U.G.T. (Union General de Trabajadores), was predominant in heavy industry and transport, and in Bilbao existed its most moderate wing. The U.G.T. was a powerful, disciplined force. Its relations with the masters were typically Basque and hardheaded, but not necessarily hostile. And eventually working-class conditions became the best in Spain, for in all Basques there was a certain spirit of democracy which made compromise possible.

Travelling through their country, along their magnificent roads, one could see what an independent people they were, and how different from the other provinces of Spain. It was not only their mysterious, unplaceable language that singled them out: it was the way they lived.

For the Basque the basis of life, it was evident, was the farm and the fishing-boat. His way of agriculture and of country living was unlike anything else in the Peninsula. Drive through Old Castile: every ten kilometres you pass through a crowded village the colour of sun-washed earth, clustered round a church like a fortress, with a tower from which can be seen every pulse of the village's heart. Between villages the dusty and measureless grain-plain stretches into the horizon past staccato mesetas, the low and level tablelands whose upper surfaces erosion has left bald-white with scurf. Little water. Everything fierce light or strict shade, without grades between. A few figures stooping in the clear expanse: the Castilian goes out to his distant lands in the morning under the rod of the sun, and returns at night to a packed and dirty village to sleep in a humble house lacking outlook or the feeling of freedom given by an upper storey. Emblems of the central state, ancient and modern, keep through centuries a stern control upon him. The old watch-towers, shells now, look across from tableland to square tableland: in the villages their place is taken by the telephone exchange, the priest and the *cuartel* of the Guardia Civil, who with rifles slung over their shoulders walked along the straight, endless acacia-shaded road in pairs, scanning the immense landscape from under their patent leather tricorn hats for crime.

The Basque, too, is a countryman, but that is all. He owns his land. He farms maize and vegetables in green mountain valleys, alive always to the sound of speeding waters. Forests of larch, oak, beech and pine have always made the sky-rim of the world less bare; have softened the harsh cruelty of the Castilian outline and shown him varieties of colour and shade impossible to encounter under the Castilian sun. But above all he lives apart. Basque villages are small, and except where industry has turned them into country towns, seem to exist mostly for the playing of pelota and the drinking of wine and singing of songs in common. The typical Basque house is the solitary caserio, or Basetxe as it is called in *vascuence*. Thick red tiles, wide, flattened eves, a porch yawning broad, outlined by a Tudor arch, under the first floor of a building with many rooms. Farm implements lie in the enclosed porch, and the impression given by every detail is that of a solid and independent prosperity. The farm-yard is usually kept dirty to show that the Basque does not mind country smells. The self-respect of the owner speaks from the great scroll-like coat-of-arms carved in stone above the door, and the whole family takes its name from the house. As for the house, it is called after some simple feature of the country-side—Mendigurren, for instance, which can be translated "Hill, slope of." And so there was in Bilbao in June, 1936, young Don Bruno Mendigurren, aged twenty-five, and a prominent member of the Basque Nationalist Party, whose director of Foreign Affairs he was going to become. He had studied engineering in Brussels at the same university as Leon Degrelle, and he was an enthusiastic Basque. At this moment he is working in his brother-in-law Gomboa's cement business in a narrow street in Bilbao, but he likes to live in his caserio at Munguia, a village nine miles east of Bilbao on the Gernika road. Here there are vines growing up the Basetxe, and wide open windows which will one day be smashed by shells. In the speech of his country his name is Mendigurren 'tar Bruno— hill, slope of, Mister Bruno. The rural surname must come first.

Or the Basque fishes, at great risk in his turbulent Bay: from fishing villages which mass lofty, glass-fronted houses against old quays of stone. The windows are long and narrow, there are often five floors, and the basement is a boathouse closed in the solid rock. The very houses seem to love the sea, so tightly do they press against the granite margin and crane their necks to peer into the grey. At intervals between them, the old women sit among baskets of silver anchovies mending the chocolate nets. It is a dear sound to a Basque, all those windows rattling together under the north wind, and the chop of the water in the fishing quay. It unites them. And so among the men

BEORLEGUI.

MOLA.

who go out in the brightly-painted trawlers for tunny, sardines and anchovies, there will be formed a battalion of heavyweights in the coming war, with the name of the Itxas-Alde—the Seashore.

For the diversion and health of all Basques there is one of the world's greatest games: open air pelota under the plane trees. The Basques are the only people in the Iberian Peninsula who have the conception of linking leisure with exercise. A game of pelota to harden the hands and broaden the chest, a violent sweat, then a conversation with the curé and a big drink of wine at the side of the court: sweat off by playing pelota again. That is the recipe of the Basque on warm and workless days, whether summer or winter. Communal dancing and skipping, monotonous to a foreigner, begin the evening; and drinking and singing long past midnight, when each rural poet prolongs his own Homeric improvisation, close the Basque day on festivals. The Basque is no secret toper, but the very weight of alcoholic content that passes through his leading drinkers tells in the end. In the war that followed I used to pass near Derio, just east of Bilbao, what looked to me like a fair-sized model city, not yet completed. "Yes," said the young Basque at my side, "that will be our new lunatic asylum. It will be full of old men who have drunk too much." Provident Bilbao, always thinking of her social services, would thus pad the walls of her older generation. But at that moment the lower stories of the madhouse were full of machinery for the construction of trench mortars.

The bottle apart, the Basque has always been a highly moral and law-abiding person. His theory of land tenure has given him a powerful property-sense. His word is his bond, and he does not think of interpreting it. Men and women are devout and practising Catholics, with a strong strain of Puritanism which separates the sexes in church. Either the central aisle divides them, or the women sit below and the men dangle their berets in worship from the gallery; which in Basque churches alone runs all round the inner walls, in massive oak suspension.

The church is not, as in Castile, simply the place where the religious law is handed down; it is the centre of civic life. In the country villages one generally finds a wide enclosed veranda leaning against the side of the church. After mass, the local council gather in this shelter to reach their decisions for the next six secular days, the curé assisting on equal terms.

Until 1936 the Basque genius had expended itself in local improvements, for the Basque makes an admirable country administrator. The best roads in Spain, the finest seaside resort, superb hospitals, schools and children's sanatoria were built out of local money. But as the Basque country developed upon the wealth of Bilbao assembled in the 80's and 90's, the politically-minded among the new farmer-bourgeoisie complained that more revenue went to Madrid than improvements came out of her; that Basque customs and the Basque language were disregarded by the police, the judiciary, and the central universities; that the Cortes, particularly after the loss of the Spanish Empire, were corrupt and interfered with business to enrich themselves; Spain, said the Basques, was all talk and no do.

An expression of this feeling of the farmer-bourgeoisie was the founder of the Basque Nationalist Party, Sabino Arana-Goiri, many times imprisoned under the monarchy: a democratic traditionalist at heart, who found refuge from the dictatorship of Castile in intellectual as well as political life, in the study of the Basque language, laws and poetry.

The ideal of his Basque Nationalist Party was to make of Basqueness something more than a competent municipal sentiment, to give it larger claims. The Basque Nationalist doctrine laid down several principles to be attained: the return of the Fueros or local privileges of Vizcaya, Guipuzcoa and Alava, of which these provinces were deprived after the Carlist Wars; a bilingual state service and educational system; control over the raising and spending of money; devotion to the Roman Catholic Church.

Essentially, it was a democratic middle-class party making overtures to the Left, for it pledged itself to certain industrial reforms and social redressments, such as family salaries, participation in profits, and even in the management of concerns. It rapidly organised its own Trades Unions and its Catholic Nationalist schools, under a flag of great æsthetic and attractive power, a white cross and an apple-green saltire on a scarlet ground. It caught the youth, who soon became its leaders: for its organisation was intensely democratic, and even the President of the party had to be changed every three years to prevent the growth of that personalism which is the bane of Spanish politics. It advanced with speed on the formation of the Republic, securing large majorities in Vizcaya, Guipuzcoa and Alava. In return for the promise of the Estatuto which would make the Basque Provinces in many things autonomous, it joined the Frente Popular list in the elections of February, 1936. By this adhesion the Left won their first great constitutional victory in Spain.

It was to be expected of the Basques that they would keep their promises. Though they found much to displease them in their allies during the war that was now being prepared against them, particularly in the persecution of religion, they did not desert them. They chose, instead, to lose everything that is dear to the Basque, his home, his countryside, his property and his comrades. General Franco has been accused of making no attempt to seduce them from their allegiance: but that is precisely what his German allies did, twice, in Paris in 1937. But the Basques disliked military Fascism, and if they were to choose between the two parties they preferred the one which, if it was of the Left, was still democratic and constitutional.

In 1936 their city of Bilbao was doing well. Shipping had recovered, and iron was in great demand for the rearmament programmes of Europe. Everybody was very busy, though it was known that a heavy contraband in arms was running the Pyrenees between France and Navarre, where the Requetes were preparing something against the State.

Yet the proclamation of the state of war throughout rebellious Spain found Bilbao unarmed and unprepared.

On July 17th radio reported the outbreak of rebellion in the Army of Africa, under General Franco, Governor of the Canaries. The Basque Nationalists met at the offices of their newspaper, *Euzkadi*, from which they rang up the Ministry of Interior in Madrid: who answered that "the situation is in hand."

An effervescence of motor cars and cycles belonging to members of the parties of the Right was noted in the Gran Via and the other main streets of Bilbao.

With great presence of mind Aldasoro ordered all telephones connected with the military in Bilbao to be lined through the Exchange of the Civil Governor, Señor Echevarria. Aldasoro knew the ways of the Spanish Army. A leading member of the Republican Left and a founder of the Republic, this strikingly handsome and energetic man, now in middle age, had been Governor of Guipuzcoa, was a friend of the Basques, and knew where to act while they still deliberated.

A bell rang in the Gobierno Civil. Aldasoro, powerful and dominating, was with Echevarria. An ageing politico, Echevarria, ready to compromise, unwilling to take or to suffer great pains, nervous, shrewishly protective of his own peace. The telephone was a nuisance, he took it up.

"*Aqui General Mola,*" it said without further warning, "*hay que sublevarse!*"

"General Mola speaking," was the bald introduction, "you have got to rebel!"

"How?" asked the incredulous, the disturbed and trembling Echevarria. "Who is it?" asked Aldasoro impatiently, standing over this shaky monument of irresolution.

"It is General Mola in Pampluna," explained Echevarria with his hand pressing wet over the mouthpiece, while the electrical discharges of the insurgent chief grated into air out of the other end, "and he says that we have got to revolt."

"And you asked him how?" shouted Aldasoro; who then broke down and laughed gutturally, for he has a Spanish sense of humour. "Why, man, shout *Viva la Republica!*"

"I don't understand, General," Echevarria continued, trying to spin the matter out and recover the slender structure of his self-confidence. "What do you want me to do? What is this all about? Rebel against whom?"

Then two voices spoke at once, one in Pampluna and the other in Bilbao, and both in tones that showed they knew that they were dealing with an idiot.

General Mola said, pronouncing each syllable clearly, "You have got to declare a state of war."

Aldasoro seized Echevarria by his telephone shoulder and said much louder, "Cry *Viva la Republica!*" And then he had an idea. He took the receiver out of the fingers of Echevarria; it was very damp, and he roared down it, *"Viva la Republica!"* "Now you try," he said, smiling in a fatherly way, handing the machine back.

"Viva la Republica," came very feebly from the lips of Echevarria. "That's quite enough," said Aldasoro, and took the receiver from Echevarria a second time, and hung it quietly upon the stand.

The die was cast. The Civil Governor looked morosely out of the window, and pulled out his pocket handkerchief. Adieu to comfort.

* * * * * *

Members of all parties forming the Frente Popular met at the Civil Governor's office to form a Junta de Defensa; they elected the young Basque Nationalist Basaldua, a tall, dark creature with a melancholy face and a good figure, and a capacity for keeping secrets, their first secretary.

They were fortunate in finding a complacent garrison. Lieutenant-Colonel Vidal, an amiable little man with a fresh clean-shaven complexion, myopia, and dyed hair thinly plastered over a conversational face, enjoyed the air of political cafés and was a trusted friend of the Left. He had once been a good theoretical soldier, and had taught Franco trigonometry at the Military Academy in the Alcazar of Toledo. But his active years were over when they were thus rudely renewed. He was not without courage, but the nervous strings which drive a man from courage to decision were drying in Vidal. He still remained extraordinarily gay and optimistic. He was a good host and an amusing talker, especially when he tried his hand at French.

At this moment Vidal, commander of the garrison regiment of the Garellano, was valuable to the Government, at whose service he put his sword. The attitude of some of his junior officers, however, caused him sleepless nights, spent behind a bodyguard of soldiers with bayonets fixed. The rebellious captains were weeded out and shot.

There now began a great search for arms, for the aims of the enemy were not known, and it was believed that he might be advancing on Bilbao from Vitoria. Vidal could only provide five hundred rifles. The paramilitary regional formations of the Basque Nationalist Party were only armed with pistols, and the Trades Unions had little more than pistols and shotguns.

The Guardia Civil, it was afterwards discovered, had buried their stock of rifles in their gardens, and Commandante José Anglada, in charge of the reserves of the Garellano Regiment, also kept a secret store. But at the moment he was playing loyal, and generously handed over fifty rifles, regretting that he positively had no more.

Basaldua took a car and drove out the second night to the arms manufacturing town of Eibar, on the borders of Vizcaya and Guipuzcoa. He made a hasty collection of weapons in the dark, stuffing his and two other cars with a little over five hundred of the machine-pistols awaiting sale there, then drove back to Bilbao. The Plaza in front of the smart Hotel Carlton was full of men clamouring for arms, and the happy party from Eibar passed them out with open hands. This was the method of the first mobilisation in Bilbao. And ammunition—that was another problem. There were precisely twelve rounds per machine-pistol, and the Basques had to abandon high-falutin ideas of maintaining a reserve. They dished them all out, then spent an exciting night on the hills around Bilbao, waiting for the enemy to attack the city . . . .

In the daytime patrols of all the parties took their beats at the street-corners, and the search for passports was incessant. The Anarchists, very weak in Bilbao, attempted to damage property but were sternly repressed by the Basque Nationalist Party.

One church was burned. About fifteen hundred arrests were made of members of the Right, and they were put into the Larrinaga Prison. In Bilbao, unlike Madrid and Barcelona and the rest of Government territory, there were very few murders; at the most, thirty in a population of 300,000. And, unlike rebel territory, there were no judicial murders of individuals for their political opinions; the only people shot were officers in rebellion against the Republic.

Refugees from the mass terror in the province of Santander, west of Vizcaya, came pouring into Bilbao. They were pursued by a party of six Santander police, whose job was to hunt them down in their hiding places, call, and take them for a ride. This method of dealing with one's enemies shocked the Basques.

One day three of the police were garrotted in a Basque village on the coastal road to Santander. The Basques said blandly that the local population had done it; and Santander police never intruded upon the territory of Vizcaya again.

Order was soon restored in Bilbao, the pickets shifted off the streets, and a purged municipal police once more in charge. After a few days of uncertainty, the churches reopened and the congregations crowded them to the doors.

Their southern frontier, however, was still the chief anxiety of the Basques. A few days after the rebellion had broken out, a small party of Socialists with dynamite in their pockets went down the Vitoria Road to a bridge near the frontier with Alava, by name Orozco. By blowing this up, they thought, they would for ever bar the way to the enemy. The packets were being fitted and the good work was warming to a climax, when round the corner from Vitoria came a military gentleman, surely no less than a colonel, from the length and magnificence of his cloak and the splendour of the stars upon his portly front.

The gallant colonel was accompanied by three other officers, of a weedy and nondescript exterior. None could have been more startled than they when the bridge of Orozco took to the air and a party of startled Socialists to their heels in front of them.

This was the first brush. The Socialists reported in Bilbao that a whole battalion led by a General in person was on its way into Vizcaya, and that only their sang-froid had delayed the enemy's march. The Civil Governor immediately broadcast an appeal to the population, urging them to take up their arms and march to Orozco to defeat the General and his battalion, and to sell their lives dear.

At Orozco there was nothing to be found. The cloak and stars had retired, one presumes with the same precipitancy to Vitoria. In these early days, both sides in the Spanish civil war were moving on the wings of their own wind, with their overcoats streaming behind them. The moments of contact were anxious and tentative. Public alarm was only allayed when a young Basque of great height and girth, a devoted Alpinist and trout fisherman, came walking over their tall boundary mountain of Gorbea to tell them that nothing was ready yet on the other side.

The massive young lawyer, Antonio Irala, who was going to be, with Basaldua, one of the secretaries of the Basque President Aguirre, had been present in Vitoria when the state of war was proclaimed and had straightway abandoned his car, which was known to his political enemies, and his coat and tie, which made him look somebody. Seizing the nearest bicycle to hand, he had made like an arrow up the Bilbao road. He was arrested on suspicion for one night, then released. He spent a few days with his family in an Alava village; heard that the Requetes had got wind of his whereabouts, took his bicycle again, abandoned it under the shadow of his familiar mountain Gorbea, and so climbed into Vizcaya over the backyard wall.

He told the Junta de Defensa in Bilbao that the Socialists were talking nonsense, and that there were no troops in Vitoria. The Junta breathed again, in rather a more virile way now that the jocose Irala had joined their counsels.

Vidal was ordered to take an amalgam of troops and Trades Union militia to Ochandiano, the big Basque village east of Gorbea, and guard the Vitoria road. The column drove off amid scenes of intense enthusiasm.

An ingenious trick was played upon them in Ochandiano. While half their force was assembled in the village square, gossiping happily with the local girls or lying down after a tiring lorry-jolt, an aeroplane with the Spanish Republican colours, red, yellow and purple, came over the mountains. Circling lower and lower upon the square, its pilot was finally visible waving his hand and giving the clenched fist, Frente Popular salute. The raw militia stood up and cheered in a mass; whereat the wily aviator dropped six small bombs on top of them, and made off south before he could hear their horrible language.

The Basques organised a revenge. They had no bombs, but there was a Puss-Moth in Bilbao used for many years for joy-rides. The pilot Yanguash took it down, as fast as the little thing could scurry, to Villareal, south of Ochandiano, an enemy village. When he saw a large group of the *Facciosos* or factious ones, as they were now beginning to be called in Bilbao, he dropped a sackful of stones on them, which knocked the stuffing out of one Requete, causing his companions momentary shock and surprise.

* * * * * *

AGUIRRE.

LEIZAOLA.

In August, however, the war began to take on a seriousness unrealised until now.

There was no social revolution in Bilbao. A few factories,
the property of those in declared rebellion, were seized by
the State and handed over to a board of management on
which their employees were represented, but which their
employees did not control. As a direct and instant reform,
rents were cut by 50 per cent. But as I have shown, political
murders and the destruction of property (the very thought
of which was horrible to the Basque farmer-bourgeoisie)
were suppressed at once. Life and industry were safe in
Bilbao.

Nevertheless the British and French Navies paid continual
visits to the Nervion mouth on their long tours round the
coast of Spain, and insisted that every British and French
subject should be evacuated. Every visit, came the warning,
might be the last; and they painted in colours of hell-fire
the awful prospect of the Left achieving power in
Bilbao.

It is probable that they really believed what they
said.

Their views were created by four main agencies: their
social environment, the instructions from the Admiralty,
the sort of newspapers that they read, and the contact
which they had made with official Britain in Spain.

Their social environment was naturally that of the Right,
which in England felt for General Franco an instinctive
affection from the beginning. I remember myself a certain
melancholy which came over me, when early reports prevailed that he was blockaded in Morocco, and his movement broken. What made me more cheerful was the proof
that Italian military planes, the Savoia 81's which I
had seen bombing in Abyssinia, were joining him in
Morocco or falling in French territory on the way. But
revelations of this kind did not affect the Navy: did not
yet.

Admiralty instructions were to clear all Britons out of
Government Spain at once.

The papers that they read described the sticky end of the
naval officers who attempted to rebel in Cartagena. The
crews shot them, which sounds like mutiny, and treated
their bodies in the most disrespectful manner. Instead of

carrying out the service regulations for burial at sea, the uneducated tars wirelessed the Ministry of Marine, "What shall we do with the corpses?" thus exposing their total lack of etiquette. The Ministry of Marine wirelessed back, "Throw them overboard," and the piratical brutes did so without even wrapping them decently in a flag. There were other stories of similar rank insubordination and sloppiness; and the official naval attitude to the Civil War was summed up colourfully in the Official Gazette of Gibraltar, which described the Spanish Government with which its own Government maintained normal diplomatic relations as — The Reds.

The Consular service in Spain consisted largely of Englishmen engaged in business there, whose normal reaction to any form of labour trouble had become the Spanish one; which was to insist that these extremists should at once be jailed. Azaña was to them the Iberian synonym of anathema. The simplified colour-politics of Red and White came readily to their lips, with not so much use of White, a term which they regarded as rather standoffish.

So the British colony in Bilbao, which was a large one, was first terrified and then lifted off the shore. A few remained; but the shock to the business system of Bilbao was great. A large proportion of the experts in the mines were foreigners—just as much of the capital was British. The heavy industries—the Construccion Naval, for instance, on the Nervion, in which Vickers had an interest—were permeated by British technical men. The general flight of foreigners from Bilbao did irreparable harm to the Bilbao economic system, and it was many months before it began to reseize itself; and then only for war objectives.

In Guipuzcoa the threat was more immediate. The Carlists were moving up to Tolosa, and the Frente Popular Committee appealed for help.

Basaldua could find none but the fifty rifles which Anglada chose to hand over. He took them in a car to Tolosa just before the village fell.

Monzon went on a mission to Barcelona to secure arms.

Young Monzon was one of the few titled Basques; he came of a rich landed family in Guipuzcoa, where he owned a beautiful *casa señorial* in the village of Vergara, destined to house Italians before the war was over. He was a Nationalist deputy in the Cortes, the best-dressed of them and the most hated by the other side. The Spaniards are a revengeful people, and the enlightened aristocrat is someone against whom the rest of the class sharpen their teeth. Monzon did not have the force of character of Aldasoro or of another Basque, the advocate Leizaola, who was now coming into prominence at Bilbao; but he was an engaging young man, easy to negotiate with, upon whom the humane argument always worked.

Now he was after arms: and he received a shock. Barcelona and the Central Government would only spare 1,000 rifles for the defence of Irun and San Sebastian. They were willing to buy arms abroad; but the dispatch of these was always delayed. For the first time in the Civil War, the Basques became exasperated by the sluggishness of their allies, and decided to act for themselves.

They seized all the gold in the vaults of the Bank of Spain and the other banks in Bilbao, and transported it in eight fishing boats through the cordon of the *Almirante Cervera, España, Canarias* and *Velasco* then bombarding the Basque coast, in safety to Bayonne. With this luggage Monzon and Irala went first to Paris and then to Germany, buying arms on Bilbao's own account.

Then there was a Basque pirate, called Letho, a man of great strength, covered with hair and smiles. He paid a visit to Bordeaux, where since the beginning of the Civil War there had been a deal of juggling with railway coaches.

On July 19th there was standing in the railway goods yard of Bordeaux a train composed of ten units, and filled with war material previously ordered and paid for in France by the Spanish Government. The cheques were honoured: but the French authorities now began to put difficulties in the' way of delivery. They said that they were negotiating a non-intervention agreement with Italy, Germany and Great Britain, and that they would like to do nothing to prejudice, etc.

Spain protested. The French Communist Party, on the pretence of shunting the trucks round Bordeaux goods yard, unlinked three and sent them post-haste to Hendaye. One crossed the frontier; the second was stopped. Franco's friends in France entered the game, the unit travelled back to Bordeaux and after two more feint attacks upon the Pyrenees was safely delivered into his hands.

The Non-Intervention Agreement had already been signed, dried and applauded when Letho appeared upon the French scene in his little fishing boat, glowing with mischief. Two distinguished Basque advocates of my acquaintance had just stolen three French machine guns with munitions from the Bordeaux barracks, but Letho was after bigger game. He cleared a whole coach of forty heavy machine guns and rounds for a fortnight before he was discovered; then the grinning escapologist took to the open sea, and Bilbao at last had heavy automatic weapons.

Irun fell, defended by only 1,500 rifles, twelve machine guns, ten cannon, and an August the Twelfth of shotguns against the long organised secret arsenals of Navarre and Castile. San Sebastian had to be abandoned for lack of munitions, and the Basques fell back slowly into Vizcaya.

Eibar was going to be occupied by the Requétés at any moment; was being shelled and bombed. And for the first time, German aviators in a full German bombing and fighting organisation came up to the northern front. Their eighteen fighting pilots were given rooms at the Hotel Fronton in Vitoria, where at this time victory was so near that they often drank to excess. One glorious day the pilot of a Heinkel 51 (the front line German Air Force fighter), near maudlin, took his plane and stunted over the quiet little town until he hit the parish church tower and was given military honours, and taken back in an oblong box to Germany.

On September 25th and 26th they bombed a defence-less Bilbao. The Basques had no fighting planes, no anti-aircraft guns; nothing, but a panicky refugee population from San Sebastian, hardly knowing where it lived, how it was to get food, and, at this terrible moment, where it was to hide. For there were no bombproof shelters.

These German bombardments, in which the old slow Junker 52 three-engined planes were used, were the first of their kind in Spain. They were a dress rehearsal for the offensive on Madrid which was to follow at the end of October. They came first in the morning of September 25th; again in the afternoon; again at night; and in the morning of September 26th, for the fourth time. These bombardments were sheer, unmixed assault upon the civilian population, who ran in terror through the streets; the bombs were aimed not at the war industries, but at the very centre of administrative and populous Bilbao.

They caused a most violent reaction. Led by members of the C.N.T., the refugees went down to the docks when the great raiders had ground their way back to Vitoria. They massacred sixty-eight of the prisoners in the prison ships, then tethered to the shore, and thought that they had been merciful, for their own dead lay in hundreds.

To the east, the enemy infantry were always pressing forward. The so-called "Red Squadron" arrived in Bilbao to help defend her: the battleship *Jaime Primero*, cruisers *Libertad, Mendez Nunez* and *Miguel de Cervantes*, and about ten destroyers. But they did little.

Bilbao had abandoned hope. A ship appeared, no bigger than a man's hand. It came nearer. It brought arms from Hamburg. It entered the Nervion.

The navvies fell upon it like lunatics. It was lit with lamps and sweating faces all night, as they piled the boxes on the quay and split them open with chisels and axes, running up and down in scores, ceaselessly working.

Cars rushed the material with Letho's machine guns to Eibar and Elgueta, where it was distributed to trembling hands in darkness.

Next morning the Requétés attacked at both points. They were met with a furious fire and a bloody defeat. The hills were littered with red berets. As the clock struck twelve, Bilbao had been saved, by Germany and a very clever thief.

III

WITH THE FATE OF BILBAO in the balance, the extraordinary
and, it must be admitted, sadly diminished Cortes of the
Republic sitting at Valencia decided to pay the Basques
their part of the bargain: on October 1st, 1926, the Statute
of Basque Autonomy came before the deputies of Spain.

Aguirre, the young leader of the Basque Nationalist
Party, made a speech in which he thanked Parliament for
giving satisfaction, "however partial," to the desire
for liberty which had lain repressed in the Basque people for
so many years back.

"We stand against this movement, which is subversive
of the legitimate authority and hostile to the public will,
because we are forced to do so by our profoundly Christian
principles. Of those principles perhaps we shall have many
occasions to speak to you, gentlemen. But at this moment
we appear at your side for two reasons: first, because
Christ does not preach the bayonet, the bomb, or high
explosive for the conquest of ideas and hearts, but love;
and secondly because we have no fears of your proletarian
movement nor of your social emotions, for we know how
much justice there is in them and how they had to be.

"Why did Christ come to this world? Did Christ
come to the earth to aid the powerful or to raise and console the weak? We, between the powerful and the weak,
are with the weak, with the people, for we are born of the
people and are fighting for them.

"I remember now the story told by Montalamber, who
when he was in Paris saw a church in which the decorations,
and spurs, and glitter of swords shone in cruel contra-
diction of the humility and austerity with which the service
there ought to have been inspired; and he said, 'Here is

a rich church, but a people poor in faith.' He went to Ireland, and found there a wretched, broken hermitage, where a priest celebrated the same sacrifice before a great multitude of the sons of Ireland, and he said, 'Here is a poor church, but a people rich in faith.'

"We, between the poor church of Ireland and the rich of Paris, with its helmets, swords and spurs, prefer Ireland: thus we know that we obey better our Christian conscience, and we have our guarantee besides of liberty and true fraternity.

"We, who condemn with all energy (it is all that we can do) the burning of our churches wherever they are burnt, for our faith looks over illimitable horizons, and who condemn the killing of human beings for the sole reason that they have certain opinions and that their political standing is known, in the hope that such acts will not be repeated, we say to you with entire loyalty: Until Fascism is defeated, Basque Nationalism will remain at its post."

And with this speech delivered, barbed as it was for both sides, and frank as a Basque could feather it, Aguirre flew back to Bilbao, autonomy in his pocket. It was law on October 5th.

Yet the killing of human beings by Spaniards, not Basques, for the sole reason that they had certain opinions and their political standing was known, was repeated in Bilbao the very day after Aguirre spoke. The "Red Squadron," as Bilbainos called it, had struck its only blow for liberty in the Bay of Biscay, and shed its only blood.

It ranked as a revenge for the sinking of the Government destroyer *Almirante Juan Ferrandiz* at the end of September. Since the massacre of the prisoners in one of the ships at Bilbao that month, the prison ships had been taken down to the outer harbour and anchored in deep water, away from the quays.

A party of sailors from the battleship *Jaime Primero* lowered a launch, and made over to the side of the *Cabo de Quilates*, where steps were in permanence for the provisionment of the ship. The sailors' little plan of campaign had been laid in secrecy, and nobody was on the look-out.

The sailors ran up the ladder, overpowered the guard, and entered the ship with revolvers in their hands. By now the prisoners had wind of their arrival, and the drunk and dirty sailors, with weeks of beard on their faces, were running down the companion ways and corridors trying to catch them. They wanted nobody in particular. As soon as they had cornered one, they took him above, and his terrified companions heard the volley of rifle shots and the bang of the body on the deck over their heads. Then the sailors were down again, and the prisoners racing upstairs and down, escaping one pair of grabbing hands to fall into another. Always the sound of the *alpargata*, the rope-soled shoe, running after them. Forty-two were shot, one by one, then heaved over the side, before the sailors heard the Basques were coming down river and took their launch and ran back to the safe shelter of the *Jaime Primero*.

Unpopularity was already the portion in Bilbao of the seamen from Cartagena, and now they were politely invited to go. Vizcaya, the Basques felt, could be defended without them: and Prieto, Minister of Marine and a Bilbaino by adoption, was willing to recall them to their Mediterranean duties. The heavy guns of *Jaime Primero* were soon to be dismounted and used in the defence of Madrid. With her departure, murder left the Basque territory, so far as it was Republican, for three months; and only saw one more day of gala.

* * * * * *

Gernika, at the head of the lovely inlet south of Bermeo, is the historic centre of Basque liberties. The representatives of the towns and parishes of Vizcaya have met there since time immemorial, under the oak which is sown again as soon as it dies.

There has always been an oak of Gernika; though at the beginning of Basque records it was not the only revered tree in Vizcaya. Durango also had hers, at Gerediaga, and her assemblies gathered in its shade until the day when all Vizcaya was united at Gernika.

The Juntas of Gernika, from the beginnings of Basque written history, met every two years. *Procuradores* were elected by the direct vote of all men who had attained their majority, in the country parishes; in the towns, the *Ayuntamientos* or councils chose their representatives, either one or two, but with one vote only, which was annulled if they disagreed. There was no distinction of classes, and no suggestion of an upper chamber. By long tradition as well as the definition of local law, every male of Vizcaya possessed *nobleza*—was an aristocrat; and this condition was admitted by the Kings of Spain when the Basques travelled outside their country. *Nobleza* was not an empty title. Difficult as it is to conceive the possibility of it in the Middle Ages, all Basques were not only free men but had no services to render to any man. Not only were there no serfs, but almost every Basque, in a country of agriculturists, had his own house and land.

Sessions of the Juntas at Gernika only lasted a fortnight or three weeks. The first representatives always to be received, and heard, were those of the fishing village of Bermeo at the mouth of the Gernika inlet; the village's title of *Head of Vizcaya* suggests that the whole of this area, Gernika-Bermeo, formerly occupied the place of Bilbao in the Basque polity, and that the inlet was then the trading river that the Nervion later became.

The oath was taken by the representative of the Castilian King, less often by the King himself as simple Señor of Vizcaya; he swore to maintain the Rights of Vizcaya. While the Juntas sat in public to make new laws, trumpets were blown and bonfires lit on the highest Vizcayan mountains; the five peaks of Gorbea, Oitz, Sollube, Ganekogorta and Kolitza.

The oldest democracy in the world was not a talking shop. At the end of its short session it elected, by lot, not ballot, an executive council of fourteen of its members, who were responsible for the government of the country until the next Juntas met. A strong executive was therefore the essence of their ancient system, and the young Basques who were going to visit Gernika this month of October could quote history to approve their powers.

* * * * * *

It was a solemn occasion when the Basques met at Gernika on the 7th: so solemn that it had to be kept a secret until the day, for the modern Basques had to face dangers which their ancestors could not imagine. The Germans would have enjoyed to the full an opportunity to bomb all the leaders of the little Basque Republic together; they would not have waited seven months to level this quiet country town.

Under the Statute of Autonomy, it was provided that while the Civil War continued Euzkadi should be ruled by a Provisional Government with full powers. The president of this Government was to be chosen by all the councillors of the Basque *Ayuntamientos* or Municipal Councils who were free to vote, and his election was to be carried out under the temporary presidency of the Civil Governor of Vizcaya, until now responsible for the administration of Vizcaya. The new president was then to name the members of the Provisional Government, who were to be not less than five. So, with much hush-hush, the councillors were told to gather at the Casa de Juntas at Gernika.

The secret was kept: no planes appeared, though the lad in the church tower skinned his eyes for a chance to use the bell. In their tailcoats and butterfly collars and dark hats the leaders of the Basques assembled, followed by the Consular Corps; they took their seats in the Parliament Hall, and the curtains were drawn aside at the east end to disclose the altar. From the earliest days their meeting place had been a church. Jose Antonio de Aguirre was elected President by an almost unanimous vote.

They then went into the courtyard, where they stood in the sun before the Tree, an oak of seventy-seven years whose leaves were beginning to fall. In Basque, Aguirre took the oath: "Before God, in all humility, upon Basque earth, standing under the oak of Gernika, in remembrance of those who have passed before, I swear to accomplish my mandate with entire faithfulness."

Señor Echevarria, till now Civil Governor and representative of Spain, said in his turn: "At this moment, and under the oak of Gernika, I hand over the authority of the Basque country to its legitimate representative, Don Jose Antonio de Aguirre y Lekube."

Autumn leaves slowly span adrift from the oak. The Basques were overcome by a great emotion. Here, at the sacred heart of their country, they had recovered their lost liberty: they were masters in their own land. Every Basque man had regained his *nobleza*.

The President published the list of his Cabinet.

Presidency and Defence: Jose Antonio de Aguirre, Basque Nationalist.

Interior: Telesforo de Monzon, Basque Nationalist.

Finance: Heliodoro de la Torre, Basque Nationalist.

Justice and Culture: Jesus Maria de Leizaola, Basque Nationalist.

Public Works: Juan de Astigarrabia, Communist.

Labour and Communications: Juan de Los Toyos, Socialist.

Social Welfare: Juan Gracia, Socialist.

Industry: Santiago Aznar, Socialist.

Agriculture: Gonzalo Nardiz, Basque Nationalist Action.

Health: Alfredo Espinosa, Republican Union.

Commerce and Supply: Ramon Maria de Aldasoro, Republican Left.

Thus, in what was to be the Basque Executive Council, the Basque Nationalists whose Statute this was secured five votes out of twelve. They could, moreover, always depend on Aldasoro and Espinosa, of the moderate Republican parties, and upon Nardiz, whose Basque Nationalist Action though more Left and less Catholic than they, was yet more Basque than Marxist at heart. The Basques were not only free; they ruled.

These pages are the record of how their well-disciplined democracy stood the stress of modern war—perhaps the most terrible modern war seen in Europe. They are the chronicle of their successes and failures. That they lacked finesse and did not understand the control of the civil population by propaganda is certain; they were too frank. Though the finest physical material, they were anti-militarist at heart, and did not interest themselves enough in the direction of the war to see why, and with what speed, it was necessary for them to divest themselves of an inefficient and cowardly Spanish staff: they therefore lost their freedom. But they fought most doggedly against weapons superior not only in quantity, but in kind; they were beaten only by the foreigner, not by Spain. And for humanity and public decency, as moderates dominating a revolutionary situation, they have left behind them a name which will not soon be forgotten, as well as a remembrance of their natural charm and friendliness, which only those who saw Bilbao in her most tragic days will have the privilege to preserve. They sang. They were companionable. One could speak one's mind.

Their first act as a Government was the release of all women prisoners: a unilateral act, for which they only hoped Franco would give them the equivalent—in vain. On October 11th H.M. destroyers *Exmouth* and *Esk* evacuated 113 of these women to France, where the gratitude of the majority for this unexampled treatment was so great that they could only complain, not in undertones, that they had had to wash the militiamen's dirty handkerchiefs.

The Basques followed up their first gesture by an offer to exchange all their political prisoners—about 2,500—for all the Basques held by the other side, believed to amount to a little over 1,000, for there had been many executions. The negotiations were conducted under the auspices of the International Red Cross, whose Swiss representative, Dr. Albert Junod, wrote the technical report on the Italian use of gas in Ethiopia which his organisation suppressed, and of the British Ambassador to Spain. Julio de Jauregui, Basque Nationalist deputy for Bilbao, represented his Government, and the Conde de Torrubia, Franco's. Argument dragged on interminably, with long intervals for silence and rupture. The Basques were ready with a list of their prisoners, but the other side would not present theirs. The question of the bombardment of the civilian population was raised, and dropped. And then, suddenly and inexplicably, on January 6th, the Government of Salamanca, whose representative had already agreed on a basis of exchange with the Basques, broke off the negotiations: refused to make any large exchange of prisoners "because such would constitute a privilege for the Basque people," but had no objection to the exchange of individuals and small groups. Junod explained to the Basques that Salamanca might be willing to consider a totalitarian exchange with Valencia. . . .

They were furious, and so, more diplomatically, was he. To themselves they explained the matter thus: Torrubia, they knew, a Basque of San Sebastian, wanted the exchange and was grievously disappointed: so they thought were Franco's Diplomatic Office, where wealthy Monarchist Basques, such as Baraibar, Aznar and the chief, Sangroniz, predominated. But the military, who were anti-Basque and objected, won the day.

Insurgent radio stations began a campaign against Junod. He was a Freemason and a what-not. He had secretly supported Abyssinian Bolshevism, and he was a Red—a RED. The insurgent radio was at this moment falling under Italian control, and it is probable that Italy had something to do with the pelting of Junod. Yet the insurgents were strangely inconsiderate of their friends' security when they broke off the negotiations with such stupefying speed. Only two days before the last and most fearful of the prison massacres had taken place at Bilbao: over 200 of their supporters had been killed. And then they suddenly decided not to save the remainder! Perhaps they hoped the massacres would continue, to give Bilbao a bad name in the world; if so, their calculations were written in a chalk which was soon rubbed out.

IV

ONE OF THE FIRST PREOCCUPATIONS of the new Government sworn in at Gernika was to organise more thoroughly the food supply of the province of Vizcaya. The work of the Department of Commercio y Abastacimiento (Commerce and Supply) was put in the experienced hands of Aldasoro, the same Ramon Aldasoro who had answered Mola on the telephone and clinched the future for Bilbao way back in July.

Aldasoro faced a difficult situation. In the first place, Vizcaya was not a food-producing area. Her farms would next year turn out a certain amount of maize, but not enough to feed Bilbao; meanwhile they would grow vegetables and seed potatoes, which were imported in mass from Ireland.

All that Vizcaya herself could offer was an enormous stock of *garbanzos Mejicanos*, or Mexican chick peas, for Bilbao was in normal times the staple of the entire chick-pea trade between Mexico and Spain. On a ration of chickpeas alone Bilbao could have existed for two years, but Aldasoro (who knew how to live well) sought some variety from the yellow menace, as we came to call the clogging puff-balls of sand that floated in our soup.

The second anxious element in Ramon Aldasoro's calculations was the presence of over 100,000 refugees in Bilbao, mostly from the province of Guipuzcoa. From this total are excluded those refugees with friends who were capable of looking after themselves; 100,000 men, women and children were already provided with lodgings and dining-rooms by the Socialist Counsellor of Assistencia Social, Juan Gracia, and it was now Aldasoro's job to supply them with free food. Their stomachs could not be satisfied with

86

the animated pictures of Engels, Marx, Caballero and Prieto that adorned their mess-room walls.

With food to import for such a multitude, and the loaves and fishes so low, Aldasoro experienced another difficulty unmentioned in the New Testament—he had to run his food ships through the rebel blockade. It was not long before he found that he could not rely on Spanish ships alone.

Although the blockade cordon had not yet been organised at San Sebastian, Franco's navy already had the preponderance of force on the northern coast of Spain. They could pit a battleship, *España*, two cruisers, *Canarias* and *Almirante Cervera*, and the destroyer *Velasco* against the destroyer *Jose Luis Diez* and two Government submarines.

It was therefore essential for the Basques to organise an auxiliary fleet of their own, and to build coastal defences. A Basque who had formerly served in the Ministry of Marine at Madrid, and later as Captain of the Port of Bilbao, was appointed by Aguirre to the former service. His name was Joaquim Eguia, and he did not like the job, but he took it on and stuck it out until the day before Santander fell.

The Government battleship *Jaime Primero*, which had visited Bilbao in the anxious days of September with the whole Red Squadron, had shed a series of ten 101 mm. guns and bequeathed them to Eguia. This artillery, with a range of about 13,000 yards, was of little value to the battleship, which was already supplied with a secondary armament of higher power.

Bilbao possessed a deep-sea fishing fleet which went out every year to fish *bacalao*, as the Basques call cod, on the Newfoundland banks, following the tradition of over five centuries. The trawlers of this fleet were now lying in the Nervion; they were built of a strength to stand any sea or storm. They were stable and steel-armoured and made a speed unusual for their kind. Eguia took over four of them, covered them with extra plates, painted them iron-grey, fitted them with wireless, and called them *Bizkaya*, *Guipuzkoa*, *Araba* and *Nabara*, after the four provinces of the Basques. Fore and aft in their broad beam he mounted two 101 mms. apiece in turrets specially constructed at Bilbao. They were to be used for convoy at all times, and throughout the coming war they shirked their duty as little as he did. Their crews were selected from the deep-sea fishermen of Bilbao and the refugee seamen of Pasajes and San Sebastian; they had never fought a battle in their lives, but they knew as well as anyone in the world how to manage a ship. These men were absolutely fearless. Many of them were chosen by Our Lady of Begoña, queen of the seas to whom Basque fishermen make their vows, to meet a heroic end in the grey, unwearying bay that would be remembered many years by their brothers and sons, as they swept back and forth with the nets between Punta de Galea and Lequeitio, over their clean, salt-whitened bones, and shoals of starry sardines and anchovies.

Eguia besides took twenty-four of the smaller trawlers that had come from Pasajes, and converted them into minesweepers. The rebels at San Sebastian might use a mine-layer, *Jupiter*, against which provision had to be made. Five motor-boats patrolled the mouth of the Nervion at night, and by the beginning of January five batteries of coastal artillery had been established and armed the harbour entrance, of which the greater part were 6-inch Vickers guns of that year, 1936, made under patent in the Asturias. The Basques were now masters of their own territorial waters, and the neighbouring Government provinces of Santander and the Asturias arranged with Bilbao to import all their needs by the Nervion. Their own coastal defence was incomparably poorer.

In spite of the speed and efficiency with which Eguia operated, Aldasoro was still confronted with a major difficulty of the food question. How was he to carry food across the open seas? Bilbao was full of shipping, owned and registered in Bilbao; but outside the range of the Vickers guns they were at the mercy of various hostile elements—German, Italian or simply Spanish rebel. Italy behaved in a manner which, in an age less jaded by incidents, would have engaged the attention of the whole world. At the beginning of the revolt there were seven Bilbao ships in her harbours—the *Arxanda-Mendi, Maria Victoria, Vizcaya, Cilurnum, Indauchu, Jupiter* and *Kauldi*. The Italian Government calmly seized these ships and, after transferring the crews to the new Italian colony of Palma de Mallorca, sailed them under her own flag by means of an Italian

Kriegstagebuch

28. ... Befehl der Hauptkolonne 13³⁰ ... Übernacht
... nach ... 15⁰⁰ ...
... Obst ... nach Vittoria ...

27. Nacht d. Hauptkolonne v. x nach x
... in Vittoria

30. Nacht d. Kolonne v. x nach Vittoria
...

31. ... Gefecht die Kolonne auf Maggio — Elbertin
u. Jerinto ... (... Truppen, ...)
Maggio ... die Kolonne gewonnen.

2. ... angriff ... Ziel 1 u. 2 (...
(x x x)

3. ... angriff ... angesetzt auf Ziel 7.
... Kolonne ... x u. Sekundär ...
... gemeinschaftl. Sekundär ... mit
Bomben belegt.

4. ... angriff ... ...
auf Sekundär ... u. auf ...
auf den beiden ... ...

1. Teil : Bereitschaft mit 1. Welle

GERMAN WAR DIARY:
CAPTURED OCHANDIANO, APRIL 5TH, 1937.

company called the "Garibaldi," for the transport of mineral from Spanish Morocco to Germany. Formerly this would have been called piracy, but the word is considered too unkind when applied to Italy, and the incident was passed over.

By similar methods the German Government provided that German shipowners in Hamburg should receive twenty Bilbao ships caught in various European Fascist ports; they now fly the swastika.

So do many other Basque ships. It seems that Franco used this way to pay his debts to Germany. For example, the *Azkaray-Mendi*, which was seized in Melilla harbour at the outbreak of the revolt, now flies the German flag and calls herself *Helen*. And at this very moment on September 30th, 1936, Franco's navy arrested the *Manu* outside Bilbao: she suffered the same transformation as the others, and now professes anti-Semitism under the name of *Marion*, and sails on her totalitarian occasions.

The only solution for Aldasoro was to use the British flag. After November, 1936, British ships were used almost exclusively. Twelve ships, whose names recur again and again in the history of the Bilbao blockade . . . *Seven Seas Spray* . . . *Thorpehall* . . . *Kenfik Pool*—these were the victuallers of the north of Spain.

Bilbao, under Aldasoro, established commercial delegations in France, at Bordeaux and Bayonne, and in eastern Spain at Barcelona, Valencia and Alicante. She bought from her own resources, and from an allowance made by the Central Government.

Wheat was imported from Valencia, Russia and France, rice from Valencia, potatoes from Valencia and France, broad beans from France, oil for cooking from Valencia; milk, powdered and condensed, in the early days from the neighbouring province of Santander, but later from France and Holland; coal from England at first, but at the end almost entirely from the Asturias.

Wheat, rice, potatoes, beans, oil, milk, coal: these were the crude elements with which Aldasoro had to deal, and sparingly. The sea at Bilbao's door added fish to the Basque ration; and great was the excitement in the city when the rowing-boats came up-river to the centre of Bilbao, and the white-haired old women in shawls staggered up the steps with a basketful of silver on their backs, shrieking *anchoas*.

Prices were fixed at the scale of July 18th, the day when the rebellion broke out in Spain. Distributions of food were made whenever ships came in, and a stock of a month's duration was kept for population and army.

Bread was made by the State bakeries—black bread, very bitter to the taste, but not unhealthy. The Basques called it Integral Bread, which meant that in order to make up weight and put a good face on their hungriness, they kept the husks and chaff as well as the grain. After a breaking-in of a month on Integral Bread one grew not to mind it. Stories were spread about its noxious qualities. Persons disaffected to the regime were convinced that it caused abortion in one sex and lunacy in the other; but the refugees were as fruitful as ever, and multiplied, and brought more problems to the desk of Aldasoro; and as for the lunatics, had the Basques not abandoned the great super-asylum, the veritable Wembley among mental hospitals that they were building at Derio, and made trench mortars in the framework instead? But the jokes about her bread went on, both inside and outside Vizcaya. I remember well a cartoon in one of the rebel papers of San Sebastian, after the death of Salengro, Blum's first Minister of the Interior. The corpse is lying splay-footedly on a ridiculous bier—it is the Spanish tradition to pursue imaginary enemies when they are dead—and in the foreground an innocent man asks the doctor, "What did he die of?"

"The bread of Bilbao, of course," says the doctor, rising to the heights of Iberian repartee.

There were many breadless days: at a rough estimate, about ten a month. And, as is natural in war, the best-fed part of the population were the Basque army, and their families, who received the soldiers' pay of ten pesetas a day.

At this time the army was in process of formation. More arms were expected; the crisis was past. As winter drew on, Aldasoro found that he was making a daily distribution to the forces in the field of 5,000 litres of oil, 5,000 litres of cognac, and 40,000 litres of wine to keep their bellies warm where they stood on watch on the white Basque mountains.

He organised, besides, a factory where food of all sorts was canned for the troops, and brown-paper packets, neatly pinned with metal, were turned out *en masse*, each containing a day's military ration. Uniforms were imported by sea from Barcelona; but boots were made at a new factory established, like so much else in Bilbao, by Aldasoro's Department of Commercio y Abastacimiento.

And until the end he exported iron and iron ore from the Bilbao mines to Great Britain, where they were needed in gross for British rearmament. By the end of the year the system was in full working order. The people of Bilbao pulled in their belts, their cheeks fell in a little, and noticeably, for the Basques are a big-boned race. There were astonishingly few complaints, and there was never a public protest. The queues of women at the bread-shops in the early morning were very orderly, and the police were never called upon to supervise them. Bilbao and Vizcaya, except when foreign aeroplanes were bombing over their heads, maintained a self-discipline unexampled in Spain, just as Aldasoro's organisation could find no counterpart between the Pyrenees and Gibraltar.

For a whole year Bilbao was to remain undernourished: when the industries which usually pay for it are turning out war material, the importation of food is a costly business. Meat and eggs, for instance, were rarities, and the whole of her 400,000 population were well aware that they lived on a month's margin of famine and chickpeas. The slightest hitch in the regular arrival of food-ships meant that starvation was felt at once, not only at Bilbao, but at Santander and in the Asturias.

Commercio y Abastacimiento; Assistencia Social. These were phrases that carried content for the Basques, more content perhaps than the war itself. Social welfare, municipal order and cleanliness were great words to them. The whole of Vizcaya is full of the sanatoria, and poor children's schools and hospitals that they built out of their careful savings. They really enjoyed creating more comfort for the poor and the suffering, and when later I visited their country I never saw them work more willingly and efficiently than when they were supplying each other's needs, taking wounded through a series of dressing stations and spotless hospitals from the line to the base, feeding refugees, weighing

out equal rations for everybody. Visitors of Leftish leanings often noticed the inadequacy of their posters compared
with those of the Asturias and Valencia. And, indeed,
the graphic art in Bilbao streets was neither bold nor
emancipated, and they did not seem capable of originating
any new coloured concepts of the work of Assistencia Social.
Perhaps it was because they were keener on the fruit than
the skin: heavy industry had made of them a people
somewhat matter-of-fact.

V

THE DEPARTMENT OF DEFENCE had been given to the President, Aguirre: by this means the Basque Nationalists established themselves in complete control over the conduct of the war. The recruitment of battalions, manufacture of war material, construction of fortifications was in their hands. True there was a General Staff appointed by Valencia with whom they had to reckon; but so far as political influence affected the army, the influence of other parties was nil, except in the internal affairs of various battalions. It was only later that the Communists tried to establish themselves in the staff.

Recruitment went ahead with a great spurt when the shipment of arms arrived from Hamburg, and it was known that more material, planes, armoured cars, anti-tank guns and rifles were expected from Russia towards the end of October. The resistance, too, at Eibar and Elgueta had put new spirit into the Basques. Soon they had organised forty-six battalions of infantry, each 660 men strong.

Of these twenty-seven were raised directly by the Basque Nationalist Party: next in strength came the moderate Socialist contingent of the U.G.T., which provided eight. The rest were made up pretty equally of Republican Left, Communist, United Socialist-Communist Youth, and Anarchist contingents. Except in the case of one fighting battalion, the Malatesta, the martial merits of the Anarchists were written off by the Basque Government, who always alleged, quite loudly, that the roles of Anarchist on the Government side and Falangist on Franco's were inter-changeable, and that in battle both were birds of passage. On parade, however, the Anarchists were more like birds of paradise. They wore gay parti-coloured forage caps, red one side and black the other, for such was the flag of Iberian Anarchism. In order to shock the pious Basques, they marched past with the girl friends leading each battalion, scarlet-lipped and blue-overalled. All carried a full complement of bombs, which burgeoned round their waists with a fertility comparable only to Josephine Baker's bananas. Personally, the individual Anarchist was the most charming creature in the world to meet, dark nights excluded.

It was not until the year of 1936 had passed that the Basques were able to enforce a medical inspection of lady Anarchists and withdraw them from the front. So powerful is the libertarian ideal among the followers of Spain's indigenous proletarian movement. The dreadful thought of some Central Authority sending a doctor to dictate to them took two months to sink in and leaven the strange lump which fills the Anarchist head. As for women, if they want to fight, let them; and there were some wild-looking suffragettes who kept a clean bill of health and a proud place in the trenches until the campaign ended.

Of the material in the new army, the best were certain well-weathered Basque Nationalist battalions—the Itxas-Alde (which means sea-shore, and was formed of fishermen), the Gordexola, the Kirikiño, Otxandiano, Marteartu. Several of the U.G.T. battalions, which were raised on a syndical basis, were of equal value: French military observers even rated them higher than the Nationalists. Certainly the syndicate was proved by the Basque war to be a first-class military foundation: the U.G.T. men fought with an extraordinary solidarity and devotion, and by the end of the war had lost a greater percentage of dead than any other political group. But my impression of them was that they were not so sharp in attack as the Nationalists, and altogether less conversant with open country.

All sorts of trade unions offered their quota. The atmosphere was catching, and the café waiters banded together to form the battalion Salsamendi. It was not a very wonderful battalion, though fleet of foot and dexterous in manœuvre; but it gave the waiters something to do, what with coffee and drinks so very scarce in Bilbao.

On the whole the Basque infantry material was extremely good. It is a big race, solid and naturally disciplined;

not too highly imaginative, and full of moral and physical
resistances, very difficult to panic. Under the hammer-
blows of foreign artillery and aviation which were to come
next summer, the Basques withdrew very slowly. Even
when great gaps had been made in their line, and it looked
as if Bilbao would fall in a day, the unexpected and incomprehensible always happened. Without any evident assistance from a defeatist General Staff, the Basque Gudaris,
as the infantrymen were called, recrystallised and reformed
upon the next natural line of defence. They could be
pushed out of one position by a day's heavy bombardment,
but never out of two.

The organisation of war supplies was a more anxious
business than the raising of men.

Vizcaya had, before the war broke out, an arms industry
of her own. At Eibar rifles and machine-gun pistols were
made: at Gernika and Durango small arms and ammunition. There were grenade factories in Bilbao itself, and
the Basques had just perfected a new trench mortar, calibre
81 mm., which they were going to put on the world market.

All these concerns were taken over by the Junta de
Defensa in July, and now surrendered by that body to the
Basque State. But they were no longer in production:
many of their requirements, nickel, explosives, cotton,
came from abroad, and two factors which tended to keep
them there were the Franco blockade and the Non-Intervention Committee. Right until the end the French would
not even allow medical cotton-wool for bandages to be
exported to Government Spain; it might be used for
filling shells. The only war material that reached the
Basques from France was stolen or smuggled. The transport of war material on British ships was out of the question.
The only sources from which Bilbao could replenish her
stocks and feed her factories were Mexico and Russia:
the Mexican Republic had proclaimed her sympathy with
Valencia from the start, and Russia in October had decided
to break the Non-Intervention Agreement, which her Fascist
enemies, Germany and Italy, had already disregarded for
two months.

To do the Soviets justice, it must be realised to the full
that it was not until mid-October that the first Russian
material arrived in Republican Spain. Germany and Italy

had intervened with regularity since before the rebellion began: it was hardly surprising that the patience of at least one of the peaceful Powers should be exhausted.

Even so, it was many months before Bilbao arms factories were in full production. Materials had to evade the warships of Franco, and it was calculated that one in four of the ships carrying them was captured on the northern coast of Spain.

Meanwhile, the Basques experimented. With the few samples to hand, Señor Delicado, the chief of their war laboratory, evolved a new fuse for incendiary mortar shells and incendiary bombs, and carried it to a point of perfection far beyond the German product, which we were to see later over Gernika and Amorebieta, Munguia and Lemona, and destroying so many of the deep pinewoods of Euzkadi.

It was towards the end of October that the ships came in from the Baltic, and were tied fast to the Nervion bank. There was great excitement in Bilbao: nobody was supposed to know that the arms ships had arrived, but the only place where the secret was really kept was the Basque hospitals for the deaf and dumb. It took some days to unload the ships, but the German raiders did not visit the harbour; as yet their information was very scrappy, even at such public moments as this.

The first weapons to be unloaded were twelve single-seater fighters, Russian biplane Boeings with four synchronised machine-guns of the type known as I.15. With a speed of 240 miles an hour, these were faster than either the Italian (Fiat) or German (Heinkel) fighters that they were likely to meet. To the latter they could give thirty miles an hour and win the race; until March, 1937, when the Germans sent out their new two-engined bombers, Heinkel 111 and Dornier 17, these were the fastest planes in Spain. Russian pilots came with them, oldish men of thirty-six and thereabouts, who kept very much to themselves and neither drank nor smoked. Also in the crew was a large Russian fox-terrier, the pilots' pet. He greatly engaged the curiosity of the Bilbainos, for dogs had not struck them before as domestic favourites except on ships, though it must be admitted that their potentialities as a change from chickpeas were being eagerly canvassed.

FATHER MORILLA DEAD: DURANGO, MARCH 31ST, 1937.
(BASQUE MOTORISED POLICE BEHIND.)

The fox-terrier, however, survived, and was known briefly as Ruso. The fighters which were to give Bilbao security for four months were called Chatos, or snub-nosed, in allusion to the shortness of their frames and the roundness of their engines. Bilbao grew to be very fond of them.

Next from the ark there stepped twenty-five Russian armoured cars, mounting each a 47 mm. gun and a heavy machine-gun. Their Ford engines could carry them at 70 kilometres an hour, on six wheels of solid rubber, four of which were double tyred. For a country like Vizcaya, better provided with roads than any other Spanish province, these pieces of mobile light artillery were admirably chosen, and the debt of the Basques to the Russian armoured car in the campaign of April-June, 1937, was heavy. They could be dispersed and concentrated afresh at great speed; in a well-roaded country their guns could command almost any point—and what beautiful guns, manœuvreable, precise, rapid. Of all the Russian material that I saw, I was most impressed by these: while they worked in Vizcaya not one was knocked out by an anti-tank gun, and only one by an aeroplane. They held up for weeks an enemy tank force three times as strong.

When these had been unloaded there tripped along the quay about a dozen small vehicles, which looked like Baby Austins in armour; these also were of Russian make. They were very, very small, and carried a machine-gun apiece in an old-fashioned turret. They were as useless as their big brothers were invaluable, and after they had been tried out were stripped of their automatics and rather pompously called "liaison cars." In other words, they carried ammunition and nervy staff officers up to the line when a bombardment was expected, and then rushed home again as quick as their little spindly legs could carry them.

Then came about a dozen anti-tank guns, inferior to the German type used by Franco, and case after case of small arms, light bombs and rifle ammunition.

Once the material had been assembled, Bilbao enjoyed a grand fiesta. The armoured cars and the crusading Austins and the anti-tanks marched through the town in long procession, and the streets were plastered with posters inviting the Basques to pay befitting homage to Soviet Russia. And though the Basques were as instinctively anti-Communist as they were anti-Fascist, being at this time perhaps the most shining example of a humanitarian, bourgeois democracy in the world, they could not help being grateful to the one nation that had come to their rescue *in extrèmis*, and ponder bitterly on the western democracies, who had, they thought, so much more in common with Vizcaya, but who had deserted her utterly.

Above them, in flights of three, their supercharged Cyclone engines roaring merrily, flew the Russian fighters who would drive the Germans away from Bilbao. Her rulers could scarcely feel so much in the debt of England, who had refused them the only powder that could make their anti-aircraft guns fire, and left their city open till to-day to the invader.

They could not know that twelve was the largest number of fighting planes that they would ever see defending Bilbao. They and their people must have thought that this was just the beginning of the arming of the Basques.

It was, in fact, almost the end. A certain amount of artillery was to come in the next six months, but no more tanks or armoured cars or planes, except to replace losses. Meanwhile, on the other side, Germany and Italy increased their pledges and their stakes. New planes were continually arriving, and the first Italian infantry were being conscripted for Spanish service. But that was not what the young men were told as they left the impoverished land for the recruiting office: Abyssinia, they heard, was their destination.

If the Basques were slow to produce their own material of war, they did not waste time in preparing fortifications for their city. It was now, when the enemy was pressing their front at Eibar, that they laid down the first plans of their famous *cinturón*. The execution of the scheme was placed in the hands of a Basque, Captain Goicoechea, and the same Major Anglada, who, at the beginning of the revolt, apologised for his inability to supply the Defence Junta with more than fifty rifles. It was a vast plan, nothing less than the enclosure of Bilbao from the sea on the east at Sopelana to the sea on the west at Somorrostro, with 200 kilometres of trench and barbed wire and concrete machine-gun posts. The Basques set to work with truly racial industry on the trenches, little realising that the men who directed their activity were both disloyal; but barbed wire and cement and spade labour could all be found in Bilbao and the Basques only wanted something useful to do to be thoroughly happy.

They began work in the middle of October and for two months there were 15,000 men struggling daily with the fortifications of Bilbao. Everywhere they were digging trenches, chopping down trees to provide timber for dug-outs, laying out wire, clearing whole forests away in front of the lines to give a smooth glacis and a clear field of fire. It was a work of ants. To the experienced eye the *cinturón* which was taking shape was, it is true, not ill-planned on paper by the military mind; but the execution of the plan on the ground was left by the military to civilian engineers who, whatever their enthusiasm (and there they greatly out-distanced the military), knew nothing about organisation in depth and camouflage, the two main elements of modern defence. In other words, the military at the service of the Basque Government, grossly failed to do their duty. Some were determined to sabotage steadily, the others, of no fixed political views, were only too willing to let civilians do the work if they were keen about it. *They* were decidedly not.

* * * * * *

Towards the end of the year the Russian General Gurieff and a small staff arrived in Bilbao, where the Basques received them in a friendly manner. Gurieff was the man who organised the first Russian tank counter-offensive at Madrid at the end of October, which failed against Franco's right wing. He struck none of us as a genius, and the Basques resolutely refused to employ him except in an advisory capacity, where his advice was in nearly every case rejected.

I found him a likeable personality, but, as I thought, inexperienced in war.

VI

AFTER ARMY AND FOOD, the third most pressing requirement of Bilbao was a reliable police force, able to prevent a recurrence of the massacres of September and October and to keep the anarchist element in hand. A Basque Nationalist with a cigar and country seat, the well-tailored young Telesforo Monzon, was put in charge of the Department of the Interior: no Marxist he. The other side of the medal of order, in the Basque mind, was Justice: this portfolio fell to another Basque Nationalist, for inflexibility of purpose the biggest of them, the sombrely dressed and grave-faced Jesus Maria de Leizaola, whose character will appear more strongly in the last pages of this book. Leizaola was a power in the shadows; he set to work to shake from the depths of his legal knowledge, a Popular Tribunal for the trial of offences against the régime which would not be sanguinary or demagogic. Older than most of the Council, his slow and steady voice, rare scornful smile and immense weight of learning in constitutional and international law soon established an ascendency over his colleagues. When the discussion ranged wider than he wished it to do, he would take out a piece of paper, and everybody noted nervously that he was writing down little paragraphs, numbered 1, 2 and 3; voices gradually weakened till Leizaola, his writing over, would say, "We are met to decide on this, this and this. Now, what do you think about 1, Astigarrabia?" For prelude to this, a heavily-disguised expression of impatience would appear on Leizaola's face, which he always found much more effective than impatience pure and simple.

First, the Guardia Civil and the Guardia de Asalto were abolished. Elsewhere in Republican Spain they were given different names, but the Basques did not like them, and got rid of them. They had bitter memories of these Spanish police organisations. Leizaola himself when a student had been marched in handcuffs from Bermeo to Amorebieta, some sixteen miles, on a hot summer's day in front of two Guardia Civil. His crime had been demonstrating for Basque Nationalism — in other words, shouting with some other young men, "God and the ancient laws," the cry of his party. At a desolate spot on the road, to give Leizaola a fright, the Guardias behind him started rattling the bolts of their rifles. The Spanish police were the first to discover the phrase "shot while trying to escape" — the *ley de fugas*. Leizaola did not forgive them. The Guardia Civil, with their patent leather tricorn hats, Castilian cloaks and tradition of hard-fisted loyalty to the Central Government, particularly if it was Right, were sent away on holiday. It was found that they were buying rifles and ammunition.

The Guardias de Asalto, crack shots, a corps of Shock Police formed after the proclamation of the Republic, were also dissolved. Many of them came from outside the Basque country, and the rule was now established that the police had to be bilingual, speaking *vascuence* as well as *castellano*. The police of Vizcaya were reorganised on the following lines:

1. Ertzana, or People's Guard, a selected arms-carrying police divided into two sections, motorised and foot.
2. Orden Publico, an armed police for normal town use.

The Orden Publico were mostly middle-aged men, wearing blue uniform and beret and carrying rifles. Their job was the prevention of ordinary crime; in a sense they corresponded to the Guardia Civil, though they were not a picked body and did not have the tradition which meant so much to Spain's old force.

The Ertzana were, however, the more interesting innovation, all of whom were Basques and members of the Nationalist Party. Their foot battalion, all young men of a certain education, had to be over 1.75 metres tall and were trained to arms — rifles, machine-guns and tear gas.

They numbered 500. In their silver-badged berets and long blue great-coats they looked a fine body. Attached to them were the 400 of their motorised section.

These were Bilbao's, or, for that matter, Spain's most modern experiment in the way of policemen. Half of them were marked out for speed-cars, and their chief, Commandante Pikazar, had chosen the Riley, though in fact only a few arrived in Bilbao before all energies had to be concentrated on the war—the Non-Intervention Agreement caused interminable delays in the purchase of English material. The rest were supplied with fast motor-cycles.

Their head-quarters were at the town house of Manoel de la Sota, on the river; but their organisation as a shock force for the maintenance of public order spread throughout Vizcaya. Liaison was maintained by wireless cars, which later gathered new value as means to tap the field wireless of the enemy. Indeed, when the great offensive came, public order in Vizcaya was so perfect that the motorised police could be transferred to the army, and acted as motor-cyclist runners and communication service to the various brigade and divisional headquarters. Two of them became a sort of journalist's bodyguard for myself, replacing a civilian chauffeur who had leapt out of the car, pushed his head down a drain and fainted when he saw a fairly well-developed bomb explode a mile in front of us. But he was a thin and pale-faced man even when he held his head higher.

Pikazar, the chief of the motorised police, was a travelled Basque, who, besides being an aeronautical and electrical engineer, had made a special hobby of police methods. He had studied the systems of France, Germany, Britain and the U.S.A.; the *systema Yanqui* amused him most. His men were an even smarter corps than the Ertzana foot; in their glistening brown leather jackets, knee-breeches and uniform caps and their high boots they greatly impressed the people of Bilbao, and so did their revolvers. Thus Monzon's force maintained public discipline by an organisation built upon three lines of public defence: the Orden Publico, older men on the spot to handle a disturbance in its early stages; if it looked like passing beyond their control, the motorised police would

be called in to overawe with a sudden concentration of
force; and finally the Ertzana foot, if necessary, would
weigh in with tear gas and machine-guns. The Basques
were ready for all eventualities: they were only caught
napping once, on the dark day of January 4th.

* * * * * *

Defence, police, justice and food supply were, with the
Presidency of the Council, in the hands of the Basque
Nationalists and the sympathetic leader of the Republican
Left, Aldasoro. These portfolios, they knew, were the keys
of the control of Euzkadi, and it was good that they were
held in one strong hand. An army and stocks of war
material were gradually built up that Spanish means alone
could not break; and the war history of Bilbao after the
formation of her autonomous government was one of success
against Spain, defeat only at the hands of Germany and
Italy. The army was provided with a steady and consistent
supply of food, even during the January crisis. The
blockade of Bilbao was never broken, but in spite of this
Aldasoro's brilliantly organised department was able to
distribute to the public a fairer, more regular and in many
ways a fuller food ration than could be found in Madrid,
which was never blockaded. The influence of this efficiency
on the people's will to resist, and on their compliance with
the requirements of public order cannot be exaggerated;
and where sugar could not convince, there was the whip
which Monzon was seldom called upon to use. Leizaola
meanwhile conducted the public wrath against its enemies
into narrow, legal channels, where the strength and solidity
of the banks broke the force of the current. It was a testimony to the value of the measures that his colleagues took
that Leizaola, the anti-Marxist, was able to run a risk in
the composition of his Popular Tribunal. The jury was
not a reflection of the Council of Ministers: it was formed
of two representatives of each party in the Frente Popular,
and there were therefore only two Nationalists in it. But
its decisions were just, its executions very few. No other
tribunal was tolerated in Vizcaya. It was known that the
Government was determined to rule: revolutionaries could
prove their enthusiasm in the defence of their country.

What a change from the early days of San Sebastian that we saw only two months before. The hours of proletarian enthusiasm were over and those of Basque organisation begun.

The organisation set to work at once, and smoked out a spies' nest.

VII

HERR WILHELM WAKONIGG was popular in Bilbao; he had
been in the last few years a great friend of the social Aldasoro,
who was his lawyer. Ortuzar, chief of the new Basque
police, was married to his pretty daughter. So the tall,
genial German was well established with the Basques, who
respond at once to frankness and *camaraderie*, even when
these qualities are noted in an agent of Krupps.

Wakonigg had lived many years in Vizcaya, not only
selling German heavy goods, but buying for his own part
interests in Bilbao heavy industries. The pro-English
Basques had forgotten their dislike of him; for, during the
Great War he, as consul of Austria-Hungary, had organised
the revictualment and fuel service of the German submarines
operating in the Bay of Biscay. These were the U-boats
that sank so many of Sota's ships with ore for England.
Wakonigg supplied them at night, at the little port of
Plencia on the creek between the Nervion and Bermeo;
he was then chief of German espionage in Northern Spain.

But that was forgotten, as old quarrels will be. After
the War, Wakonigg ceased to be consul; but he did much
to help, and regularly visited the ex-Empress Zita in her
exile at Lequeitio. Here the Basque millionaires who
were enemies of the Basque Nationalist Party paid her
constant court, and Wakonigg agreed with them in all
things. Zita became godmother to his younger daughter.
But the Basques were not bitter politicians; he was easy
to get on with, they therefore liked him.

The Civil War broke out; less to the surprise of Wakonigg,
who was in on the date, than of the Basques. Wakonigg
received a wire from Vienna, saying that he should consider
himself Austrian Consul once more; and some days later,

another nice wire from Berlin, asking him to become German Consul when the permanent man left Bilbao. Neither of these appointments was confirmed at Madrid. But what did that matter? In the happy disorganisation of government at Bilbao when the Junta de Defensa was taking over, and availing himself of the general esteem in which he was held, Wakonigg marched into the Junta with his telegrams to wave as sufficient credentials, and immediately set to work, before the assumption could be questioned, to negotiate the export of German and Austrian citizens in a most official way. Slapping backs heartily and being slapped back again, Wakonigg found his re-elevation to the consulate as easy as falling off a log.

German men-of-war were often in the harbour, and Wakonigg always found some Teuton to ship away, and went aboard himself for a chat with the officers, and maybe handed them some documents worth passing on to General Franco, if they ever chanced to have a quick one with the General round the corner. For Wakonigg knew a lot of things and people.

He kept open house in the so-called International Zone at Las Arenas, where consuls and foreigners lived, as well as those Bilbao millionaires who were not now in smaller rooms and on stricter diets than formerly. Franco had promised not to bomb the International Zone, but one day in October he just happened to bomb it, no doubt by mistake and thinking that it was Madrid, or perhaps because he had forgotten his promise for a moment.

The consuls were much enraged by this slipshod behaviour on the part of General Franco, none more than Herr Wakonigg, who expressed himself most violently and said that it was no good sitting down under this treatment, but they ought to send a deputation to protest to the Embassies at St. Jean de Luz. This struck all as an excellent idea, and a deputation was formed of Stevenson, the British consul, and the consuls of the Argentine, Switzerland, Belgium, and naturally Herr Wakonigg, titular consul of Germany and Austria, who would be a most useful member, seeing that his government was believed by some to be on fairly talkative terms with the bombers. The British destroyer *Exmouth* was commissioned to take the party to France.

The embarkation was to take place on October 28th. To the surprise of the consuls, the Basque police very politely told them that their luggage would have to be searched. Stevenson naturally complied, and without opening his bag they chalked it off; so also with the consul of Switzerland.

Wakonigg protested. He said that a consul had diplomatic rights, and that it was a breach of procedure to open his luggage. But the Basque police said no, it was their information that consuls did not have diplomatic immunity in this sense.

The German still refused to open his valise, and it was noticed that a small unhappy compatriot of his, Emil Schaeidt Schneider, an employee of the Consulate, was making nervous signs to his master with his eyebrows and nose, and at more critical moments by twitching, jerking and snapping his fingers.

To break the ice which was now forming Wakonigg said that he could not permit his valise to be opened, as a matter of principle, but that if they persisted he could only compromise with them by sending the valise back to his house, reserving all rights to protest, etc. Thereupon he put his hand on the valise-handle, but the Basque police put bigger hands upon the corners and said that, now the valise was in their possession it must remain there until examined; and they discreetly suggested to Wakonigg that he should, if he still had doubts, come with them to the Ministry of the Interior to see Monzon.

"Well," said Wakonigg, "I don't know what all this fuss is about, but as you insist, I'll open the bag myself here. I've nothing to hide," and he opened it, in a light-hearted and careless manner.

The police began poking about, and the first thing that appeared were a lot of jewels, which it was forbidden to take out of the country. Wakonigg said that they were his own, but could not explain where he wore them. So they took him off with Schneider, whose nose and fingers were still in tiresome activity, to see Telesforo de Monzon.

A fine haul of documents was made in the valise. First came a report by the Captain of Engineers, Pablo Murga,

on the form of construction of the Bilbao *cinturón*, with
minute details about the fortifications; on the position of
factories making shells and fuses for artillery, rifle ammunition; and details of the powder used by the Basques.
Murga wrote that the best way for the rebels to hold up
work on the Bilbao defences would be frequent visits of the
aviation, particularly using machine guns. Murga, who
was in the Second Section of the Basque General Staff, was
also able to inform his friends that an offensive was being
prepared in the Otxandiano sector.

Second was a letter signed by the banker Hernandez
Mendirichaga, with details on Bilbao banking interests.
Third, a letter from Julian Munsuri, entitled "Information
on the Basque Nationalist Movement." More important
was document number four, which bore the signature of
Commandante Jose Anglada, the same that had said he
had no arms in the early days; it included a full description
of the failure of the rebel movement in the Garellano
regiment at the beginning, and listed the officers according
as their sympathies were for or against the régime.

These documents were unaddressed; Wakonigg also
carried private letters. One was from unhappy little
Schneider, and contained highly derogatory descriptions
of members of the Basque Government. It was, besides,
full of the praises of Herr Wakonigg, whose services to the
rebels he said were immeasurable; Herr Wakonigg, he
wrote, could rest content that after all this was over they
were going to erect a beautiful statue to him, as indeed he
deserved, and as big as the statue of the Sacred Heart in
the Gran Via. This was the biggest statue in Bilbao, so
they were clearly going to immortalise Wilhelm.

It was discovered on examination that the consul of
Paraguay was involved in the espionage affair; and
Anglada, when questioned, handed up a thousand hidden
rifles, and was able to tell the Basques that a German
warship had carried away two Spanish Air Force officers,
a captain and a Carabinero Commandant, and left them
with the rebels at San Sebastian.

So Germany was not only sending war material to destroy
the Basques; her own consul at Bilbao had organised a
service of espionage against the people to whom, as he said,
he was accredited; and her ships, while pretending to

take away German refugees, had been carrying espionage and recruits to the rebels. No wonder that Basque dislike settled upon the Germans as a race.

Anglada and Murga and the Paraguayan consul were shot; Schneider, by a typical act of Basque clemency, was sentenced only to life imprisonment. He is now at large.

Wakonigg was tried in public by the Popular Tribunal on November 18th, under the presidency of the Judge-dean of Bilbao, and found guilty of espionage and sentenced to death. Leizaola and his son-in-law Ortuzar visited him to comfort him in the evening, and as in the old days had a long and friendly talk. Next morning at 7.15, after he had dressed very neatly and taken a parting pull at the knot of his tie in the glass before he left the prison, he was shot at Zamudio with eyes unbandaged. The firing squad shook hands with him before the volley, and his death was inscribed in the municipal register of that village.

VIII

NOBODY KNOWS WHY IT happened on January 4th. There seemed to be no point in it. The front was completely quiet, and Franco did not make up his mind to attack Bilbao until two and a half months had passed. It was a raid without object, a play without continuity: but the climax was more horrible than if it were part of the most skilfully written tragedy, and as an object lesson in the new *mystique* of the air it must always lead.

At three o'clock in the afternoon on January 4th, the Department of Defence was informed by telephone from the southern front, south of the great mountain Gorbea, that a large air fleet had passed over from Vitoria, and was making for Bilbao. The Department of Defence advised the Gobernacion, Monzon's Ministry of the Interior, and the wailing sirens struck up their terror-tune along fourteen kilometres of the Nervion, from the city to the sea.

The former polo-ground of the Bilbao rich, a small spread of level ground between the river and the hills at Lamiaco, next to Las Arenas, was now the air port of the Russian fighters. There were eight of them now; the rest had been sent to Santander. And the Russians had succeeded so well in training Spanish pilots that of eight who stepped into the aeroplanes now, four only were Russian. They gained height flying upriver towards the city, and when they were over Bilbao climbed rapidly, to the uneven beat of their supercharged engines, then turned in two streams and made off unexpectedly to sea.

Everyone in the town who saw this was very angry. "Those Russians," they said, "anyone could have told that they would run away." Then they ran away them-selves. The sirens changed to a most melancholy song of

two notes, one high and the other low, signifying peril.
The women of Bilbao had already seized up their children
and gone below with streaming hair into the refuges;
the men now followed them hotfoot. Bilbao became a
city where only police lived, and Red Cross men stood
ready at their cars; in a few seconds all noise of circulation
had gone, except the flutter of old paper along the streets.

In three closely organised flights, in the flat viperish
arrowhead that the Germans affected (for it greatly strengthened the defence of each unit), nine great Junker 52 three-
engined bombers slowly stepped across the sky of central
Bilbao. Those who saw them coming say that they were
a terrifying sight; it was as if a great bar was being drawn
across the sky, full of menace for the city. So perfect was
the marching formation that the Germans kept.

The observers looked up again; it was about 3.15, and
they saw far above the bombers, in glittering shoals of
three, twelve fighting planes that sparkled white as their
wings feathered the afternoon sunlight, and as quickly
vanished again. They kept about three thousand feet
above the bombers, who had no side escort but their own
machine guns.

With appalling deliberation, with the slowhandedness of
experts in political torture, the foreign fleet passed over
the cringing city of Bilbao. Then suddenly, the liquid
noise of machine guns high in the air was heard. From
either side of the river, three Russian fighters had suddenly
appeared over the valley rim, flying at the same altitude
as the Germans, whom they immediately engaged.

The Germans, like wolves, hunt in packs. They do not
fight singly against Russian material if they can help it.
As organised units they were the equal of anyone in Spain;
they stuck together at all costs, waiting for the moment
when they could rake the enemy with three planes at a
time. They always re-formed before they attacked again.

It was under these conditions that the machine gun
battle raged between the twenty-one Germans of Vitoria
and the six Russians of Bilbao.

Fighting singly, five of the Russian fighters made for the
four flights of German, whom they now saw were Henkel 51.
The sixth, flown by a twenty-year-old Spaniard of whom
his Russian tutors were proud, swung left and dropped at

great speed towards the leading Junker, which was now nearly half-way down the Nervion.

A flight of Heinkels, seeing that the convoy was broken, disengaged themselves from the dogfight in the higher air, and followed Felipe del Rio, but they were much too late. The young Spaniard had drawn blood.

Junker 52, to the civilian eye, is an ugly-looking monster, and the noise of its three engines seems to signify the power that it brings to battle. But in point of fact it is only a wonderful plane when there is no opposition. Its defences are very poor.

As it has a third propeller, there is no room for a forward machine gun turret. There are two turrets to the rear, one above the fuselage which covers the tail and sides of the plane, and the second suspended below the fuselage, shooting forward and downwards at an awkward angle.

Attacked frontally the Junker 52, even when it flies in formation, has a poor chance of survival and almost no chance of victory. That is why, in the attacks on Madrid of the previous two months, the Junker was frequently escorted to right and left as well as above.

His four machine guns rattling furiously, Del Rio put his plane straight at the central propeller of the foremost bomber. The Germans must have seen danger already, for the bombs had started dropping wildly on to the riverside and into the river, which fountained water and sizzling metal. A jet of fire struck out of the Junker forward, as Del Rio climbed out of range with a wing full of bullets.

Two little specks fell out of the bomber, fell downwards, unrolled, and suddenly hung effortless on air as the parachutes tautened in whiteness above them. The Junker was now rolling in flames, and pitched forward spinning into Mount Arraiz, west of the Nervion. It exploded as it struck the ground; two bodies were found in it completely carbonised.

The eight Junkers dropped their entire load without stint into the river and turned for home. Above them could be seen the power dives and the acrobatic tumbles of the fighters, who continued the whirling battle back to the front; one Heinkel and one Boeing were shot down. The whole raid was over in seven minutes. Del Rio's dramatic intervention had shortened the casualty list to three dead and three wounded. The Russian planes had done a remarkable day's work.

On Arraiz there was pandemonium. The police cars and Red Gross could not set out in time as the parachutes descended. A furious crowd was already there.

Adolf Hermann, twenty-four years, domiciled in Berlin, of German nationality, Lieutenant in Franco's aviation, had the misfortune to land at the back of a group of houses on the road leading up to the range of Pagasarri. He was immediately surrounded and in a few minutes he was dead.

Bilbao, so orderly at other times, went flaming Red under air bombardment. Such is the *mystique* of the air.

The circumstances of Hermann's death are not clear. Some say that he pulled out a gun and fired at the crowd, killing a woman and a militiaman; whereupon the survivors jumped on him and pulled him to pieces. The members of the Basque Government, however, to whom the modern military conception of editing the truth was alien, told me that they believed that the militiaman first fired at Hermann, missed him and killed the woman; that Hermann then fired rather better at the militiaman and scored a bull; and that the population then started jumping, with fatal consequences for Adolf Hermann. The second story sounds rather more muddled and by that more credible than the other. When there was nothing much to keep the population jumping, they picked up the flattened pieces and carried them down to Bilbao, where the police took them in charge and dispersed their bearers. Much of the German's documentation was preserved, including a receipt for 2,284 litres of gasoline for his plane, Junker number 25:147, dated Sevilla, November 15th, and written in Italian.

Karl Gustav Schmidt, the anchor of the other parachute, was luckier than his compatriot. A gust of wind caught him and took him to the other side of the river, where he banged his back on landing at a place called Enecuri. As he came down, a Russian pilot in a Boeing knocked out, but not destroyed in the battle, followed him solicitously and landed in rough country beside him.

The feeling of hatred for the German aviators was spontaneous among all the Basques. It was not only the town mob, the proletariat of Bilbao, that wished to take violent measures against them. As they saw the parachute bellying down, the country people who lived on the ridge between Bilbao and Derio raced to where they thought it would fall with guns in their hands. The blond young Schmidt drew his revolver and tried to defend himself, but was disarmed. He would have been killed at once if the Russian had not warned the crowd away with another gun. And so the Nazi owed his life to the Muscovite. Not that the latter's motives were wholly humanitarian. He wanted to know as much about the aviation of Herr Hitler as he possibly could, and by the time he and his fellow Russians had wrung young Schmidt dry they had learnt a lot that never came my way.

This boy of twenty-one was a radiotelegraphist. He told the Basques that he had been sent out to Spain in September by the National-Socialist Party, of which he was a member, and that he travelled from Hamburg to Cadiz in a German man-of-war. Like all German prisoners taken on this front, he said that he had come to Spain to suppress Communism.

Whereupon the Basques laughed heartily, and the boy blushed somewhat. He had a nice silk parachute which was impounded with the recognisable remains of his aeroplane. It issued from the German factory on an interesting date, twenty-four hours before the signature of the Non-Intervention Agreement.

Dusk was falling on Bilbao as the Russian brought Schmidt down to the General Staff in a closed car. As they looked through the windows they saw a strange effervescence in the town, along the riverside at the Arenal and up the Gran Via. Everybody was walking fast and running into the Old Town, and going up the hill. There were Anarchists carrying their black and red flag, and many wild faces and much shouting; all the thousands of refugees seemed to be in movement, as they had moved once before in September. Only then it was to the riverside and the ships.

The Russian remembered that the prisoners had been moved from the ships after the last massacre, and were now behind the walls of Larrinaga prison and of two Convents, the Carmelo and the Angeles Custodios, in

Begoña above the Old City. And that was where the crowd was marching. The landless, penniless, homeless refugee population of Bilbao had once more gone Red-mad, and nobody was stopping them.

Drawing the curtains of his car, the Russian drove his prisoner down the Gran Via and put him in safe keeping at the Presidencia, in what had once been the Carlton Hotel.

All the Basque Ministers were there, very worried. The mob was gathering in thousands round the prisons, yelling to the warders to open. Sticks and stones and bricks were being hurled at the roof, the walls, and through the windows. The prison governors had telephoned down to the Ministry of the Interior demanding instant help. They said that if troops were not sent at once to disperse the mob, the warders of the Left parties would open the gates and murder would begin. They rang off shouting that revolvers were being used outside the prisons.

A quick decision had to be taken at the Presidencia, for over two thousand human lives were in danger. Obviously, a battalion would have to be sent up: but which? There were in Bilbao reserve battalions of all the parties, but the council of Ministers knew that the nerves of the town were on edge; that they would have to go very carefully. Dictatorships can act on such occasions with drastic speed; but a system like the Basque, based on a compromise, had to consider. It was part of the price of their liberty.

The Basque Nationalist Ministers did not want to send one of their battalions up to restore order. They might have to shoot on the crowd, none of whom were Basque Nationalists: and the last thing that they wanted was civil war between the parties.

The Socialists agreed to the proposal that a Socialist battalion should be sent up to the prisons. If they had to shoot, the political consequences would not be severe. The Socialist battalions of the U.G.T., besides, could be relied upon to do their duty. From the first they had been, with the Nationalists, the strongest partisans of order, and had combined with them to suppress murder in the first frantic days of July. A U.G.T. battalion was dis-patched to the prisons, which were still holding out against the infuriated people.

But the *mystique* of the foreign aviation had infected the sober U.G.T. As they marched up the road to Begoña, they talked among themselves of the iniquity of the German raid upon civilian Bilbao that they had witnessed that afternoon. They were as red as the mob when they reached the prisons.

Of these, two stand on the western or lower side of the same road, separated by one of the steep streets that lead down to the river. The converted monastery of the Carmelo is about a quarter of a mile from the others, up the dusty hill-side. The governor was one of the monks formerly established there, but now withdrawn to a single wing of the building.

The U.G.T. battalion carefully placed picquets on all the streets giving access to the town, with instructions to stop any police who tried to interfere. They then went up to the gates of the Larrinaga and demanded that they should be opened "in the name of the Government." The porters of the Left parties were only too willing to open first the outer gate and then the inner, letting the troops into the Central hall, from which the prison dormitories opened off the ground floor, while three further storeys could be reached by stairs and galleries of wrought iron. The whole scene was dimly lit by electricity from the distant murky roof. As the prisoners ran in terror along the openwork galleries, and slammed the doors of their cells and piled their cheap beds and boxes against them, a hundred soldiers in the spotlight, in the very centre of the prison, started firing their rifles at the scattering figures, and lobbed hand grenades wherever they could see an open door.

In the diseased, yellow light of the rationed electricity of Bilbao, illuminating through a haze of dust raised by the militiamen's feet the Normal Prison of Larrinaga, bodies could be seen dripping blood slowly through the grating of the first, the second, the third floor corridors on to the ground and walls. The building was crowded with political *detenus*, of Bilbao and Vizcaya, and from San Sebastian. In the narrow dormitories along the ground floor there lay, on iron bedsteads mattressed with sacking, with their few dirty clothes hanging from rough wooden shelves above them, cooped together thirty to a

room, the men who could not bar their doors in time.
They were pulped with grenades. Sixty-one men were
killed in the Larrinaga as the maddened U.G.T. ran
round shooting and bombing: and thirty-three more in
the annex of the Casa de Galera.

Meanwhile another detachment stormed the convent of
the Angeles Custodios, which was to prove this evening
so cruelly misnamed. The convent had less adequate
defences than the Normal Prison, and most of the prisoners
who lived here were elderly men, less capable of defending
themselves and raising barricades than any of the others.
The crowd followed the troops into their flimsy refuge,
using knives and sticks: they killed ninety-six here, and
the stairs and floors were slippery with blood. For many
of the people were now little less than lunatic with hate,
and pursued the prisoners round the convent, shouting
"You are the men who brought the Germans to kill our
children. You have lived your lives, and are fitter to
die." The refugees of Guipuzcoa then not only killed,
but mutilated. Such is the *mystique* of the air.

The third part of the U.G.T. battalion went up to the
Carmelo, which was farther away, and therefore fore-
warned and better prepared to meet them. They were
able to batter down the doors; but six Basque guards
with rifles had already got in, and a party of officer
prisoners laid with them the plans that were to save the
lives of all but four. These were caught at the bottom
of the stairs, and were run through with knives. The
rest piled beds, mattresses and broken doors on the winding
wood staircase, and as the troops came up threw bottles
filled with water on to their heads. From below came
a hand grenade: it missed an open door, struck the lintel,
and bounced back to burst among the crowded shouting
militia. Then, as the six guards fired over the heads of
the mob, at a signal from an imprisoned captain, all the
electric lights throughout the monastery were knocked
out together. The troops thought that the explosions
which they heard were more bombs coming from above,
and bolted out of the prison, just as the five hundred men
of the Basque Motorised Police came up the hill, led by
young Telesforo Monzon.

Franco's friends were always very hostile to Monzon,

who had done his utmost during the last two months to get rid of all the political prisoners of Bilbao by way of exchange with Basques held by Franco, on the not un-reasonable theory that if both were with their own people their chances of survival would correspondingly rise. But Franco had rejected exchange, and here was Monzon coming to clean up the mess of his forebodings.

He was a brave man, and he went straight in to the Normal Prison without an escort: the militia were still chasing people up and down the dirty iron stairs and openwork galleries of the Central Hall, and battering at resistant doors with rifle butts. The dead lay tossed around, some had fallen from the top storey and lay crushed on the ground. The rationed unhealthy electricity of Bilbao still half-lit the scene of her people's insanity.

Monzon took an officer by the shoulder of his revolver arm, and said: "If you do not clear your men at once from the prison, they will all be shot inside it." The shooting ceased to a shouted order. In the high, drab hall with the turn-key's empty office of broken glass in the centre, and the dull walls nicked with bullets and the slow shake of dust in the air and movement of some of the bodies at Monzon's feet, there was a rare silence. The faces of the militia, only a second before starched stiff with fury, suddenly relaxed, whitened, took a look of incomprehension as if they found themselves waking from an unreal world. They trooped out of the prison: some of them vomited at the outer gate. Such is the *mystique* of the air.

In front of them they saw the Basque motorised police, their shiny leather suits reflecting the street lamps of winter like the skin of tall metal robots, and their hands on their guns.

In the Angeles Custodios and the Carmelo the game was finished. The crowd had blackened out into the night. Only the militia remained, pale-faced like men who feel an icy tune in their head, and know that they have drunk too much.

They were formed up and marched down to their barracks, where they were disarmed. The officers were placed under arrest. Everybody was pale now—the troops, the police, Monzon.

The behaviour of the Basque Government on this occasion was nothing short of incredible. At this time, it should be remembered, true stories of the killings in Madrid could only be smuggled out as uncensored articles by unknown correspondents: with Franco, the situation was even worse. If a foreign newspaper dared to publish any statement about atrocities in his territory, its correspondent — whether responsible or not — was immediately expelled.

For the Basques, the word conscience was possessed of dynamic meaning. They had, as best they might, to expiate the horrible crime committed by the air-maddened population of Bilbao. Though they were at war, they gave orders to the censor to let all truthful descriptions pass.

Leizaola, at his Ministry of Justice and Culture, affixed a list of all the dead. At the bottom he admitted eight names "mutilizados" — the dead who had also been mutilated. The representatives of the foreign press were allowed to broadcast all these facts, and so was the Bilbao radio.

The relatives of the dead, who till now had been able to visit the prisons and talk across the bars and cage-wire which set the boundary of liberty, and had brought parcels of food and omelettes and cigarettes every day of the week, were now permitted to pay their final service. They were free to lead funeral processions through the town, and did so. All the churches tolled their bells for the dead — inglorious martyrs to the modern mechanism of war: one hundred and ninety-four killed, and thirty dead of their injuries. Music began and ended the drama: the sirens and church bells sounded pastoral indeed, judged by the staccato standard of the musketry in between.

A special secret court was set up to try the leaders of the U.G.T. battalion responsible — if one can use such a word of the crazy condition in which they reacted to the thunder of the skies. In unnerved Bilbao it was impossible to make any striking example of them, but by the end of January six had been condemned to death. The sentences were passed upon them in a room near the President's, and a heavy guard with fixed bayonets and sub-machine-guns stood in front of the door.

It took a long time for the excitement in Bilbao to die

down. From now on detachments of Basque Nationalist
militia, on leave from the front, protected the prisons. I
visited these a fortnight later, and talked freely with the
prisoners: by that time the Angeles Custodios, behind
its flimsy railings and its broken glass, had been abandoned, and the men were now concentrated in the Larrinaga and the Carmelo, around which the Basques were
building concrete walls with loopholes.

A concentration camp was half-finished at Sondika,
five miles outside Bilbao across the eastern range of the
Nervion valley. It looked a healthy place with clean
dormitories, copious sanitation, room for exercise: all
things lacking in the old buildings of Larrinaga and the
Carmelo, where lavatories were square boxes trimmed with
sacking at the corner of each bedroom, beds jammed twelve
inches apart, and the only space for walking the dreary
courtyard, cement underfoot and cement walls above.
At Sondika there was light, and flowers, and turf: the
prison buildings were long bungalows painted in the
bright marine blues, greens and whites of an English
yachting club, and as fully windowed. I told the prisoners
about it.

They had been saying that the one thing they feared
was another air raid and the repetition of January 4th.
The only thing that they wanted was the *canje*—the exchange of prisoners with Franco, which he himself had
turned down. As a journalist, could I help them? It
seemed too cruel to tell them that their own side would
not save them. So I turned the conversation to the new
concentration camp, to find that my audience was growing
lukewarm, even hostile.

The concentration camp? It would, of course, be well
outside the town, and therefore safer: and machine-guns
in the turrets at each corner would help keep off the
crowds. But to think of moving there would be quite
impossible. They were, thank you very much, comfortable where they were, and the old walls of the Larrinaga
and the Carmelo kept them warm. At Sondika it might
be healthy, but in the prisoners' view ventilation meant
draughts, and draughts meant catching your death-of-
cold, an end which they seemed to regard as stickier than
others. No; they were naturally grateful to the Basque

Government for the kind thought behind the concentration camp, but they must regretfully turn the idea down, in the politest manner possible.

I left the prison with my tail between my legs, while the fug-fans blew clouds of self-satisfaction from their long cigars behind me. Spain is a queer place. At the prison entrance visitors' day was once more in full cry. Round about thirty aunts and sisters and grandmothers were shrieking at the tops of their voices at round about thirty prisoners behind the wire cage, who were shrieking competitively back. The din was like that of an enormous parrot-house, enraged. They stood holding the bars and wire, elbow to elbow, shaking and yelling. Now and then somebody seemed to hear something, and grinned and threw up his head in interpretative triumph. The practice is called by foreigners who love Spain individualism: give me Hyde Park.

Outside, in the city, the popular excitement spread. The Anarchists of the C.N.T., reputed the toughest organisation of the Left, felt that they had been outdone by the U.G.T.: they must retrieve their reputation, and if possible establish themselves in the Government of Vizcaya, from which they had been excluded.

Wednesday, January 13th, was a dark night, and the Anarchists staged a test mobilisation. Their militia picketed street corners in the centre of Bilbao, and party members went round with buckets and paste sticking up little pink posters by hundreds.

"The F.A.I. and C.N.T., with 360 syndicates, 36,000 organised workers, 8,000 combatants and 16,000 in mobilised industries demand a place in the Government." (The figures were round almost to bursting point, but fierce-face pays in the Iberian Peninsula.)

It was a feeble show: the Basques were fully prepared. The police were out, and swept the pickets off the streets before two in the morning; and a new mobilised industry and other buckets were provided for the C.N.T., who had to march round tarring their posters until daybreak.

It was a tiring time for the police, who had to escort refugees of the Right next morning to a British destroyer which would take them to France. But this was the last kick of the C.N.T. until they ran out of the line in April. Aguirre seized the opportunity to ban their paper, the *C.N.T. del Norte*, and disperse their meetings, which were only allowed henceforward by special permission of the Ministry of the Interior. The C.N.T. had no backbone, and they crumpled up. From now on there were no massacres and no murders in Bilbao: the police ruled, and energies could be concentrated on the war.

Only a fear remained. The blockade, the large refugee population with nothing but children to lose, the uproar of another air raid on a great city, would act as a violent acid on the emotions of a proletariat whose nerves were already near the skin with hunger, and must keep the authorities always at the ready.

IX

THERE WAS A LONG SWELL flattening out towards the Bay when we stopped off the Puenta de Galea, where the river Nervion limits its estuary upon the east. We lay five miles out to sea, slowly dipping and climbing in the soap-suds. Bilbao, the iron city, lay behind the hard brown headland, where the cliff was overlaid with solemn pine and blurred by a light drizzle. The other side of the river mouth the hills rose higher to pyramid peaks, exuberantly green, and the Basque mountains in blue and grey paved the horizon behind them. In the sense of altitude it was an abrupt coastline, and the white-hot violence of the waves at its foot conveyed the same impression. But the surface of the country-side to right and left said no. Pasture and small farms smoothed the transition from mountain to the turbulent sea. They triangulated every corner of the hill-side, and only the precipices sheared their mathematical boundaries clean away. As we went in, we were to see cows cropping at a fantastic number of degrees off the horizontal. Every acre of hill was used.

A week before, General Franco's minelayer *Jupiter* had set out from San Sebastian under the escort of the battleship *España*, carrying a cargo of one hundred massive globes. A destroyer of the British Navy had noted her, and estimated their number. On a dank night, when Basque vigilance after three months without discovery of a mine was relaxed, the harbour mouths of Bilbao, Santander and Gijon had been lightly sown. The Bilbao survey plane, skimming low, spotted twenty-five black balls in the water when sky and sea were clear. The trawlers had accounted for eight and one trawler had been blown sky-high on the job, her crew a total loss; they were now

123

sweeping a channel on the western side of the harbour mouth, within the range of their shore batteries and reflectors.

We were in a destroyer and had to lie outside. It was interesting to note the change in the officers' attitude since July, when all was Red: for at this time Italy was landing fifty thousand conscripts fully supplied with arms, artillery, tanks, motor-lorries, red cross units and supplies, in Franco's Spain. Italy was not popular. We see-sawed on the Bay until Eguia, the port captain and chief of the Auxiliary Marine, foamed up in his big speed-boat at our side.

Big-nosed, gaunt, broad-shouldered seamen in berets took the luggage. The Basque flag—white cross and green saltire on a red ground—unfolded and tautened at our stern as we slit the rollers shoreward, over the mines, at an exhilarating pace. The 500 horsepower engines sang their materialistic hymn very sweetly. Eguia, his beret jutting over his big forehead, told us the news in broken English learnt when he sailed before the mast; then he became silent. The race does not talk much, except at wine. One liked Eguia at once. There was something frank and genial about his broad face, and the long nose coming to a plastic point over the small mouth marked him out as a whimsical of no common type. He was stout, but he had clearly been stouter: the blockade in his view was a damned nuisance.

The helmsman played the wheel, and we were past the Puenta de Galea. Suddenly we saw that the farms were a mask, for the river Nervion opened up to us a landscape unimagined from the open sea.

Between two lines of hills running north and south lay the narrow river valley, an industrial ribbon packed with tall black chimneys, gasometers, foundries like giant dark pill-boxes, grimed steel stairs and bridges, clattering trains, soot, crumble-faced slums. Iron-ore tilts at the end of trailing steel aerial lines hung empty in the air, backed by steep brown peaks of mine-waste which climbed the hill-side behind them. Dozens of cranes stood at their full idle height, paraded at ease along the solid granite quays of the Nervion. Shipping, Transatlantic and Continental, lay anchored side to side in rusty black as far as the eye could reach. Trawlers were tethered in phalanxes of a hundred. From Portugalete, on our right, the poorly-dressed working class looked across the river at two deserted steam yachts, whose white paint and gilt were scaling away, and at Las Arenas behind them, once the home and yellow beach of the Bilbao millionaires. These now served in the Red Cross hospitals which had once been—and would again become—their houses. But the poor still looked at them; the thousandfold poor swollen by the refugees of San Sebastian who were quartered at the water-side and had nothing to do but wash their clothes with rare rationed soap, and sit on the ugly iron benches on the stone flags, and watch the river slip by them and their innumerable children, and get thinner. Both rich and poor had cheeks which were becoming hollow; at a glance, one could see that Bilbao was nearly desperate for food.

For fourteen kilometres we sped up the Nervion, past factories mobilised for war and houses shattered through six storeys by German bombing planes. One or two British ships which had slipped through the mine-field in ignorance were loading iron. A few armed trawlers, painted grey, stood ready for sea. But otherwise the industrial riverscape was the same—hard stone quays at head-height, gaunt cranes and swinging tilts, drizzle on black foundries and chimneys, crowded tenements peeling soot, mountains of sad brown slack; all rising in close tiers which rimmed the Nervion green, and peopled by men whose eyes looked spectrally through big, strong sockets from big frames. A working race are the Basques, and they were hard put to it in January, 1937. In fourteen kilometres we had passed the packed living and labouring places of three hundred thousand of them, and of a hundred thousand refugees. The quays were a mass of them in their drab, worn clothes as we shot between the tall river-side houses, all glass, of old Bilbao, to tie up alongside heavy barges that had lost their paint. A great church of the eighteenth century, squarely built in ochre-brown stone, stood above us. Frente Popular posters fluttered in half-holding paste against its west door, while worshippers passed in and out. Men respectfully took off their berets, women put on the black hair veil. White gulls, mewing, planed overhead in the soft *sirri-mirri*, the invisible permeating rain of the Vizcayan coast. We stepped ashore.

They invited us to drink at a bar. It was very bare: nothing like the smart furniture of the Bar Basque in Franco's San Sebastian, or the cloudy cafés of Salamanca. Little smoke, for there were few cigarettes. We drank a kind of whisky. No, beer had been rationed out. No, there was no change, but local five-peseta notes and "claims" on the bar, for the Basque Government call in all Bank of Spain paper to realise abroad, and metal to convert into instruments of war. I noticed a lot of newspapers; newsprint was well stocked. Even the local sporting paper was still publishing, for the Basque is a great soccer player, and the best professionals of Spain are bought out of Bilbao.

I was taken to my hotel. Coal was running short. "Hot water," said the landlady, "on Thursdays and Sundays." The Torrontegui was once the leading hotel in Bilbao. Its long restaurant was on the top storey of, I think, seven; and there, looking out upon the river and the avenues of yellow artificial light, I dined in silence, surrounded by families of the Right waiting permission to leave Bilbao. Nobody seemed to care to speak over elbow range, and what they ate would have made a strange dinner to them once, I fancy. Bean mash, fish, horsemeat not intolerably sweet, and small cakes made of an entirely inoffensive and tasteless flour. And that was my introduction to the ancient capital of the Basques, the wealthy, well-organised progressive city of iron and steel, soccer, pelota and shipping, now the stark centre of Republican resistance in the north, and the single fortress in Spain where the democratic middle-class existed.

Or, as I noticed when I went down the corridor to my room to an early bed, where the political Right could live while the political Left carried arms. At each door lay an emptied tray, and the key was the other side of each door. They lived a cavernous life: there were too many trays to believe that all supported invalids. Gradually I warmed to an understanding of their situation; there were some who never dared stick their noses outside their doors, and there were others whose turn it was to enjoy a special meal, with an omelette or maybe a lobster prepared by the Torrontegui family, who begged them to enjoy it in

the shadows and not to rouse the jealousy of the boardless
up stairs.

Only when the sirens shrieked did all the doors open
and reveal many pale ladies and old gentlemen with distinguished sallow faces, who tumbled into the lift and down
the stairs to the air-raid refuge wearing black dresses rather
meaner than their features. The covertness and the ghastly
silence of the hotel were utterly unnecessary: not one of
these people at the passport turnstile of the Torrontegui
would ever have been hurt. And one by one Monzon let
them go away to France in British destroyers. But the
events of January 4th had left their mark, and the un-
expressed fear of the Torrontegui's clientéle transferred itself
to everybody that they met—porters, waitresses, maids and
even for a moment to passengers like myself. The girls
who served us at table moved through the restaurant in
long black dresses, and did not wish to converse. The
wine-waiter, who still kept a small stock, preferred to
remain out of sight, and when he put on his white gloves
to pour water for the refugees he did it with a cold, iron-
handed ferocity that made me wonder when he would
crack their heads with the jug. The only relief was to be
gained from a garrulous night-watchman and from white-
haired old Mrs. Torrontegui, with a face of beef and a
stout bosom covered with crumbs, as she moved from table
to table cheering us all up and commenting upon the
imaginary qualities of the food which we had to push down
our throats. A huge radio put a sort of strength into our
silences.

At ten o'clock all the lights went out over Bilbao, the
cinemas and soldiers' cabarets closed, and one looked out
to see a skeleton city, drawn in lowered street lamps over
two hundred yards apart.

* * * * * *

January was the month when Bilbao suffered most, when
the stocks of food dwindled to zero; a few ships entered
through the mine-field, and rations were reduced until
they reached starvation point. Aldasoro was almost at
his wit's end; every ten days he was able to issue 500
grammes of rice, 500 grammes of chickpeas, 500 grammes
of vegetables and 250 grammes of cooking oil per head.
The value of this square but scarcely cubic meal was six

pesetas, about three shillings at pre-war and one shilling and threepence at current exchange. Bread also failed half-way through the month. There was no milk for mothers or babies, and even the hospital food stores, which after the army were first served, were running out. Next day I visited the great city market on the right bank of the Nervion.

It was full of echoes which make wretched food. The two long halls which composed the market were almost entirely empty. Half of one was given over to the meat trade; but the meat trade was not booming, and there was only one stall open, with a pathetic show of sausages and ham, for which a little knot of Bilbainos were bargaining. The fish market was fuller, for the sea lay at our doors. In the fruit and vegetable market there were shrivelled witch-like lemons from Valencia, poor cider apples and onions at threepence each, which were rapidly slipping into people's pockets.

The papers carried daily lists of merchants fined for profiteering—e.g. nine or ten pesetas (four to five shillings at par) for a dozen eggs. An embarrassing scandal was exposed on January 26th, when it was found that 2,000 refugees were drawing double rations; but, as the officials of Assistencia Social said, it did not seem to have made them any fatter. There was no soap, and bread was becoming more and more integral before its failure.

The domestic cat has always been viewed as a delicacy by the poorer people of Bilbao. But in time of peace the cat was elaborately dressed for the table. First the cat was caught, then laid in salt for twenty-four hours, then basted. A magnificent sauce of sherry and mushrooms and various spices was then prepared to drown the last carnivorous flavours of pussy, and the whole was said to resemble jugged hare, and even in the case of plump lady cats to give jugged hare points and a beating.

In January, 1937, the cat was still a delicacy; only the leading elements that had made it a delicacy were sadly lacking. There was no salt, few occasions for basting, sherry belonged to Franco, mushrooms were found only to be eaten at once, and Aldasoro could hardly be expected to import spices. But the cat was skilfully tracked when he dared to come out at night. British ships' cats, however black and sacrosanct, did not return from lonely

DURANGO FROM CHURCH TOWER:
MARCH 31ST, 1937.

walks on the quay. The people who ate them said that they were not palatable, really; but one must have meat.

Chickens at this time raised between one pound and thirty shillings—forty and sixty pesetas. As the banks could only issue 250 pesetas a week per head, chickens were beyond the purse of most people. A substitute chicken, however, was found on the seashore and along the river: lines were baited with fish and seagulls hooked up for the pot. If seagulls were not rising, one need not despair; one could still eat the bait—God be thanked for His small mercies.

How the people of Bilbao were able to support this diet without demonstration or protest is still a mystery to me and to their rulers. There was only one complaint ever made to the Ministry of Commerce and Supply: towards the end of January two hundred women signed a pitiful letter asking if it was not possible now to distribute milk to their children. It was not. They accepted the answer. Against all the laws of medical science the children of Bilbao appear to have survived that terrible January, when the arrival of a food-ship was more valuable than a fleet of aircraft.

There can be little wonder that when air raids were made on Bilbao all the suppressed suffering of the people broke the chains of self-control. Months later, when the river-side of Bilbao was being bombed nearly every day, and the dead were adding up into hundreds, I remember wondering why the people did not massacre the Right again. For the river-side, menaced on January 4th as well as in April, was the home of the refugees, who from the day that they had come from Guipuzcoa had acted as a solvent to Bilbao in every crisis. They were desperate people: why did they not run wild in April? I believe that it was because there were stocks of food in April, while in January there were none. That month the concentration of hunger and bombs was too much for everybody: the refugee volcano discharged and the whole people went up in red flame. The Bilbao of January was a key example of civilian psychology in a case where blockade and the air arm are operating to the enemy's advantage. Contrary to the text-books, the people's will to resist does not weaken: it increases. But the poorer part of the population, starved and unnerved, is liable to outbursts of fury which may bring them into opposition with their Government. In this sense it was touch and go at Bilbao at the beginning of 1937. What pulled the Basques through a crisis which would have broken another community was their natural sense of discipline and order.

There was a striking similarity between the Basque massacre of January 4th, 1937, and the Paris shootings of February 6th, 1934. After each even the participants were horribly shocked; a limit of behaviour had been exceeded; in France logic, and in Bilbao they said con- science had stopped the political decay. But I fancy these two words are synonyms, and that they only flourish in democratic states, giving them a strength and braking power incomprehensible to others.

X

SIX DAYS WAS THE LIMIT of my stay in Bilbao. I had to leave at a few hours' notice in a Basque minesweeper, which, with lights out to slip the blockade, steamed on a zig-zag course to France via Castro Urdiales to the west of Bilbao, reaching the port of Bayonne after thirteen hours of rolling in the Bay. Six days was enough to see a great deal of Basque civil administration.

The morning after my arrival I visit the Carlton Hotel, where the Presidencia had been installed ever since a German bomb had fallen beside the old Bilbaino Club, their late headquarters. The new-comer received his first shock at the entrance, which was guarded by elderly police in blue tunics and red berets; and he had to read his Basque history again to find that the red beret—brilliant war-like dress that it is—does not represent the Carlism of Navarre, but is the traditional Basque cap for war, fiestas and communal dances. These bearers of the insignia were the Mikeletes, or guards of the Provincial Council of Guipuzcoa. They marched in white gloves, rifles shouldered, with an easy carelessness tempered only by rheumatism, up and down in front of the Presidential portico.

This was reached by crossing the bridge which separated Old Bilbao, with its narrow tortuous streets, massive churches and high houses, from the New Town on the left bank of the Nervion. Here, pivoted on the axis of the broad Gran Via, business Bilbao spread itself behind the classical pilasters, heavy granite courses and prosperous bas-reliefs of cornucopias, grapes and shipping, bouncing Cherubs and cushioned nymphs of the nineties, when Bilbao saw her great renaissance in trade with Great Britain and France. There were holes for bombs, empty windows for no commerce.

At the Presidency to which this avenue of stability and old money conducted there was a second surprise in store. One was introduced to the chief of the Department of Foreign Affairs, Don Bruno Mendigurren, and saw that Euzkadi's Mr. Eden was even younger than oneself. Further inquiries established that he was twenty-five.

Young Mendigurren, who later duplicated his work with that of chief of the Basque Press Bureau, was a god-send to the journalist. An ardent Basque Nationalist with a torrent of political French, in which references to the "purple Basque" took the lead of one sentence out of three, Mendigurren's idea of a Press Bureau was that it existed to let foreign journalists see and hear what they wanted to, not to tell them what they were to put in their messages every day and expel them for what they added of their own accord.

Bruno was in civil life a constructional engineer, and partnered his brother-in-law Gomboa in a concern which was prepared to enlarge cities overnight with massive buildings of cement. He had learnt his job in Brussels, where he was proud to be a junior contemporary of Degrelle: there he had also learnt his French.

A slight young man, always in a dark blue suit and beret, like many Basques, Bruno differed from others in that his physical force did not seem to maintain the high standard of the enthusiasm of his eyes, tongue and arms. He was fair, with a narrow head and tip-tilted nose, and when he spoke of his country his bright eyes bulged out of their sockets with excitement. To emphasise the decisiveness and determination of the Basque race, he had a peculiar fast-cutting motion of the forearm from the shoulder downwards, which only just stopped short of breaking itself for ever on his office desk. Until I met Bruno I thought that Basque Nationalism was something crankish, like a movement of the Isle of Man for the islanders; now I saw how deadly serious they were about it, for Bruno, with his strenuous eyes and arms, was the spear-point of their persuasion. He left me in no doubt: "White and Red in Spain, they are the same."

He was charming. "What do you want to see?" he asked when his introduction to Basqueness was over and his slender frame was recuperating from the delightful effort. At moments such as this Bruno Mendigurren had shot his mouth and was democratically waiting for you to shoot yours. He was all democratic ears. I began to feel Bilbao congenial.

As he turned his head to the window I noticed in a chance opening of the shirt below his black tie a suspended cross. It was tied by a thread round his neck.

Taking a deep breath, I said: "I want to see your schools, hospitals, social welfare"—nice harmless things, and tensing my voice a little—"your prisons, barracks and the front"; and then, with a last struggle between the tongue, tonsil and the saliva and the feeling that, after all, he'd said they were so free and democratic, so why not let him have it?—"your defences, aerodromes, planes, mechanisation and war industries." The breath failed. What an awful thing I'd done! Still, my last cry against the shooting wall would be "You asked for it: you said you were democratic."

"Right," said Mendigurren, "we'll arrange all that for you." That was the third shock of my second day at Bilbao. A long time afterwards I asked him why he was so confiding. "Oh," he explained, as if it was as logical as engineering, "you were English, and we like them, and you were introduced to us by your Consul, Stevenson. He's never cheated us with fake passports for the refugees, like all the others." I suppose it was a reasonable rule of thumb.

"Now," said Bruno, "come and see the President." A paternal usher in the Presidencia uniform came in, and said, "Jose Antonio sent me to tell you he's ready." It seemed unnecessary to this free-shouldered old servant to use the President's surname in the presence of a foreigner. Another jolt: imagine a Nazi telling *The Times* correspondent in Berlin, "I'm sorry, Adolf can't turn out to-day, what with this terrible hoarseness and all." The Four-Year Plan would collapse in a minute; Germany would be humiliated again.

We went into a small square room looking out on the wintry Plaza. There was a tall cross of ebony on the desk, with Our Lord nailed to it in silver. On the wall there were specimen clips of rifle ammunition made by the mobilised industries of Durango, now concentrated at

Bilbao. A man who was working at the desk got up as we came in and walked two paces towards us.

Jose Antonio de Aguirre, who extended his hand, was at this moment thirty-six years old. He was short; but the first thing that one noticed about him was the extraordinary fineness and delicacy of his features. The second that he walked with a slight swagger: the Irish would call it a chesty walk. For Jose Antonio had been a great soccer forward in his day, when the crowd, to distinguish him from another player of the same name, often applauded Chocolate-Aguirre in allusion to his parallel prowess as a manufacturer.

Aguirre was also a lawyer, and had led the battles of the Basque Nationalist Party ever since 1931, when his organisation sprang fully armed from the dead head of the monarchy to win an overwhelming predominance in Guipuzcoa and Vizcaya which it was never to lose, even when the provinces were conquered by Franco. For it was a political movement founded wholly on the Basque youth.

He had lived through lively days when in the first Republican Cortes his colleague Leizaola, now Basque Minister of Justice and Culture, had been plugged full in the nose by an indignant Socialist for defence of the Catholic Church against the encroachments of the State. In those days, when Spaniards were merely sparring, the Basque Nationalists were allied to the Traditionalists of Navarre. But the union of ardent Catholics did not last. The Navarrese movement, without in the least losing the enthusiasm of the Navarrese peasant, slipped more and more into the hands of the provincial aristocracy. Big money backed it: it entered into relations with the army officers and with the centralising parties of the Right, who would be the last to give the Basques autonomy. For did not their leader, Calvo Sotelo, whose murder was the signal for the long-prepared revolt, say at San Sebastian, in the very centre of the Basque country, "I would rather see Spain without God, without the Church and without the family than a Spain divided"? The Basques, under Aguirre, had to turn to the Left for their autonomy; it was a great wrench, and one could see the traces of the struggle in Aguirre's face.

A fine-drawn face, with very nimble, rather humorous eyes. His brows, long, straight and black, had in the

centre the puzzling lines that every man carries who compromises in order to achieve an ideal. For Aguirre, like
all his party, was an idealist first and last; the quality
sprang like a flower from his public speeches, which even
in the bitterest hours of Bilbao were never demagogic,
always explanatory in the closest sense, pierced through and
through with the appeal to history, to the law, and formed
as thoroughly by a humanistic appreciation of the two. It
was astonishing to hear him in the great closed pelota court
of Bilbao, the Fronton Euzkalduna, where he sometimes
addressed the crowd before the days when twelve-inch
shells landed upon it. The voice, which he forced into a
certain hardness in his brisk private conversations, was
beautiful and active in the extreme. The people, though
seldom of his own party—they were at the front—listened
spellbound. Yet he spoke to them, not of bread and peace
and guns and butter like the dictators of to-day; but
the mercantilism of Old Spain, the virtues and vices of the
economic liberalism of the nineteenth century, the proletarian movements to which they gave rise, the efforts of
the bourgeoisie to reach a human compromise with them,
the failure and success of that movement throughout
the world. He did not, like noisier orators, say that Bilbao
was untakeable; the historical thread of his argument
proved rather how much she was worth preserving. With
every paragraph, his voice, naturally sweet and clear,
tautened to an officer's rasp; till he came to his conclusions,
he walked up and down his platform with the slight
footballer's roll that I saw now. His only gesture in
a land where they are grotesque was to pocket his
hands.

Below him, Republican Left, Socialists, Communists,
Anarchists, craned their heads in wonder. Here was the
man who solved all their contradictions; whom for that
reason the organising chiefs of Communism, for instance,
could not bear, since he stood in the way of their plans to
control the Basque army. But the Anarchists, for whom
the personal factor is always a weighty thing, ate out of his
hand; whenever their rank and file misbehaved, they
assembled before Aguirre in the deepest contrition, promising
never to do it again. And even the Communists, though
they whispered against him, did not come out into the

open until Bilbao fell, after two and a half months of continuous offensive; then Larriñaga, their young Political Commissar with the General Staff, was able to make a speech in Santander comparing Aguirre with the Louis XIV of "L'état, c'est moi," and to prophesy that the resistance of Santander, united and proletarian, should be a different proposition altogether from that of Bilbao. Which it was: it lasted less than two weeks.

Aguirre in front of whom I now sat was, besides, the last person to compare with Louis XIV. He was not a despot; he was a young political ascetic, who in the end would have to practise his faith in the wilderness. His fine thin nose, thin straight mouth with upper lip strangely tightened in the use of self-control, rather gaunt athletic face were features rather of a man trying to find the right way than to enforce it.

Not that Aguirre did not know his own mind. He was very clear about what he wanted, long or short term. He wished, for the moment, he told me, to exchange all his political prisoners in a block for the Basques held by Franco: 2,300 on his part for 1,000 on the enemy's, but the difference in figures did not matter; it was humanitarian, he said, to get rid of the prisoner problem at one stroke, and he was unwilling to consider the proposals of Salamanca to give a few selected Marquises and Counts special treatment. No! He brought his right hand down flat on the glass table top, and his marriage ring rattled to the emphasis.

Middle term: he was determined to fight on the side of the Republic to the finish. He told me this because the Basques knew that henceforward a well-organised propaganda in England would attempt to drive a wedge between them and the Spanish Government. It was an ill-informed propaganda at best: with a military movement based on the dogma admitted by Calvo Sotelo that Separatism was worse than Marxism, there could be for the Basques no compromise; and besides, the quality that they hated most in the Spaniard was his militarism, partly because it was inefficient, and partly because the Basques just preferred fishing. It was therefore a propaganda unbased in reality; and since it reflected upon the Basques' honesty (for they had pledged their support to Valencia in return

DURANGO CHURCH PORCH:
MARCH 31ST, 1937.

for autonomy), it was foolish. Honesty was the Basques' proudest quality. And behind it all, there was something utilitarian in the Basques' moral code. If they fought for Franco, they would gain nothing; but if they fought for the Government and the Government won, Spain would be so enfeebled that they could negotiate for much more than the Estatuto de Autonomia. If they lost—well, they could not lose more than by submitting to Franco in the first place. Not even in man-power, for he would send their youth to fight his battles all over Spain.

And that brought Aguirre to his long term calculations. If he lost, worse luck. But if the Government were victorious he would press for a Statute granting Euzkadi the equivalent of Dominion Status. He did not say this in a way offensive to Spain; he was, in fact, one of the few Basque Nationalists who never uttered a harsh word about the Castilian, and that was why he was so successful in the conduct of the Government of Vizcaya. The perfectness of his manners, the obvious decency of his intentions, his way of constantly consulting his colleagues, established a remarkable record in Spanish Administration. At a time of war, when the Governments of Valencia and Barcelona were continually quarrelling and reshuffling themselves, and when Franco himself had to suppress and imprison his Falangist supporters and shoot down rebel officers in Morocco, the Government of Euzkadi under Jose Antonio de Aguirre not only remained identically the same until the end, without even the rumour of a crisis; more, from October 7th, when the Council of Ministers was constituted, until June 19th, when Bilbao was abandoned, *they did not once proceed to a vote*; the rule of law in Vizcaya and the conduct of the war was secured by unanimous decisions.

When one saw the inflammable tinder in Bilbao, the rawbone faces of the poor, the depression of the middle class, dwindling food-magazines, the rows of once prosperous shops with dusty, empty windows starred with paper against air raids, the rows of locked doors and tight, rusted steel shutters where before there was trade; the peace and agreement in the Government seemed a miracle. Partly it was due to the Basque character, which is experienced in provincial administration and knows that material progress demands material compromises. But a larger part was due to the chairmanship of Aguirre. There were perhaps stronger characters in the Council than he: Leizaola, for instance, his older chief lieutenant—but he was known as an anti-Marxist. There were more experienced men of the world; but Aldasoro for all his charm could not present quite the same transparent mind to his colleagues and the masses. Idealism, the effort to accommodate, friendliness and honesty were the qualities needed. Aguirre had them: he was a great conciliar.

He had no axe to grind: he lost his fortune in the war. And long before it broke out, he had taken small profits from his business, for he practised his principles and, instituted family salaries and profit-sharing for the workers. He was proud of it. He was also proud of the humanitarian record of his Government, which alone in Spain had taken up the initiative of the International Red Cross and the Foreign Office with enthusiasm. He and his Basques were horrified by the ruthlessness with which the Spaniards fought each other: the killing of prisoners in the field or of political rivals at the back door were not to their taste. "Look at our police," he said, "and find out for yourself how many murders there have been. See if we keep women prisoners. Ask at your hotel how many wretched members of the Right we have saved from the Asturias and Santander.* Ask your consul how many we have permitted him to carry away to France, and how many of the people whom we have rescued are now working against us for the rebels."

All these imperatives look rather pompous on paper, but Aguirre uttered them in a cheerful, unaffected voice, his eyebrows pursed together quizzically and a smile turning on the corners of his mouth . . . Take it or leave it: but we fancy we've done quite well. There was something rather sporting in the way he looked at it; he was captain of a soccer team again, and even if they lost they were going to obey the whistle and the rules. No biting; no hacking; no tripping. Not very Continental, in fact. And the Basques were not. As one went out into the drizzle again, it looked a bit like Liverpool, with the shops shut, and the

* I found out later that his mother ran the Escaping Club.

Irish away at Blackpool and the Protestants decently staying at home and keeping the King's Peace.

* * * * * *

It seemed a convenient moment for me, with the aid of a few local experts, to add up the number of political murders, executions and massacres that had taken place in Vizcaya. The Popular Tribunal had sentenced less than thirty to death, including Wakonigg and his spy gang. Excluding the Santanderinos killed by their police in July and August, the individual murders were thirty also. Sixty-eight prisoners were massacred after the September air raid, and forty-two by the sailors of the *Jaime Primero*. Then a prison guard in a rage had shot a prisoner for waving a handkerchief at a German aeroplane after he had been told not to do so. Two hundred and twenty-four died on the terrible day, January 4th. That made three hundred and ninety-four. Enemies of the Basque régime could not go further than five hundred. There was no city in Spain that could hold a candle to Bilbao for the control of homicide. Madrid, Valencia, Barcelona, Toledo, Sevilla, Badajoz notoriously have the record for the highest political death-rate in Spain. But take the towns in Franco's hands east, west and south of Bilbao. In San Sebastian, a quarter of Bilbao's size, there had been six hundred executions since the Franco occupation; in still smaller Pampluna, over five hundred; in Vigo two thousand. These are rough official figures. Within my own experience, when I drove through Old Castile in October, 1936, the province of Valladolid, with a population of 300,000, a deal less therefore than Bilbao and her refugees, had lost five thousand men and women to the punitive revolvers of the Falange and the Guardia Civil and the military courts; they were still being executed at the rate of ten a day. The proportion of dead, therefore, in the heart of Franco's territory was ten times as great as in Bilbao. In small villages of Castile, numbering only a few thousand souls, like Venta de Baños and Dueñas, I found that the dead were one hundred and twenty-three and one hundred and five, including "Red" schoolmistresses and wives of murdered men who had complained that their husbands were unjustly killed. The Basques killed no women until the last week of their war, when the Anarchists ran amok in Las Arenas; and I only once knew them kill prisoners in the field — the same week.

Yes, it was true what the Basques said. They did seem different from Spain. They had not, perhaps, the charm, the ease or the finesse of Castile, but they seemed strangely averse to the shedding of blood. Very old-fashioned.

XI

IN MARCH THE BAY OF BISCAY, the *Mar Cantabrico*, as Basques and Spaniards call it, is a changeable, moody sea. A storm blows up from nowhere, and the grey wings of the *Mar Cantabrico* batter and plane wildly against Vizcayan cliffs, and the spindle-shanked vegetation that grows man-high in the seaward fields leans south and lets fly its few early leaves, grey with ill-health and stunted by a wiry will to live, over outcrops of rock, to where the pines begin.

Centuries of this flagellation have torn granite islands off the Basque mainland, or stripped it into narrow penin-sulas, into knuckles of redoubtable rock joined to the land by causeways as narrow as an Indian's wrist. To these sacrifices to their sea the Basques attribute a particular virtue and holiness; and not least to the little peninsula under the western cheek of Cape Machichaco. A Hermitage whose small solemn walls of stone melt into the grey of the rocky extremity, gave to this ancient mysticism the blessing and the shadow of the True Cross. Pregnant women, it is known, have only to make a pilgrimage across the isthmus to the shrine, and they will be fortunate in the painful event. And on March 5th some of them were witnesses, as they prayed to the loud organ-stops of naval artillery, of the most gallant sea engagement of the Spanish Civil War.

But in March, as I say, the *Mar Cantabrico* often changes its mind. A north-westerly wind rolls up cloud, and as it nears the coast, drops mist like a train of gauze and seems to stroke and charm the sea into the semblance of mercury. The rounded sea rolls back and forth, but noiselessly, without harm to the coast; erosion takes a holiday, and the fishermen of Bermeo a day's work. On March 5th they were preparing their blue trawlers and loading their chocolate nets, when the battle drove them home again.

Aguirre, two days before, had ordered four of the armed trawlers in Bilbao to proceed to Bayonne; there to convoy the Basque Government despatch trawler *Galdames* back through the blockade to Bilbao. At this time the blockade was enforced by the battleship *España* and the cruiser *Canarias*, the destroyer *Velasco*, one large armed trawler, the *Galerna* (captured from the Basques in the autumn and converted into a fighting craft), and smaller trawlers fitted with wireless. The German submarines based on Pasajes, the port of San Sebastian, passed frequently along the coast; their form of intervention was to watch for the insurgents the movement of Spanish Government shipping, or of vessels flying the flag of countries unrepresented on the Non-Intervention Committee.

They had to be discreet and careful, for the Control was about to come into operation, and the B flotilla of British destroyers was patrolling the northern Spanish coast, mist or storm.

Nabara, Guipuzkoa and *Bizkaya*, with the smaller *Donostia* in line, arrived safely at Bayonne. It is in no mood of preciousness that I spell the names of the Basque provinces in the Basque way; the idiomatic B for V, K for C, were printed on their nationalist bow and stern.

The *Galdames*, their charge, carried a precious cargo: two hundred people returning to Bilbao, of which a half were women and children. Amongst them was Formiguera, a well-known Catalan industrialist and politician of the Centre, whose life had been threatened by the Anarchist organisation in Barcelona: he and his family, who accompanied him, were old friends of Aguirre, who offered them asylum at Bilbao, the only tolerant city in Spain. The whole of the new Basque nickel currency was in the hold, and the captain was entrusted with valuable secret correspondence and cypher. It is a nine hours' journey from Bayonne to Bilbao, and the convoy left port in the evening of March 4th.

The mist lay off the coast, outside territorial waters, on the morning of the 5th. The look-out on Machichaco, high on the cliff beside the old battery of 105's, could see nothing of the expected fleet. They were late, somewhere in the mist.

Punta Galea, the 155 battery at the mouth of the Nervion, suddenly rang up the Marina headquarters at eleven o'clock. "Cruiser sighted to the west moving slowly eastwards, accompanied by small steamer." At the Marina they said, "That must be the English patrol"; but Galea telephoned urgently again, "Steamer flying Estonian flag. And cruiser is the rebel *Canarias*."

On orders from Eguia at the Marina, Punta Galea opened fire. Clearly the *Canarias* had captured an arms ship and was taking her to Pasajes.

On the edge of the mist, four flashes like matches lighting along the *Canarias'* lean side. Then a deep-throated answer from the shore. *Canarias* veered northward to get out of range; it is probable that she was struck in the first encounter.

At this moment the mist rolled back, and out of an alleyway of ghostly light came the *Bizkaya* and the *Guipuzkoa* together, manning altogether four guns of 101 (4-inch). They did not hesitate to open fire on the *Canarias*, and she responded with her 8-inch.

Out of the mist stepped *Nabara* and the little *Donostia*, armed with 75's. The look-out on Machichaco 'phoned the Marina, "Armed trawlers sighted but no sign of *Galdames*."

She was lost in the fog. *Galdames* had struck a wrong course. Suddenly she too appeared, far to the west of her convoy, under the very guns of the modern cruiser *Canarias*, who recognised her and sent five shells over her dirt-caked funnel.

The women and children began screaming and skidding over the deck, still slippery with mist. A few more shells dropped short; they shrieked to the captain to surrender, and he, poor man, shrugged his shoulders as far as the women who had rushed his bridge would let him, and shook himself free and ran up the white flag; his own death sentence.

Canarias, signalling to the Estonian boat to await her, steamed over to *Galdames* under a pepper fire from *Guipuzkoa* and *Nabara*, upon whom she now turned her heavy armament. *Guipuzkoa*, who had to lie well within range to

score with her 101's, was struck three times. *Nabara*,
however, persisted.

It was the dogged insolence of these two Newfoundland
trawlers that enabled the *Bizkaya* now to carry out a
manœuvre unrecorded in naval war.

She went full steam ahead and signal flags ready to the
Estonian tramp, which lay there becalmed and bewildered
between *Canarias* and Cape Machichaco. She drew up on
the leeside of the Estonian, ran up her flags and ran them
down again.

They asked, "Who are you and where are you going?"

The Estonian answered, "Carrying arms and forced to
go to Pasajes."

Another flutter of flags, as quickly withdrawn.

"Follow me to harbour." And the Estonian said,
"Cannot, am threatened."

Bizkaya hoisted her final warning, "Turn at once," and
swivelled her two 101's and her two machine guns upon
the arms ship. And she had to comply.

As they lay, it was impossible for the *Canarias* to read the
questions flagged the other side of the Estonian, whose
name the Basques now read as *J——*. The earliest sign
of misbehaviour that she detected in her first capture was
when the tramp followed *Bizkaya* round Cape Machichaco
towards Bermeo.

Canarias was now engaged with *Guipuzkoa* and *Nabara*,
and with the prize ship *Galdames*. In the Basques' belief,
Canarias thought that Bermeo was too small a harbour
for the *J——*, and that she could therefore retake her
at will.

Indeed, *J——*. at 1,600 odd tons was the biggest ship
that had ever entered Bermeo harbour, and it was a miracle
that she scraped into the quay. The port captain, in
abnormal pride and dignity, put on his best beret to inspect
the ship's papers.

These were beyond the powers of any port captain to
comprehend.

To this day the identity and the seafaring motive of the
J——. remain a mystery to both sides in Spain. The
Canarias had captured her, therefore she was not carrying
arms for Franco; but neither the Basques nor Valencia
were expecting her.

Everything about this remarkable ship was elusive.

Most ships, however large, are satisfied with one captain, but this 1,600-tonner boasted three. One was Estonian, the second English and the third, a tired-looking man who was probably telling the truth, said that he was Spanish and that he took neither side in the civil war.

She carried a few thousand rifles and some million rounds of rifle ammunition. Where were they bound for? Her papers said, quite clearly and without blushing, "German Arabia." Now, it is known that German Arabia figures only in the maps of "Wonderland," and in the dreams of Wilhelm II, and that no ship setting out from a physical port has ever been able to find it, and that it has never so much as figured in Nazi claims.

The Basques, however, are realists. They soon stopped scratching their heads over the *J*——. dossier, and settled down to an inventory of the arms she carried.

Outside, as the mist drew away to sea, the battle of the four 101's against Spain's most up-to-date cruiser continued.

It was a sad sight. The *Guipuzkoa* was already in flames, the *Nabara* had been hit four times, but was still firing regularly. *Canarias* hovered over *Galdames*, and stripes of fire jerked from all her armament. The little *Donostia*, with her petty 75's, lay off to sea nervously watching and wondering.

Between three and four the fire on the *Guipuzkoa* was threatening the munition locker, and she turned away in a ribbon of smoke for the Nervion. Her engines, too, were damaged: she only just limped past the mole of Las Arenas. A quarter of her crew were dead and laid in line on the sooty deck. She was a fire-ship as she came into port.

Nabara had made up her mind to stick it out. She fought *Canarias* single-handed until nightfall.

The history of the sufferings and the tenacity of her complement will, I hope, be one day described by the survivors: if, indeed, they survive their second ordeal, that of imprisonment in San Sebastian.

Canarias now, who had been struck more than once, described a wide semi-circle round *Nabara* on the very limit of the trawler's range. But as she passed backwards and forwards, sending broadsides about her, *Nabara* grimly presented her side to give her both her guns. It made her a dangerous target. But perhaps she felt that by putting forth all her strength she would enable the *Galdames* to escape.

There were long intervals in the firing, as the afternoon sky weighed like lead on the water. Gradually the 8-inch guns of the cruiser, manned by German gun-layers, began to tell. The *Nabara* was burning fore and aft. But she made no attempt to get away, even into Bermeo. *Donostia* watched her eagerly, to see if she hoisted the white flag, but her only signals were the two flashes every five minutes, economically measured.

A boat was lowered from *Nabara* at about five o'clock and rowed painfully over to the *Donostia*, As it came nearer they saw that the crew were all wounded men, and they and the oars mucked with blood. They imagined that they had abandoned ship, seeing that the flames were high, and as they came alongside the captain of the *Donostia* shouted, "Quickly, come aboard and we'll get into Bermeo," and let down a ladder.

"No, no," the bleeding men answered, "we're going back at once. But we want watercasks to put the fire out and we have run out of bandages. Give us your store; then, our officer says, you must make for safety and leave us. We're going to finish this game of *pelota*."

The captain of the *Donostia* begged them to come aboard. But they only cursed him for being so slow, and he burst into tears as he lowered the casks into their boat, and his medical stores. Then they rowed away, and he turned for the shore.

Nabara fought *Canarias* for two hours more. She carried 190 rounds, and when her forward gun was knocked out she turned about and went on fighting aft. It was seven when the last shell had parted. The earlier fires had been mastered, but there were new ones now. The engines were smashed and the ship was filling and sinking. The deck was all holes and jagged teeth of iron, the funnel was scrap. This Newfoundland trawler would not visit the deep seas or fish cod or ride out the storms any more.

Of her crew of fifty-two all except fourteen were dead; the captain and all the officers except one were dead; all the engineers except one were dead; the chief gunners were dead. The fourteen, who included the wireless operator and the cabin-boy, were badly wounded. Dead lay all over the decks, and some were already burning.

They looked from the shore, and no doubt from the *Canarias* as well, for a white flag. But *Nabara* never surrendered. As night settled down, so did she in the waters, a flaming torch soon to be quenched.

With great difficulty the fourteen lowered a boat, half wrecked, for the second time and clambered unsteadily into it. They tried to pull for the shore. *Nabara* sank by the stern in crimson flames behind them, and thirty-eight of the brave dead sank with her in a viking's funeral.

Canarias lowered a launch, which made after the rowing-boat and soon overhauled it. They came close to make the Basques easy prisoners, and received the surprise of their lives.

As they drew level the fourteen wounded, or those who still had the use of their arms, threw hand-grenades at them. They were their only weapons left.

When they had expended all their bombs the *Canarias* launch made them fast, knocked them out and took them to the cruiser. *Canarias* herself had lost eight or nine men in the action, and had fired an enormous quantity of shells.

The fourteen were landed at Pasajes and imprisoned in San Sebastian. In more ordinary circumstances they would have been shot. But the captain of the *Canarias* put in a plea for mercy, saying that they were heroes and deserved to live.

It is strange that their story, the most gallant of the civil war, should not have been told before. The British press did not interest itself in Bilbao until the blockade became a subject of party politics. And it is true that the duel of the *Canarias* and the *Nabara* did little to alter the course of the war; the Basques lost their nickel and their despatch-boat, and a good armed trawler, and gained a valuable shipment of arms.

But I cannot help feeling that there are some things in this world more important than arms or nickel. That is why the fortitude of fifty-one Basque deep-sea fishermen and a cabin-boy, all equally unused to war, shall not be forgotten.

The dead lie off Bermeo, the ancient fishing village which

in 1351 signed a treaty with Edward III of England, establishing the master principle of the freedom of the seas. They lie in the passage of the small ships which sailed to the undiscovered west, after neat building along the Gernika inlet, where the great Basque navigators of the New World, from Labrador to the Horn, had learned their profession. They had died in a great tradition, the risk and freedom of the seas. In the modern world they had confirmed the view of Walsingham the English historian, who wrote after the sea battle between English and Basques in 1350: *They preferred, because of the rudeness of their heart, to die rather than to surrender.*

XII

TOWARDS THE END OF MARCH preparations were being made for the great offensive on Euzkadi which was to end in the fall of Bilbao. Throughout the six months preceding this offensive the ground had been made ready, in a general sense.

A loose blockade had been maintained by the battleship *España* and the cruiser *Almirante Cervera*, whose crews early in December were found to be hatching a mutiny in Ferrol, where a hundred of the battleship's complement and forty of the cruiser's faced a firing squad. A machine-gun rattling against a dockyard wall cleared the way for Falangist lower-deck men, and German gunnery experts. These in the *España's* log were always given the prefix Herr, never an officer's title; so far did Spanish pride still assert its dominion. But the Germans fired the guns.

At Pasajes, the port of San Sebastian, where a narrow passage between heavy fists of headland opens the way from the harbour pool to the Cantabrian sea, the *bous* or armed trawlers of the insurgents found their base. Others were equipped with German wireless to establish a reconnaissance cordon across the southern half of the Bay of Biscay. Behind this line of sea scouts the rebel warships cruised east and west, informed continually of all sea movements in their corner.

They caught the *Mar Cantabrico*, a liner stuffed with second-hand planes, guns and small arms from Mexico — the same *Mar Cantabrico* that the papers featured when she won her race against Congress and reached the limit of territorial waters before the United States passed their arms embargo and the coastguard cutters could stop her. She was the *Adda* now, repainted and reflagged in English;

149

but espionage is powerful in Mexico, and the rebels were prepared for the false whiskers that the *Mar Cantabrico* was wearing. They caught her in the blinding stare of their German searchlights and conducted her to Ferrol, where the Spaniards in the crew were executed.

Queipo de Llano, in a loud after-dinner broadcast from Sevilla next week, announced that the war material in the *Mar Cantabrico* was worn and useless. But the Government area in the north of Spain sorely needed it. Bilbao in particular was very low for ammunition.

Other ships were captured—ships of Sota's company, going out of Bilbao to England with iron ore and coming back with food. That was how the Basque Government paid for their food. Aldasoro, the Minister of Supply, found that his stocks were getting low. They were well under the month; the border-line of famine was now something like three weeks. Bilbao went many days without her dark sour bread.

Low ammunition, low foodstocks, low spirits in Bilbao. All who knew anything about her situation knew that she could not hold out if vigorously attacked from land and sea and in the air. It was at the height of her and his depression that Goicoechea, the Basque officer of the former regular army who had supervised the *Cinturón*, packed up his plans in a small portfolio, took his car to the front and passed over to the other side through one of the wide gaps between positions.

Just as Pepi Urresti, Sota's partner in Bilbao, had entered the plain of Vitoria in January to collect cows for his farm-carts. But Goicoechea sought a hole in the war-line for more sinister motives.

The Basques were always fair to Goicoechea in their unmilitary way. Other people would have pounced on his property, molested his family, stigmatised him in public as "The Traitor." But the Basques did none of these things. They often talked to me about Goicoechea during the campaign which followed his monstrous defection. "We knew him well," they said. "He's a pleasant fellow, and got on very well with us. He isn't at all a Fascist; he's a Basque at heart. In his case it wasn't ordinary treason; he was just terrified by the poverty of our re-sources at the time when he went. He was frequently in the party (Basque Nationalist) offices, and we could see that he really favoured our cause."

The Basques were like that. A good fellow, he had our confidence; some power outside himself drove him to this stupidity.

El Liberal, the Spanish Socialist paper of Bilbao, used occasionally to try and slip in a reference to the treachery of Goicoechea. The Basque censor as regularly blocked out the traitor's name. It looked funny on the page, but it had a purpose. The public, you see, in the Basques' view, had a right to know that — had betrayed the secrets of the *cinturón*; but if they only knew that — had done it they would not be able to vent their wrath on —'s friends and relations. In this way feeling against the vile — was volatilised; one could use the most horrible words, such as — and —, against him, but wherever one launched out more seriously one hit a blank wall.

So the mild-faced, smooth-shaven Goicoechea passed over, and handed every detail of the defences of Bilbao and of the new front-line fortifications around Villareal to General Mola, the commander of the rebel *Ejercito del Norte*, Euzkadi's special enemy. He was able to tell Mola also the precise number of guns, rifles and ammunition stocks at the command of the Basque army. He also gave information about the sites of the Basque war factories, which at this moment were being tuned up to their full productive capacity.

Goicoechea came as a god-send, a spring shower to open the leaves of the rebel cause and green them over with new life. Since the death of the German, Wakonigg, their information had been sketchy, often false. Now they knew everything about Bilbao, at a moment when they had just learnt a little too much about the rest of Spain.

* * * * * *

March in Spain had been a dead month for the rebels, full of disasters and cruel forebodings that they would never take Madrid; more, that their new allies, the 55,000 Italian conscripts, were valueless in the field.

February had gone well; with the fall of Malaga and the penetration in Andalusia towards the mercury mines of Almaden, the first employment of the Italians where no opposition was to be expected proved useful enough, and at Pozoblanco they were near guaranteeing their paysheet.

But in March their grandiose descent upon Madrid was broken north of Guadalajara; against a superior air force it was found that the Italian without ideals was as fast a mover as ever across country. They were driven back from Pozoblanco again. Everywhere the rebel cause was faced with disaster, with defeat on the circumference and dissatisfaction in the centre, where the Falangists were intriguing for power and the Spanish officer class protested against Italian domination of the staff.

It was an ugly moment. Some action had to be rigged to carry the interest of Nationalist Spain and International Fascism until they could prepare a newer and more elaborate attack upon Madrid. And at this ugly moment the little white dove flew into the lurching ark, with a sheaf of plans in his beak and a report that not far off to starboard lay a comfortable city, unarmed and ill-fed, called Bilbao. Here one could easily cast anchor and pay the crew. For Noah it was better than Mothersill; he rose from his sick bay refreshed.

The offensive on which Generals Franco and Mola set their heads to work was to be more than a side-show; they decided to make of it the most advanced operation of the Spanish Civil War. They had cornered an opponent whom they considered weak. By a tremendous display of force, with all the heavy arms that they could muster on land and in the air, they aimed at the surrender of Bilbao within twenty-one days.

Bilbao would have no time to reconstruct her *cinturón* or her front-line defences, import food or arms. Under an enormous weight of aviation and artillery the Basque militia would break and run.

The attack would be launched from two bases to the south and south-east of the Vizcaya front— Villareal, Mondragon. Twelve thousand troops would be used, of whom a third, Moors, were to occupy the mountain positions of Maroto, Jacinto and Albertia, captured by the Basques in the offensive of December, when they all but entered Villareal. Goicoechea carried the plans of their fortification, the shell-

DIGGING OUT DEAD: DURANGO CHURCH,
MARCH 31ST, 1937.

like pill-boxes, inadequate dug-outs, communication systems, head-quarter layout—everything, down to the types of machine-guns, which were discordant and manifold, and the issue of cartridges per man.

Otxandiano, the Basque base in this sector, would be taken in two or three days. Durango, knot of communications for the whole south-eastern front, would be occupied in a fortnight, and the rebels in Durango would cut off most of the Basques to the east as well, in Udala and Elgueta on the Guipuzcoa border. Thus in a fortnight one could make a hole fifty kilometres wide in the Basque defences and press on quickly against the *cinturón*, now an open book and an easy one at that—an elementary primer, as simple as spelling cat. Bilbao herself, pressed by the sea blockade, would surrender at the end of the third week of April.*

The way for so rapid an advance across mountainous country was to be blasted by the air fleets of Germany and Italy. The secret of this offensive was to be the use of air-power on a scale not yet seen in Spain or in the world at large. A new aerodrome was constructed at Vitoria under German supervision. Fresh orders for German pilots and planes, types Dornier 17 (heavy bomber) and Heinkel 111 (cruiser bomber), were placed in Berlin. The eighteen German pilots who had lived, bar accidents, at the Hotel Fronton in Vitoria since September were now sent out on ceaseless reconnaissance over the central sector of the Vizcayan front, between Durango and the firing-line. Hundreds of packing-cases arrived at Vitoria containing bombs, machine-gun ammunition and new fighting planes in parts, type Heinkel 51.

During the week-end of March 27th and 28th General Mola arrived in Vitoria with Franco's chief of air staff, the Spanish General Kinderlen, and with the German air staff which took a more active interest than he in the course of operations on the Vizcayan front. The aerodrome was now ready, and the German Air Force aviator, Captain Carsten von Harling, was selected to command the ground organisation.

The muster of aviation at Vitoria was to be so important

* My authority for this statement of objective is Walther Kienzle, German pilot captured Otxandiano, 5th April, 1937.

that the airfield at Talavera, once the chief aerial base for the Tagus valley, was stripped of chasers. Part of the German force at Avila (Germany's headquarters aerodrome in Spain) were also sent north.

The members of the First (German) Squadron J.88 under Ober-Lieutenant Walther Kienzle, who till now had been charged with the protection of Talavera, record the fact in simple military German in their War Diary.

"Dates (March) 27. Departure of the Advanced Detachment.

    28. Departure of main column 12.30. Spend the night in ——. Start of squadron for Avila 12.00. Start of Ober-Lt. Kienzle for Vitoria; arrival of Advanced Detachment in Vitoria.

    29. March of main column from X to X. Arrangements for billeting, etc., in Vitoria.

    30. March of main column from X to Vitoria. Arrival X o'clock. Start of flight in Avila at X o'clock, landing in V (itoria) X o'clock.

    31. Stand ready with one flight . . ."

By March 31st, the day on which the offensive was to open, there were gathered in Vitoria over sixty bombing and pursuit planes. Two squadrons of pursuit planes were of the German type Heinkel 51, and a third of the Italian type Fiat CR.32; each squadron consisted of twelve planes, formed in four flights, of which one flight was always in reserve. There were therefore thirty-six fighting planes ready in the aerodrome in formation. Heavy bombers at Vitoria added ten more planes to the total. (At this period, however, when General Mola was not certain what aerial striking power the Basques might develop, he kept his newer bombers farther from the front than Vitoria; Burgos, Soria and Logroño held their planes in readiness for the attack on Bilbao.

Five or six of the new cruiser-bomber type, the rapid two-engined Heinkel 111, lay like long hungry basking sharks on the Vitoria greens. These, like the new German heavy bomber Dornier 17, were to have shown their paces first in the Guadalajara battle, when their silhouettes were issued to their Italian allies on the ground to save them the trouble of running from their own planes. But hard weather in the Sierra, and the mastery of the air by the Government fighters, kept these new types at home in March. They were to prove themselves first against Vizcaya, and we grew to hate the Heinkel 111 more than any other plane. She slid over us at a terrible noiseless speed, she was a born spy, beautifully turned out as Mata Hari, with as evil a nature. She machine-gunned us at any angle: she was as beastly and as unexpected as a Frenchwoman with a jewelled revolver.

Besides this tigress plane in Vitoria there were a random series of older Breguet bombers, Germany army co-operation fighters type Heinkel 45, bringing the total to over sixty.

Bombers and aerodrome-protection fighters at Burgos, Soria, Logroño numbered perhaps another sixty, of which a proportion of two-thirds were given heavy work on the Vizcayan front. The summed assembly of German and Italian aviation for the offensive against Bilbao was about one hundred, therefore, of which more than half were ready for work at a distance of only fifteen kilometres from the front, and only seventy kilometres from the enemy base, Bilbao.

A huge stock of German-made bombs was distributed between various empty factories at Vitoria and Burgos, ranging from 1,000 pounder high explosives to the little two-pounder aluminium incendiary with which the Germans were to experiment, and on which they were prepared to improve, during the next eighty days.

Except that optimism divided that period by four.

New maps of the southern Vizcaya front were issued to the German aviators by the reconnaissance service, with the enemy's positions marked and numbered, from 1 to 16, for wireless reference. Old Paul Freese, a good-natured, white-haired German who had long lived at Zarauz in Guipuzcoa and risen to the proud rank of Stützpunktleiter in the Nazi foreign organisation, holding membership card 774, was appointed interpreter to the Vitoria 1.J88 chaser squadron and their German crews. Old flossy-haired Freese described the country and the maps to them in preparation for the morning of the 31st. He told them that, after many years' residence in Zarauz, he had found the Basques to be the best people in Spain, hard-working, honest, simple and free. These complimentary epithets, however, did not discourage old Freese from sketching out the plans for next day's bombardment of Durango.

* * * * * *

More troops were also brought up to Vitoria.

It was settled that the offensive would begin with 12,000 men, Moors and Spanish levies; but that the whole force against Vizcaya would number about 35,000. Apart from the column based on Villareal and Mondragon, there would be other columns at the extreme south-western corner of Vizcaya, opposite Orduña; at Vergara in preparation for the occupation, one hoped painless, of Elgueta to the east; and at Vera, where the Italian organisation of Flechas Negras found its base for the attack along the sea-coast. And reserves.

French journalists travelled up from Vitoria to Salamanca with the Italians. They noted and tried to count large numbers, long dusty columns of the totalitarian volunteers. Spies did the rest. There were probably 10,000 of them at first, stiffened later by a reserve of 5,000. But the exact number of Italians used in the Bilbao offensive will always be difficult to determine, for the Black Arrows organisation itself remained until the end a mystery to the Basques. Sometimes a brigade of Flechas Negras was found to contain two pure Italian battalions and one mixed battalion with Italian officers and Spanish rank and file. In other brigades the officers were all Italians and all the men were Spanish. In others Spanish and Italian rank and file were mixed freely throughout the battalions. Interrogation of Italian officer prisoners might have solved the puzzle; but of the only two Italian officers ever taken prisoners in the Bilbao offensive, one was so severely wounded that the Basques did not care to question him and he later died in hospital, while the other was shot out of hand in the last fighting on the crest of Arxanda, before the city fell. His was the only case that I was able to find in Vizcaya of the killing of prisoners. It was a pity that on the only desperate day when the Basques broke their record for good behaviour, they gave the quietus to a man who would have been anything but quiet had he survived.

A large force of tanks, mostly Fiat-Ansaldo two machine-gun whippets, was assembled for the war. In Bilbao their numbers were calculated at about eighty and their concentrations were marked at Vergara and Vera in particular. There were among them a few larger tanks, with a turret mounting two machine guns, and a few larger still carrying a tank gun, supposed but never proved to be German.

Their behaviour in this offensive was, until the very end, to be disappointing. Their tactic before they reached the *cinturón*, two months and two weeks later, was to follow the roads in waddling unimaginative blindness; where the fast auto-canons that the Basques had bought from Russia had the better of them in every engagement. The tendency of the insurgent tank corps therefore, was to keep its nose prudently round the corner and lurk on the shady side of the hill, attacking only rarely where a feint had proved that no anti-tank gun existed.

But the main support of the insurgent infantry, after the aviation, was their artillery, which found a general park and store in the Bull Ring at Vitoria. It was calculated that for this offensive the insurgents could muster forty-five batteries on a single point, ranging from 210 mm. (8-inch) to the Italian 65 mm. field artillery. The 155 mm. (6-inch) guns were believed to be old Spanish Army stocks, but all the other calibres, in which Italian 105's, 89's, 75.27's and 65's predominated, were either Italian or German. The foreigners picketed their own batteries and did not allow the indigenous insurgent infantry near them.

Five big siege guns, 310 mm. (12-inch) were held in reserve for the last operations on Bilbao and its harbour.

The infantry were, of course, equipped better in the case of the Flechas Negras than the new Spanish levies who filled up the holes in the line; but all units had more machine guns than the most heavily armed Basque battalions, and at the beginning of this war, even after the Santander and Asturias armies had sent men and material to help

Vizcaya, there were still twenty battalions out of the seventy-nine of the defence who had no machine guns. The Basque artillery, with the forty new field Schneider's that arrived just before March 31st, was still only 50 per cent. the strength of the enemy; who, it was to be seen in the coming weeks, could silence the Basque guns all day by the mere song of their aerial engines and the shadow of their taper wings.

Six fighting planes, Russian Boeing 1.16, were the total of the Basque air fleet; they were manned by young Spanish pilots whom the Russians had trained since November, and were led by the boy Felipe Del Rio. I forget. There were seven old Breguet bombers, dismally slow, who, compared with the German attack much as undertakers compare with public executioners. They once bombed the enemy.

In every way except in numbers of men the insurgents were superior. The Basques could put into the field 45,000 men. But over the huge front of one hundred and twenty kilometres which they had to defend 45,000 men poorly equipped with machine guns was not an army to be proud of. Success would certainly march with the side that could preserve the initiative manœuvre and penetrate; and the insurgent mastery of the air would obviously give them that. While their enemy was tied to the ground during the day, they could move troops and material freely from front to front.

It was obvious that the Basques had no chance. Mola and Franco entered upon the offensive in the gayest and most expensive manner, for it was bound to be over in three weeks, and the iron ore to the west of the peasoup Nervion would pay out Germany handsomely.

Germany also prepared to protect her interests in the northern coast of Spain; she kept at Pasajes two submarines, the U27 and U29, with their own refuelling service for a long stay. They rested in the day and worked at night.

Everybody is in line, waiting for the whistle which will signal the advance upon Bilbao. The propaganda pamphlets are printed, containing the famous menace to the civilian population which set the compass for the whole campaign.

"*I have decided* (they read) *to terminate rapidly the war in the North. Those not guilty of assassinations who surrender their arms will have their lives and property saved. But if submission is not immediate I will raze all Vizcaya to the ground, beginning with the industries of war. I have the means to do so.*

GENERAL MOLA."

XIII

"MARCH 31ST.—STAND READY WITH one flight . . ." reads the German war diary. The pamphlets signed by General Mola were issued to bombing and fighting pilots. At 7 a.m. punctually the bombers from Burgos were over Vitoria, dappling the plain, where Wellington had once fought, with standardised heavy-shadowed T's. The jerky pulse of their engines in the distance, carried in waves of sound which tickled the ear-drum, made the eye look up, grew into the roar of a great factory; singing a higher note, two squadrons of German pursuit planes took off from the aerodrome, climbed speedily in arrow abreast and after one circle were above the tri-motors. It was a fine day, they glittered like fish doubling backwards in the light. A flicker of their wings and they were lost, swallowed high in the blue mouth of a fairweather heaven.

The air fleet divided into three parts.

Nine bombers and nine chasers made north-east towards position 1 on the German air map, where they began to bomb and to dive to the attack on entrenched positions; and again the Germans in their war diary are able to describe the day's activities in the simplest terms:

"1. Dive-attack (*Tiefangriff*) of flight towards Maroto, Albertia and Jacinto" (the three mountains which dominated the Vitoria-Bilbao road to the north-east of Villareal) "(start, landing, targets, one hit in the ——, spent munition and bombs)."

"Maroto taken with aid of flight."

"2. Dive-attack (high approach) targets 1 and 2 (*Uncella* XXX).

"3. Dive-attack ordered on target 7. Motorised

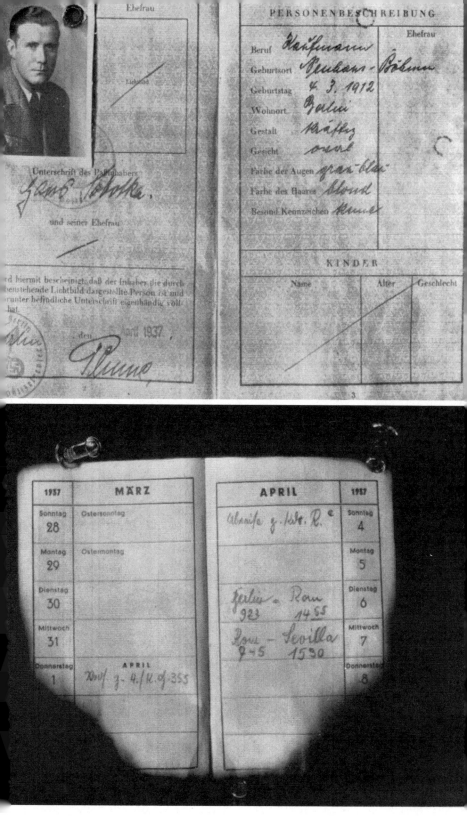

SOBOTKA'S PASSPORT: BERLIN, APRIL 5TH, 1937.

SOBOTKA'S DIARY: FLIGHT BERLIN–ROME–SEVILLA,
APRIL 6TH–7TH, 1937.

column between X and Ochandiano brought to standstill. Tank hit and fired, Ochandiano bombed.

"4. Dive-attack on the same vehicles, on Ochandiano, and on lorries on the two roads north of Ochandiano."

Other bombers and chasers attacked the Basque villages of Elgueta and Elorrio, where lay the headquarters of the Basque commander of the South-Eastern Guipuzcoa sector.

A third, consisting of four heavy bombers and nine chasers, appeared at 7.20 precisely over the country town of Durango, on which they began to drop 500-lb. projectiles.

The work of the German and Italian aviation in this, their first specimen offensive may therefore be divided into four parts. First, they attacked the front line with bombs and machine guns; secondly, they laid down a control on road traffic, bringing it to a standstill; thirdly, they bombed villages which acted as baseline H.Q. to the Basque front, Otxandiano and Elorrio; and fourthly, they attacked Durango, a typical centre of civil population established on the lines of communication between Bilbao and the front. Their activity on this day corresponded exactly to their activity on April 26th following, when Gernika took the place of Durango in the destructive scheme. But they were not yet using incendiary bombs behind the line.

It was a new method of war, more terrible than any practised against Madrid. So, while the mountains over the Vitoria plain were cross-patterned with kilometres of fulminating smoke, and the roads lay in dreary silence awaiting the machine guns' rattle, and the bases were underground struggling to make telephones talk that were cut to tangled pieces by flying knives of metal, there began the most terrible bombardment of a civil population in the history of the world up to March 31st, 1937.

The object of this bombardment, part number four of the German staff plan, was to terrify civilians, and to knock so many houses across the roads that they would be impassable to motor transport. Civilian morale is an extremely important element of war in any voluntary or militia system; where the conduct of war depends not so much on direction from above but on willingness to fight for an ideal, an army and the civilian population which it protects are so tightly linked that changes in their feeling, either towards fear or enthusiasm, become common property at once. The more so with the Basques, whose militia at only forty miles at the farthest from their homes in Bilbao were constantly visiting, eating with, receiving letters and washing from their families. Mutual reactions on morale were immediate.

The Germans wanted to strike terror into everyone who lived in Durango, everyone who passed through it, and everyone who heard of it.

* * * * * *

Durango, the town which they chose, was one of the prettiest in all Vizcaya. The main road from Bilbao ran through it, as well as an old-fashioned narrow gauge railway and country tramline. To the right, another road led through the mountain pass of Urkiola to Vitoria; the train rattled on through Abadiano and Elorrio to Guipuzcoa. A cluster of communications therefore.

The little town itself had played a certain part in Basque history, for during the Carlist Wars of the middle nineteenth century it had been the headquarters of Don Carlos himself. It had flared with scarlet berets, creaked with top-boots bowing to absolute monarchy. There were still many in Durango who remembered Carlism and called themselves still Traditionalists. The life of the town did not make for change.

A narrow river, flanked by much greenery, flowed through Durango; but when it was in the centre of her, buildings packed up against it on either side, and strangers would call the river a clear-watered canal. Plane trees with flimsy chiffon leaves lightened the weight of old houses, grey stone and long slabs of falling plaster, over cobble walks. Crimson petunias with lips of velvet hung in languid vanity over the lucid river, against hards tone quays. There was a narrow gateway with a gorgeous scroll of arms and prancing animals carved to face Urkiola, near the Convent of the Augustine sisters dedicated to St. Susana. The affectionate lazy-making sun shadowed out its embossment in drooping eyelashes of black, and made of the plane avenue in the Paseo de Ezkurdi alongside a cool tunnel of indolence, with seats for conservatives to sit on. The river induced sleep, as it passed through Durango in soft frou-frou of silk skirts, past wide Basque windows and rusted frames warming sun-parlours and tasselled furnishings within. In the spring, Durango was beginning to put off her rural winter slumbers, and turn over with half-open eyes to a summer drowsiness; she was just beginning to wake to half-life when Germany settled her style for ever.

In the very middle of Durango the houses and the tall sun-balconies in their bulging glass grew taller, more elbow-cramped, and the streets played narrowly between them round unexpected corners and gutters which brought lorries up with a jerk. The streets, indeed, were most irregular; for a lovely creation of Basque art had tres-passed on their space and knocked them quite askew. This was the ancient parish church of Santa Maria, whose tower dominated Durango and whose enormous oak porch could have covered half her population from the Vizcayan drizzle. In a long shallow curve, the wood sprang clean from the massive stone walls of the aisle, till it nearly reached the massed houses to the northward, square pillars stopping it dead. In a very proper way this porch represented the life of the Basque church. It gave shelter to many outside the holy ground; square mud-coloured farm-carts lay tilted on their shafts in the straw underneath, luminous-eyed oxen were tethered to rings in its stone, old gaffers in berets talked high politics and smoked on its long benches, and only children were forbidden to play pelota near it most strictly. A prohibition quite disregarded.

From the high tower in brown stone, banistered about in the careful Basque way, one could see and size the whole of Durango in a second. A small sleepy town in a valley of a rich peaceful green. Thick red tiles lay undusted by any wind like the paving stones of a square over the tight mass of houses. Wide roofs with gables low almost to the point of invisibility, so broad was the angle of the eaves. White plaster showing dully in the narrow intervals between houses and elderly fragile half-timber framing the wide flat foreheads of house-fronts with black cheeks. It all looked very sunburnt and friable; of an unrestored anti-quity that should not be washed or touched.

Nearer in, the houses had put on modern provincial faces—of the last century. Much iron work and square tiling and flat glass; but they did not look unpleasant for they were so careless of themselves. They did not glare or hit the eye, they just stood next to each other in a sort of ramshackle discipline.

Farther out, the Elorrio road ran down the Paseo de Ezkurdi with its green papery stream of plane trees, past houses more wistaria-laden, more significantly detached and shuttered, behind garden railings and small iron gates which carried enamel plates of the thin-lettered Spanish provincial type; reading Doctor Don this and Advocate Don that, printed like the legs of spiders. These houses were all empty now. The *facciosos* were in prison, the *good ones* were in Bilbao working for the Government hospitals and offices. The houses stood very square in their smalltown plots, toned into Durango by grey stone and greying plaster.

In the same Paseo, the new yellow church of the Jesuit Fathers. Beyond the Paseo, green fields and a smooth transition to Basque mountain side. But to the south, rocks and hard grey teeth of horizon, over which came now four grey bombing planes.

Durango was a religious and well-ordered town; at seven-twenty there were many people at Mass in its three churches, of whom nearly half were secretly, sentimentally, only by their mode of conversation detectably, on the bombers' side. And they spoke little.

The bell of warning broke the Mass in the church tower, but the officiating priest, Don Carlos Morilla, refugee from his "Red" parish of Jove in the Asturias, did not believe that his flock would be attacked.

Four Junker bombers circled over Durango, seemed suspended for a moment like ugly Christmas-tree toys as they turned, then came lower. The fighters shook tinsel light above them. Women in houses ran down to the refuges with their children in their arms and their dark hair on their shoulders. The congregations in Santa Maria and the Church of the Jesuit Fathers, and the nuns in the chapel of Santa Susana could now hear the oppressive noise of the engines of the Junker bombers.

I am told that these came down as low as 1,000 feet. Then the bombs fell, singing to themselves.

Four tons of heavy bombs were dropped, and what the

people of Durango called light grenades were thrown into the streets as the fighters too swung down and skimmed noisily across the red tiles.

Which opened and flew all over the town. Which split and leant and fell into the street. Which stripped away with whole plastered sides of houses like torn cloth. Which cascaded glass into the streets like shining arrows.

A heavy bomb shot through the roof of Santa Susana's chapel; fourteen nuns were mangled and killed there on the spot, and thrown in pieces with pieces of church chairs and images and strips of tapestry all round the chapel. Good shot! A heavy bomb shot through the roof of the Church of the Jesuit Fathers. Father Rafael Billalabeitia was bending over the faithful to communicate the Body of Christ; at this tense moment the roof and the bomb fell in upon Father Rafael, and the faithful, and the Blessed Sacrament. Beams, stones, the great blocks of arches, the dangling roof fell in to obliterate the faithful. All that ever got out of this church was the vicar, whose confessional box supported the avalanche, and the stained glass, which escaped through the windows. Good shot!

A heavy bomb shot through the roof of Santa Maria. Her massive tower shook, stood, shook again as a fourth bomb hit the porch, then stood firm and hard. Within, the Reverend Don Carlos Morilla was elevating the Host. As the heavy roof and the thunderclap of high explosive came down, Morilla was crushed to the earth, the chalice snapped into two pieces as the stem rolled to his dying, bucking feet. Good shot? Good God, sir, a bull's-eye. Teach him to escape from his "Red" congregation in the Asturias.

And with that the walls of the choir and the top of the nave shook apart, and slipped, and fell in like Samson's last curtain call upon the shrieking people, who died in grotesque attitudes of fear and despair. The whole nave was deep in stones and tiles and rubble, and long beams like savage spears sticking out of the quarry which had been a beautiful church.

Bombs fell all over the town, tearing wounds in the old houses, shaking the very air with their explosions. Dust in enormous inverted cones shuffled up to the sky, like blood pouring thick and clogging from deep thrusts of the knife. Though the churches were now all open wide to the daylight, they were darker now than ever they had been with their roofs on. The bombs fell again all over the town, blotting out with their fearful detonations the groans of the dying pinioned people. Durango stank with high explosive and dust and the dissolution of her houses.

It lasted less than half an hour. And then, when the smoke cones had lifted towards the morning mist, still dissolving on the mountains, and tilted away on a light north wind, the anguished survivors looked round their town. The bombers had gone; the fighting planes were going, machine-gunning as they flew off.

The dust, ground by friction of thousands of beams and stones blown to pieces, was scattering in the churches and letting in the light, which shone through speckled, choking air upon the tangle of wreckage which had been Santa Maria, Santa Susana, the Jesuit Fathers. Here hands and feet, sometimes heads, stuck out of the rubble, and sometimes they were attached to bodies, sometimes they were shorn free, and sometimes their association was so loose that attempts to pull them out disestablished it for ever. Some still gently moved, like dying worms.

From a house opposite the shattered porch came the crackle of fire; in the indolent Paseo de Ezkurdi cars lay upside down in flames.

In the silence, more horrible even than the noise, could be heard glass slipping prettily to earth, tiles crackling far away; rarely some queer balancing trick of a table five storeys up on a broken floor breaking down and the whole crashing to the cellar. Then silence, broken by a little moaning.

Not at once, but gradually, with appalling foreboding, unwillingly even, the people came to the churches to look for those that they had lost. They were right to tremble. Very few were not dead.

Like a shipwrecked fleet on a rocky sea-bottom, the giant rubbish heap lay there three to four feet deep. Above it in hollow contrast the rococo gold and white plaster, the twisted columns and fat silver leaves of the altars and the chapels, and the robed saints with their eyes fixed wistfully upon the skies. Which they now saw for the first time in full spring glory, indifferent and blue, as the dust cleared away through shattered roofs and windows and doors blown smartly into the street.

Parties of the Basque motorised police arrived from Bilbao in their glister tunics and breeches, with special break-down gangs to clear the corpses. The work was painful and lasted all day, being broken at evening by another more modest bombardment.

By then 127 corpses, not counting unexplained pieces, had been dug out in dangerous conditions, for roofs were continually shedding more beams and stones. Many unrecognised, and many of these women and children. Thus in the police list one reads, "Male, approximate age four years," and "Male, approximate age six years," and "Girl of two or three years," among the unidentified bodies. So terrible was the panic, so rigid the moral paralysis that seized the people of Durango: children, loved in Spain, unrecognised dead in Durango.

Slowly the bodies were lugged out of the masonry and laid on slabs in the cemetery of Durango and ticketed 1 to 127. All blue in the face, dried blood streaking in thin lines from their nostrils and their eyes and the corners of their mouths to their necks. Mouths sagging open in the senility of death. Their hair and torn, dusty clothes matted with blood, and bones showing jagged from their crushed hands. They looked a fashionable congregation.

They were buried in two common graves, and in the tombs of their families. Lorries took the wounded back over a bumpy road to Bilbao, where 121 more died in the hospitals. The people of Durango were not great weight-lifters.

I do not know the number of the wounded. Nor were all the dead found on the first day. The next week was full of unpleasant smells and feverish excavations.

There were strange things to see in Durango. There were houses which looked fairly solid and whole outside, except for broken windows; but within all the floors had been shaken to the ground by a bomb. There they lay, like the fragments at the bottom of a kaleidescope, only not so nice to look at.

Parts of cars could be found in houses, and sometimes

parts of bodies in the street. The dead cats and dogs, of course, lay around for a long time.

The Germans did not carry out the second part of their project, which was to block the streets with wreckage. In spite of their narrowness, the streets could still be passed. The bombing, you see, lacked finish: incendiaries had been forgotten.

Durango was bombed again on Thursday, April 1st, and again at a special performance for the Dean of Canterbury and his party on April 2nd, when the fighting planes machine-gunned the civilian population as they took to the fields. And on April 4th also; but they could not close the houses over the roads, and the passage through Durango remained free but perilous.

They had not, however, completed their religious bag on March 31st. On April 2nd the machine-gunners scored two more excellent hits on two Sisters of Charity serving the wounded in Durango hospital as they ran to shelter across a field.

Salamanca was prepared for a denial of the raid on Durango, just as she was prepared on April 27th to deny the totalitarian destruction of Gernika. The principle of lying and continuous prolonged lying enunciated by Herr Hitler in *Mein Kampf* was thus tried out for the first time in war, like the rest of the German air method of which it was an important part.

Thus Radio-Club of Portugal announced "The socialists, anarchists and communists in Durango were annoyed at the renewal of religious worship and taking advantage of the fact that the Nationalist Aviation had bombarded certain military concentrations in revenge would not allow the faithful to issue from the churches and caused the death of some 200 of them . . . the churches were burnt. . . ."

A communiqué of Salamanca told the same story. And General Queipo de Llano, loud-speaking from Sevilla, said, "Our planes bombed military objectives in Durango and later communists and socialists locked up the priests and nuns in the churches, shooting them without pity and burning the churches."

All of this was rather bad lying, as none of the churches showed any trace of fire, nor the corpses of priests and nuns signs of death by shooting.

* * * * * *

On the front, Mola had pulled off a great surprise.

The day that Durango suffered first he bombed and machine-gunned the mountains of Maroto, Albertia and Jacinto from the air. These were the positions that the Basques had captured north of Villareal, on the very edge of the great Alava Plain in the advance which they had undertaken in late November to relieve insurgent pressure on Madrid. Fortified by Goicoechea, they were now betrayed by him.

The three mountains fell like nine pins—one, two three. It was an easy game. The plans were there, for the artillery to shell the strong points; the reconnaissance by air of the line had been intense. A great, quick-firing barrage of Italian and German guns opened. The Basques, at the presence of the aviation, went underground. Six thousand of Mola's infantry infiltrated between positions. When the Basques came up to resist, 1. J88 and the other two flights of chasers dropped to machine-gun their heads.

As the German war diary curtly said: *Maroto taken with aid of flight*. And Albertia and Jacinto were taken with the aid of another. Before the chasers, heavy bombers passed over the hills in an endless chain, raising smoke in gigantic hedges patterned momentarily with the running bloom of fire, which dies at birth.

Next, the planes turned their attention to communications, for in this first phase the Basques were to learn that they could not move convoys, reserves, munitions in the day-time. Lorries were smashed behind their advanced headquarters, Ochandiano; a Russian armoured car, with a lucky shot not to be repeated in this war, was blown off the road.

On the wings of the attack next day the Moors pressed forward on the right to Mount Amboto; the Requetes to the left scaled the high boundary mountain of the Basques, Gorbea, and planted their flag in its summit snows. At this the Basque militia reacted violently; on April 2nd they counter-attacked, stripped away the hated red and gold and unfurled once more their own beautiful flag, the white cross of St. George, upon a green saltire. Gorbea remained theirs for two more months.

But in the centre it was going badly. Ochandiano was being strongly encircled from the south and east. On

April 4th a most drastic attack of aviation was mounted; I spoke to many who survived it, and it was the most horrible memory of all. From midday to five there were always forty great planes in permanence; towards the end they counted fifty-seven. The staff calculated that 5,000 bombs were dropped in relay after relay from Vitoria. Ochandiano was shattered, and the lines defending it. The militia passed in chaos from the east, leaving whole companies interred, the fields sopping with the dead cut down by the light bomb in flight. As they all converged on Ochandiano, there rose a great cry, *estamos copados*—we are cut off! This was the profoundest fear of every militiaman, for to be captured by Franco was to be shot in Spain. Their faces were thin, white and strained with terror under the intolerable, unexperienced, inescapable thunder of great bombs, they turned at nightfall in shepherdless droves from the north, to be reformed, such battalions that were not decimated, upon the passes of Barazar, Dima and Urkiola, where three roads led across the mountains from the south to Bilbao.

Mola reported 600 dead and 400 prisoners; but there were many more dead whom he never troubled to dig up. They lie there, in the Basque soil, smothered by his foreign aircraft.

They were conscientious workers, his Germans, always pushing ahead and trying to speed the Spaniard up. Next afternoon the commander of Squadron 1. J.88, Walther Kienzle, went a little too far on his ground reconnaissance. With Von Harling the young superintendent of the Vitoria airfield (the German monopoly) and his lieutenant, Schulze-Blanck, and old Paul Freese, the interpreter, he fell into Basque hands at the pass of Urkiola on a quiet day. Harling tried to run (his head being stuffed with stories that the Basques were Reds who cut off the limbs of their prisoners); Harling was therefore killed, and Freese wounded. The other two were lodged in the Larrinaga Prison of Bilbao, where I talked with them. Both were members of the German Air Force. Kienzle was one of the most charming people that I have ever met, and the Basques became very fond of him; Schulze-Blanck was out to smash everything in the way. He told me that he had come to Spain "to smash Communism," and with a glint of supreme pleasure in his little eyes he lifted up one of his big legs encased in a boot and ground it into the prison floor. He justified Durango. "We have in Germany a saying," he told me, as if it were an honour to claim the authorship, "that the end justifies the means."

Both were confident that Mola would be in Bilbao in three weeks; but they had calculated without the natural resistance of the Basque, who is a creature of unlimited peasant stubbornness. Next day the Germans had a new surprise in store for him; they literally burnt off the tops of the hills that he held over the passes with thermite. Puzzled a little, he edged farther back. Then the rain came down, and the sirri-mirri of Vizcaya kept the planes at Vitoria. He dug furiously, called up three extra classes in Bilbao, counter-attacked with great determination—I remember seeing one battalion lose all its officers—and pinned the enemy down. The offensive from the south was over, and reinforcements from the Asturias and Santander poured into Vizcaya.

In the world outside the success of the aeroplane caused much surprise: the world suffered from a fixed and stolid assumption that mountains were impregnable. In fact, mountain positions, especially if they are thinly held, are a superb mark for the bomb. The Basque army, 45,000 strong, covered a front of 120 miles; its line could not be continuous and its fire-power was small, for it lacked automatics. Infiltration was as easy as walking uphill.

* * * * * *

A fortnight afterwards I was in the little fishing village of Bermeo, and entered the batsoki, or Basque Nationalist Party house there, a magnificent building with library, reading-rooms, rest-rooms, dining-rooms, cinema. It was a fiesta day.

Upstairs in the biggest dining-room we saw the Saseta battalion, which lost two-thirds of its effectives at Ochandiano, celebrating its renaissance. It was now on coastal defence. The gaps had at once been filled with recruits.

They were having a square meal, and it was going down no round holes. The battalion was eating and drinking without a shadow of doubt; and after the meat and wine, which was served by speedy girls in black dresses and light Basque dancing shoes of white, cross-gartered with white tape, the whole battalion broke into Basque song and began to dance about and upon their long tables. They were not drunk; this was just Basque camaraderie. The pipes and *xistu* were brought in, and played the Basque Nationalist Hymn and the Basque marching song, two superb tunes. Then came the new flags, with black silk streamers, which were greeted by a roar, and everybody was up in the tumult as they passed along the benches, and every hand was trying to catch the hem of the flags to pledge loyalty.

Prizes were given in the intervals of song: for Basque accomplishments—the lifting of heavy stones, wood-chopping races, dragging stone weights with oxen, all, like their Basque language, sports kept clean and unaltered from their prehistory. It gave one the impression of a people stable as a rock, over whom the present waves would pass as lightly as the Saseta battalion seemed capable of forgetting Ochandiano.

They sang and danced in the batsoki all the afternoon, between wall frescoes of their country life, big-eyed oxen and wooden carts, pelota courts and apple orchards, and gravely beautiful, long-featured women: through the windows at the end of the room, framed by their flags, they could look at their other immortal playground, the Bay. *Mucha allegria, los vascos,* said my friend.

XIV

THIS OFFENSIVE, THE MOST COMPACT and modern that Franco had yet dressed against his enemies, was not to last the twenty-one days which he planned; it was to limp on into May and June, and to end in his victory at the cost of his best general, his only battleship, about eighteen planes, an unknown quantity of tanks and 20,000 dead and wounded. Also a no uncertain but soon forgotten smell in the world on account of Gernika.

With it his lieutenant, Mola, instituted the daily raids over Bilbao, which in fine weather sometimes caused as many as fourteen alarms and scurries in the city within ten hours, but were discontinued when the drizzle and mist screened the Basque mountains with folds of grey, impenetrable gauze and the Germans thought it too dangerous to fly.

I came back to Bilbao at this time and went down to the front at the passes of Barazar, Dima and Urkiola, to find in officers and men a deep depression which made me fancy that Bilbao would change hands in a fortnight. But I had misjudged the Basques.

They believed, because they were told, that the aeroplanes which they expected would soon be there. I think that it was this belief, never realised, that enabled them to fight so long without modern weapons. Their leaders, the Basque Government, promised them that they were coming, for the Government was itself a creditor in promises, writ large above the signature of Madrid.

Cisneros, the chief of the Spanish Republican aviation, visited Bilbao as soon as the offensive began. He saw the unbearable torture that aviation, used competently and in mass as the German handled it, could inflict on mountain positions well reconnoitred. Something would have to be done to meet this menace: the puzzle, what? The enemy had the advantage of interior lines, and of a fleet that operated; it was, therefore, impossible to supply Bilbao with the anti-aircraft guns necessary for the protection of an air-fleet on its aerodromes. Yet such protection was vital, if an air-fleet of any size was to be sent to Bilbao; for the bombing force of the defence would be obliged to lie within less than twenty miles of the enemy lines: an air raid signal could not hope to raise enough fighters off the ground in time.

The second prejudice to the formation of a Basque air arm beyond the six fighters that they owned lay in the shortness of suitable aerodromes in Vizcaya. It was a hilly country, worked into small fields, sudden slopes and tufts of land, outcrops of rock, farmhouses, streams, roads in network, pine-woods: all tumbled together in rural amity at the feet of granite mountains, and fitted for anything comfortable except the receipt of aircraft. There was the big airport of Sondika in the Derio valley which the Basques had cemented flat, but that was all. Lamiako, on the banks of the Nervion, was already too small for the fighters that it had to carry. A small field was possible, and was later developed, at La Playa de Somorrostro, north-west of Bilbao. But where else could room be found, short of planing away ridges and blowing up houses? Vizcaya was inhospitable: as always, she wanted to be left alone.

These technical reasons were very weighty: I adduce them because it has been too lightly said that the Republic deserted Bilbao in the matter of planes. Nevertheless Cisneros did promise fighting planes before he went away, and said that bombers, too, would come if they could be spared. The Basque militia lived in hope of these. Looking back on the war from a desk confronted by a row of grey windows and chimney-pots, I can see that even if aeroplanes had not been promised, it was necessary to say that they were. The soldier must feel that there are reserves behind him: reserves of power, not only of men. They must always be coming out of the future, with an enormous onset, like the planes and artillery which did, in fact, save Madrid when her life was at ebb.

And I believe that the longer the soldier waits for these elements, the more he is ready to sweep aside in his enthusiasm when they come. Certainly Bilbao waited long enough.

But the *mystique* of the air, to which the Basque soldier bowed, is a weapon which stabs as well as cuts, and can be used in either hand. It calls for an all-round defence, and this the Basque Government did not provide.

It is not enough to say that aeroplanes are coming and the balance of force will be restored, particularly to irregular troops, as the Basques still were. Though soldiers will resist more vigorously on promises, they will nevertheless retreat steadily before the promises are fulfilled. They will show doggedness; but they will not show drive. They will accept local defeats, hoping next day to redress the balance. And that is, in fact, how the Basque militia behaved, sustaining often grave losses as they withdrew.

Morale in a regular army is a delicate thing, to be ridden carefully and humoured much; but in a force of militia whose barracks are the home, the beast is not only delicate but wild, and despotic measures must be taken to control it; else it will struggle away along any path of easy escape.

The German aviation menaced both the front line and Bilbao: from his girl to his commanding officer, it mastered the conversation of everybody that the Basque soldier met. Between the front and the base he passed its butcher's shop, and saw the real stuff on the slab.

His emotions ought to have been controlled by the papers, by *Euzkadi* and the Socialist *Liberal* and the Communist *Euzkadi Roja* that filled his trenches. For the militiaman, whatever his party, was out to read and learn: the war was a liberation for him, and his ten pesetas a day gave him a new status of which he honestly wished to be worthy. But, in fact, the newspapers did not control his natural reactions to this the first mass use of aviation that he had seen: they showed him the path of escape, and after that he did not feel the reins on his mouth any more.

The newspapers were untruthful: they explained things away to the militia and the people. It was not that they disguised retreats and losses. That would not have been unwise. They were censored, as they should have been.

But what they did disguise from the militiaman was the true material calculus of his fears. They justified him.

Every paper sprouted with phrases like these: Terrible attack of aviation and artillery: Germans bomb in mass: is this non-intervention?: our brave *gudaris* resist heroically, in spite of appalling bombardments: forced to retreat by overwhelming barrage: our brave *gudaris* reform: typical enemy attack with enormous weight of aviation.

Now this was not—and never will be—true. The *mystique* of aviation in the field is based upon its physical dominance; it is always making menacing noises above, not like artillery, less menacing noises off. It gives the impression of selecting its target in a secure and leisurely manner: it does not hide behind rocks and camouflage. It therefore makes the infantry believe that it is superlatively brave, and he quivers: and it looks as if it were coolly aiming at only him, and he sticks his head under cover, quivering rather more comically.

The *mystique* of aviation in the field is based, secondly, on the appalling noise, the reeking obscurity, and later the enormous cavities caused by bombs of five hundred pounds and upwards. The row exceeds that of any artillery: it deafens, stupefies and shakes one into semi-consciousness. The obscurity is horrible, for one fears that anything from a Moor to a tank may come out of it: and one cannot see if more planes are overhead or not. The holes ought to give the show away, for they mostly lie at 100 yards from the target, and only a few bombs have struck anywhere near the trench. But as interpreters, the holes play quite a different role from what they should. Everyone points at them, and notes their remarkable size, and estimates at fantastic figures the weight of the missile which caused them: digging starts for the few dead, and one wonders whether one can stand the next aerial round. Some others are dead of concussion: a queer, ghostly death to see.

In point of fact, aerial bombing is still far less accurate than artillery, even where artillery suffers from inexperienced hands. The bombers that can carry great weights, and whose dispersion of load is therefore less wide, are still vulnerable—an easy mark for the fighter: faster bombers are still inexact, and carry too little weight to impress. Therefore, the air arm thinks out a new hocus-pocus, and adds a third element to the *mystique* of the air: it drops fire behind the troops. Now there is noise, smoke, and fire, too. The thing's a circus.

Now, if one admits to a force of militia that this aerial form of attack is terrible, unheard of—German and Italian and overwhelming—one has given them the excuse to go home. And if one tells them and their families in Bilbao that they resisted bravely, their attitude is a shrug of the shoulders and a grin, which means in militia language, "You see that I did my best: the papers say so."

The men who survived the raids on Maroto, Albertia and Ochandiano, and were able to read the newspapers next morning, were not brave. The brave were those who stayed at their posts when the line broke right and left, and who were blotted out. But it was the others who felt themselves justified, and who built up a tradition that it was bravery to resist heroically against overwhelming force, and then to retire with honour. The newspapers of Bilbao instead of lauding the whole Basque army, ought to have commended the dead alone; but there was no directing hand to shape it that way. The town was a democracy, the party papers were out particularly to defend the name of their own party's troops, and the State was paying the price.

The irregular nature of the militia, and the fact that Bilbao was being continually raided, set the price very much higher. To a civilian population naturally uneducated to the aeroplane—for Spain is a backward country— and biased in the direction of ignorance and alarmism by the influx of what was largely a lower class refugee mass from Guipuzcoa, the daily arrival of the planes over Bilbao and the incessant bombardment of fourteen kilometres of riverside and port meant that they were suffering the same cruel fate as their fighting menfolk. The riverside and the port, and Las Arenas were precisely the parts of Bilbao where the poorer classes lived and the refugees were quartered. Scattered among them there was shipping; there were war factories; there was one aerodrome and one important bridge. It was the fault neither of the poor of Bilbao nor of its government that they lived near such targets of aerial war: if of anybody, it was the fault of a capitalist system which encouraged the workers to live near the great factories of Basque heavy industry in time of peace. And so they suffered.

I neither desire nor intend to make any claim that the German aircraft which made its daily mess of industrial Bilbao were out to kill civilians. They wanted to hit factories; and more often than not, they missed. They did, however, break the Air Warfare Rules drawn up at The Hague in 1923, which expressly forbid the bombardment of military establishments or depôts, or factories constituting important and well-known centres engaged in the manufacture of arms, ammunition or distinctively military supplies, where such localities cannot be bombarded "without the indiscriminate bombardment of the civil population."

Now, on an average during these bombardments of the Nervion, nine Basques were killed per raiding day; and it was calculated by the Direction of Mobilised Industries in Bilbao that the material damage done to the machinery or stocks under their control was considerably less than the value of civilian lives lost, if one assesses a Basque life insurance policy at £500 a piece. And the bombers knew this: they went for the same factories again and again. An instance was the Lunatic Asylum where trench mortars were made at Derio: I personally saw it bombed three times, without injury to machinery, but one peasant and one worker were killed in a field, and several villagers given the *quietus* in Derio itself.

This bombing was therefore indiscriminate bombing: the repetition of attacks on the same target in many other places than Derio proved that the bombers knew their chances of accuracy were low. At Portugalete and in Las Arenas, indeed, I am generous when I acquit them of deliberate attacks on the civilian population: the military objectives that existed there were so petty, and so far from the bomb-holes, that inaccuracy seemed too weak a donkey to carry the blame along. But there it is. Let them go.

What they knew when they bombed the Nervion was that if the factory was missed, the civilian population would get it in the neck. And that was why the bombing was worth while. Not only was a trifling damage done to Bilbao's war industry; not only was the working capacity of the men in mobilised industries reduced (though to a far less degree than in the case of London workmen during the Great War, and only appreciably in the last fortnight of the fight for Bilbao): but there was always a last, dependable reserve in the overbearing argument of their bombs, that the lesson of air dominance would be written red in the blood of the terrified poor, and that their memories would be stamped with a heavy imprint, whose lines were the torture and whose paper the pallid faces of their brothers, or sisters, or children in death.

Theorists too easily assume that bombardments killing civilians break down their resistance in the end, and make them sue for peace. This was not true of Bilbao: the raiders were hated, and even when the town was occupied by the conquering army, whom the raiders screened, the masses of Bilbao did not receive them with pleasure. A bitterness, an opposition lasted: the first night of the victory was celebrated with doors shut, lights out, and silence in the streets. The Basques had been handled too brutally to wish to mask their feelings.

The raids, however, did terrify; they dazed the people; they were a sharp and acid solvent of normal life. One never knew at what moment of the day—but not of the night—they would come. The Germans seemed averse, during the great offensive, to night-raids: perhaps the mountain barrier south of Bilbao embarrassed them. There were only two occasions when they flew at night, on one of which they dropped bombs in an untenanted pinewood south of the *cinturón*, while the other was dedicated to the machine-gunning of the civilian refugees on the road to Santander. But in the day the *sirena* would shriek, whether one was eating or washing or cleaning the house. Then one would have to gather together the small corps of children with which every Spanish family is blessed, and bolt into the *refugio* and perhaps hang about for an hour doing nothing but see how much Bilbao needed aeroplanes; and calculate when they were coming. Then there were the dead and the damage to see, and the excitement of the Red Cross cars and police dashing round on the bombers' trail, and the sudden re-opening of the roads to a lunatic traffic. And there were special spicy days, as when the driver of the up-train from Las Arenas did not hear the warning, ran slap into a tunnel where people were hiding, and cut six of them in half, which drove him mad. And the children became little nuisances to their mothers, for they had nothing to do: the schools closed their doors before the impossibility of conducting classes which might suffer fatal interruption at any hour.

The *sirena*, the grind of engines in the air, the dash for shelter, the explosions, and the *sirena* again became an abnormal, over-rapid rhythm of life for the ill-employed Bilbaino family. They invented funny words for the new elements in their existence: the planes, because of their noise, were called *tranvias* (tramways), and the biggest plane of all—the Junker 52—was called *pajarito*, which is the diminutive of bird. There were jokes about the *sirena* and the helter-skelter in plenty. But it was a bitter sardonic humour, showing how deep the terror had sunk in.

And so the alarm of the militia was condoned.

Did not civilians read in the papers every day of the terrible bombardments upon the front line, when (both in legend and in fact) far more bombs were dropped in an attack than the Nervion saw in a week; and was it not added that the *gudaris* had resisted bravely, but had at last been forced to fall back on second-line positions? It was perfectly comprehensible. When they saw the damage done at the river-side—and every bomb-hole represented to them a deliberate aim—the *gudaris* must have seemed heroes to resist at all. They never thought to ask whether the bombs at the front had hit *anything*, when at Bilbao they always hit *something*.

A spirit of sympathy was built up for the militia, where a spirit of resistance ought to have been consciously created. And the deep-rooted reasons for it were two—and they were twins born on the same democratic day. Because he was an out-and-out democrat, the Basque was essentially sympathetic and humane: he was sorry for the sufferings of individuals, and could not think of cauterising the wounds of the mass. As a democrat, too, he detested propaganda and the control of thought. Censorship, yes; but a department to control the civilian population, no. The idea of the suppression of certain unpleasant military details he understood, but that a new-fangled hortatory organisation should lay down the lines of each day's Press was intolerable and degrading.

Every night at eleven-thirty in Bilbao a young Commandant of the General Staff, called Arbex, would yawn, stick another cigarette into his amber holder, ruffle his kinky black hair a little more, run down the Presidency stairs and step into his car, which he would drive like one insane as far as the Ministry of the Interior. Arbex was an engaging lazy young man, a son of a General of Engineers, a member of the General Staff before Azaña's reforms, axed by Azaña, a visit to Hollywood, a harebrained film company, a glass of cognac and a rich wife left to her own devices. The rebellion found him in Madrid: to save his life, he signed on as an officer again when officers were sorely needed. He had run with the militia and General Asensio all the way back from Talavera to Madrid. He was not a coward, but he lived on alarms and cigarettes, and his day was a patchy affair, made of jerks of energy, sudden suspicions that he was overworked, tired, sleeping on sofas, shouting down telephones, and very great personal charm. He liked Biarritz: I am not so fond of it, but I was very fond of him. He passed over to Franco three days after the city of Bilbao fell. Arbex was not a man for a crisis.

This friend of mine is now stranded at the Ministry of the Interior, with the five morning papers of Bilbao before his still agile but sleepy eyes. Thank God, he says to himself every night, there aren't six: for the *C.N.T. del Norte* had been the biggest — — of the whole — — lot. He runs through the series with a blue pencil, clipping this and that out of the story of the War Correspondents, who—as this is Bilbao—have seen much more than any other indigenous journalist in Spain, and have the heart to say what they saw, with much adjectival employ of the concepts of bravery and terror. Arbex leaves that sort of literature in, and cuts only the passages which might prove of strategic value to the enemy. He yawns and stretches, says *"que conio,"* runs down the stairs, and steps on the gas for home.

Arbex was an artist: he could draft perfect maps. He really loved the cinema: in his indolent way he thought politically. But that such a man should have been the only control over the Bilbao Press is the measure of the extraordinary confidence which the Basques had in human nature.

Under their eyes, the *mystique* of the air was drugging their troops and rearguard; and the rearguard re-injected the troops with the opium in double portion. It was solely their natural peasant virtues; the undertow of resistance fathoms deep in them, formed by their timeless tradition as free men, that enabled the Basques to fight so long and, towards the end, with increasing bravery. Defeatism was always to be detected below their surface: it could have been cleared out of them, but no one ever tried to organise that simple service. They stand, therefore, as a warning to democracy—that some freedoms should not be tolerated in war.

XV

MOLA WAS EXPECTING NEW planes from Germany. On April 7th one, at least of them, arrived in Seville, with a blond crew direct from the Fatherland. The pilot was a young man of twenty-five—Hans Sobotka—and the plane was the fast medium bomber Dornier 17.

Dornier 17 is an attractive-looking plane, with a long slip of a body on whose account Germans call it the Flying Pencil. Its two engines develop a speed of 270 miles per hour, and Sobotka was therefore faster than the fighters at the service of the Government in Bilbao, or the insurgent escorts in Vitoria. He could carry 2,000 pounds weight of bombs over a distance of 1,500 miles.

In the July 28th number of the *Aeroplane*, it is written of the DO. 17 that "it is doing useful work in Spain." And it was no doubt in high hope of so doing that Hans Sobotka set out from Berlin on April 6th, at nine-twenty-two in the morning, with a pocketful of lire and pesetas from the German Air Ministry—generous souls!

That same day the Police President of Berlin had given him and his two companions (one of whom was a strange-looking boy; of him more hereafter) special passes for a journey "to and through Spain." *"Nach und durch Spanien,"* reads the interesting formula, which shows that there are aerodromes in Spain under German control.

Since the DO. 17 is a well-known new type of warplane, and a machine gun stuck out of a turret between the wings, it must have been clear to the Police President of Berlin that Sobotka and his vehicle were fit to receive special passports to Spain, in consideration of the Non-Intervention Agreement of August, 1936, and the Volunteer Agreement signed by Germany about a month before the young airman flew south. A good-looking fellow with a broad face, well greased hair, smallish eyes and thin lips, cleft chin, in a loose, rather overthick suit of heavy tweed, too broadly peppered for English taste.

April 18th was a Sunday in Bilbao, there was nothing doing at the front, but the rebel planes were a great bore, and kept our sirens constantly shrieking. They came at half-past nine, when one was shaving, and at ten, when one was pulling on one's shoes, and again during lunch. Curiosity on the latter occasion took me out into the Arenal in front of the Hotel Torrontegui. Little to be seen, but suddenly two two-engined bombers shot across a patch of blue between clouds. Then a confused noise of engines zooming and picking up again, and covering each other as it seemed; a loud explosion, a furious racing of engines, and suddenly across the hill of Begoña in front of me fell a line of bombs at top speed. Lightning, thunder, thunder, lightning, prolonged thunder and smoke.

There was a great mob of people under the old bridge. To the south a plane came out of the cloud smoking, and another pitching a little. The first was losing altitude fast; it crashed in flames on a hill west of the Nervion at Galdakano.

It carried Hans Sobotka and his two German friends.

This third raid of Sunday, April 18th, I learned, was carried out by three Dornier 17's and two Heinkel 111's. The fighting airport on the old polo ground at Lamiako, near the Nervion mountain, had been warned by the lookout posts in the south, and four Russian fighters with Spanish pilots had gone up. They were led by the young Felipe Del Rio. They had lain low in the cloudbanks where the valley tightened around old Bilbao; as the Germans came on through open space, they pounced on the three Dorniers from the rear, unseen. The machine gunners of all three were looking forward. It was hardly a fight.

In a minute the machine guns of Del Rio's Boeing had drilled the forward Dornier, in which Sobotka flew. Another of the Spaniards took the Dornier a little behind, to the right; a bullet must have penetrated to the pilot, for the plane began to lurch.

All three Germans turned; they could do that. The

two injured planes dropped all their bombs at the same
time, and from Sobotka's issued fire and smoke along the
fuselage, between two ends of the box-kite rudder, streaming
over the Flying Pencil like a narrow veil. Del Rio followed
him shooting, till he fell at Galdakano in a great fireball,
from which little men detached themselves too late. Then
he and the three other fighters tracked the second wounded
Dornier to a similar fate over Villareal.

All the girls of the city began to trek out to Galdakano,
where the wreckage was still burning among heather, and
the aerodrome mechanics followed in heavy lorries, while
Pablovitch the Russian sharpened his pencil to take down
some German notes.

We found that the Dornier had a crew of three. Sobotka
and two other of his people. Sobotka and one of the
unknown carried German passes which marked their
departure from Rome on April 5th. The third had no
papers, but was obviously German.

Sobotka lay on the ground on his back, half carbonised,
stiffly curved upwards along the spine. Part of his intes-
tines which were fried into a good imitation of sausages,
hung out of his rather corpulent body. His two arms were
held in dead stylised terror across his face, as he must
have raised them in the last agony before he hit the hillside.
And his face—well, it looked less handsome than the
photograph.

The two other Germans had fallen into the Nervion.
They had tried to jump, but the parachutes had no time
to open, and they hit the water hard, and died of shock.
One was dull enough, but the other caused the Basques
to wonder.

The Basques were not a bit like that. It was new to
them. They turned the tall blond body over. The face
was bruised, but even so it struck them as extraordinary.
For the eyebrows were plucked, and the mouth was painted
red; not with blood, which passed out of the
corner of it.

They looked at the hands, which were white and fine;
at the nails, which were prettily manicured and enamelled,
and drawn to points. Very odd.

The simple Basques put the body rather confusedly into
a car and sent it to the Sanidad Militar. Fancy the Germans

using women war pilots they thought; what will they be up to next.

In Bilbao, however, at the Sanidad Militar, were doctors and men of the world. They undressed the corpse and scrutinised it more closely. Its hair had been plucked from under the armpits, and it wore feminine pink silk underwear. But it passed, it just scraped past the standards of virility: and they jotted it down in their case books as one of the queerer incidents of the Civil War.

As the July 28th number of *The Aeroplane* had said, the Dornier 17 was doing useful work in Spain.

The balance of the three-minute bombardment was 67 dead and 110 wounded. A ribbon of destruction stretched taut over the Old Town and Begoña, from the shattered quay on the riverside where the women sold anchovies.

Blocks of cheap flats were torn open and exposed to the street like untidy bookshelves kept by a blind man, who pushes his volumes back sideways and upside down. The streets in this poorer part of Bilbao were a sea of glass, on which lay wrecked trams and cars.

Through the streets of Solocoeche and Iturribide, San Francisco and Las Cortes, the Incarnacion and Autonomia lay the plumed disaster. Bombs penetrated to underground lavatories, to railway tunnels, and to refuges marked secure by the Department of Passive Defence.

One such lay beneath the rubber and shoe factory of Señor Cotorruelo, which caught fire. Soon the stone streets under the grey sky, on the tip-tilted hillside of Bilbao, were running with water. The Basque motorised police cordoned off the factory while for four hours the whole fire brigade of the city worked upon the flames. Between four and five they were able to start digging under the dripping machinery and sodden floors for the people imprisoned below. They worked all that evening; but the people were all dead, crushed, suffocated, drowned. Their pulpy bodies came up slowly. First a small child, of about five years; then a youngish man; then a pregnant woman. A whole family of the past and future wiped out by one bomb. Their hair lay wet and straggly over their bruised faces, hung in damp black slabs of gauntness as they were carried away.

On the woman they tried artificial respiration, why I knew not; she was long dead. But the Red Cross orderlies who stood there in their white overalls with bottles of medicine had to do something, with the firemen and police working so hard.

The grave gave up its dead through the machinery and the smelling rubber all night to the drip of water from the thin ragged factory walls and the light of street flares. The pink silk underwear of the Aryan who helped to set this bizarre scene was hung on exhibition in the Basque Department of Defence.

* * * * * *

A few days later the Heinkel 111's came again and took their revenge. Del Rio misjudged their speed and was shot down clean on the shore, near the Nervion mouth. Seven planes to his machine gun was not a bad record for a Spaniard of twenty-one years. He was given a public funeral and banner headlines signalled his obituary in the Bilbao Press.

His death broke the morale of the Bilbao aviators for good. The three fighting planes had done their work well against Junker 52 and Heinkel 51, and they were good enough for the Fiat fighters too. But the new two-engined bombers that now appeared on the Northern front out-classed them; even if they had not, what were three against so many?

Bilbao now awaited the fulfilment of the promise of Cisneros. They were told that a force of aviators would be coming any day from Catalonia. But in the Presidency they were already cynical. When I dined with the War Department I found that Unceta, the doctor in charge of Sanidad Militar, had invented a new song, which he was strumming on the piano.

Dicen que van a venir que van a venir los aeroplanos,
Mataremos al Fascismo con los denies y los manos,
Dicen que van a venir que van a venir los aeroplanos,
Veneran veneran pero nunca llegaran,
Quando el Fascista tira la bomba, tira la bomba, tira la bomba, (with
   expression)
Quando el Fascista tira la bomba, tira la bomba y (with much
   hopefulness) *no explota.*

(Translated.)
They say the planes are coming, meanwhile
We'll kill Fascism with our teeth and hands,
They say they are coming.
They're coming, they're coming, but they will never get here,
When the Fascist drops his bomb, his bomb
And it doesn't go off.

This became our theme song and could raise a laugh in any hot corner. I must admit that its risible potentialities rather surprise me now; but I suppose any effort to make light of one's condition when it is known to be grave, ranks as humour in war time.

After singing it, Unceta, who was unmistakably a wag, made a speech in mock German, and with it many striking Hitlerian gestures welcoming his German aviators to Bilbao on behalf of the Basque Government, and offering them the freedom of the air over the city.

We learnt this song, which after all was simple enough, at top speed, and sang it at the end of every meal. One's memory fondles it still. It was an accurate prophecy.

XVI

UNTIL APRIL 6TH, THE DAY on which *Beagle* took me back to Bilbao, Franco's navy on the North Coast of Spain had always given the right of way to British cargoes. But I remember how we suddenly leapt into speed that day, and how the crew stopped spitting and polishing the little bronze beagles that decorated the destroyer and the decks were clearing for action and the torpedoes put their warheads on as we entered Bermeo bay. The radio had spoken.

It was *Brazen* who was talking, and she said that the British steamer *Thorpehall* was held up by warships between Santander and Bilbao. *Blanche* and *Brazen* were going to her assistance, and they wanted *Beagle* to come too. Everybody was somewhat excited in our destroyer, and there were happy whispers forward of "dirty work."

Stevenson, the British Consul in Bilbao, was picked up at Bermeo as interpreter-in-chief, and a megaphone thrust into his hands for purposes of parliament. Off dashed *Beagle*, to find indeed a lively huddle on the high seas. There, five miles from the shore, lay *Thorpehall*, threatened by the cruiser *Almirante Cervera* and the armed trawler *Galerna*, with the German pocket battleship *Admiral Graf Spee* nosing around rather parkerly in the middle distance. Up from the west there raced *Blanche* and *Brazen*, line ahead and their decks cleared for action and signalling like mad to lay off British shipping, which they said they would defend. This was rather a brave thing to do, for *Almirante Cervera* could have polished off *Blanche* and *Brazen* easily. But now one of the Admirals had seen enough; *Almirante*, forgive me, *Admiral Graf Spee*, said, "Thank you" and horizonwarded, and the rest of the foreign cast began to quit when dear old Stevenson was seen clinging to the rail and bawling quite unlike a consul, funnelwise, that it was time to end the play. It was clear that the insurgent fleet had orders not to quarrel with the Royal Navy. *Thorpehall* was allowed to pass, and brought in a cargo of food that afternoon.

That was all that the British public heard about it until a special Cabinet met at 10, Downing Street on the night of Sunday, April 11th, and after deliberating for two hours decided to keep British ships out of Bilbao; in other words, to hand the city over to Franco, for only ships protected on the high seas were capable of making her territorial waters; and the only other power besides Britain able to protect her shipping was France, who was bound to follow British policy in all matters. The fate of Bilbao was sealed.

She had, as before, supplies for three weeks to a month. After that it would be chickpeas and lunacy. The Basque Government faced the biggest crisis since their constitution, and began to think out telegrams for British Members of Parliament as a hopeless last resort.

News of the British Cabinet's decision was not allowed to enter the papers of Bilbao, which became a raw mass of scratches and botchings. If the people had known, with the German planes overhead every day, order would have been swept into the river and the British Consulate with it.

* * * * * *

The history of the blockade thus instituted was only divulged afterwards, and that in tantalising pieces. Some of which, such as certain material which came into my hands, was never published for it was too revealing.

Sometimes Sir Samuel Hoare dropped a clue, sometimes it was Sir John Simon, and the Special Correspondent of *The Times* at St. Jean de Luz was able to lever a certain portion of the truth out of the official British world around him.

One by one, the reasons why the Cabinet decided to keep British ships out of Bilbao were these.

The same day as the *Thorpehall* was stopped, the commander of the insurgent fleet announced that no supplies would in future be allowed to go into Bilbao or other Government ports westward to the Asturias (*Times*). This threat was accepted in all seriousness; it was forgotten that the insurgent fleet to cover this coast of two hundred miles consisted only of a slow old rusty-sided battleship and a cruiser. With them went a small destroyer and an armed trawler which could never afford to travel without heavier escort: the Government had two faster destroyers prepared to snap them up.

It would be wrong to find fault with the commander of the destroyer flotilla at St. Jean de Luz for all that he did. He did not have a superiority of force on the north coast of Spain, and to avoid incidents he was right to re-establish such a situation by asking for heavier guns. H.M.S. *Hood*, flagship of Vice-Admiral G. Blake, was therefore sent to St. Jean de Luz, leaving Gibraltar at nine o'clock on Saturday night, April 10th.

But the commander of the flotilla did make a grave mistake. On April 6th he reported that in his view Franco's blockade was effective (Hoare, April 20th). This was not true; and later events proved how ill-founded an opinion it was.

The Admiralty reported that Bilbao harbour was mined (Simon, April 14th). Mr. Baldwin, though he never stated his source, even went so far as to allege that it had been mined by both sides within territorial waters, though an explanation of the reasons why the Basques had mined waters well within the range of their shore batteries, into which insurgent vessels had never intruded, was not vouchsafed. Indeed, it could not be; for it was not true, and it was later proved not to be true, that there were mines within or indeed without Bilbao territorial waters, laid by either side. But the mining yarn went on. On April 21st, Sir Samuel Hoare repeated it. "In quite recent days we have received further information," he said, "that mine-laying is still going on by General Franco (*sic*). There is no doubt that General Franco has mined there." This again was untrue. It is not astonishing, it is in the nature of things that the mine myth should have lived so long for the Royal Navy never was in position to get information about Bilbao territorial waters. For months it had not come within five miles of the Punta de Galea, which formed their eastern limit.

On the same day, the sadly misinformed First Lord of

the Admiralty, answering an interruption of Mr. Noel Baker, declared that insurgent warships could enter Bilbao territorial waters. His information, he said, did not bear out the information given to the House by another Labour member, that the fortifications and the guns of Bilbao were capable of keeping the insurgent warships outside territorial waters. His information was that insurgent ships had been *frequently* within the three-mile limit, that they had not been fired on by the shore guns, and that they had themselves fired on the shore fortifications.

All of this was untrue; indeed, it must be well nigh impossible, reading the reports of Parliamentary debates, to find another passage so tightly packed with inaccuracy. Insurgent warships could not and never did enter the territorial waters of Bilbao; later, the trawler *Galerna* once stood upon the limit to fire across an English merchantman's bows; but she received such a sprinkling of 6-inch shells from the shore that she turned round for home, never venturing forward again. The guns of Bilbao proved themselves perfectly capable of keeping insurgent ships more than three miles away: the preferred distance of these was nearer eleven. Insurgent warships had never been within the three-mile limit; they had been fired upon, and hit by the shore guns much farther out, as in the *Canarias* episode. That makes four gross inaccuracies. One tires of counting. But again, there is nothing astonishing in them. Neither the Royal Navy nor the British Consul had ever seen the guns of Bilbao, or possessed any information about them whatsoever. They had not even seen half the batteries in action; they knew neither their calibre, nor their number, nor, except the Punta de Galea, their emplacement.

Thus the Government case rested upon two major misstatements of the truth, that there were mines in Bilbao territorial waters, and that this three-mile stretch could not be protected by Bilbao coastal batteries.

* * * * * *

What was the truth?

To my certain knowledge, for I saw the guns, the mouth of the Nervion was defended by five batteries of three pieces each, of which three batteries were Vickers 6-inch (one with

SOBOTKA'S BOMBARDMENT: FIGHTING THE SHOE FACTORY FIRE, BILBAO, APRIL 18TH, 1937.

SOBOTKA'S BOMBARDMENT: THE DEAD CHILD OF THE FAMILY.

naval mountings) and two 4-inch. The range of the big
guns was over twenty-three kilometres, and they were
served by intelligent crews trained by one of the best
artillery officers in Spain, Guerrika-Echevarria. So much
for the guns; they could hold enemy ships outside territorial
waters, where, according to the rules which the British
Government laid down, it would have been improper for
the insurgents to shoot on British shipping.

Mines were laid at Bilbao by the insurgents three times,
by the Basques never. The first batch, in September,
1936; were cleared on November 1st. The second, on
January 16th, 1937 I were cleared on March 15th. The
third were laid later on May 1st, on a black-browed night;
searchlights discovered the *Jupiter* at work, and though the
España came to her aid the shore batteries drove both off.
Next morning a wide passage was swept clear, and the
whole harbour mouth was free in five days. So when
Mr. Baldwin and Sir John Simon and Sir Samuel Hoare
made their statements about mines, there were no mines
in Bilbao territorial waters at all; in the period March 15th,
when the Basques found the last (empty) mine of the
January brood, to May 1st, during which all the talking was
done in Parliament, the entry to Bilbao was completely
clear.

These facts, which were known to me at the time, were
later confirmed by the laborious researches of Commander
H. Pursey, R.N. (retired), who came out to Bilbao in May
to inquire into the operation of the Non-Intervention
Agreement. Amongst other sources, Commander Pursey
was able to use the log-book of the man who laid the mines
before Bilbao, which was washed up with a mass of other
material from the mined battleship *España*. It must have
come as a peculiar sensation, if not a jolt, for this gentleman
to realise, as the big ship settled by the stern off Santander
on April 30th, that here was the only sizeable victim of his
art to date. He was an inveterate diarist, and all his
dates and figures coincided with what the Basque Marine
Department and the skippers of their minesweepers had
told me, and with what Pursey himself had established.

Why was Bilbao so little and so inefficiently mined?
First, because the Auxiliary Marine of Euzkadi, being
wholly in Basque hands, was admirably organised, routined

and active. Sixteen to twenty-four sweepers worked territorial waters and at least a mile beyond every day. On moonlit nights three, on dark six, patrol motor-boats covered the three-mile limit, aided by searchlights and studied obsequiously by the shore batteries. Secondly, because of the haphazard mine-laying methods of the *Jupiter*, and because the mines that were laid were either veterans or dummies. Both in January and May the mines were laid with supreme incapacity; a third were too deep, a third were too shallow and broke adrift, in which condition they were harmless. And in January, when the Basque found in the end that eighty-five mines had been laid, thirty-seven proved to be impotent, containing no explosive. That was the blockade of Bilbao.

It was strange, therefore, to read in Bilbao the arguments of Mr. Eden and Sir Samuel Hoare that there must be mines in Bilbao territorial waters if they were swept every day; for every sailor knows, and Sir Samuel at least should have found plenty at the Admiralty to inform him, that in time of war, sweeping, whether there are mines or not, is a daily routine of all navies, including that which Sir Samuel administered. And it was more than strange—it left one a little ashamed of the honesty of the House of Commons—to read that both Sir John Simon and Sir Samuel Hoare stated, in a context which was understood to refer to the present situation in Bilbao, that two Basque minesweepers had been blown up at their work; for one knew that this event took place in January, three months before the British Government began to worry about Bilbao, and that it had been reported in Consular correspondence at that, its correct date.

Such were the false and such the true premises of the political problem which we must consider. But meanwhile, how did the problem present itself after the commander of the flotilla at St. Jean de Luz had given the Admiralty inaccurate information on April 6th?

* * * * * *

As a temporary measure before the arrival of *Hood*, which should restore the balance of power in the north of Spain, all British merchant ships within a hundred miles of northern Spanish ports were ordered by the Navy to proceed to St. Jean de Luz and there await further instructions. Six had entered the little harbour by Friday morning, April 9, and were joined by the British flotilla (*Times*).

This concentration, according to the same source, caused the local agents of General Franco to ponder. He was informed that a convoy was assembling for Bilbao, and immediately sent a message to the British Ambassador, Sir Henry Chilton, at Hendaye, through his military governor at Irun, across the International Bridge—the very Comandante Troncoso himself, at that time a teller of fairly tales but later a stealer of submarines and now a penitent in French prisons.

Franco, talking through his loud mouthpiece, the combative Troncoso, declared that he was determined that the blockade of Bilbao should be complete and effective; that he regarded the denial of foodstuffs to that and other Government ports as even more important than the denial of war material; and that he would resist any attempt to break the blockade by force, whatever might be the consequences (*Times*). This message was received in London on Saturday, April 10th (Eden, April 19th). Referring presumably to the same message, Mr. Eden divulged in the Commons on April 19th that in a note dated April 9th the insurgent authorities informed Sir Henry Chilton that mining would be intensified between Cape Vidios and Cape Machichaco—i.e. across the territorial waters of Bilbao.

It is interesting to see in passing that this, pressed out of Mr. Eden by a question of the Socialist, Mr. A. Henderson, was the first reference on the part of a member of the Government to a menacing message received from General Franco just before the Cabinet meeting which decided on a policy with regard to Bilbao. Hitherto when they had described the course of events leading up to this decision (e.g. Simon, April 14th), they had omitted to mention this obviously important element; and even now the facts were squeezed out rather slowly, for it was only towards the end of question time on April 19th that Mr. Eden admitted, to a direct query of Sir Archibald Sinclair, the visit of Troncoso with his menace to British ships on April 9th. The Foreign Secretary resented insinuations on the point. He said that we had yielded to facts, not to threats. Clearly the cat was jumping about not a little in the bag, and would soon be tearing a way to the outer world.

It was next day, indeed, that its horrid little head appeared, in an unguarded answer of Sir Samuel Hoare. Said Mr. Attlee, with unaffected innocence: "Where does our Ambassador get his information if he is at Hendaye?" to which Sir Samuel replied that there was only a bridge between the Ambassador and Spain.

The joke clearly being that the bridge led to insurgent territory only and to our newly-found friend Troncoso. But it was rather an esoteric joke, and the Opposition did not get there yet.

* * * * * *

To put it very briefly, the effect of Troncoso's threat was as follows: On Friday, April 9th, according to Sir John Simon on April 14th, the British Government decided to inform British ships of its views, which were transmitted in a letter by the commander of *Blanche*. The letter read: "You are not to leave St. Jean de Luz for any port in the hands of the Spanish Government on the north of Spain *until further orders*. This order will be confirmed in due course by the Board of Trade through the British Consul." And on Saturday, April 10th, the Board of Trade came through in a message rather more diplomatically framed: "Inform British ships now in St. Jean de Luz that British Government desire them not to enter Basque ports *for the time being* on account of the dangerous situation there, and to wait at St. Jean de Luz *for further communications*."

Troncoso's threat was presented in London on the morning of April 10th. A special Cabinet meeting was called for April 11th, and it came to the following decision: the very phrasing of its first sentence shows that it was framed in an atmosphere of menace.

"His Majesty's Government," it read, "cannot recognise or concede belligerent rights and they cannot tolerate any interference with British shipping at sea. They are, however, warning British shipping that in view of conditions at present prevailing in the neighbourhood of Bilbao they should not, for practical reasons, and in view of risks against which it is at present impossible to protect them, go into that area so long as these conditions prevail."

In other words, on the presentation of no new facts but the threat of Comandante Troncoso, the provisional measure of mustering the ships at St. Jean de Luz to await further orders had hardened into a policy of preventing their entry into Bilbao at all. It is amusing to note that before this policy was in operation the source of news was Troncoso only, for the British Consul at Bilbao was not asked for his views at all until after the decision was taken, and the storm was gathering in Parliament. He could at least have sent the information of Eguia (who knew a considerable amount about mines, and had until policy intervened been regarded as the Royal Navy's authority upon them for Bilbao) against the information of Troncoso. But he was not asked to do so; I suppose that the International Bridge between Hendaye and Irun was a shorter walk.

More, it was in the testing of Basque information that the Government actually broke their word to the House. For on April! Mr. Lloyd George asked whether President Aguirre's message about the absence of mines in Bilbao territorial waters and the power of his batteries had been communicated to the Admiral in H.M.S. *Hood*, and whether he had been asked for his opinion on the statement made. Mr. Eden answered that if the Admiral was not in possession of it the information would certainly be given to him. But on April 19th, when Lieutenant-Commander Fletcher inquired whether *Hood* had been instructed to verify the declaration of the Basque Government, Sir Samuel Hoare replied that the answer was in the negative.

Briefly, Troncoso's views are heard and acted upon; but Aguirre's are not examined even when the Foreign Secretary of Great Britain has promised that they will be.

* * * * * *

Well, here we are with Bilbao beginning to starve again and a new kind of blockade established about her by the Royal Navy in French territorial waters, while at times

España and *Almirante Cervera* condescend to take a hand,
though they are always careful enough to keep over ten
miles from the shore when they pass in front of the batteries
of Bilbao. Gradually the news is creeping into the Basque
press, and the author of this book, as a representative
Englishman, undergoes a period of unpopularity, a diet
of chickpeas being proposed for him. He, however, takes
upon his shoulders the mantle of prophecy, and tells the
Basques in a patriotic flush that in England the truth
usually wins: this blockade will not last.

At St. Jean de Luz a great time is being had by one and
all; funny stories about Potato Jones break every day,
and the potatoes themselves are bursting into flower for
the occasion. At Bilbao, behind powerful guns and mine-
less waters, people are eating daily the value of forty centimos,
which is twopence. On April 12th Aldasoro publishes a
list for the first distribution of food for twelve days, and
he says that it will have to last a fortnight. Each person
is allotted a pound of soup paste, two pounds of rice, half
a pound of sugar, a pound of chickpeas and a little less
than half a pound of cabbage. But on April 15th, as people
are getting anxious, Aldasoro, who likes a finesse, decides
to gamble against the blockade: he announces that the
next issue will be April 20th, quite soon. I am more
popular among the neighbours.

In the House of Commons the storm is rising higher and
higher; it is beginning to resemble the Bay of Biscay.
One roller after another, and much official queasiness.
The threatening wave of question after question is inter-
spersed by the yawning, weary and bathetic trough of
answer after answer. And, forgive me if I must mix my
metaphors, a large box of red herrings is unloaded by the
back-benchers on the Government foreshore. There it is,
a jazz design, Low at his lowest; Sir John Simon craning
his neck rather painfully over one bulwark; Sir Samuel
Hoare leaning unhappily over the wheel and trying to
eradicate error by studying between waves a little book
on the practice of sweeping; the Foreign Secretary a trifle
paler in the bows, clinging to his hat and looking for mines,
while all the time the ship of State lurches most horribly
beneath them. The herrings are dragged hither and yon,
but even that will not still the raging of the waters or give

the old ship a settled course. Gloomily, Sir Samuel puts back into the hated port of Bilbao.

I have collected here six herrings from back-benchers, and two from the First Lord of the Admiralty himself. The herrings are of different sizes, and one at least of them is very old and worn and has been dragged around many times before. But let them issue forth in chronological order, as one by one they were exposed upon the foreshore.

1. On April 12th Mr. Duncan Sandys asked, apropos of Bilbao, whether the policy of denying belligerent rights to the combatants would not create an international precedent which might prejudice our rights on some future occasion. This peculiar phrase, if logically analysed, suggests preparations for a civil war in England, which is certainly a far cry from the situation at Bilbao. As a herring it gained very little support and was soon returned to store.

2. On April 14th Mr. Winston Churchill said that food was as much a part of the war-making capacity of a country as anything else, the suggestion being that on high moral grounds it ought to be kept out of Bilbao. An inflated herring this, which was received with Opposition cries of "Oh!" and burst.

3. The same day Mr. Harold Nicolson, who might be expected to offer rather a resourceful fish, declared that "to provide one side with the elements of defence and to deprive the other side of what military advantage it might obtain by a campaign of starvation would be definite intervention." I cannot help thinking that when Mr. Nicolson had pulled the little thing past the Opposition front bench he must have noticed that it only had one eye. For by the same argument, to deprive one side of the elements of defence and to provide the other with what military advantage it might obtain by a campaign of starvation would equally be intervention; and that was what the Government was doing. Drop that fish. It smells of something. Can it be partiality?

4. On April 14th also came the king of red herrings. It has for some five years been a common British practice, whenever it is proposed to do something, however trivial,

to say that no, one should not take the risk, because something is part of a Wider Problem, and Europe is a Powder
Magazine and that means War. This is the herring referred to in a previous paragraph: it is old, as I have said,
and worn with constant traffic, and through the holes in
its person one can see how thoroughly filleted it is. At
times, indeed, it seems to have no backbone at all. It was
Mr. Emrys-Evans who brought it out of the box. The
Spanish problem, he said, was only part of a much larger
one, and showed itself as a minor problem beside that of
Germany and Central Europe. The danger of an attack
on Czechoslovakia would be increased by intervention in
Spain and diminished if we followed a policy of non-
intervention. The danger . . . filleted people are expected to shiver.

5. April 14th, which was the date of the first big debate
on Bilbao in the House, seems to have been a very fair
day, for it encouraged the herrings to come out and sun
themselves in large numbers. Mr. Crossley said that he
supported the people who were standing for the right of
freedom of religion and the rights of property, but he
believed in the most rigid non-intervention. This was
perhaps the most confusing fish that ever took the floor.
For on the face of it one would have said, knowing Spain,
that Mr. Crossley was referring to Bilbao, which was the
only part of the Peninsula where real religious freedom
existed; but no, Mr. Crossley referred to General Franco's
territory where professing atheists were bumped off, and
by a concession which can only be described as noble
Mr. Crossley was foregoing his right to support General
Franco. A versatile herring this: a slippery Jim.

6. On April 20th Mr. Bernays debunked Potato Jones.
He was no philanthropist, he said; he was a sailor of
fortune. He stood to make as much as £2,000 if he was
successful. Why should the British Navy be exposed to
unjustifiable risks in order that Potato Jones should reap
rich profits? To which the answer is quite simple: that
the duty of the Royal Navy, the reason why its officers
and men are paid and its ships built out of taxpayers'
money, is to protect British commerce on the high seas;
and the profit made by the skipper of a British ship has
as much to do with the question as Mr. Bernays' speech

had to do with Bilbao. And the answer can be embellished: there were no risks at all for the Royal Navy, unjustifiable or not. Nothing was sunk or hit: no warship, no merchantman. The whole policy with regard to Bilbao was beginning to smell of muddle and the suppression of truth, and by April 20th support for it was growing weak indeed.

After all, the only point to be established now was the safety of Bilbao territorial waters, which had carefully been faked unsafe since the beginning of April. If British ships could pass them safely, either way, then the blockade was fantasy, and in the week preceding this debate of April 20th four British ships sailed out of the port of Bilbao without molestation or injury, including the s.s. *Olavus*, whom we shall have occasion to mention later. Soon the Government would be accused of bad faith, and they knew it.

Yet one of the last of the herring-sellers was Sir Samuel Hoare himself. For on two separate occasions on April 20th he spoke of "pushing ships into Bilbao," as if any help were asked of his navy but that which was promised from the first by Cabinet policy—protection outside the three-mile limit. And, as the event proved and the Basques had said all along, no more help was needed.

And finally, when naval information on his and Mr. Eden's admission had so utterly broken down—for he had himself informed the House that the Navy had not been within Basque territorial waters for two months, and Mr. Eden had said that naturally the only other source, the Consul in Bilbao, could not give an opinion on naval matters—Sir Samuel brought out the queerest piece of evidence of the whole long controversy. To stun the House, he read a telegram from the master of the *Olavus*, sent on April 19th to his shipping company: "At day-light proceeded into harbour," it read. "Passed un-knowingly through mine area. Saw one mine and kept clear. . . ."

Now, as Mr. Attlee pointed out, this could not be claimed in justification of the Government decision, for it had only come to their notice nine days after the decision was made. But the researches of Commander Pursey in Bilbao went even deeper. He found that the *Olavus* entered Bilbao on April 8th; that the master of the *Olavus* made no report to the captain of the port or the office of the Director-General of Mercantile Marine, as it was his duty to do if he had sighted any object dangerous to shipping; that he saw his agent on numerous occasions, but that his agent said he did not mention anything about the mine or mine-field; and that Joseph Ducable, an old-established ship-chandler and British subject who provisioned the *Olavus*, saw a great deal of the master, who never mentioned mine or mine-field to him either. Indeed, it was a strange mine, which only needed to be reported eleven days after it had been shaved.

And all this while, when Government arguments grew shallower and shallower, the food-ships had to wait at St. Jean de Luz. Potato Jones had sailed into the blue. But the rest knew very well that Bilbao waters were clean and safe to any ship that could claim protection on the high seas. Even Sir Samuel Hoare had to climb down about the efficacy of the Basque guns, for when he was pressed to give chapter and verse for naval information on the point, he made the following answer: "On April 19th I was informed that the commanding officers . . . have frequently observed insurgent warships *within the range of the Bilbao batteries.*" Which was twenty-three kilometres. In other words, when on April 21st Sir Samuel said that insurgent warships had frequently been within the three-mile limit, he had no evidence for the statement. He meant twenty-three kilometres, which is quite a big difference.

The food-ships were becoming restive; the Opposition in the Commons were jubilant; the Basques were hungry; myself more weird and prophetic. I said that the truth was bound to win.

Eguia had a talk with me. He showed me the request sent to a certain ship at St. Jean de Luz, that it should arrive in daylight on April 20th. The shore batteries would then be more useful than at night; it was the 19th—would I be awake at 6 a.m.?

* * * * * *

Seven Seas Spray, captained by Mr. W. H. Roberts of Penarth, South Wales, and adorned by his twenty-year-old daughter Fifi, who was suitably dressed in light blue polo sweater and grey flannel slacks, made harbour at Bilbao at

nine o'clock in the morning of April 20th and docked
without any incident more alarming than the public
enthusiasm. Another lady was also to be seen on deck,
a stouter blonde: Mrs. B. M. Docker, of Swansea, wife
of the chief engineer had come to look after him during
the festivities. *Seven Seas Spray* carried a general cargo of
3,600 tons from Valencia, including salt, wine, olive oil,
hams, honey, flour, beans and peas. Her gallant, somewhat inexpressive master with his boyish little daughter,
Mrs. Docker, six British officers and cheerful coloured crew
were to be for many days the heroes of the city and fêted
from pillar to post.

Spray belonged to the Veronica Steamship Company,
directed by Mr. Thomas Blazquez McEwen, of Edinburgh
and Spain, and engaged since December, 1936, in the
coastal trade between Spanish Government ports. With
her owner aboard, and the two ladies out to see a bit of
fun, the ship left St. Jean de Luz suddenly at 10 p.m. on
April 19th. Great was the display of nerves upon the
official shore, from which a semaphore palpitated frantic-
ally, insisting that she should stop; but Captain Roberts,
who had grown white hair in the traditions of British
seamanship, turned the blind eye. "A good sailor," he
explained to me in deepest confidence, "doesn't look
astern."

The ship did not use her steering lights, and the voyage
until six-thirty in the morning was entirely peaceful and
undisturbed. Fifi and Mrs. Docker slept like two tops,
and so did most of the crew except Fifi's father, who paced
the bridge looking in an automatic and sailorly manner for
mischief, of whose material proximity he felt bound to
admit the most unqualified doubt. "Do sea-serpents
really exist?" he said to himself, as *Seven Seas Spray* made
forward past Cape Machichaco.

It was here that a shape loomed ahead, but it was not a
sea-serpent; it was a British destroyer. In international
code she signalled "Where bound?" and the shameless
answer flew back, "Bilbao." The conversation changed
to the more intimate whisper of semaphore, "Enter at
your own risk"; Captain Roberts made a very good
reply, "I accept full responsibility." Naval reserve broke
down at it; as the destroyer moved off she patted him on

the back with a parting "Good luck." "Thanks," said Captain Roberts, as she turned the Cape for the last stretch before Bilbao territorial waters.

In the great port everything was ready for him. Coastal batteries were manned and a small flotilla consisting of the Government destroyers *Ciscar* and *Jose Luis Diez*, with two armed Basque trawlers, sailed out to greet him. Like playful porpoises, as sleek as Panope and all her sisters, they threaded their way about the harbour entrance and territorial waters to show how free these were of mines; smoky hollows between the rollers and stout little bodies of black on their crest showed where the Basque fishing fleet were plying their industry unmolested, miles out in the Bay. The insurgent warships *España* and *Almirante Cervera* were reported fourteen miles off the coast to the westward, but nobody seemed to care, while *Spray* passed the mole at eight-thirty on a free course without asking for a pilot.

We joined her in a launch, as the armed trawlers passed to their moorings upriver. We ran up the rope ladder and jumped over casks, well tarred and heavy, until we reached the ladder to the bridge. The first man we met was the mate, who said "Danger?" in a most manly and sarcastic voice. "It was as safe as going to the bank. We could have done it blindfold." A tall, smooth-haired, dark, clean-shaven gentleman, in a smooth dark suit, with a long Spanish face and a diplomatic manner, looked down at us from the rails above; he impeccably held a cigarette. He was most distinguished and grave; he was diagnosed infallibly to be the owner. And he took us along to see Captain Roberts and his daughter Fifi, who settled us with powerful handshakes, and to drink the first decent whisky that we had tasted for three weeks. We waited for the river-pilot. The mate popped his head in: "Congratulations," we said, in our most formal manner, waving empty glasses for more. He grinned at full stretch, and answered more breezily, "Aye, we're the boys."

Nine Russian chaser planes, the Bilbao force supplemented by a flight from Santander, were already performing acrobatics over the river, and as we stepped forward they dipped to welcome us, very low. Del Rio led them; this was the last time that I saw his young face, smiling. The

Captain, middle height, white hair and fresh-coloured cheeks, took his position on the bridge; he stood very erect in a uniform carefully brushed, with a smart white cover to his cap. W. H. Roberts was ship-shape, a real master; we stood beside him trying hard not to let the ship down. And what a sight! Eguia's story was out, and all the town seemed to know it. Mile after mile of the Nervion trough, the grey quays and waterside, was crammed with people. There were tens of thousands of them watching the English ship, with the Red ensign that they knew so well in times of peace trailing at the stern, over green river. These were the bombable districts, where the refugee women and children of Guipuzcoa and the Asturias were quartered by the Department of Assistencia Social. They cheered and shrieked, and ran out of houses to stand on waste blocks of stone and cement at the river's edge. It was not roses, but old handkerchiefs, twice-read papers and thousands of shreds of washing all the way, shaken from drab and grimy windows. Many raised the clenched fist, and the Captain and Fifi answered in our more English fashion. Yes, the Captain was a good figure as he stood at his bridge as we went upriver. The little clubs of women and children who even now were making a practice of spending all day at the air raid shelters, came out of their caves and yelled. One could hear from the quays cries of *Viva los marineros ingleses* and *Viva la libertad*; but the women were rather more carnal, and shouted *Vino y aceite*, wine and oil! So sharp was the lack of all things in Bilbao; there was nothing to cook with. Above it all, there came the guttural shout of a Basque sailor, in English, *well done*. The militia turned out of their barracks to salute the ship which had broken the paper blockade, and it was a great moment for the captain when he could take his megaphone at last, as we came among the high houses of Bilbao city, and the ship slowed down to the right-hand dock, and he called, with a quiet voice, *"Make her fast where she is now, Mister Bo'sun."* What a comfortable journey; and the Basques had begun to believe that an English sailor would never take the risk.

Fifi and Mrs. Docker stepped ashore to see if they could do some shopping.

* * * * * *

It was now clear to the world that Bilbao's minefields had been, to say the least, undersown and overwritten. Though Sir Samuel Hoare maintained an unmistakable belief in their existence when he addressed the House of Commons that afternoon, the Navy and the merchant skippers were entering upon a period of scepticism as advanced as Fifi's. It was also clear that a night journey would probably beat a blockade maintained by only two warships at a time. All that had to be proved now was the efficiency of the coastal batteries.

British policy was changed by executive order. British ship-owners, who were beginning to be alarmed by the mounting claims of the Basques for non-delivery of cargo, were told that the Government could not advise them that ships were able to enter Bilbao. In any event protection, if asked for, would be given to ships on the high seas. Whereas ships before this date were definitely warned against going into the Bilbao area while dangerous conditions prevailed, they were now only informed that the Government could not advise them that the entry was free.

The Royal Navy now, with its usual generosity when it recognises an error, laid ingenious plans with the British ships remaining in St. Jean de Luz to conduct them safely to the Bilbao three-mile limit. *Hamsterley, Macgregor* and *Stanbrook* left St. Jean de Luz in complete darkness before midnight on April 21st; and at the same time H.M.S. *Hood* was seen to turn for the open sea, a constellation of lights that grew smaller and more spent till the horizon extinguished it.

Morning broke with a mist lying off the Vizcayan coast, in the slipaway of the clouds from highlands above the sea. *Macgregor* led, *Hamsterley* and *Stanbrook* followed under this cover. But it cleared before they reached the sea at the mouth of the Nervion.

This time, Franco knew; his ironclads were there. The three British foodships were warned by the destroyer *Firedrake* when they were over ten miles off Punta de Galea. The *Almirante Cervera* and the trawler *Galerna* were waiting for them, the former well out to sea, but the little ship not far from the three-mile limit. And there, too, was *Hood*, the finest fighting craft in the world.

Macgregor, still outside territorial waters, was ordered by *Almirante Cervera* to stop; she immediately sent out an S.O.S. and the *Firedrake* summoned *Hood*. Vice-Admiral Blake asked the insurgent cruiser not to interfere with British shipping outside territorial waters. To which *Cervera* replied that her jurisdiction extended six miles from the coast.

This was the final bluff of Franco in the Bilbao blockade. Having pretended that he had laid mines in Bilbao which he had not laid, and that he would resist the entry of British ships by force when he had not the force to do so, he brought out the old Spanish claim, never accepted by Great Britain, that territorial waters extended to six miles from the shore. And this bluff, too, was called; her eight 15-inch guns ready, *Hood* replied that she did not recognise the claim, and *Macgregor* received the message *"Proceed if you wish."* She did. *Cervera* was silent. The Royal Navy's duty had been done.

As *Macgregor* approached the three-mile limit, the little insurgent trawler sent a shot across her bows; and was warned by *Firedrake* to lay off a British ship. The Basques meanwhile had been standing on the shore, itching to show off their coastal batteries upon the international shipping gathered in front of Punta de Galea. They chose this moment to open, with a certain wildness but recognisable enthusiasm. Indeed, the batteries on Galea tried their weight impartially upon friend and foe. While some shells flew screaming over *Firedrake*, others fell only ten yards from the trawler *Galerna*. The battle of the Cantabrian Sea was over; the last chain in the argument had been established. The Basque batteries proved themselves capable of protecting an area even beyond their territorial waters, into which the British convoy now cheerfully proceeded — for *Galerna* had turned tail.

Two Basque armed trawlers, the *Bizkaya* and the *Ipareko-Izara*, accompanied *Macgregor, Hamsterley* and *Stanbrook* into harbour. The same enormous crowds cheered as the procession of three red dusters passed slowly up river.

They carried a cargo of 8,500 tons of food, of which the most important element was 2,000 tons of wheat. Men in the patrol boat which preceded them up the Nervion shouted *"Pan! Pan!"* and the women on the shore were mad with joy. The political doldrums of St. Jean de Luz may have added years to some of the tomatoes, but the population clearly entertained high hopes of all the rest.

Two more British food and coal ships, *Stesso* and *Thurston*, arrived on April 25th without incident; and next day a third, *Sheaf Garth.*

Insurgent warships no longer interrupted the course of free commerce to Bilbao. Troncoso went over the International Bridge to raise his voice, no longer in warning but in resonant exasperation, before the staff of the British Embassy at the other end. When four British ships, *Marvia, Sheaf Field, Thorpehall* and *Portelet* entered the outer harbour of Bilbao on April 29th, twenty-two insurgent bombers tried to hit them and the big bridge across the river mouth and missed all five objectives. That was the end of the blockade of Bilbao, for good and all. It was a scrap of paper, and the truth had won.

Afterwards, in England, the friends of reaction bitterly complained that the policy of the Government, forced by the facts to protect British ships up to the three-mile limit, was an intervention in the Spanish civil war. Over-simple souls. The first warning to British shipping to avoid Bilbao, based as it was on inaccuracy and lies, was intervention in far grosser form. If the policy had persisted it would have brought Bilbao to her knees; she would have been bound to lose. When it was abandoned, it did not follow that Bilbao would win; she might either win or lose, and in fact she lost. Which of these two courses, on grounds of the most elementary logic, would have influenced the civil war the more? That which forced a certain issue, or that which left it open? That which was based on truth, or that which was based on Troncoso?

I take to myself the credit that I, before anyone else, exposed the fake in the blockade and recovered the truth. A journalist is not a simple purveyor of news, whether sensational or controversial, or well-written, or merely funny. He is a historian of every day's events, and he has a duty to his public. If he is kept from his public, he must use other methods; for as a historian in little, he belongs to the most honourable profession in the world, and as a historian must be filled with the most passionate and most critical attachment to the truth, so must the journalist, with the great power that he wields, see that the truth prevails. I did not rest until I had torn this falsehood to pieces.

XVII

ELGETA WAS A PRETTY sky-village, at the head of the pass which the road had to mount between Vergara in Guipuzcoa and Durango through Elorrio in Vizcaya. Here, as at Eibar graveyard, the insurgents had received a bloody check when they tried to press forward in October, when the arms arrived with the sea-wolf Letho.

One passed up to Elgeta through winding hills. Old shell-holes marked the village, and one saw the sky through a simple plastered gateway above which lived, in peace time, the mayor. But now it was the headquarters of the sector. The enemy knew this well and had often tried to hit it; but only a glancing shot had knocked off a few tiles in six months' lazy hostilities.

The front here had seen no change since October. It was considered more or less bad form, a rupture of long-established custom, to fire between the lines. In the deep scoop of the valley between Elgeta these indeed quite lost touch with each other. Nobody knew where the enemy was, except that he was bound to be somewhere down there in the green valley, among the square patches of mustard, which lost themselves in an all-pervading yellow towards Vergara. One could see it all from the shell-pocked square, for the drop to the valley from the pass which Elgeta crowned was steep, and the square opened to the east like a balcony on it. Some overcareful person had placed sandbags here, on which we used to stand to enjoy the view of the fresh mustard, and of the enemy lines on Asensiomendi, six hundred yards away half-right. Here the enemy were said to hold at least two machine guns, which were ill-trained and taciturn even if one held field-glasses to one's eyes, and publicly blinked at them.

Down the long valley peasants went on working in no-man's land. Cattle munched maize stalks strewn over fallow, but were gradually being sold off to the militia on either side. The old farmers had ploughed and sown and were prepared to reap. They professed no political views; as Basques they committed no crimes and needed no police; and as privileged inhabitants of no man's land they paid no taxes, posted no letters and told no stories. Such were their inter-territorial rights.

Asensiomendi, which rose in mass to the south of the valley, was in effect an eastward-running spur of the Inchorta range, which in three leonine hills grass-covered to the top ran due south from Elgeta to the Basque bastion marking the south-eastern corner of their front, Mount Udala. Asensiomendi was almost entirely in rebel hands. It was joined by a narrow neck of ground to the Great Inchorta; in the middle of this neck lay a little lake and a hermitage, once a rebel observation post, but long ago battered by gunfire into total blindness.

The Basque trenches had in October been cut in a crude rectilinear fashion across the forehead of the Inchortas. In this form they were, in the French phrase, *nids d'obus*, an easy target for any artillery attack. But in March a new commander, Beldarrain, had taken over the position, with a new battalion, the Marteartu, Basque Nationalists to a man.

Beldarrain was a small dark shy-faced creature who, before the war was a turner-mechanic, and like a fair number of people who are interested in machines was utterly tongue-tied; more, unwilling to talk. He dressed abominably, in an old blue woollen jacket and shabby artisan's trousers, and a worn beret which carried no insignia of rank. His features were long and melancholic, with very steady brown eyes; the only fine thing about him. He seemed incapable of smiling, or of ceasing to work. On first encounter, Beldarrain appeared not to understand ever the questions put to him; he was so profoundly silent by nature that he simply could not answer. One asked oneself whether the man was really a melancholy maniac, or simply a turner-mechanic ashamed of drilling a carnival army. When military advisers of the Basque Government told him to do this and that, they would find him equally wordless. They scratched their heads and went away. The man was a post.

When they came back next morning, as black with pessimism as Beldarrain was with his silences, to their astonishment they found three-quarters of what they had advised perfectly done. Over the other quarter the gloomy little statue would begin to talk; slowly at first, then gathering enthusiasm. It was a ridiculous idea, he said, when one worked it out; for reasons a, b, c, d. None of which had anything to do with the morale of his troops; his reasons were always technical, turner-like. He was almost the only commander who never bothered about morale, and his troops adored him for it.

Half the terror of the aeroplane in this war was provoked by ignorant officers, who spoke of their own fears in the presence of their troops. Beldarrain, incapable as he was of expressing his feelings at the best of times, remained quite dumb after the heaviest bombardments; seemed not to notice them. His men took them in the same spirit. There was none of that anguished discussion about the process of the aeroplane, obvious and occult, which one heard with gathering alarm in other sectors.

Beldarrain had made a clean sweep of the old fortifications on the Inchortas. The rectilinear trenches, of which there were two lines, were half filled; so that they should continue to bluff the enemy artillery but provide no footing for his infantry. Behind these abandoned graveyards Beldarrain constructed new defences, interlocked and irregular, covering each other in quincunx with a perfect crossfire.

Communication trenches connected the various positions, but were turfed over from the air. Over the key-like positions themselves Beldarrain laid natural camouflage; turf was even spread upon the sandbags. Not only deep, but enough deep dug-outs were constructed to protect the whole battalion, and look-outs were established away from the main system of defence.

Until now, as Beldarrain knew, the Basque line had been broken by penetration following air bombardment. He had to work out a system of dispersed defence to avoid the evil effects of the latter. He did this by placing the bulk of his men in concealed positions behind the crest of the hill.

His system was a series of small earth fortresses in front of the Inchortas, invisible from the air and inexplicable from Asensiomendi; and behind the Inchortas deep covered shelters cut like galleries into the hillside.

Nothing protruded. Even the barbed wire was wound round the branches and bushes, to remain invisible. Elgeta and the Inchortas were the only sector in the Basque line prepared to meet a modern attack, against every weapon but gas.

He was the only commander who realised that the Basques had not enough troops to defend a continuous line over 180 kilometres of mountain country, and that mountain tops were not in themselves ideal positions if the pine-wood passes at their feet were bare of men. He closed all passages where tanks might move, with mines. His system, allied to his own personal example, was to prove the ineffectiveness of the German aviation when properly met. For they were to concentrate all their fury upon Beldarrain.

On April 20th, with fair weather clearly outlining the Basque mountains against a pure blue curtain, and the supple mist wreathing away past the great organ loft of Mount Udala, before whose flinty sides the birds rose in spring song, Mola released the offensive which he had been preparing for the last three weeks, and the Italians were told that they could move forward.

Two points of attack were chosen, the solitary hill of Tellamendi to the south-west and the Inchorta position to the east of Elorrio. Elorrio was the major objective, and it was hoped that by a rapid occupation of the village the whole south-eastern corner of the front round Udala and Kampantzar would be cut off.

There were large musters of rebel troops in Vergara and Mondragon, and in the first town a column of Italian tanks to force Elgeta. Once Elorrio was taken, the road would be free to Durango, while the other columns would press northwards from Elgeta to cut off Eibar and Markina and the whole Basque line to the sea.

The aerial preparations for this had already been made. Among documents found on the dead Sobodka was a note of the flying time from Vitoria to Vergara.

On the morning of April 20th the great air fleet appeared

once more in the skies of Euzkadi. On the clustered visible trenches of Tellamendi they dropped a few tons of bombs. Where they could, the militia went underground. The rest cowered with fear in shallow trenches, which were now roofed in with quick-firing shrapnel. Meanwhile the rebel infantry moved tranquilly through the pines on either side of Tellamendi, and sent a few machine-guns up the slopes to east and west. When the bombardment was over, and the mere noise of it in their shaken smoky dug-outs was enough to disorganise the Basques, they came out to find that they were being shot from behind. The terrible cry of panic arose that had broken the line before Ochandiano—*estamos copados*! In the Spanish Civil War, where the rebels made a practice of killing all prisoners taken arms in hand, and all officers whatever their *tenue*, the militia—when ill-led—did not think it worth their while to fight a battle in a salient. "We are cut off!" they shouted, and away they ran down the back of Tellamendi between the flanking machine-guns. By midday the red and yellow flag floated from the summit of Tellamendi, and the militia were scattering southward in the fresh brushwood below. Flat wooded country now lay open all the way to Memaya, the ridge behind which lay Elorrio. Ideal country to defend if there had been commanders capable of woodland war; but they followed the directions of the General Staff, who never visited the front. They did not think for themselves, like Beldarrain.

The bombers passed on to Elgeta. Two squadrons of twelve, reloaded and carrying over a ton each, they advanced in flat, viperish arrow-head, close-marching German formation, to the vicious drumming of their engines, across the Basque sky to the lion-head Inchortas. Chasers played above: they no longer bothered to flank the bombers from our fighting aviation.

Over the Inchortas the twenty-four bombers released their load. They could see nothing but the old straight trenches below, and the top of the ridge where they knew from experience that Basques were also to be found. As they took aim, all their machine-guns fired a sharp, menacing signal together. Three bursts—r-r-r, r-r-r, r-r-r-romm: repeated three times, a domineering and masterful noise, to tell us that they were the overwhelming, disciplinary lords of the air; and that we should bow and submit to the winged metal.

The lion-head of the Inchortas curled with heraldic flame. On the neck beyond, the earth trembled to explosive tonnage. Not a man was killed: not one man.

Their fighters came down as was their wont, and saw empty, useless trenches; no comprehensible system of defence; no one to machine-gun.

Their artillery opened a devastating fire on Elgeta; hundreds followed hundreds of shells. Three passed through the mayor's gate-house, and dodged—as shells do—from room to room. But the command were cheerful after the failure of the great aerial bombardment, and drank coffee in the basement. Hundreds of shells fell behind Elgeta, and gashed her tidy fields. About six people were killed.

Their artillery turned to fire blind at the Inchortas. Five men were killed, mostly in look-outs. Towards midday the rebel infantry moved forward from Asensio-mendi: a battalion of Moors in white turbans—so sure they were of a peaceful occupation—a battalion of Regular infantry along the saddle of the Ermita, and a third battalion of Falangistas advancing more prudently to the southward.

Beldarrain had forbidden fire until the Ermita was reached. Then the Basques opened at 300 yards, flattening the attack to the ground. The rebels refused to obey the orders of their officers to advance. They clung to the ground near the Ermita.

Beldarrain had expected this moment and prepared for it long before, with his artillery, which lay well behind Elgeta to the left of the Elorrio road, among trees so large that the smoke of shooting tangled and was dissipated in the branches before the enemy aviation could place it. The guns were laid, dropped shells four a time on the enemy crouching round the Ermita. It was the most prettily-conceived action in the Spanish war, thought out by a dumb mechanic. For all their superior means they withered away.

Beldarrain, you see, had not bothered so much about the morale of his own troops, which meant that they did not bother about it either. But he *had* bothered about enemy morale: in his long periods of silence he had realised that they placed all their confidence in their aviation, and that their infantry would be at their wits' end if the aviation failed them. All that Beldarrain had to do was to plot the geographical position of their dis-illusionment, and the time was just after twelve-thirty. The rebels scattered westwards, losing men to wounds in the back.

They repeated the attack, unwillingly, twice that after-noon, with aviation, artillery, mortars, and all the apparatus of war. But the regulars only reached the lake-side: the four guns at Beldarrain's disposal shortened their range, raised jets of terrifying water that sparkled into the summer sky, and the machine-guns darted furiously between the fountains. Elgeta and the Inchortas were impregnable.

When night fell—after three heavy bombardments of aviation and artillery—a man came in with sopping trousers to Beldarrain's headquarters. The deserter from Logroño had, said he, stood with exemplary patience in the lake from two p.m. to sunset. On the margin he had left forty of his fellows dead, while shells passed over into the Ermita. From the top of the Inchortas one could see the khaki forms lying there, more than two hundred of them. The fire relaxed, stretcher-bearers came out un-molested with dusk to carry away the wounded. Their failure had broken the hearts of the troops on Asensio-mendi, and they withdrew into the pines; all except the man with the stomach-chill and the dripping trousers, and the two hundred dead. He was warmed up with brandy and transported enthusiastically to Bilbao.

But behind Tellamendi it was a different story. As we drove away that evening from the Elgeta triumph, we could hear continuous machine-gun fire in the valley to the south. It sounded nasty and nearer; too low down in the dark valley to please. Besides, the battle by Spanish rules should have stopped with dark. They persisted. In Elorrio Vidal was trying to get news of the Tellamendi battalions, but the 'phone was cut, and the *enlaces* (the runners) did not come in. A great crowd of officers chattered round the map in the *Casa Señorial*.

"Embrace your men for me," Vidal said on the tele-phone to Beldarrain. But to the south all was dark and mysterious, except for the sleeplessness of their machine-guns.

It was only towards morning that the true situation north of Tellamendi was known. The Staff attempted to organise a rapid counter-attack with four battalions, but it was too late. They would not march in daylight, and they were given no definite orders: they waited a little, then melted away.

Next day Elgeta was bombed again by a squadron of Germans; but the insurgent troops on Asensiomendi would not move out of the pines. The great squares of mustard stood motionless; no Moors made them shake apart behind the caserios, whose chimneys smoked peacefully: the whole valley towards Vergara was quiet. To the south of Elorrio only they were ranging their artillery now, three batteries in line, upon the ridge of Memaya, and their aircraft were carefully plotting our positions for the third day's attack.

Their shells fell through the heat haze, where solitary peaks of rock stuck out of the eastern flank of Mount Udala, barely descried and, in the distance, conveying no impression of strength. But we knew that Udala was now outflanked on the western side, and that the militia would withdraw as they had done from Tellamendi. At night there were rumours of political dispute among the routed militia, but all was very vague; nothing was confirmed.

Gradually the front took shape to the south. A battalion —the Guipuzkoa—came into the trenches at Memaya before sundown very tired and depressed. And on the hills behind Elorrio even, where the road led north to Berriz, trenches were being finished and lightly wired, and steel sheets from Bilbao naval works were being laid down against the aerial machine-guns which the ill-led militia disliked so much, and to which they gave such excessive military value. A foreigner came among them as they worked, and when the aeroplanes flew over the light-traced branches of the apple orchard where the new trenches lay, he took a rifle from one of the Socialists and jumped on to the parapet and fired until the barrel was hot in his hands. Then a few men took up their guns and shot, and a few more: the General Staff at Bilbao had never thought of encouraging fighters to fly higher

by this means. All that they could think of was the construction of more and more trenches, single lines of defence
without bomb-proof shelters, persuading the militia continually to fall back. But the force at Elgeta and the
Inchortas stood like a rock, because it took no notice of
the General Staff, and thought instead of talking.

XVIII

IT WAS THE THIRD DAY of the offensive from Guipuzcoa.

Elgeta and the leonine hills of the Inchortas to the south had held firm: the direct attack on them was abandoned, had cost too many lives.

I went up to the front that morning. We had just passed the corner of the Santa Marina ridge on the Galdakano road when we saw police in furry blue jackets running in front of us. We went slower.

Where the big new bridge crossed the Nervion to the chimney stacks of Dos Caminos, five or six lorries had stopped. On their radiators flapped the black-red flags of the Anarchists. Men and women militia jumped off them with furious eyes: there were bombs and machine-guns in their hands, and the black-red forage caps stood askew on their heads, to show in the most defiant and piratical way possible how fully they meant business.

The lorries and the men and women in blue overalls, bulging with grenades, were facing Bilbao; and facing the lorries were half a dozen Basque police—long-featured, gaunt and tall—possessed of a melancholy calm, with bayonets fixed towards the C.N.T.

The C.N.T., two battalions strong, had decided to leave the front. For political reasons, they said: they wished to have a place in the Government and publish their paper again. But it seemed strange to us that politics should be so important when the line was broken south of Elorrio, and the enemy pouring through the gap which the C.N.T. had left, two battalions wide.

Yet if one had said to the C.N.T. that they were cowards they would, to their own satisfaction, have proved one a liar with a hand-grenade, or a machine-gun for preference.

An argument to which, at thirty yards' distance, there is no answer: and the six police knew best not to use it upon the C.N.T., who stood there working up their faces into fanatical proof of the nobleness of their motives.

We drove faster past the death's-head emblems and the overstrained features. There must be something queer in the line.

There was. At Elorrio we found Vidal in his command-post looking restless, but saying nothing. Sometimes he tried to ring up his line at Kampantzar, but the telephone was cut by bombardment: a few messengers came in, but very few from the line. He seemed to have no control over his front. His little myopic—not unkindly—eyes blinked nervously behind the thick spectacles as he walked up and down, affecting a concentration of thought.

His honest Asturian A.D.C. sat out in a chair in the sun, reading a paper under apple trees. Over the ridge of Memaya there was a little artillery fire, eight by eight, Italian style: grey bushes of smoke on Kampantzar. The enemy aviation flew in eights and nines above Memaya, rather puzzled, changing altitude, dropping no bombs. Sometimes fighting planes stooped to the level of the long ridge, but they seemed uncertain: the machine-guns were fitful.

Before lunch we saw men coming down to Elorrio, under cover. The colonel sent a messenger into the village to find who they were. Basques of the battalion Guipuzkoa, abandoning the ridge.

We could see more huddling along the gulleys, where bushes and shade sprouted from hill-springs. Over open patches they ran half-bent, their helmets stiff cowls concealing faces which hung forward. The whole battalion was in retreat.

A mortar shell had fallen in one of their trenches, killing a boy: their flanks to right and left were laid bare by the defection of the C.N.T., and they believed that the moment had come to leave. But, unlike the C.N.T., they were not politically conscious: they were quite unable to give philosophical reasons for the abandonment of Memaya.

Memaya was degarnished. The key to the valley of Abadiano and to Durango, to Elorrio and Elgeta was no-man's-land. Colonel Vidal grew very hot, and called for his walking stick.

We marched with him down to the village of Elorrio: it was sunny, and the fields were full of blue columbine. Not a shot could be heard, and the birds were singing. A lark competed with the aeroplanes over the hill.

In Elorrio we found the Guipuzkoa battalion sitting under the wide porch and veranda of the church, and in the nave under the tower—safe from air bombardments—among piles of sandbags. Many were already asleep. Vidal bustled round for their commander, whom he accused of cowardice.

Just above us the ridge was still vacant: you must reoccupy it, said Vidal, shaking his stick. The captain showed no sign of initiative: he had evidently long ago decided that positions were neither to be held nor recaptured. For by now the *mystique* of the *cinturón* was entering into the heads of the field-commanders, and joining with the louder *mystique* of the aviation convinced them that retreat was safer, and Bilbao not so far behind them.

Vidal told the captain that if the hill Memaya were not re-attempted, he would lose his head. Literally. His head would be severed. With a dignified unwillingness, the captain said that he would try.

The troops were woken up and rolled into line. There were many who said that they were lame; but when two bombers flew over Elorrio—white silhouettes against the blue—their feet recovered nerve immediately, and the corns fell like scales from their toes as they scattered for shelter. It was a long time mustering the battalion Guipuzkoa from the dark religious sanctuary where it would lose itself.

Vidal stood in the open under the planes, shouting for them to reform. Painfully the Guipuzkoans dragged themselves out into the open. It took them an age to find all their equipment.

"Are you workers or señoritos?" shouted Vidal to each man as he passed; "Basques or Spaniards?" The men grumbled at that. "All right, we'll go," they said. "Look at the boys at Elgeta," shouted Vidal, "who've stood out three frontal attacks without flinching . . . heroes . . .

and you run before a trench mortar." "But their trenches are better than ours," they said slowly, as they trudged by in line. The reputation of Beldarrain's forethought had spread far.

Vidal shook his stick at each one as they went up the hill, behind long garden walls over flag-stone paving crumpled by mountain-water. Then under trees: there they stopped and looked timidly at the aeroplanes, who had not noticed them.

The captain said that he would go forward and reconnoitre. He went forward and wasted time examining the empty ridge with his back against a tree.

His column behind him moved like a caterpillar on a stalk. A heave forward of the front part, a great tension of the middle: after a long wait the rear is jerked up, and the caterpillar enjoys a rest and a nibble. The battalion Guipuzkoa lagged behind bushes and walls, and spread its blankets to sit down until the captain had finished his reconnaissance.

One daring stranger walked to near the backbone of the ridge unarmed. He climbed in the hot scrub until he was two hundred yards from the top. Then, peeping through bushes, he saw men in his own histrionic image: a handful of Fascists lying on their stomachs above, peering with equal anxiety down.

And so the aeroplanes had signalled forward the enemy to Memaya, and the ridge had fallen into their hands. On the eastward slopes their machine-guns were spitting between the pine-boles, and in Bilbao the motorised police picked up a message radioed by Mola: "My headquarters are at the Ermita on Kampantzar."

We could see the Ermita perched on the rocks above us, a pretty target for the artillery, which was ordered to fire, and remained silent. A silence as strange as the *mystique* of the aviation, or the blue-grey haze which curtained the precipices below the Ermita and, like the lark and the columbines, made us forget war, such a cascade of beauty swept down with it to the pines.

Vidal wept. The whole of the southern front was broken. Elorrio, Elgeta, all would have to go. On the way home I visited the General Staff in their chalet at Galdakano.

This was the first time I had seen Colonel Montaud, the defender of San Sebastian and now Chief of the Basque General Staff. He had been a professor of military fortifications before the war, and he looked, if indeed he inadequately played, his part.

A middle-sized, round-headed man, he came into the room in a check lumber jacket, tightly fitting him, khaki slacks and carpet slippers. His eyes were the straight eyes, a little protruding and unclear, of a false witness, and lay in wait behind powerful glasses. A full, brown, muddy face, with a short moustache covering a thick upper lip. Obvious capacity, obvious disgust with his position. He spoke perfect French with a full, bunched mouth, at whose corners flecks of white appeared when the argument became complicated.

Montaud looked German, without German will-power.

He began to talk at once. Considering that this was our first interview, he was astonishingly frank about his own opinions. When I asked him about the military situation after the fall of Memaya, he laid bare his entire lack of confidence in the militia whom he commanded. "They have not the social drive of the troops in Madrid," he said. "Our peasantry, if you want to know the truth, is at heart more at one with the other side than with us. And peasants make the best soldiers, alas!" He shrugged his shoulders, looking at me steadily with his emotionless brown eyes through the goggling glasses. He spoke deliberately, at every word testing my face.

"What can we do? Talk of forming a regular army, but that will change nothing. The militia will remain militia whatever you call them: slow, untidy, often disobedient, always incoherent. And they are beginning to get a little tired of this war. What material have we? No planes. If I order a counter-attack on Memaya tomorrow, the troops will be cut to pieces by their fighting planes before they close. They are bombed whenever they show themselves at day. And artillery? We have no mules, no mountain guns; but they can carry their guns wherever they like in our hills. All that we have are heavy pieces that can't be taken off the roads. And not much ammunition either. Machine-guns? A quarter of their number. What can we do?"

"I don't," he said with impressive insincerity, "at all despair. I believe that we are moving towards the final stages of a *siege en régle* when we will be able to use our artillery and hope to receive aviation, which we must have. My object now is to withdraw my men gradually upon the *cinturón*, without loss of effectiveness or material. There perhaps we can meet them; and, fortunately for us, we have an enemy who wastes his munitions terribly."

Montaud repeated all this not as I have written it, but with slow, rounded phrases which made of war a whole philosophy, or at least a system of overweight generalisations which the Germans would have honoured with that name. Planes were bombing us as he talked.

He told me that they would counter-attack on Memaya next morning with three battalions, at break of day. Then he walked out of his office with me carefully and slowly like a tired conspirator, and said good-bye between guards giving the clenched fist salute. He looked at them as if he were their prisoner. Yet he was supposed to be loyal enough; all that Montaud lacked was comprehension of the militia. His false witness was a false witness to their qualities, for he resolutely set himself to judge them by the standard of Toledo and Zaragoza, where he had taught.

Clearly, these fellows with clenched fists and wills of their own would never have passed a Spanish Military Academy. Neither Montaud nor Vidal stopped to think that perhaps it was their own fault that no alternative means had been used to train them.

* * * * * *

"*Les milices marchent très lentement*," explained Vidal that night at Amorebieta, when we came to sleep at his head-quarters. Three battalions were going to come by train from Bilbao, then take trains for Abadiano, and thence travel in buses to the point of departure for Memaya. At midnight they had not yet arrived at Amorebieta and nobody was quite sure that they had left Bilbao.

But Vidal's instinct was not to be angry on the telephone, but to sit and wait, and finally after giving orders for the troops' reception at Elorrio to go to bed. His staff were very genial and comradely. We ate well, and drank the powerful spirit *saltaparapetos*—jump-out-of-the-trenches—before lying down to sleep against the great counter-attack.

MINES SWEPT IN NERVION MARK: MARCH, 1937.

Left to Right: SEÑORA ALDASORO, THOMAS MCEWEN, CAPTAIN ROBERTS, FIFI ROBERTS, SEÑORA MONZON (WIFE OF MINISTER OF INTERIOR), SEÑOR RAMON ALDASORO (MINISTER OF COMMERCE): APRIL, 1937.

We were away in the dark before five, taking the northern road after Durango, for the route under Memaya to Elorrio was no longer considered safe. At Berriz dawn was breaking, a lifeless grey. Grey forms of buses came out of the mist, disembarking troops of the Battalion Azaña, of the Republican Left. They stood on the dull grey road in line, waiting for orders to move.

With Vidal we drove down to the command post outside Elorrio. No one was there. Not a single battalion was in place against Memaya. The clefts in the hill-side, sprouting cover to near the top, were empty. Troops were just beginning to man the second-line trenches north of Elorrio, of the Battalion Prieto.

Behind, our artillery began to fire at the three little crests of Memaya, where one could see non-commissioned officers gathering to study our line. They scattered. We went on firing, not ill. But no troops were yet in place.

It was six o'clock, the sun was up, the film of cloud between the stark mountain Udala and Memaya lifted, the mists shrank up the three clefts, Memaya was no more a floating island, Memaya was obliterated, only the roots of her were pure green and at last Memaya existed, solid, untakable, crowned with infantry, as a clear day shone again, and their aviation came out to bomb our second line.

That was the end of our great counter-attack which never came off.

From behind Memaya they began to shell the Elorrio-Elgeta road, as cars passed with sudden jets of fire when their windscreens snapped the rays of the sun.

Nine Junkers came from the south over Elgeta; they dropped their total load on the little village, near fourteen tons of bombs, all in a second. It was a terrible sight in the pitiless sunlight as the great block of smoke rose, half a mile long, over the pass to Vergara, and the noise banged about in the heat from hill to hill, among the blue columbines.

In our apple orchard on the hill-side stood an ox-cart loaded with farm furnishings: beds, hats, chairs, meat and the like. The black-dressed women in the farm-house were moving off, talking quickly and low to each other in toneless Basque. Fighting planes sprayed us in passing. Our artillery stopped talking.

Ten great bombers swept up the ridge to the west of the Inchortas, dropping incendiaries. The heavy slope of pines became of a sudden a field of flax, which thickened and fattened past the dreams of Pharaoh, till it was all white, then all crackling flames. That was how they dealt with our reserves.

Above us, circling for ever, were their fighting planes.

We attempted one movement. Half a battalion was sent out to a hill between Elorrio and Elgeta to check the penetration there, among great oak trees. They spotted them from Memaya, and their quick-firing artillery corrected aim. There were nests of Italian shrapnel in the oak trees.

Their machine-guns to the east of Memaya became very insistent. The direction of their movement now was obviously the rear of Elgeta and the impregnable Inchortas. No defences had been made to meet this menace.

As they progressed through the woods their aviation stopped every movement of ours through the day. One could do nothing against it for fourteen hours out of the twenty-four; the militia sat moody and dissatisfied in their trenches reading the Bilbao press, with its savage jokes about the Non-Intervention Committee.

The terrible thing for them was that while everyone else was doing so, they could not intervene. Over there the infantry, if it did no fighting, could at least march forward.

Shells burst over Elorrio. It was clear to both sides that there were no troops there. We suffered it without moving until sundown.

It was towards eight o'clock when the heavy moths were fluttering about the orchard where our trenches lay, and the foreigner who had molested the enemy planes saw a movement on the ridge of Memaya—a movement downwards, in orderly fashion. At the head of the men, who he could now see were marching in column, went the red and yellow flag. It was bold; it printed on us a great impression of daring and mastery; it was the spirit of victory that led them on. Then they burst into song, the jaunty *"Viva el Rey"* of the Requétés: too dark to see if they were wearing their scarlet berets or not, as the four Traditionalist Tercios swept down into Elorrio. Nobody shot at them; in our lines there was a total lack of authority which boded ill for Bilbao. Men loaded up, waited for the order to fire which never came. Our guns flung a few shells into the deserted village as they coolly ran up their flag on the solid square church tower with the Basque crown dome above it. The Battalion Largo Caballero could bear it no longer: without orders, with mass spontaneity, they turned their rifles on the hated emblem of reaction, and one could hear the nick of the bullets against the brown stone, with senses sharpened by the dusk as the Requétés' song faded.

One wondered what had happened at Elgeta. We knew that Vidal had sent no orders for retirement to Beldarrain, and now the last road of communication was broken. But Beldarrain got away.

That afternoon his men had heard the shooting behind them; the enemy were penetrating between Memaya and the Inchortas. Beldarrain sent away his guns and his armoured cars. When his road to Elorrio was quite cut off he evacuated all his material across country to Berriz, and followed with the Battalion Marteartu to second-line positions. They were immediately recalled to Bilbao after sixty days at the front without a break—something of a feat for the militia. Beldarrain was somewhat embarrassed by the official embrace with which he was received by Montaud. It seemed to him a showy, rather than Basque gesture, too military in the Castilian sense for a simple mechanic. But he knew at the bottom of his inexpressive heart that he deserved it, extravagant though it might be.

XIX

IN A WIDE HALF-CIRCLE the whole of the front between Tellamendi and Elgeta had caved in. Battalion after battalion was in plain retreat. Mola drove his men on remorselessly. Eibar and Berriz were his next objectives.

Immediately south-west of the arms town of Eibar, whose factories had been moved back to Bilbao many months ago, lay the high hill of Santa Marina Zar joined to the ridge of Mendizuko. The deep pinewoods that smothered their sides protected the Bilbao-Eibar road and lay upon the flank of Berriz.

Jaureghuy, the Frenchman, was asked to visit these hills on the night of the 24th, when they were to be occupied by two Basque Nationalist battalions. I decided to amuse myself and to go with him; it was our first journey together.

I had noted him before in the Torrontegui, where he took his meals at a table alone, with a map in front of him worn in squares by his pocket and fitted against his water-jug like an Englishman's newspaper. He was a stout little man, rather bald, in an untidy suit, a face fresh and pink, and the short, thick moustache over a thick mouth that made me think at first that Jaureghuy was a Russian officer. But the sad, nun-like girl in the black ankleward dress who superintended the restaurant of the Torrontegui said no, he was a French journalist who lived in the next room to me. A room full of maps, as one saw when the door was ajar, and when it was ajar enough to see that the little Jaureghuy was not there, I went in to read his reports on the military prospects of the Basques, written in a round, orderly hand from which violent criticism in every paragraph protruded: "trenches too rectilinear . . . no military organisation of the ground . . . attitude to warfare like that of the Basques at their last victory, gained against Roland at Roncesvalles . . . . You must learn to occupy the passes, not the mountain-tops . . . ." And even at this early period of Jaureghuy's work in Euzkadi he was writing unashamedly about "treason of the General Staff."

He used to come down to the Presidencia at the Carlton, where journalists assembled in Mendigurren's office. I did not yet talk to him, but was near enough to notice that his eyes were hard blue of an exquisite clarity and intelligence. Then old Corman found out that he had been a colonel of Chasseurs Alpins, a member of Foch's staff, and was now a leader of *Anciens Combattants*. He presented his reports to the President in person daily, his eyes twinkling. Military weaknesses were for him always a cause for merriment. He spent his whole days at the front. I think that he had come to Bilbao mainly to sell arms, but the fighting fascinated him; he seemed to abandon commerce and money-making to reacquaint himself and the Basques with his old profession.

He carried a Leica camera which he never used. When queried about his work, Jaureghuy replied with a crinkle of eyelids that seemed to engage his eyebrows too, and a twist-pout of his mouth which relaxed to show a row of small square fighting teeth, that he was the Special Correspondent in Bilbao of the Salvation Army and wrote regularly for their paper, *Blood and Fire*. He was willing, he said, to lend the editor's camera to anyone, provided that they could show him how to work it.

In his pert beret and his soft leather zip-fastener jacket which fitted comfortably over a well-rounded paunch, and adding a certain elegance with a narrow Basque alpenstock to movements naturally brisk and determined, J. was obviously the man to be chosen eponymous hero of the Press Association which the war was gradually drawing to Bilbao; and guide and humorous commentator to the Basque front which he already knew better than all the staff officers combined.

Delighted to believe that the first thing the enemy would do if they captured him would be to shoot him, J. learnt up the Basque cry, *"Gora Euzkadi Eskatuta"* — "long live free Euzkadi" — for final comic use against the wall, and spent the rest of the offensive getting encircled and pistolling his way out again. The greater the risk the more crinkled and bluer the eyes of J. "How the editor will praise my work! General Bood will give me a rise," he used to say as he pushed another charge of thirty into his Astra machine pistol, made in Gernika, 1935.

To himself Jaureghuy said that he had come to Euzkadi to defend France; but it was quite evident in the heat of battle and the overwhelming fear of retreat that Jaureghuy was capable of forgetting all interests less immediate than his own excitement and the practice of his own quick-wittedness. He was a French officer. War was his game, and to make it a game worth playing every manœuvre had to be executed as near the touchline of danger as possible. He made a great impression on the Basques, but found himself unable in the end to move their General Staff.

It annoyed him that every time he entered their suite in the Carlton, Lafuente was looking sadly out of the window into space, and Arbex, with much relief, seized this opportunity to distribute cognac, and asked him if he would go on the *bombe* with him that night. Then Jaureghuy's blue eyes hardened and his eyebrows formed a sharp line, rather cruel, Oriental, downwards to the bridge of his nose, and his lids discovered a series of loose, cynical folds, and he asked the Staff if they had visited the front that day or would they care to come with him to-morrow?

We went off towards Berriz at about eleven that night, and after one o'clock we were at Zaldibar, where some of the troops were assembled to mount Santa Marina Zar. The road was uncomfortably wedged with lorries, and in the bottlenecks between the shattered unpeopled houses of Durango we had to wait twenty minutes, wondering when the withdrawal would end, as every kind of car squeezed through carrying hundreds of men in blankets, sleeping and swaying.

Of the battalion which was intended for Santa Marina Zar, one-third were still in their cantonments when we arrived. The confusion was great, men grumbling and officers quarrelling in a higher key; it seemed that two officers in particular refused to lead their company out to the position supposedly prepared for them in the pines. They said that nothing was ready and that there would be no covering support, with many protestant gestures and much seizing of one another's lapels. We struggled up over the damp, glossy carpet of pine needles, along the crest in night and mist, until we reached Santa Marina Zar at about two-thirty; our way was quite deserted, we heard and saw no one.

At Santa Marina the sappers had been working to lanterns since midnight. They had carved out a single shallow trench facing south and west from the crest, with two other trenches to communicate over the hill. There was no wire and no sandbags. The troops around us looked about them and found that they had no trenching tools of their own. There were no anti-aircraft shelters. So the battalion begged the sappers to leave them a few picks and shovels, and a party went down to Zaldibar to play upon the patriotism of the peasantry, returning later with two scythes and a hatchet, very useful.

There was no food, no reserves of grenades, and the battalion possessed only one machine-gun. Munitions were low, and a runner was sent back to order more. It was a heavy job digging shelters in the clogging mist. We went on to Mendizuko.

Mendizuko was empty. A battalion had gone off without waiting for its relief. But at six, when the trails of moisture within the pines were becoming palely luminous, a Basque battalion came up to occupy Mendizuko. It was followed an hour later by Comandante Castet's battalion, which took over the ground prepared on Santa Marina Zar, being one of the twenty Basque battalions which had no machine-guns. Its so-called "machine-gun company" was armed with four short machine pistols. It had no ammunition reserve, but about this time the munitions ordered by its predecessor arrived at Santa Marina, and were found to be of a smaller calibre than Castet's.

Among the hungry, ill-supplied troops there was a lot of talking in groups, and on backs. It was obvious that they were nervy, uncertain of themselves. They were convinced that the western approaches of Santa Marina were not covered, except by the mist.

Their restlessness was increased when a counter-order sent away the battalion which had first occupied Santa Marina Zar. It left at eight o'clock. As it was moving away and the mist on the mountain thickened, a burst of machine gun fire on the south-western slopes showed that the enemy had made contact with our patrols.

On our side it was rifle fire, and a few light machine pistols. A message was sent after the battalion withdrawing, but its commander refused to offer help. They were going back fast.

Our patrols ran in to the trenches. Below, the sea of mist and pine seemed full of machine guns, firing over our heads.

Castet marked one down quite near, in a separate wood. He walked out with a party to turn it, and was shot through the brain just below the trench. No one had been selected by the command to succeed him in such an emergency, and while Jaureghuy, good marksman, cleared with his pistol the post which had accounted for poor Castet, the junior officers spent twenty minutes deciding who was to lead the battalion now. Now that Castet was lying down there, with his mouth open to catch flies at midday.

Yet in spite of this appalling disorder the Basques stood their ground and beat off three attempts to attack before eleven o'clock. The enemy was not pressing hard; with his superiority of means he seemed as confused about his objectives as the Basques were. And at eleven the Basques had spent all their ammunition.

Their machine guns now were stripping the whole western side of the position, and a retreat began along the ridge. J. was left behind with his pistol, gleefully firing from the top of the hill as they scrambled up to the trenches. Then we escaped, Heaven knows how; for on the north side of Santa Marina Zar, where we ran, the mist had lifted and we could see the enemy progressing now on both flanks of the mountain. And when the grey curtain rose higher, we could see his flag upon the summit.

Everyone had gone.

We came to the road without seeing a soul. A car passed, and we drove to Berriz.

The enemy were advancing on Berriz from Elorrio. The trenches where the men had read the Bilbao papers the day before were evacuated without a shot fired, and sections of infantry were taking cover now behind walls and hedges and haystacks. Our artillery did not know where to fire.

It was at this moment of chaos in the line that General Mola ordered the bombardment of Eibar with incendiary and high explosive, and the attack by the Italian Division Flechas Negras to the east of the town. Eibar already wrecked by artillery crumbled to pieces, a smoking ruin, an enormous grey smudge on the Basque valley. Sunday, April 25th, saw the first of the incendiary bombardments from the air, which were to be aimed at the Basque communications rearwards next day as far as Gernika.

Bombed to pieces in Eibar, assailed frontally to the east and to the south-west at Santa Marina Zar, the Basques fell back in disorder towards Markina. Only the coastal corner of the original line was left, near Ondarroa, and orders were sent to the battalions here at once to retreat before the road was cut.

From the sea to Tellamendi the Basques were in disorganised movement homewards. It looked like the finish. Certainly the staff did nothing to save the situation. It was only the natural discipline, the astonishing power of recrystallisation of the Basques that enabled them to defend Bilbao for nearly two months more. I do not think that any other force, led and equipped as they were, would have done it. Particularly after the morrow, when the attack was aimed at the village which was the centre of their national feeling, and destroyed it utterly.

XX

THEY TOLD US AT THE General Staff that afternoon of the bombardment of Markina, Bolibar, and Arbacegui-Guerricaiz. All the villages had been smashed up on the way back to Gernika.

The destruction at Arbacegui barred our way. There were four dead near the church. Two cottages sprawled in smoking pieces across the road, and we climbed over them and down the fields to see the biggest bomb-holes we had ever seen, warm and stinking of metal still. They were over twenty feet deep and forty feet wide. They were moon craters. We looked in wonder at them. Suddenly on the hillside behind us the bell of the little church began to tinkle. We saw the two old priests and a few villagers stumble across debris and torn green grass into the tower door. Then silence in the village; nothing to see but the smoking houses and walls smirched grey with fire.

Over the ridge to the north-west, from the direction of Gernika, came six fighting planes in echelon. They were flying very fast, level and straight, and their engines made a noise which meant immediate war. In a few seconds they were on the village. They were so low that one could see with the naked eye the pilots and every detail of the planes down to the split wheels and characteristic pin-nose of the German army fighter, Heinkel 51. These were the same planes that Kienzle and Schulze-Blanck said that they had flown from Vitoria—six Heinkel 51's in battle formation.

Christopher Corman and I thought that the bomb-hole was the best place. We reached the bottom in two jumps. It looked less safe from down below, for the sides were unusually wide and one could see too much sky. But it was a hole, and we lay on the shady side face down in tumbled clay and jagged bomb splinters.

There can have been no movement visible in the village, and there was no traffic moving or stationary upon the road, except our car. But they dropped a few light bombs and machine-gunned the place until they must have shot all the dust off the roofs that still stood.

Then they circled and spotted us. For between fifteen and twenty minutes they dived over our hole at full throttle, loosing off their double guns at us from anything down to two hundred feet. The only thing was to pretend to be dead already, and sometimes we wondered whether we were. Old Corman was spinning a long story about the ineffectiveness of aerial machine-gunning on entrenched positions, but somehow to-day he sounded much less impressive, and I asked him to be silent and to wait and see. It struck me, too, as very undignified for an English-man to eat earth before the German aviation; but I was bothered if I could think of any safe alternative. It was difficult to think at all. As soon as the very material process known as the collection of one's thoughts was nearly com-plete another bloody little fighter was roaring down at us, and we were spreadeagled and passive again.

Of course, it's all noise. The shooting was wild, and after a quarter of an hour of it we could not find a bullet in the bomb-hole. And when they had gone we recol-lected how often the pilots had kept on gunning when the planes were soaring upwards fit to hit the stars. Terror and noise were their weapons, not death.

I had been machine-gunned a few times before and was machine-gunned many times afterwards, but I never figured in so pretty a target. It impressed me. My experience must be much the same as that of any young recruit. Continual strafing from the air does not frighten; it paralyses. We pulled ourselves out of the hole very slowly. We didn't look about us much. We were thinking all the time of the experience which we had suffered, and not a thought did we give to the future or the present. We were raw material for any surprise.

None of the villagers were hurt, but they stayed huddled in the blackness of the church tower, I suppose till night-fall. Their terror was real, not half-exorcised like ours.

We turned our car in front of the burning barricade. It, too, was untouched. The chauffeur was told to go straight back to Bilbao.

As we made homewards we had to stop twice and wait for enemy aeroplanes to pass. Their type was the light bomber Heinkel 111, and we saw several fly across to our right towards the Gernika inlet. The same alarm chained the peasantry to their holes and hedges; the fields were tragically deserted and bare. As we passed the level-crossing we heard bombing to the north, where the inlet settled down into green valley. We saw nothing, for there were hills between. The bombs must have been dropped by the planes which passed us. We had experienced quite enough that day, and we went on without stopping to Bilbao to write our stories.

It was about four-thirty by the clock of our car on Monday, April 26th.

* * * * * *

Monday was the weekly market day of Gernika, when the town existed. At about four-thirty the market, in summer, was at its fullest. The civil war had not made great difference to the Gernika farmers who brought in their animals and produce for sale from the rich valley. Rather there was better business. In Gernika, where the population was usually seven thousand, there were now an additional three thousand refugees and two Basque battalions, who had plenty of pesetas to spend. A few of the factious rich had been jailed or run away, but only a few. Their fine stone houses with the floreate blazons engraved hugely over wide doors were shut; but they never had used the market much, and most of them visited peace-time Gernika little.

Gernika remained a modest Vizcayan country town. The population behaved itself, the priests walked about in the cloth, mass was held in the churches all day and every day. The two Basque Nationalist battalions quartered to the north of the town, where a water-green avenue of plane trees rippled out towards Bermeo, were popular with the people, and in Gernika itself there was the usual post of Basque motorised police. There were no troops retreating through the town. The armies were beyond Markina, miles to the east, and at Oitz, miles to the south. Gernika lay well behind the front, on part of its communications with Bilbao; to destroy it would cut off the retreating armies from the General Staff and their base.

After four there were farm carts coming into Gernika, rolling on solid wooden wheels and drawn by oxen whose heads were shaded under fleeces of sheep. Basque peasants in their long puckered market smocks walked backwards in front of them, mesmerising the oxen to Gernika with their slim wands, with which they kept touching the horns and yoke gently. They talked to the oxen. Others were driving sheep to market. There was an assembly of animals near the parish church, a stately structure cavernous, tall and dark within, standing upon a flight of thin steps like leaves piled one upon the other.

It is improbable that anyone was thinking about the war when at four-thirty the church bell rang out loud. All over Spain a peal on a single bell is an air-raid warning. The population took cover, and the sheep in the square were left to their own devices.

There were numerous air-raid shelters in Gernika, constructed after the terrible raid on Durango on March 31st. Any cellar was covered with sandbags, and the entrance protected in the same way: a cardboard at the door painted ornamentally *refugio* showed where the people had to dive. Though there had been few raid warnings at Gernika since the war began, the whole Basque population by now took their church bells seriously.

In a few minutes a Heinkel 111 came over and dropped six medium bombs, probably fifty-pounders, near the station, with a shower of grenades. A director of the railway company who was in the office rang up Bilbao to inform them that an aeroplane was bombing Gernika.

A few minutes later another Heinkel 111 appeared, to bomb the same area, but nearer the centre. The telephone with Bilbao was now cut. The plane from its slant and speedy sides machine-gunned the town at random, then veered homeward.

The parish priest, Aronategui, left his church with the sacraments, for dying people were reported near the railway station. He went calmly through the deserted streets with the holy oil. No fires had yet started.

Fifteen minutes passed, and the people were coming out of their shelters. A heavy drumming of engines was heard to the east. It was what we called in lighter moments the *tranvias*—the trams—the Junker 52's, who were so clumsy that they seemed to clang rather than to fly. These were the heaviest bombers that Germany had sent to Spain.

Over the town, whose streets were once more empty trenches, they dispersed their load a ton at a time. They turned woodenly over Gernika, the bombs fell mechanically in line as they turned. Then came the crack of the explosions; smoke stood up over Gernika like wool on a negro's head. Everywhere it sprouted, as more heavy bombers came.

Besides many fifty- and hundred-pound bombs, they dropped great torpedoes weighing a thousand. Gernika is a compact little town, and most of these hit buildings, tearing them to pieces vertically from top to bottom and below the bottom. They penetrated refuges. The spirit of the people had been good, but now they panicked.

An escort of Heinkel 51's, the same perhaps that had molested us that afternoon, were waiting for this moment. Till now they had been machine-gunning the roads round Gernika, scattering, killing or wounding sheep and shepherds. As the terrified population streamed out of the town they dived low to drill them with their guns. Women were killed here whose bodies I afterwards saw. It was the same technique as that used at Durango on March 31st, nearly a month back.

The little fighting planes came down in a line, like flashing dancing waves on shingle. They burst in spray on the countryside as they merrily dived. Twenty machine guns working together in line, and the roar of breakers behind them from ten engines. Always they flew nose towards Gernika. For the pilots it must have been like surfing. The terrified people lay face down in ditches, pressed their backs against tree trunks, coiled themselves in holes, shut their eyes and ran across sweet green open meadow. Many were foolish, and fled back before the aerial tide into the village. It was then that the heavy bombing of Gernika began.

It was then that Gernika was smudged out of that rich landscape, the province of Vizcaya, with a heavy fist.

It was about five-fifteen. For two hours and a half flights of between three and twelve aeroplanes, types Heinkel 111 and Junker 52, bombed Gernika without mercy and with system. They chose their sectors in the town in orderly fashion, with the opening points east of the Casa de Juntas and north of the arms factory. Early bombs fell like a circle of stars round the hospital on the road to Bermeo; all the windows were blown in by the divine efflatus, the wounded militiamen were thrown out of their beds, the inner fabric of the building shook and broke.

On the shattered houses, whose carpets and curtains, splintered beams and floors and furniture were knocked into angles and ready for the burning, the planes threw silver flakes. Tubes of two pounds, long as your forearm, glistening silver from their aluminium and elektron casing; inside them, as in the beginning of the world in Prometheus' reed, slept fire. Fire in a silver powder, sixty-five grammes in weight, ready to slip through six holes at the base of the glittering tube. So, as the houses were broken to pieces over the people, sheathed fire descended from heaven to burn them up.

Every twenty minutes fresh raiders came. And between the explosions and the spurts of flame as the burning metal seeped into curtains and beams, doors and carpets, while a grey pall stood over Gernika supported from below by white pillars where fires were starting, in the pauses of modern battle the population ran about the street to clear away the doors of smothered refuges, to pull children and other small worthless belongings from houses afire.

There was much groaning in Gernika, much breathless work to dig out wounded people before the next planes came. Twenty minutes was the interval between fire, and the priests spoke to the people to keep them calm. By now something like a spirit of passive resistance had been built up in them. Gernika's face was turning to ashes, everybody's face in Gernika was ash-grey, but terror had reached a condition of submissive stubbornness not seen before in Vizcaya.

In the intervals people moved out of the town, but the fear of the fighting plane and separation from their families persuaded many to remain in Gernika. And then the

planes returned with their tinsel tubes to shower over
Gernika, and another part was destroyed, and more were
buried in the *refugios*.

I do not know whether you have ever sat in a railway
station having lost one train and waiting for another which
will come in two and a half hours time. A country railway
station, where you can buy nothing to read or smoke or
eat; and the hours take days to pass if you cannot go to
sleep. Now in Gernika it was well nigh impossible to go to
sleep, except in an obligatory sleep which had no morrow
in Gernika, or Vizcaya, or this world. And since there
was nothing to eat or smoke, and fumes prevented one
from reading, no other diversion remained but to allow
terror to expand those hours past days into months and
years. Years half-spent in dug-outs that might crash at
any moment, and half-spent in streets of an unrecognisable
town looking for people who may now be unrecognisable.

And so you see that to be in Gernika when it was destroyed
was, in a limited sense, like waiting for a train in a country
station. Time in both cases passed slowly.

Soon there was little of the town to move about in. The
Church of San Juan was burning fiercely, with a huge
bomb-hole through its roof and its altar and pulpit rippling
fire. Even a few isolated buildings were touched; at the
old Parish Church of Andra Mari, in the corner of the square
where the sheep had been gathered, the chapel behind the
altar was aflame.

As the people not trapped in the refuges moved northwards before the general fire the planes that raided Gernika
came very low. It must have been difficult for them to
sight their target in the smoke and grit which rose from the
spreading campfire below them. They flew at six hundred
feet, slowly and steadily shedding their tubes of silver,
which settled upon those houses that still stood in pools of
intolerable heat; then slipped and dribbled from floor to
floor. Gernika was compact as peat to serve as fuel for
the German planes. Nobody now bothered to save relatives
or possessions; between bombardments they walked out
of Gernika in front of the stifling smoke and sat in bewildered
hundreds on the roads to Bermeo and Mugika. Mercifully,
the fighters had gone. They no longer glanced down to
mutilate the population in movement and chase them

across the open fields. The people were worn out by
noise, heat and terror; they lay about like dirty bundles
of washing, mindless, sprawling and immobile. There was
nothing to save in Gernika but the few old mattresses and
pillows, kitchen tables and chairs which they had dragged
out of the fire. By seven-thirty that evening fire was
eating away the whole of crowded little Gernika but the
Casa de Juntas and the houses of the Fascist families.
These, being wealthier than the others, lived in stone
mansions apart from the rest of the people; their properties
did not catch the infection of the running fire, even when
under pressure of the wind it stretched its savage arms to
stroke them.

At seven-forty-five the last plane went away. One could
hear now, through ears half-numbed by the engines of
the heavy bombers and explosions of the heavy bombs,
the nervous crackle of arson all over the town and the totter
and trembling collapse of roofs and walls. Gernika was
finished, and as night fell and the motorised police stumbled
along the road to ring up Bilbao to say that all was over,
the total furnace that was Gernika began to play tricks
of crimson colour with the night clouds. Very gently and
softly they throbbed reflections of her death movement.
They lay over her like a crimson-cushioned ceiling, like the
hangings of a dying monarch, billowy and rich, stirring to
the Gernika light.

Around the corpse of the Basques' oldest village caserios
aflame in the hills made candles. The aviation had spent
the residue of its fire upon them and had struck many.

Beginning to talk and to try to understand their experience, the Basques asked each other how many planes had
attacked their town. Some said eighty, others one hundred,
others two hundred, others more. They could not tell;
but those who were outside Gernika the whole afternoon
say that between forty and fifty German planes attacked
her, including ten fighters. The bombers reappeared
again and again with fresh loads.

To the people within Gernika it was not a question of
figures, but of inquantitative and immeasurable terror.
All they could hear was the drumbeat of the engines and
the split of the explosions again and again until they
sounded dull enough. They could see no more but the

trembling doors of their refuges and their own helpless faces, and sometimes if they were in the streets the points of fire where the silver tubes struck; these fell many at a time, for they were dropped twenty-four together on a single spinning rod. Sometimes, too, before they bolted below they saw through the smoke the stiff, stubborn wings of the planes which molested them and heard the wingless flight of the metal that spurted blindly all over the town, crushing walls and roof tiles and stripping trees of their leaves and branches.

When they crept back to the town between the soft breeze of the flames now blowing on every house they saw what I saw later that night.

* * * * * *

At Bilbao we sent our day's story off; it dealt with the bombardments all along the communications that day, from Markina to Arbacegui-Guerricaiz. Some time about seven Arbex told me that Gernika was being bombed; he said that they had had news earlier of it, but there were no details. He did not seem to give the bombardment much importance. I did not mention it in my story that night.

We were having dinner at eight-thirty in the Torrontegui that evening; quite a number of us. Captain Roberts of the *Seven Seas Spray* and his daughter Fifi, Arbex, Christopher Holme, and some other journalists sat down with me in the wide sombre dining-room, peopled by the near-ghosts of women and old men of the Right, who talked in a whisper and glided rather than walked. The dinner was going fairly well, when at ten o'clock Antonio Irala rang up. "Gernika is in flames," he said.

We got cars, threw our napkins on the floor, and drove out into the dark towards Gernika. I recollect the mood in which I went to that fire; the same mood as that with which many people in England heard the news of it. Irala must be exaggerating, I felt. The whole town cannot be burning.

We followed Arbex's car through the countryside along the road which we had followed that morning. Arbex drove like a lunatic, with a cigarette-holder sticking out of his open glass. It glowed ahead of us, until we lost it against a brighter sky.

* * * * * *

Fifteen miles south of Gernika the sky began to impress us. It was not the flat dead sky of night; it seemed to move and carry trembling veins of blood; a bloom of life gave it body, flushed its smooth round skin.

Nearer it became a gorgeous pink. The sort of pink that Parisians have dreamed of for centuries. And it seemed enormously fat; it was beginning to disgust us.

It still had no source. Gernika was hidden behind the hills through which we careered. But we could see now that the fatness was great bellying clouds of smoke and the pinkness the reflection of some great fire upon them. The skies in their vague, all-embracing way were mirroring Gernika, and pulsed more slowly to the destruction that danced a war dance over the home of seven thousand human beings.

Out of the hills we saw Gernika itself. A meccano framework. At every window piercing eyes of fire; where every roof had stood wild trailing locks of fire. The meccano framework was trembling, and a wild red disorder was taking the place of its rigid geometry. We drove down the street which led into Gernika from the south carefully, for it was a street no longer. Black or burning beams and tattered telephone wires rolled drunkenly, merrily across it, and the houses on either side streamed fire as vapour rises effortless from Niagara. Four dead sheep lay to our right in a trickle of blood, and as we approached the central place over huge bomb-holes and volcanoed fresh earth before the Casa de Juntas, we saw a dazed score of militiamen, Batallion Saseta, standing by the roadside, half waiting for, half incapable of understanding, their orders. The fire of the houses lit up their spent, open faces.

In the plaza, in the dark shadow of the Casa de Juntas which made the only shade in Gernika that night, people sat upon broken chairs, lay on rough tables or mattresses wet with water. Mostly women: some hundreds of them were littered around in the open space, and as we passed they groped about, fiddled with dirty pillows, tried to sleep, tried feebly to walk. We talked to them: they told me all that had happened. This stricken people were my authority for all that I have written. Two priests were with them: Aronategui was not to be found, and they supposed him dead. They conversed in tired gestures and words unnaturally short for Spain, and they made the funny noises of bombers poising, fighters machine-gunning, bombs bursting, houses falling, the tubes of fire spurting and spilling over their town. Such was the weary, sore-eyed testimony of the people of Gernika, and it was only later that people who were never in Gernika thought of other stories to tell.

Some of the witnesses were quite dumb. They were digging them out of ruined houses—families at a time, dead and blue-black with bruising. Others were brought in from just outside Gernika with machine-gun bullets in their bodies: one, a lovely girl. The militia cried as they laid her out on the ground in the broken hospital: they could give no reason for their tears—they just cried.

A fire brigade with a feeble jet was playing on the chapel of Andra Mari. I went up into the shades of the Casa de Juntas. The gardens were torn about, windows were broken; but behind the Casa stood the oak of Basque civil liberty. Untouched! The black old trunk, under which, when it flowered, the Catholic kings promised to respect Basque democracy, stood there in its mummified death, untouched between thick white pillars. The seats, engraved with the arms of Vizcaya—tree and lurking wolves—where the Señor of Vizcaya took the oath of suzerainty and respect, untouched and green. A few rose petals lay on the stones around—pink confetti blown there in the twilight by the bombardment of Gernika.

In the centre of the town the smaller tongues of fire were turning into a single roar. The motorised police, with Monzon, Minister of the Interior, stood helpless beyond the plaza, where streets tightened and intertwined to make the heart of our conflagration. We tried to enter, but the streets were a royal carpet of live coals; blocks of wreckage slithered and crashed from the houses, and from their sides that were still erect the polished heat struck at our cheeks and eyes. There were people, they said, to be saved there: there were the frameworks of dozens of cars. But nothing could be done, and we put our hands in our pockets and wondered why on earth the world was so mad and warfare become so easy.

We talked with the people round the great furnace for two hours. I smoked a number of cigarettes to settle my mood, drove back to Bilbao, and slept on my story.

Government lorries and ox-carts carried away the refugees. Our headlights illumined the slack shoulders and loose blankets of hundreds who walked slowly towards Bilbao and Munguia.

Between cigarettes I played with three silver tubes picked up that evening in Gernika. The argent thermite distilled itself slowly from their bases; they came from the German RhS factory in 1936, said their stamp. And over the legend stood a symbol in miniature, the Imperial eagle with scarecrow wings spread.

XXI

THE DESTRUCTION OF GERNIKA was not only a horrible thing to see: it led to some of the most horrible and inconsistent lying heard by Christian ears since Ananias was carried out feet foremost to his long, central-heated home.

The night after Salamanca had read the *Reuter* telegram about it in the world's press, Radio Salamanca (an Italian station) gave the air to Señor Gay, who had read a lot about Goebbels, and was now chief of Franco's Propaganda. Señor Gay appropriately described his talk as *"Mentiras, mentiras y mentiras,"* which means "Lies, lies and lies." The title conveys not only the substance but the spasmodic style of little Gay's address.

In the style of Queipo de Llano, after the bombing of Durango, Gay declared roundly that Gernika had been destroyed by the Reds. He could provide no evidence, and did not even trouble to invent any. His statement was official; and how Salamanca could—a day after the bombing of Gernika, and two days before they entered it—know that it had been destroyed by Reds when it was still ten miles the other side of the retreating Basque army, I leave to you, gentle and complacent reader. No means have ever been suggested; no declaration of an eye-witness was ever put before the foreign press working with Franco.

On April 28th the Government of Salamanca were openly dishonest. They stated officially that no plane had left the ground on the day that Gernika was said to have been bombed, and offered to show pressmen with them the in-and-out books of Vitoria aerodrome for

April 27th. They may have deceived a few of the more helpful kind by this means; but the rest knew very well that Gernika was not burnt on the 27th but on the 26th. And Mr. Gerahty, the correspondent of the *Daily Mail* at Vitoria, has written in his book, "The Road to Madrid," that he saw a fleet of heavy "Nationalist" bombers passing northwards into Vizcaya on the 26th, the very day itself.

A "Nationalist" communiqué declared "we have eye-witnesses to the bombing of Gernika by the Reds; witnesses to their work with incendiary material and petrol." But these eye-witnesses had to wait four months before they were produced; to convince, not experienced journalists and impartial inquirers, but itinerant British officers of Fascist sympathies, convinced in their cradles.

All these statements were denied by hundreds of real eye-witnesses with whom we spoke: from the two priests— Don Alberto Onaindia, Canon of Valladolid, and Father Aronategui, priest of Gernika itself—and from the Mayor of Gernika to the humblest human salvage from the smoking ruin.

We spoke to all of them without constraint or interpreters. Not only myself; but the correspondents of *Reuter*, the *Star*, the *Daily Express*, and *Ce Soir* of Paris. They told the same story: if there had been a tale of "Red destruction" to tell, they would have been the first to cry out. For they were peasants with politics more of the Right than the Left, and they had lost all their property in the fire.

We saw the great bomb-holes in the plaza, the churches, the school, round the hospital—all of us with our own eyes. They were not there when I passed through Gernika the day before. We picked up unexploded German incendiary bombs and bomb-splinters, and saw people dead of bomb wounds and machine-gun bullets. There was no sign of petrol.

"It is possible," read another of the "Salamanca communiqués," written on May 2nd, "that a few bombs fell upon Gernika during days when our aeroplanes were operating against objectives of military importance." Before or after April 26th? No: for April 26th was the only day on which Gernika was ever bombed. It was strange for us to read in the same communiqué that "Irun suffered a similar (i.e. *Red*) fate under the eyes of European journalists and witnesses from Hendaye, in the same negligent or culpable silence." For both Holme and I had reported Irun truthfully and in full, as it is reported in this book. This was just another of their falsehoods.

Indeed, their story was beginning to collapse of its own inanity. The day that Gernika was destroyed, the Basque front lay between Markina and the sea: the troops were retreating. What army in the world would try to destroy its own communications (for that was the motive which the "Nationalists" gave) fifteen miles behind its own front, on a day when no retreating troops were ever able to pass through Gernika, to which the roads were blocked already by the German aviation, as we had ourselves seen at Arbacegui-Guerrikaiz.

The troops of Franco entered Gernika, as we shall see, on April 29th. I was near them—in the field. There was hardly any fighting: it would have been quite safe for foreign journalists to enter. And, in passing, be it observed that Sandro Sandri, the Italian journalist, entered; but not the less reliable correspondents of the British Press.

They had to wait five days. There were a lot of holes to be filled in, and witnesses had to be collected and talked to a bit, and advised of their patriotic duty, and the smell of petrol had to be propagated.

At last, *The Times* correspondent with Franco was allowed to send a little piece about Gernika, on May 4th. It was pronounced an eye-witness opinion; but, in fact, it was mostly a rewrite of a document published for the whole foreign and "Nationalist" press at Vitoria, and purporting to be a report by civilian engineers of the causes of the burning of Gernika.

Franco must have been very cross with them. They did their work very inadequately.

"That Gernika, after a week's bombardment by artillery and aircraft, should not have shown signs of fire . . ." they began, feeling their way feebly towards a compromise. Very feebly; for Gernika had never been shelled or bombed before April 26th. But the engineers showed goodwill. They had to explain away some of the holes that could not be covered in time.

Next, they admitted that Gernika had been bombed "intermittently" over a period of three hours. This was what the Basques had said already; but not what Gay and Franco had said. Oh, no! They said that no aeroplanes went up.

A local dentist was roped in to say that when he returned after watching the bombing from a little outside Gernika, there were only a few small fires. But residents who survived the bombardment and fire were "for the most part unable to help the investigators much": which says a lot for the stubborn truthfulness of the Basque even when he is captured and menaced.

In the investigators' final opinion, it would be difficult to establish exactly how the fire started. Good God! After Gay had *known*, on April 27th, because he *had eye-witnesses* that the *Reds had done it*.

Let those who found comfort in these "investigators" make of the contradictions of Franco what they will; but admit with me, that if by any chance he has been lent "Mein Kampf" by one of his friends, with a signature upon the fly-leaf, he has learnt the lesson about powerful and consistent invention very, very badly.

Even the conquered population were not going to submit to this propaganda. A typical story of a stubborn old Basque peasant was told six months afterwards by a special correspondent of the *Sunday Times*. The correspondent was invited to visit Gernika, scene of Red arson, by one of Franco's Press officers. He found that the race was as truthful and intractable as ever.

"Gernika was a lonely chaos of timber and brick," he writes, "like an ancient civilisation in the process of being excavated. There were only three or four people in the streets: one old man was standing inside an apartment house that had four sides to it but an interior that was only a sea of bricks; it was his job to clear away the débris, which seemed a life work, for with each brick he threw over his shoulder he stopped and mopped his forehead.

"Accompanied by the Press officer, I went up to him and asked him if he had been in Gernika during the destruction. He nodded his head, and when I inquired what had happened he waved his arms in the air and declared that the sky had been black with planes—'*aviones*,' he said, '*Italianos y Alemanes*.'

"The Press officer turned pale. Gernika was burned, he contradicted. The old man, however, stuck to his point, insisting that after a four-hour bombardment there was little left to burn. The Press officer moved me away. 'He's a Red,' he said.

"We talked to two more people, and they both gave us the same story about the aeroplanes. The Press officer relapsed into silence, and when, later in the day, we ran into two of General Davila's staff officers, he brought the subject up. 'Gernika's full of Reds,' he said, 'they all try to tell us it was bombed, not burned.'

"'Of course it was bombed,' said one of the staff officers, 'we bombed it, and bombed it, and bombed it, and, *bueno*, why not?' The Press officer never mentioned Gernika again."

Because I told the same story I received threats from two different sources abroad that if I was caught alive I would be shot at once. This added a great zest to the remainder of my time in Bilbao. As my work took me daily to the front, I now carried a machine-pistol of the type of Jaureghuy's, to be used *in extremis*, for a getaway. Fortunately I never had occasion to fire it—for I was never shown how to do so.

* * * * * *

In the military sense, how far was the bombardment of Gernika effective? Its object was plainly the same as that sought at Durango on March 31st, and the heavy bombing of the line and the road between Markina and Gernika on April 26th correspond also to major bombardments in the Durango prototype. The quadruple scheme was in operation again: line, bases, roads, civilian population, on the communications with Bilbao.

Gernika, like Durango, was bombed in order to terrify

the civil population, and through them the militia: and in order to break communications to the rear of a retreating army, as I saw them broken in the afternoon of April 26th at Arbacegui-Guerricaiz.

But Gernika was a town which meant more to the Basques than did Durango. It was the town of their ancient liberties, of which they were treacherously deprived in the nineteenth century. The Casa de Juntas was where their Parliament had met to administer the Fueros, their provincial rights: the archives of the Basque race and language were stored there. And before the Casa de Juntas was built—with its oval walls darkly decorated by the faces and figures of the Kings of Spain, Señores de Vizcaya—the Juntas had met under the oak tree, whose renown was set to patriotic music in the Basque song, "Gernikako Arbola." Gernika had existed before Bilbao and its iron mines had been thought of. Some of the earliest ships to sail to America were built on her long inlet, then skirted with ship-timber mountains. She went back long beyond that, to the Basque stone age and the beginnings of their corporate life: and they called her, therefore, the Foral Town.

To the Basques the destruction of the village in the flat valley came, in Aguirre's words, as a blow to the heart. Their reaction as a race was not that of wild hatred, the unsparing desire for revenge that some peoples feel when their dearest objects suffer: the Basques tended rather to profound mourning and sadness, and to wondering how they would ever forget the grief that the bombardment of so sweet a village had caused them. The Communists and Socialists, on whom the loss of Gernika was not so heavy, declared roundly that this was a monstrous crime, and that the guilty should be punished: but the Nationalists, for whom Gernika meant the fount of everything Basque and lovable, did not think of crude things like sanctions.

"The *Facciosos* are going to destroy everything," they said. They did not mean that such a prospect terrified them. They were, on the other hand, determined to resist even more bitterly than before: and the next few days were to show what remarkable powers of re-crystallisation they had. But now they were anæsthetised by their grief and their forebodings, and it would obviously take them a long time to come round.

The *Facciosos*, meanwhile, had three or four days to do exactly what they liked. Surprisingly few of the Basques in the line were killed or taken prisoner, but the whole army was heading backwards in a rout that looked as if it would not stop before Bilbao.

Mount Oitz, the great massif south-east of Gernika and north of Durango, was occupied by the Moors that same day without a struggle. Next day they had come into Arbacegui-Guerricaiz, and that evening a dear old Fascist lady, pushing on rather too fast with comforts for the soldiers, entered Gernika in her limousine, and was shot up by a surprised Basque post—the rearguard now of their retreat. Her pretty daughter travelling with her was killed, the charitable lady herself was taken prisoner, and the comforts divided among the Basques. Next day Durango itself was taken, and Gernika was entered by the troops of Franco on Thursday without resistance.

The General Staff were staggered by the series of reverses for which they would not accept, but on whose narrow shoulders we lay, the responsibility. Montaud now advised the President to withdraw the whole Basque army to the *cinturón*.

The *cinturón*! Unfinished between Munguia and the sea, unfinished at Gastelumendi, left just as it had been when Goicoechea reported the plans to Mola. Without aeroplanes or machine-guns to defend it: manned by an army in flight, without reserves reorganised to stand and steady the shock of failure. The *cinturón*—for half its length on the eastern side a single line of trenches, to penetrate which at one point meant the collapse of the whole; without air raid shelters, or machine-gun posts, or overhead cover.

For a moment the President played with the idea, which would have handed Bilbao over to the enemy before the end of April. The man who saved Bilbao in this crisis was Jaureghuy, the Frenchman, who wrote such a bitter report on the rewards of cowardice that the Basques, hard-headed as they were, winced and thought again. Very slowly their eyes were being opened to the game of their General Staff.

It was decided to hold a line running from Bermeo through Mount Sollube, west of Gernika, to Urrimendi, between Durango and Amorebieta. But not before even Bermeo had been lost to a daring raid of Requetes, followed by Italians.

Everything was as black as it could be painted—and the Basques were not much given to art of that kind.

Here is one of Jaureghuy's reports, made on the day when Gernika was taken, indicative of the disorder existing after the terrible bombardment. He writes in his special report to the President, on the evening of April 26th:

"After a journey in the back areas of the front, the impression of disorder continues. It seems that no liaison now exists between certain battalions and the High Command.

"Certain commanders of battalions, full of good will, do not know where to go. Even in the large villages it is impossible to find a place to get information or an officer who can tell stragglers what they have got to do.

"It is easy to cope with this disorder, but it is necessary first to have a *will*; to re-group the battalions, give them each their mission, and appoint a garrison Major at each important point of concentration.

"I fear that alarm caused by the aviation may have cooled the ardour of our engineers: we have seen very few people at work. Positions ought to be barred now with impenetrable lines of barbed wire, and sown with strong bomb-proof shelters. That is more important than continuous trenches—'*Nids à obus*.'"

And in a supplementary report:

"All the battalions must be got into hand again. It is intolerable that the men of certain battalions should be dispersed in five or six different villages. *Attention!* After demoralisation one is near to panic: then one can no longer hold troops who have learned the habit of retreat."

The disorder increased on the 27th and the 28th, when Jaureghuy and his adjutant visited Gernika to try and establish a defence of this key position. Gernika, at the head of its fjord, closed the road to Mundaka and Bermeo, and to the whole of the promontory which ended in the cliffs of Cape Machichaco. It was only necessary to keep troops here, in the still smoking village, and the whole northern sector was guarded by the wide uncrossable river.

Two brigades covered the ground between Bermeo and Ajanguiz to the south, and the line ought to have been impregnable, even in view of the disorganisation of the militia. But with communications, the command also had broken down.

The two brigadiers were without instructions. Jaureghuy found the post of the Northern near Mundaka, and his troops uselessly lining the river-side. The Southern briga-dier occupied the mountain to the west of Ajanguiz: he did not wish to descend into the plain or sit in any village, least of all Gernika, which lay open, ruined, not even mined, awaiting the invader in ashen impassivity.

The commander behind Ajanguiz was alone at his post, without telephone or liaison, without even a runner. One of his battalions—the disciplined and hardy Com-munist unit, Rosa Luxembourg—held Renteria and the ridge to the south-east of that village; the rest were scattered on the roads.

The commander near Mundaka was equally unwilling to oblige. He said that his orders were to stay in Mun-daka (which even now he was avoiding, and from which he was ready to run at the earliest opportunity), not to go near Gernika: Jaureghuy, therefore, sent three urgent messages to the Staff in Bilbao insisting on the immediate mining and destruction of the roads leading to Gernika. In vain. Nothing was done, though the telephone conver-sations were arduous and prolonged. It seemed almost that there was a conspiracy to let the enemy enter Gernika unopposed.

At five in the morning, however, the Staff acted. Colonel Yartz arrived in Gernika with two younger officers from Bilbao; an old, tired but rigid-minded soldier, it would have been better for him and his army if he had never come. But he made a show of energy, if in an incompre-hensible direction, on this his last day of active service.

Yartz took a very strange decision. He was going to advance south-east, he said, in the direction of Marmiz and Mount Oitz and reoccupy the heights lost on Monday. The peculiar obsession of the Spanish soldier in favour of mountain-tops was to-day to find its most devastating expression in Yartz.

Yartz stood with his glasses in the farm-house at Ajanguiz, happily watching his troops advance south-west without sound of fighting. Jaureghuy pointed out that this movement endangered even more profoundly the position of Gernika, but Yartz replied, "The enemy won't dare to pass. I am going to hold these crests here," with a possessive sweep of the hand.

The Rosa Luxembourg at Renteria sent in a message that the enemy was concentrating in the north and looked as if he was going to send tanks against their village. They asked for help, but Yartz was already making progress up the mountain.

Cristobal, the commander of the Rosa Luxembourg, was no fool. He was, like Beldarrain, one of the civilian discoveries of the war. But evil tongues said of him that mechanics had not been his trade; living at Vera, near the French frontier, he had probably seen that smuggling made a profitable and at the same time a lively profession. Cristobal, at any rate, was a first-class shot with a flair for improvisation. And indeed these qualities may formerly have been found valuable in his relations with the police. Like Beldarrain, he was a fighter, with a rich stock of courage. He had made of the Rosa Luxembourg a crack battalion, disciplined, pliable, well equipped and keen.

Cristobal broad-shouldered his way into Yartz's headquarters to describe the danger on his left; at least three enemy battalions and their artillery was beginning to shoot; but to no avail.

They were now coming on. Their machine-guns opened as they trotted easily across bare ground. On the left the fusillade was very loud, and pink shrapnel softly powdered the hill, feeling this way and that like a puff on a rounded cheek. And under this beauty treatment the wounded began to arrive. "We can't hold out any more . . . the enemy is pressing the left . . . very well . . . but the tanks are forcing us along the road; the line is breaking."

This was the first time that the little Fiat-Ansaldo tanks had been active in Vizcaya, for the enemy were pushing us into smoother country now, and the mountain war was nearly finished. There were great pine-hills and uplands of gorse ahead, but no giant walls and pillars and slabs of stone grating the feet of the mountaineer. The valleys were no longer locked by forests; everything curved sweetly to the crude Basque plough, for south of Gernika the flats spilled through easy passes, cultivated to the top, into the rolling plain of Munguia, whose surface was threaded only with small silk gleaming rivers until it folded upon the feet of the *cinturón*.

The tanks, with little machine-guns, like whips had forced our left. We had no anti-tank guns near. The Rosa Luxembourg fell back in order.

Jaureghuy paid a last visit to Yartz at Ajanguiz. He found his brain as dry-set and unresponsive as before. "*Mon Colonel*," said Jaureghuy, "you are going to be turned. I beg you to call your battalions in and throw them on to your left to counter-attack the enemy. He is near Renteria."

"I am in command here. I know what to do," said Yartz, with a sudden burst of cold temper. "Do not insist, señor. I need neither you nor your advice."

Half an hour later Yartz and his two adjutants were taken prisoner at Ajanguiz. They were interrogated and shot that night.

Gernika was occupied by the enemy at one o'clock that afternoon. A Frenchman, correspondent of the *Petite Gironde*, entered it from the other side at the same time, with his young guide, a poet who was chief of the Propaganda Department of the Basque Nationalist Party. They had come to see the ruins, but the free tourist traffic was now arrested.

The young propaganda man was shot (this was the kind of boy in whom the rebels really enjoyed cutting off the springs of poetry). The Frenchman, in spite of a recent decree of General Franco's establishing the death penalty for all journalists previously with him now found with the "Reds," was eventually released and wrote articles favourable to the Generalissimo.

Another Frenchman was now footing it across the flats, with as much dignity as possible in his present alarming position, for two machine-guns newly installed in Ajanguiz evidently took him for the whole Basque army. Every

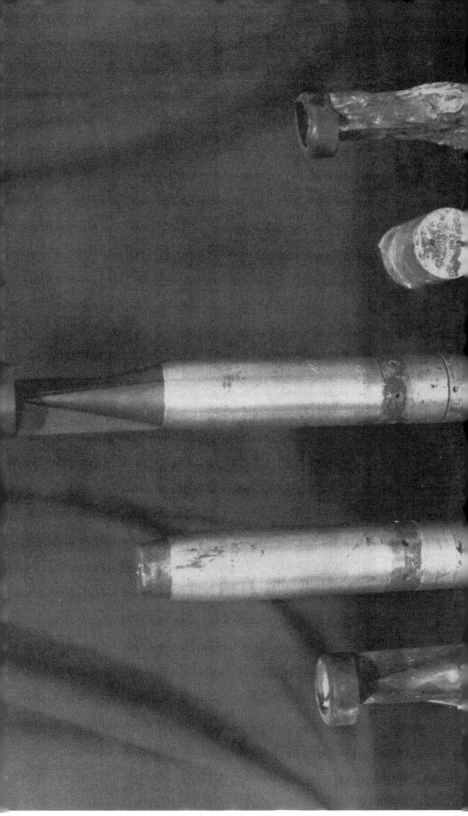

GERMAN INCENDIARY BOMBS: GERNIKA
APRIL 26TH, 1937.

now and then this small, round man would stop behind hedges to laugh. "I told you so," he said to himself, "didn't I?" His eyes sparkled with clear Gallic perception of the humorous situation in which he might soon find himself, and as he went he rehearsed the phrase, "*Gora Euzkadi Eskatuta.*"

XXII

YET I WONDER WHETHER atrocity pays as a weapon of war.

The bombardment of Gernika, lengthily documented by the Press on the spot, was undoubtedly the most elaborate attack upon the civilian population staged in Europe since the Great War, and more concentrated than any of their experiences in that holocaust. Its international repercussions were immense. The evil conscience of the people who had planned this war-like method in Germany was stirred, and came bubbling to the surface in a wave of Anglophobia artificially directed from the centre of the German nervous system. Coming on top of the blockade, with its unhappy memories for those who had at heart the prestige of Franco, the story of the bombing of Gernika caused a violent reaction against Great Britain in insurgent territory, and as violent a dislike of the insurgents among the majority of English people.

Bombardments of cities have always meant more to the British, who have to defend the greatest and most vulnerable of them, than to any other people. Assuming a German mastery of the air, the destruction of Gernika, with 10,000 souls, by a series of about forty planes in relay, would correspond to the destruction of a borough with 200,000 inhabitants by the size of fleet that Germany might send against Great Britain: in the same time, three and a half hours. The blotting out of Hull, for instance, with a fair number of bombs left over to polish off her shipping. Or the end of Portsmouth.

In a less mathematical way, the people of Great Britain grasped this point, and it led them to take measures which went even further to estrange them from General Franco and his allies, who will long remember their wordy conflict with the English over the siege of Bilbao.

Popular feeling forced the Government of Great Britain to take two decisions: to admit 4,000 Basque children refugees to the United Kingdom, and to agree to protect all shipping, whether British, foreign or even Spanish, which was taking children, women and men past military age away from the horrors of Bilbao. For the bombing and machine-gunning of the Basque villages and country roads, and the continual menace of the aeroplane over Bilbao and the river, was stretching nerves until they were going to snap.

* * * * * *

Bilbao at this period was indeed a tragic sight. Every day there was a bombardment in the industrial areas, which were those of closest population; and then came the funerals, the pathetic little cortéges of thin and pale, weeping women. In the earlier weeks of my stay in Bilbao women and children used to run to the *refugios* from their houses when they heard the *sirenas* whine. But now, with at least half a dozen raids a day the women spent all the sunshine hours, from the early bread-queue to the bells for vespers, squatting outside their bolt-holes, reading, knitting, playing with the children, doubtful whether they should dare go home and prepare a midday meal. In the early morning it was not so bad: you would see them reading the papers aloud from cover to cover and back again, but at last that pleasure palled. Then the old women in black shawls and the young with their many babies and their bare heads would build paper hats out of party politics, and sport them with unconscious humour against the power of the mounting sun; for it was a Spanish May. By midday they were tired and sprawled in unhappy angles over the protective sandbags at the *refugio's* mouth. The children were desolately howling and the mothers were losing their tempers with them and with one another. By nightfall they were worn out, and went back to eat a small dinner worth twopence. The only normal part of their lives was the night's repose.

Into this nervous mass more and more doses of nerve-stimulating compound were injected—the refugees from

Gernika, Mugika, Durango, Amorebieta and many smaller villages, with their stories of horror. The routine of the cellar-mouth was only broken by the alternative routine of the cellar blackness. And these intervals lasted long. Bilbao was a long city, and the *sirenas* did not shriek the all clear until the bombers had passed along its tired and lanky limbs, done their damage and returned. About this time the Basque Government had to issue new orders for discipline in the *refugios*. Where people were crammed together, they said, all should speak in the lowest possible voice and as little as possible; talking loudly or too much (a common failing south of the Pyrenees) expended air and got on everybody's nerves. There were sometimes quarrels in *refugios*; not often, but sometimes. And yet the tension could not be relieved, for silence made them think more deeply of the terrors to come.

It was now that a rumour ran through Bilbao; it was heard, too, in the outer world. It was said that General Mola had made a radio speech in which he threatened to raze Bilbao to the ground, "and its bare and desolate site shall make the British people regret for ever the aid which they made to the Basque Bolshevists." I was never able to find whether the General really used these words, and I do not yet believe that he did. But they had their currency in our city, and it moved from hand to hand as quickly as any fearful inflation. Bilbao was trembling; only the men at the top kept their nerve.

Their solution was to prepare the largest evacuation of a people in the history of modern war. France was willing to take their women and children without limit; England to take as many children as private subscription would support, and that was 4,000; Russia, Holland, Belgium, Czechoslovakia would take others. The protection of the Royal Navy was assured.

And so modern war enters upon one of its new phases. The attack upon the civilian population leads to the retreat of the civilian population. The period of the great migrations of people begins once more, with a flight of women and children of a kind forgotten since the invasions of the Tartars.

This is not the place to write of the great evacuations from Bilbao, which in the end placed well over 100,000

Basque non-combatants north of the Pyrenees, away from the rattle and roar of bombardment. Once started, it could not be stopped, and from May to August it went on continuously, ship after ship bucketing across the right-angle of the Bay to the serenity of France, their holds a vomiting, rolling mass of refugees; with more elegant departures, too, as of the stately Transatlantic liner *Habana*, 10,551 tons, and of the steam yacht of the Sota family *Goizeko-Izarra*, a pretty, glittering toy in gold and white.

The protection granted by H.M. ships exasperated Franco and his supporters, and in fact they were right when they said that it helped the Basques to resist. It was not, as they roared, a matter for the Basques of so much less mouths to feed, but of so much less panic and disorganisation in the great city, for every man who walked there heard the talk and felt the terror of his women-folk all day. Franco could congratulate himself that his own aircraft were responsible for this change.

This moment, climax as it was of the attack upon the civilian population of Bilbao by air and by blockade, must remain for many months the greatest object-lesson in Europe of the effects of modern war upon the international conscience. This entity, of whose real existence many had been in doubt, is to be found in countries where freedom and therefore diversity of self-expression survive; in others it lies hid, becoming, as it were, an international sub-conscious. There it struggles in subliminal darkness against the savage and extravagant forms of national order and discipline which try to keep it down; its voice only speaks in cries of individual fear, in the deep, indefinable clamour for peace which hampers the diplomacy of all the dictatorships. For they can say that they are military, and even militaristic, but there is something that drags at them from below when they think of a war on their own frontiers, or an open European war at all. They choose Abyssinia and Spain; they work in the shadows. In the democracies this feeling springs rapidly to the surface —in the case of Abyssinia, Vizcaya and China it has been an unmistakable nuisance to Governments that would side-step. It forced the issue here. The Government of Great Britain was bound to give the humanitarian aid demanded by Bilbao.

The Confédération Générale du Travail agreed to take 2,300 Basque children under its care in France; Russia to take the children of Communist families. In Great Britain the Roman Catholic Church, whose Press had throughout the struggle shown itself a bitter enemy of Catholic Basque Nationalism, was obliged to associate in the work of the Committee which was to receive the Basque children; their humanitarian motive was expressed by a leading Roman Catholic prelate in England, who wrote: "We are most anxious to help in this work of saving and of caring for the poor victims of the cruel war."

Habana and *Goizeko-Izarra*, with the Red Cross flying at the fore (not because they were hospital ships, but out of respect to the Royal Navy escorting them), left Bilbao on their first voyage on May 6th, carrying 1,000 women and 2,300 children. These latter had been selected from a list of over 10,000 children whose parents wished to send them abroad; they were gathered under cover of darkness, so that they would not scatter irrecoverably at the sound of the *sirena*, and embarked at Portugalete. The Bilbao Press rang with the praises of *our brave expeditionary infants* who were daring to leave their country at such a tender age and to face the horrors of the Bay of Biscay. Each child was issued with a tart weighing half a pound and a packet containing twelve cream caramels.

Bilbao gave them a great send-off. Carabiniers conscientiously searched the children's luggage, while the children, like experienced travellers, told them to hurry up or they'ld miss the boat. All had been vaccinated and carefully weighed and measured before they left. As the ships steamed down river fishing-boat sirens hooted triumphantly but softly, to suggest pleasure rather than an air raid; and to each wide-eyed youngster was served a meal of coffee, milk and fried eggs.

Three French ships left Bilbao on May 9th with over 2,000 old men, women and children, half of whom were paying for their voyage and could maintain themselves abroad, and belonged mostly to the parties of the Right. In concert with Stevenson, the British Consul at Bilbao, the Basques were carrying out their promise of political nondiscrimination to the letter.

A week later Habana and the yacht had returned for

more. They left for Bordeaux in the morning with nearly 4,000 refugees. In the evening before the embarkation began six insurgent bombers tried to hit the dock at Santurce: the people went aboard at night. The saloon floors, cabins, decks, alleyways were a cross-word of mattresses, and in a cabin at amidships sat the old Lady de la Sota, widow of the Basque Nationalist millionaire Ramon who was knighted for his services to Great Britain during the war, when many of his ships and men settled to rest on the floor of their stormy home, the Bay, with cargoes of iron which would make the world safe for democracies more cynical than Gernika's. Eight of her grand-children sat round her; we talked at length about the past. It was raining dismally; I remember how falsely, where the water fell, the rain-coats on the river front shined in the ship's light. About 10,000 had now left Bilbao.

And at last, on May 21st, the 4,000 children sailed for England, with Mrs. Leah Manning, organiser of the expedition and the commission of four doctors with their assistants who had examined the children in accordance with the instructions of the Home Office and the Ministry of Health; they were at Southampton on the 23rd and were driven immediately to Stoneham Camp. The Air Ministry had to give instructions to pilots to avoid, as far as possible, flying near the children's camp. Though interpreters were always explaining to the children that the aeroplanes were *nuestras, our ones*, the youngest would not be convinced that the enemy had not followed them from Spain, but threw themselves on the ground at the appearance of every superannuated English kite and cried, "*Bombas, bombas.*"

The feeling of ordinary English people for the Basque children was reflected in their gifts: taxi-drives from a Southampton taxi company, fifty loaves of bread weekly from a Southampton bakery, free laundry on Sundays by the employees of the Southampton Corporation washhouses, nominal rent for a camp of thirty-six acres, voluntary labour of all kinds, a daily ration of chocolates, 20,000 oranges, boots and underclothing.

Later more distinguished persons were to notice that these war-terrified children sometimes stole apples, broke windows with stones, teased little girls, and on one occasion used knives upon a cook who had inadvertently first cut

one of their number. The anti-Red herring fleet came out
to drag again. It is well known that no English children do
anything of the kind. In my own youth I always refused
to receive stolen goods, reported other boys who did nasty
things immediately to my mother, would not touch girls
with a bargepole and fell off apple trees whenever I tried
to climb them. In this way I kept carefully out of the
Juvenile Courts, and it was only when I was at Oxford
that I first heard the sound of broken glass. And I learnt
there, too, of the existence of Borstal institutions, which
figured then in comic songs; but I was persuaded by the
Archdeacon that the worst crimes for which boys were
confined in these unmentionable places were verbal errors
in the recitation of the Catechism, and that English youth
was becoming so word-perfect that most of the Borstal
branches were closing down.

But this propaganda broke loose only after Bilbao had
fallen. Until then Gernika was remembered. It caused a
breach between the destroyers of Gernika and the democratic powers at a moment when the former most wanted
a rapprochement, with trading agreements, belligerent
rights and sterling to follow. And as much as it alarmed
the civilian population of the Basques, so it seemed to
provide for their export. In the last analysis, I think, it
was not so much these bombardments of Bilbao and her
villages that won the war, but the enormous weight of
German and Italian material that fell on the Basque front
line and the utter *inconscience* of Bilbao's allies from the
Asturias and Santander.

XXIII

In the field it looked like ruin; yet on May 1st the Basques had their first wholly successful day all along the line, from Bermeo to Gernika, and from Gernika to Amorebieta.

Ten new batteries of Schneider 75's and 105's had made a difference; but the greatest part of the gap in our expectations was recovered by the natural stubbornness of the Basque. Quite automatically he sat down; and once he was thoroughly seated, his old orderliness reasserted itself. He reformed line.

On May 1st a general attack launched by Mola failed at every point. The insurgent field radio, intercepted by the Basque motorised police, reported to headquarters a total of 2,500 dead and wounded. Throughout the day their wireless was a constant clamour for more and more ambulances; and by the day's end they had taken only one small hill, Urrimendi to the east of Amorebieta where the Santanderinos in their charming manner ran away. They had quite an original explanation for their cowardice: "They're just Fascists like the other side, these Basques," they said.

When the insurgents occupied Bermeo on Friday, April 30th, they had fallen into a trap prepared for them by the Basque command. In the end it was a trap which broke; the German aircraft, after much hammering and swearing, let their struggling allies, the Italian infantry, out. But it cost them many lives.

As a German journalist said to a colleague of mine in the Bar Basque, St. Jean de Luz, "We have got to get those bloody Italians out of a hole again." The hole was Bermeo.

Pushing forward along the only road to the fishing

village, that which lay under the steep *massif* of Sollube along the western side of the Gernika inlet, nearly 4,000 men of the Italian division Flechas Negras entered Bermeo without resistance, rang the church bells, ran up their national flag, and occupied the whole road-sector from Bermeo to Pedernales. Two thousand more poured into Gernika (but not the British Press; they had to wait). On May 1st these troops and the Spanish division to the south of them attacked along the new line; it was the first *general attack* of Mola's, and he thought that he would break through to Bilbao.

He made an enormous mistake. If he had only sent his tanks along the Durango-Bilbao road after the fall of Durango, when Montaud was on the very point of retirement to the *cinturón* he would have smashed his way to Bilbao at once. Neither Amorebieta nor the *cinturón* would have been held. His troops would have poured through an enormous gap. The Basques between Durango and the sea would have been isolated. The Biscay campaign would have been a brilliant affair, finished in two days, not two months.

But Mola was sluggish and his Italian allies forced his hand. He attempted a general frontal attack when he had not the man-power to execute it, and it was a dismal failure, leading to the encirclement of Bermeo.

In spite of the presence of aircraft, on one side only, the front was too long for constant supervision and the concentration of aerial force. The Basques were quite ready. From Mount Truende, where the road from Bermeo wound painfully up the pass to Bilbao, the 8th battalion of the U.G.T. counter-attacked simultaneously over the slope and drove an Italian column downhill towards Bermeo after a short fight. Then was to be seen a sight to lighten the darkness of any Abyssinian. An Italian officer led the rout on a bicycle, with a funny little Italian flag between the bars; his men followed hot foot, abandoning machine guns, trench mortars, machine gun rifles, cases of mortar shells, boxes of machine gun ammunition, hundreds of rifles coming from Italian army stock, packets of Italian Army first-aid, loaves of white bread (a great gift to the Basques), and over two hundred camouflage waterproof cloaks, in whose properties of obscurity their fugitive owners could have put no trust. A few Italian prisoners were taken, including a cook and a captain, the latter dying of his wounds a week later in Bilbao; but the rest were too fleet of foot and kept up with the bicycle. A young private told me that he belonged to the 92nd Regiment of Italian infantry, and that his "Brigade" consisted of two battalions, one of which was wholly Italian and the other half Spanish; he had been mobilised for Spain and left Naples on February 17th. There were many dead. The Basques said 368, but I was unable to confirm this.

Jose Rezola, Aguirre's young Secretary-General of Defence, tired of office life, had taken a rifle and gone out to Truende in mufti to enjoy the sport. Here he had harangued the troops, who were much impressed by his tall body, loose sporting shoulders, clear blue eyes, shaven hair and jutting chin below a long, covenanting face. His speech was gruff and short. "Now," said Rezola, "up and at 'em." Whereat the peculiar figure in a tweed coat and flannel trousers led the way, over the brow, and the Basques were goatishly bounding after him, in their long hairy breeches, from rock to rock; but the other side ran faster along the straight.

Jose came back to the Defence Department that evening with his personal booty, an Italian steel helmet, an Italian trench-mortar, three Italian rifles, two Italian gas-masks and thousands of rounds; and a loaf of white bread. After him came the wounded Italians, who had been told they would be murdered if taken by the Reds. Instead they were X-rayed. One was confessed by a Basque priest as he died.

South of Truende that day another Basque battalion drove the enemy back from the great gorse-mountain Sollube, until the coastal road at Pedernales was under the fire of their machine guns. A third Italo-Spanish force which advanced from Gernika on Rigoitia, on Sollube's southern foot, was first held then forced back with loss. South of Rigoitia the Spaniards failed again at Zugazteitia, on the Gernika-Amorebieta road which they greatly coveted, for it would have given them perfect cross-communications and the power of manœuvre which they needed. And south of Zugazteitia a bloody battle raged at Urrimendi, attacked three times by Moors who had

mounted Oitz: the Basques held under the terrible flail of
the Fascist artillery, the politically-conscious men of Santander abandoned the Hermitage of San Miguel.

It may have been the reorganisation of the Basque Army
into divisions and brigades that brought about this change;
the sinking of the battleship *España* certainly made a great
difference to the morale of the troops. But I think above
all it was the Basque nature; they had been given a
breathing space, and they were solid again.

Had they any aviation to exploit their success the battle
of May 1st would have developed into a second Guadalajara,
followed by the surrender of the Italians in Bermeo *en bloc*.
Next night the Basques descended on the coastal road which
was Bermeo's only landline to the rear, and blew up the
long bridge at Mundaka with dynamite. The trawler
Galerna entered the port with a battery of artillery and
more machine guns to stiffen the morale of the defence;
as the guns were mounted in the old *plaza*, Bermeo fish-
wives looked moodily on.

On May 3rd, the Basque communications between
Truende and Munguia were bombarded ferociously. A
single road, it smoked as I passed along it; and the fighters'
bullets were flying. Thirty enemy planes took part.
Rigoitia was attacked by planes and tanks, and Urrimendi so
far as the Basques held it. But the aviation could not
break the ring. Many mountain tops were burning.
Messengers were swimming across the inlet from Bermeo
to the eastern shore, where Mola was feverishly laying
batteries to blow the Italians out of their hole. All that
the insurgent communiqué could say was that they were
consolidating their positions.

Every day Mola's bombers were out, unopposed: May
4th, May 5th, May 6th, Sollube, on whose muscular rearward flanks they dropped thermite bombs, was smoking
like a great volcano; a great curtain of white rose hundreds
of feet above it. The Basques, looking at the German
war-game with a pacific wonder, thought of those earlier
days, when the bonfires were lit on Sollube and Oitz for
the meeting of the Juntas at Gernika, which would not
meet again for many a long day.

May 6th was a terrible day. We went up to the front
early, and walked all over the line with Rezola; the

bombs and shells had driven the Basques off the long bridge at Mundaka, but no farther. We started at Truende and walked south.

At Truende we took morning coffee with the commander of the San Andres battalion, a Basque Nationalist. Before he drank, Rezola crossed himself. And after he had drunk, the bombers passed over the cottage where we were, dropping much to right and left. But Rezola and the commander went on drinking, unperturbed. I lay on the floor; so did old Corman.

We left, walking down the mountain front to Sollube. I love to see the lay-out of a battle. The battalion Munguia was the next that we met: a bad battalion, morale at lowest, officers rare, dirty and bearish. Soldiers talking of immediate withdrawal if no aeroplanes came from Madrid. They sat there among the pine needles without digging trenches, and dreamed in their muddle-headed way of home. They were sent out of the line at once as we passed along; a fresh battalion took their place.

It was impossible to climb to the top of Sollube, which a battalion of Basque Nationalist Action held: the gorse was thick as jungle and chest-high, and thorns remained in my body for three months. The hill was trenched and manned. We walked along under pink shrapnel, badly laid. It flew past us not too fast, for it was fused to burst very high.

That day they attacked again, on a shorter front, for they had learnt their lesson. Sollube, Truende, Machichaco to the northward, a stretch of four miles; over 3,000 Italians went up to the attack on the first two positions, and 1,000 more on Machichaco.

The aerial bombardment began at eight in the morning, after the Battalion Munguia had been removed, and it was continued by relays of machines throughout the day. Our sky, a cloudless background, was never empty of great bombers striking fountains of smoke out of the long mountain ridge, or of fighters machine-gunning the road back to Munguia. The back of Sollube was a great African bush fire again, and the smoke swept upward foaming in an enormous high-tide through the gorse and pine, trying to choke the Basques on the summit; but they held their ground stolidly. The four-inch guns on the Pedernales road, and the six-inch guns across the inlet battered the crests; before sunset *Almirante Cervera*, which lay off Bermeo Bay behind the steep whaleback island, took a hand with her heavy pieces.

It was at ten o'clock in the morning that the insurgent infantry began to advance up the slopes westward of Bermeo and Pedernales, in their three columns. One force moved north-west of Bermeo in the direction of Cape Machichaco; but the Basque positions were well hid here above the village cornfields where the forest began. The Italians were soon driven back to Bermeo cemetery, and did not stir for the rest of the day.

A second column struggled up the spurs of Sollube, through clefts knit close together with gorse and along platforms in the mountain system which were lapped in pine. Anetu, below the crest, was occupied; but here they found themselves between two fires, and in spite of renewed intervention by their aircraft could not drive farther on.

The bulk of the attack, however, fell on Truende, where the Basques sat in light trenches on either side of the Bermeo-Munguia road. It was very steep here; and four of their new Schneiders were placed at the top of the pass, to gaze on the bay and the Italian flags, but to fire seldom; for the enemy's eyes, his aviation, were always looking down, as eternally effortless as stars.

Bermeo road, a good tarmac surface softening a little in the sun, wound in a right angle to achieve Truende. Here all that the Basques had done was to lay three logs across it. They were reconnoitred by Heinkel fighters for an hour. It was at nine that the bombers dropped their first incendiaries, but the terror of these missiles in pinewood was beginning to wear off. White pillars stood behind the U G T 8 and the San Andres battalions, whom the artillery then shelled for two hours. Their cessation was the sign for the infantry advance from Bermeo.

Italy came up the hill in the most ludicrous formation conceivable in war; the Italian general in Bermeo, considered simply as a soldier, must have been the biggest fool in Spain on May 7th.

Along the narrow, winding road came eighteen tanks in pairs. Up the hill the Fiat-Ansaldos climbed, but they never left the road. They made a terrible noise as they went, and perhaps they thought the Basques would run away when they heard it. The Italian and insurgent flags were painted ablaze upon their plates. Infantry deployed into the cornfields on either side, and made their way gingerly up water-gullies between the crops; which swayed.

They were taking a terrible risk, for if the Basques at the top had an anti-tank gun, the little mechanised procession was blown to glory. And the Basques did have one Russian anti-tank gun, with a long barrel. What a superb moment for the gunner.

He tried to fire it. It jammed.

Fortune still smiling on their turning tracks, the Fiat-Ansaldos came nearer. They could not move off the road to right or left, before or after the right angle where the Basque trenches lay. The fields rose or fell too steeply. So the tanks had to be used for road work; and on a road where they were not fitted to fight in crocodile. For where the road lay parallel to the trenches and they could turn to give the fearful broadside from their double linked machine guns, the trenches were too high above the tanks for the guns to fire into them. The bullets could only glance upwards from the parapet. When, on the other hand, they had passed the right-angle they were confronted by the three logs, which were too high for the little two-man tanks to straddle; and in this uncomfortable *cul-de-sac* they could only use the guns of the leading pair, for by turning at right-angles the road ran frontally into the Basque positions.

For these reasons I regard the Italian commander in Bermeo as the leading military ass of my experience in Spain; and I was there for a year, and met many officers whose ears were unmistakably long. The Italian tanks could not pass the trunks, could not sidestep them, and could not fire into the Basque trenches from below them. So this ingenious regular sent eighteen up, just to make it a party.

It was indeed very alarming for the Basques. Thirty-six machine guns in line firing over your head are not really lethal, but the noise and song of them is exceptionally loud, and it sounded as if the whole sky was ripping itself to pieces above us. Perhaps they thought that their own infantry would move up to the assault while we kept our heads down. But the Italian infantry preferred itself to keep its head down, in the clefts below. Machine guns chattering from the woods above, that the Italians in the tanks could not place because of the infernal row that they themselves were making, kept Italian noses to the ground between the cornfields. The men in the trenches lobbed grenades down the hill, and when one cared to pop one's head above, one laughed to watch the tanks edging backwards and forwards nervously as the bombs rolled towards them. The sound of some explosions evidently resembled artillery, for they withdrew at noon, to return later at four,

The defence were now in great heart; but it was typical of the staff arrangements at Bilbao that no anti-tank weapon had yet arrived. Towards half-past five I drove up with an *enlace* in a dangerous vehicle; for the back of it was full of special anti-tank grenades made in Bilbao, a highly penetrative specific.

Aeroplanes bombed and machine-gunned us the whole way. I have never undertaken a more uninviting journey; but it was the only transport to Truende, and filled with alarm as I was for the safety of my back, I dearly desired to see the little Fiat-Ansaldos going home.

It took a long time to reach Truende. We had to hide at times behind rocks, and the driver would at other times discover that his car could go no farther. We passed behind a Sollube swallowed up in flame. The *enlace* said: "Perhaps we are too late and Truende is taken." There were signs of merriment on the skyline.

At Truende the men of U G T 8 and San Andres were drinking wine out of skins and dancing very manfully. They had broken the hearts of all the tanks except six an hour back, they said. And then a Basque had been bold. Taking a grenade, he had crept up to the leading tank on its right side, where it was blind; and with a delicate hand he had placed the grenade under the tank's behind, and fallen back into a ditch. As grenades will, it exploded; and after the day's failures, that upheaval was enough for the leading tank, who turned round for home and hustled the others downhill in front of it. General booing was heard in Truende.

So the boys did not need the *enlace* so greatly, and were drinking and hopping round in a commendable manner, after a victory of a kind somewhat superior to that of David over Goliath.

Despite the fires and the artillery and the tanks, the line was solid. That night an Asturian battalion was put into the position of Sollube.

What they did will perhaps never be known. What they said was this.

Between six and seven next morning, said the regretful Asturians, they were enjoying a nice cup of coffee in their shelters behind Sollube crest. It was lovely warm coffee, and no fault of their own, when suddenly they looked up and saw twenty Moorish faces in their trenches above them and a Monarchist flag being brandished on a pole. There had been no aviation or artillery; it was all a horrible surprise and gave them quite a turn. So they all went down the back of the hill.

Another view held in Bilbao was that the Asturians, afraid of one day's bombardment like those which the Basque Nationalist Action had suffered, without flinching, for five, withdrew at daybreak without even a surprise to excuse them. The position was then occupied by the Italians.

The loss of Sollube, the red and yellow flag showing on the highest point for miles around, led to utter chaos. The men at Truende and Cape Machichaco, fearing that their retreat was cut and receiving no orders, for the road to Munguia was soon under the enemy machine guns from Sollube, fell back along the coast. The four Schneiders limbered up, and tried to make speed down the road; but under Sollube the driver of the foremost lorry was shot dead, and the commander, Rezola's brother, severely wounded in the chest. They abandoned the guns on the road, and made away with the groaning officer through the pines below, into the plain of Munguia.

The shattering of the line came with terrifying suddenness. Even to the south of Sollube battalions melted away. Italian columns, defeated continually in level war, exploited the Asturian weakness to the full. Cape Machichaco, Truende, Sollube were at once consolidated, and the insurgents advanced steadily along the coast.

Aguirre had one of his very uncommon rages when he was informed of the fall of Sollube.

A Council of War sat to try the Asturians, some of whom were shot. On May 10th, in his capacity as Councillor of Defence, he sacked the Chief of Staff Montaud. Commandant Lafuente, a tall thin creature with New Fabian Research eyes and sloping shoulders, was made nominally Chief of Staff; nominally, for Aguirre himself took over the High Command, and the rest were now no longer his fellow-mourners after the event but his advisers before it. The change was a radical one, and was meant to cut short the discussion, argument and apathy which had knotted up the General Staff until now.

Aguirre demanded a new General from Madrid, with a new Chief of Staff; and ordered a strong counter-attack upon Sollube.

The disasters consequent upon the fall of the great *massif* were still working their way out. On May 10th Rigoitia and Morga, south of the mountain, were abandoned by the Asturians. Asturian Battalion 23 had held Rigoitia against incessant attacks for ten days, and they were particularly proud of bringing down one fighting plane, which I saw in a field across the valley, by concentrated rifle fire as it tried to machine-gun them.

A terrible disaster followed on the morning of the 11th: pursuing their advantage, non-Italian forces at the service of Franco struck south of Morga and east of Mugika to occupy the great chain of Vizkargi. Once more the Santanderinos ran away from a position as valuable as the Hermitage of Vizkargi, which was to prove the key to the *cinturón*. For it was from this magnificent observatory, below which the *cinturón* lay only two miles distant, that the operation of June 12th was planned and the aim of the massed artillery directed to smash it to pieces.

Close fighting continued on Sollube for four days, on Vizkargi for seven. Without aviation and with a minimum of artillery, against low-flying fighters of whom they shot down three more, the Basque Nationalists struggled again and again to wrest back the crowns of Vizcaya that their allies had lost.

Two fighters of the enemy crashed in flames behind Sollube; a third was shot down west of Vizkargi, type

Heinkel 51, and a young German boy called Hans Joachim Wandel parachuted out to bump his head on landing, for the militia cheerfully punctured his umbrella with bullets as he floated down. Hans was a rattish personality who amused me a lot. Of him hereafter.

Pursuant of their methods of Gernika, but perhaps afraid of promoting another international uproar, they bombed Amorebieta with incendiaries on Sunday, May 14th, but not continuously: they did not want to start a huge fire and another nasty story. I saw this bombardment, and picked up the unexploded incendiary bombs. They were of a slightly smaller German type than those used at Gernika, and Delicado the inventor found that the thermite mixture was more active.

Altogether the Germans used three types of (roughly) two-pounder incendiary bombs in Vizcaya. They were most clearly experimenting in horror. In order of trial the bombs became lighter and the charge more active. The latest type were used on Amorebieta; the second had fallen on Galdakano on April 29th, where Corman collected something like ten unexploded incendiaries with the other pressmen.

The fires continued for four more days in Amorebieta, which was bombed once again on the 16th. Then they took the town, and said that the "Reds" had done it.

On May 19th, the day after Amorebieta had been lost, and after the counter-attacks which had brought the Basque Nationalists almost to the summit of Sollube had been abandoned, the Santanderino Battalion 105, unattacked, abandoned its positions on Gondramendi, the last ridge before the village and plain of Munguia, which rolled gently up to the northern sector of the *cinturón*. The Santanderinos were to be met retiring all along the road to Bilbao, well loaded with chickens and fresh farm produce, and telling an unsummable number of lies about the alarming nature of the attack which had never taken place. Eventually the Italians must have noticed that the trenches were empty, for they occupied the whole ridge above Munguia that evening, and Mount Jata to the north as well, where the Basques had stood a week of bombing and burning without a move, but were now turned on the flank by their allies' withdrawal.

It would have been difficult to estimate the disinclination of Basques for Santanderinos that evening. Aguirre acted swiftly. Gomez, a squalid and incompetent lieutenant of Carabineros who commanded the 1st Basque Division where these misfortunes befell, and who had done little to prevent them, and whose large staff lazed about his headquarters devouring his substance, was deprived of half his troops. Beldarrain was put in charge of the reconstituted division, which was now named the 5th Basque, and after a hurried conference with Jaureghuy that night it was decided to hold Munguia at all costs. To cover these preparations, four Russian armoured cars with anti-tank guns were assembled in Munguia, and a counter-attack on Gondramendi was staged for the morrow. A Basque Socialist battalion recaptured half the ridge and took two Italian machine-guns and two Italian machine-gun rifles.

I was astounded to see the effect of the change from Carabinero Gomez the dirty to little turner Beldarrain the silent and neat. Though Munguia was considered by the General Staff indefensible, and they wanted on the night of May 19th to evacuate, not only Munguia, but the whole of his line on that day was reorganised and held by Beldarrain until the week before Bilbao fell, which was a month later. Then he withdrew in obedience to orders only.

That was the limit of Italy's active service against the Basque capital. On two different nights after May 19th there were nerve storms at Bilbao headquarters, for the motorised police had picked up on these two occasions messages from General Mancini, commanding Italy in north Spain, to take Munguia at once.

Beldarrain did not turn a hair. He said that he was fully prepared. All that the Italians did was to sit conveniently in the trenches and shoot with all the violence that a rifle can give a bullet into Munguia. In other words, they made a terrible noise and did not stir.

Every day, beginning on the night of May 20th, incendiary mortar shells were lobbed from their trenches into the little Basque town. Fires spread because this was the fighting line and no fire engine would go near it. The evil conscience of the other side must continue to account for Gernika: they wanted to show a fourth town burnt by the Basque Reds in their retreat. I and the other journalists were amused to follow the first stages of this puerile propaganda as we counted the incendiary shells falling in front of us. Every day the insurgent wireless innocently announced: *Fires have been rising in Munguia, and it is feared that the Reds are burning the whole town before they abandon it.* Children and matches.

Held as they were by Beldarrain between Munguia and the coast of Plencia, the contribution of the Italians towards the fall of Bilbao can be well estimated. Actively, they did not show to great advantage; as the German in his wine said, they got the army into a hole at Bermeo, and the German aviation had to blast them out of it. Though better armed with automatics than Mola's troops from Navarre, they made no daring stroke like theirs, which gave him Vizkargi. Their use of tanks was inexperienced and thoughtless, for at Truende they were held up by three trees, and at Munguia by four Russian cars of whose quick-firing guns they manifested the most heartfelt alarm, never daring to poke their humble nose round in front of Beldarrain's positions.

Their infantry was sluggish; its advances were not due to engagement, which it seemed to shun, but to the work of the German aviation, which was brave, to the regional and selfish spirit of the Asturians and still more the men of Santander, to the showing of the red and yellow flag on a high mountain, with all the fears of capture and execution that the waving badge aroused.

But passively the Italians were of enormous value to Mola, for they were perfectly equipped for a defensive war and could hold miles of front for which he could not have found the men. This, then, was their rôle—the passive fire-power of the defence. Gradually they learnt it, and from Gondramendi to the sea the Basque hills stiffened to the steely sparkle of their barbed wire.

XXIV

I AM OF THE OPINION that the Basques, had they had bombing aircraft, would have finished off the Italian division Flechas Negras on the crucial days of May 1st to 3rd, and with that disaster the attack on Bilbao would have been over. We shall see how the world conspired to prevent such a set-back to Fascist aims.

It had already been agreed that in spite of the difficulties of accommodation in Vizcaya, planes should be sent by the Republic to support Bilbao; the figure mentioned in secret messages was sixty, of which forty were to be fighters and twenty Katiouskas (two-engined Martins, Russian patent SB, capable of a speed over 425 kilometres an hour, they were the fastest bombing machines in Spain).

The problem now was to get the planes from Eastern to Northern Spain. The bombers could not be safely sent unless there were fighters to protect their arrival, particularly in the absence of anti-aircraft defence. Fighters had therefore to blaze the way, but the Russian fighter I-15, flying from Madrid or Aragon to its landing grounds near Bilbao, would, it was calculated, find itself at the end of its journey with only fifteen minutes of fighting time in hand if it were attacked. Its fuel content was not large enough, and if it were chased on the way its superior speed would always save it from the enemy; but acceleration shortened its range even more severely.

Cisneros definitely did not want to send his planes direct. How else to do it? He thought of France.

On this part of the story I am less fully informed. It is enough to say that Cisneros was not discouraged in his purpose of sending his planes through France, where they could refuel and take off speedily for Bilbao across the Bay.

The execution of this plan was postponed over the critical period of the Bermeo battle by the super-civil war of the Trades Unions in Barcelona, for it was arranged that the Catalan aviation, long idle, should go to the aid of Vizcaya. Once more the extreme left agreed with the Asturias and Santander to give the Basques slow torture.

But at last, on May 8th, the worst moment had passed. Fifteen military aeroplanes belonging to the Spanish Government landed in full military formation at Toulouse airport at nine-thirty in the morning. The pilots said that they had left Barcelona for Bilbao, but meeting strong head winds, were afraid of running short of fuel over enemy territory and were forced to land at Toulouse. Could they please continue their journey after filling their tanks?

Bar the use of Fiat-Ansaldos at Truende, this must rank as the most foolish manœuvre of the Spanish civil war. The French, of course, were prepared to say yes; they had the petrol all ready. But the Non-Intervention Officers, who lived at Toulouse, were ready too, and wide awake at 9.30 a.m., and could scarcely have missed the sights and sounds of fifteen military planes in formation, even if they had not been informed beforehand of the little scheme by the disbanded *Croix de Feu* at Franco's service.

Briefly the Spaniards muddled all the arrangements. They arrived in full daylight instead of at dawn. They came in military formation instead of singly. And they landed on the wrong airport, for they would have to re-fuel a second time in France if they wanted to reach Bilbao from Toulouse, and that would undoubtedly cause the French much pain and anxiety, not to mention jumping from one foot to another as democrats love to do.

So the Control and the authorities of Toulouse airport entered into a pious pow-wow, drawing a veil over what they knew of each other's activities, and it was arranged that the Spaniards should be allowed to return to Barcelona, escorted to the frontier by French aeroplanes. They left next morning; the Basques were wild. *That's Spain*, they said, and laughingly we answered, *That was*.

A week later I found Mendigurren in his office at the Bilbao Presidencia looking mischievous. He was reading the confidential wireless news bulletin which we received every day—Madrid's claims, Franco's claims, German and Italian claims, and occasionally the claims of Mr. Eden set in a minor key. "You've seen," he said, "that we have lost our planes?" which puzzled me a little until I saw his eyes.

It was announced from France that a group of twelve Boeing (I.15) fighters and five Katiouskas had landed at Pau in the morning of May 17th. That was getting warmer: Pau is a little west of Toulouse. The officer in charge said that the planes had left Santander on a reconnaissance flight and lost their way in a great big fog. The French were all for letting the planes go back to Santander, but by now the Control were thoroughly woken up.

Colonel Lunn, head of the Non-Intervention Board on the Franco-Spanish frontier, came to Pau. There was a scene with the Spanish flying commander; it appeared that somebody was not certain that the truth was being told in its entirety. Lunn finally objected to the release of the planes, and the question was laid before the French Government. On May 22nd the planes were sent back to Barcelona by order, escorted as before, but first, all except three were deprived of their machine-guns and ammunition. The Spanish Government were informed that if they tried to send aeroplanes to Bilbao in this way they would be held in France.

The position of Bilbao was now very grave indeed. Cisneros decided to take the risk; he sent ten fighters in direct flight over enemy territory. One was shot down trying to protect the others as they landed near the city, and two crashed in a hurried landing.

They fought for a week or so, their scanty and restricted aerodromes always in danger. Then one day there was a sudden unexpected raid of the type which Cisneros had feared on the aerodrome at La Playa de Somorrostro.

It was the Italians this time, Savoia 81 bombers, accompanied by Fiat fighters. On June 5th they swooped down to La Playa field, to find six fighters on the ground together; in twenty minutes, with the machine-gun and the light bomb, they had set all six on fire. A patrol of four fighters from Santander exacted immediate venegance, shooting down a Savoia in the sea and a stunting Fiat on to the beach of the pretty cove.

On the dead pilot was found a letter . . . he was Guido Piezl of Bolzano . . . his parents had written the letter, which was forwarded by the Air Ministry in Rome. It mentioned the salary of the young Tyrolean, and showed how surprised they were to find that the Ministry would remit his salary to his parents while he was away. They were proud to hear of *the great honour* paid to him and of "his brave efforts for the Fatherland and the Duce."

Next day the Roman papers announced the death of Guido Piezl, "a great Italian pilot who had shot down twenty-three of the enemy," and who had been awarded a medal by the Duce.

After that day the Basques used no more planes. The bombers never arrived.

* * * * * *

Now let us consider the case of Hans Joachim Wandel, shot down between Vizkargi and Larrabezua on May 14th in a Heinkel 51. For with Hans Sobotka and his Dornier 17 he provides valuable evidence for the working of Non-Intervention.

Wandel was a small twenty-three-year-old from Silesia. His diary showed the word Garnika (sic) on April 26th, the day when that town was destroyed. Now, where Kienzle was gentlemanly to question, and Schulze Blanck brutal, the method of Wandel was sharp-nosed and altogether rat-like. He said Garnika was a girl's name—which it may be by now—in Germany. Wandel admitted that Gernika had been bombed, but said that as a pilot of a pursuit plane he did not take part. He flew over Gernika on the 26th, "but it was still standing then." He had accompanied German bombers on other expeditions when they destroyed Basque pinewoods with incendiary bombs, which, he said, were highly efficient. He seemed at the same time very nervous and very frank, but as the bump on his head got better he began to lie terribly and to remind me of a Santanderino.

Wandel, unlike other Germans who had been shot down, said that he was not seconded from the German Air Force for service in Spain, but was by profession an architect and flew as an amateur. Later we disbelieved this statement, for after photographs had been taken of his diary he was given the book back again, and fell into a trap which I thought was beyond the Basques. I suppose that guile was growing upon them. Wandel changed some words in pencil, and then to his horror the book was re-impounded and the photographs of its earlier condition shown to him. He had altered entries of the German word for "staff" to "S.A."; clearly he belonged to some military formation before he came to Spain, and wished to hide the fact.

His diary supported his statement that he was recruited in Berlin for service in Spain in the middle of April, signing on in an office near the Wilhelmstrasse, "which is always changing its quarters." The offer was of 600 pesetas a month while in Spain and a bonus on returning to Germany.

He and his diary told me that he left Berlin on April 22nd for Rome in a commercial aeroplane. Next day he flew from Rome to a Spanish aerodrome, from which he took a train journey of about two hours into Seville, where he stayed in "a foreign hostel." The following day he handled a Heinkel 51 (he said for the first time) and practised machine-gun fire at a fixed target from altitudes of 3,000 to 300 feet.

Sobodka, it will be remembered, left Berlin on April 5th in his Dornier 17 bomber, over a month after the Volunteers Agreement had been signed, and reached Seville via Rome on April 6th. Wandel admitted to leaving his country even later by the same route. And, indeed, the air in these parts was known to stink of German and Italian bombers flying into Spain.

* * * * * *

That is the short story of how the world's diplomacy conspired to prevent Bilbao from receiving planes, while the enemy could receive planes and pilots daily even when the Volunteers Agreement had been signed and the Control imposed.

Spanish-owned planes, piloted by Spaniards, could not pass through France to Bilbao. But foreign planes not yet painted in Franco's colours, piloted by Germans and Italians, could pass any day from Italy to Seville.

The Control was very enthusiastic about its jurisdiction over French airports; but nobody on the Non-Intervention

Committee dreamed for one moment of establishing or even suggesting a Control over Italian airports. Such equality of treatment for a democracy and a dictatorship was fantastic.

To do so would have put Mussolini in a bad temper, and it was essential that he should be kept cool, come what might to Bilbao. For it was known that when Mussolini was in a bad temper or felt hurt in his feelings, everyone else spent sleepless nights. And everyone wanted to sleep.

A special insulation was therefore required for the bed-chamber of the democracies, and, like all patents, it had a long name. It was called the Non-Intervention Committee, and consisted of persons agreed to differ. In frank reverse of the parallel lines of Euclid, however many times it met, it refused to be extended.

XXV

ON MAY 29TH THE BASQUES lost the Peña de Lemona to the usual assault in mass of aviation and artillery, not upon the position itself, raised though it was in culminating grandeur to spy upon the enemy in Amorebieta. Their bombs and shells fell on the wooded line in front of the peak, and as night came down the enemy pressed over conquered ground and skirted the Peña itself, which fell to a surprise assault in the mist, and to cries of *Viva Espana*.

The terror of being taken prisoner once more played a master part in the progress of the war. The militia scattered away like heavy sheep in the highland mist, huddled in their woollen blankets and thick baggy pantaloons. Once more the Basques were faced with a position to recapture. The Peña de Lemona was of supreme importance. At 368 metres altitude and a distance of only three miles from the El Gallo *cinturón* it was a superb point of observation for an enemy bombardment of the lines before Bilbao, where they were supposed to be strongest. If only to delay a day which everybody had seemed to think must come, the Peña had to be retaken.

At seven o'clock in the evening of May 30th, we were with Goritxu at his command post, in a white farmhouse in the front line of Hill 306, where the Anarchist Battalion Malatesta lay. Ahead of us, like a horseshoe opened towards us, was the Peña itself; a long ridge across the horizon, fringing which one could see with the naked eye the little pins that held their barbed wire in place, stuck carelessly this way and that. Our maps marked the ridge 368, and the two spurs of the horseshoe which jutted towards us 306, to the northward, and 365 to the south. Their 306 faced our 306, across four hundred yards of hilltop country, dry and timbered only in its hollows. We roofed the pine forest.

To the south 365 rose in sudden domineering granite from the light hill soil, and from its rocky summit, under two lonely splay-footed firs, their machine guns, after long intervals of silence, spat hard metal at us.

Behind us and beyond the valley to whose upper edge we clung lay the dusty uncamouflaged lines of El Gallo, the little grey pillboxes in cement, the tumbled screes from our sappers' long excavation. Thousand upon thousand of pines laid low many months ago, now chocolate brown as the old fern in autumn that the Basques gather in their carts from the mountain-sides for winter fodder. A deep valley, comfortably pillowed in pinewood which moved slowly to the wind, separated us from the too visible *cinturón*.

Two batteries of ours opened fire down there. Their shells came lobbing up over our heads into the Peña, wreathed it here and there with white gossamer, between seven-thirty and eight. Then they ceased.

The attack had to be carried out with three battalions. The Basque Nationalist Bolibar against 365 on the south; the 225th of the Asturias frontally and against 306; the 230th of the Asturias to break in from the back of 306 and take 368 in the flank. All battalions had to climb.

At eight o'clock the Bolibar and the 225th were in their positions, and the 230th could be seen, in their skull-fitting dun-brown felt *kepis*, the Asturian uniform, advancing in great disorder through the scrub. An enemy plane, warned by our artillery, flew over the scrub at speed without doing anything. The 230th was seized with panic, and ran back down the hillside. We could see no officer trying to stop them, all were convulsively running and hiding, hiding and running.

About five minutes later came four more pursuit planes, who machine-gunned the scrub from 1,200 to 1,500 feet. The panic of the 230th continued. They suffered no losses. At eight-twenty the planes had gone. But as the 230th was not ready to attack, or indeed in view, Comandante Goritxu sent the ugly black-bearded man in the Asturian forage cap, who commanded the battalion, an order to re-establish liaison with the 225th, after regrouping his men, and report to the 225th when he was ready to attack.

Mist came down at eight-forty-five, and the brigade could have attacked at once, but there was no movement in the scrub. At nine-thirty night fell; no movement. An hour later the black-bearded man came to Goritxu's command post, saying that he had been unable to make contact with the 225th. Nor had he regrouped his own battalion, as we found later that night, when we stumbled across men sleeping in the pines far behind the line, and munching bits of sheep.

Goritxu summoned the commanders of the 225th and the 230th and gave them final instructions to attack at four-thirty in the morning of the 31st.

At four-thirty in the dark and the mist, the Bolibar, which had lost Peña de Lemona, went up to the attack alone. They reached the trenches and penetrated the wire at three points; led in person by their commander, Etxe-goyen, they settled down to a full hour of fighting with the grenade. Across the tilted black roof of the hill one could hear for an hour the flat explosions, see the dull spread of light which illuminated their doggedness and perseverance in battle.

Neither the 225th nor the 230th moved. At six Goritxu received the following note from the commander of the 225th:

> Before the immediate danger of approaching day, my forces have withdrawn downhill (Se han replegado abajo) without orders from me, abandoning the slopes of Peña de Lemona. Situation of battalion thus left alone somewhat compromised.

No news came from the commander of the 230th.

* * * * * *

Goritxu's first two plans of attack had been set for times at which the enemy aviation were supposed not to work. If his artillery had shot half an hour later, say between eight and eight-thirty, the planes would not have come. That was his error. But all the other errors were to be set at the door of the Asturians, the ever-open back door as we came to know it. The Asturians were useless outside their own country. They dug good trenches, they worked hard in the line. But they treated Vizcaya as a foreign land, and looked upon the Spanish War in the petty way of all regionalists. For them the Peña de Lemona meant nothing, just as Sollube and Jatamendi and Rigoitia meant nothing. They were not cowards, but their long-range programme was to go back to the Asturias with as many cows and poultry as they could mobilise in neighbouring provinces.

They excused themselves by saying, like the Santanderinos, that Basque Nationalism was as Fascist a movement as that against which they had taken arms. My impression of these men was that they were sincerely of the left, Marxist in permanence, anti-sacerdotal and anti-capitalist until their dying day. But they wished to postpone that painful moment as long as they possibly could. They would, I felt sure, fight like demons when they were cornered, but it would take all the ingenuity of Franco to coax them into that final situation, so fluid were they in the open field.

* * * * * *

On June 2nd I was with the commander of the 8th Asturian Battalion, at four o'clock in the morning, opposite the Peña de Lemona's southward spur. The little *caserio* between hills 306 and 365 gleamed dully through the curtain of visibility before dawn, and the quadrangle of pines above it seemed to throttle the neck of the mountain with a deadweight tonnage of black, thick and motion-less.

At four-thirty the 8th of the Asturias were to advance on the right against the rocks of 365, while the 25th of the Asturias Were to make a large turning movement and attack from the north.

The 8th led off at four-thirty, and was soon stopped by grenades and crossed machine-gun fire at the foot of the cliff. And the 25th? Nobody knew what became of the 25th of Asturias. It maintained no contact with the 8th, and it was not possible to hear, although we strained our ears, any fire to the north. The action broke off. It was then that I noticed that the High Command had disinter-ested itself completely in its progress from the beginning. The chief of the Brigade attacking the Peña was throughout the attack in Bedia, a village to the west, on the Lemona-Galdakano road, without liaison with his battalions.

The troops were very depressed at the failure of their

command, and the absence of artillery support was another element which disappointed them.

* * * * * *

Cristobal, the Communist commander of the Rosa Luxembourg, who since his adventures in front of Gernika had been made chief of a Brigade, was given charge of the operations in front of the Peña de Lemona; he used three Basque battalions, the 4th, the 22nd and the 35th.

Cristobal laid his plans carefully and quickly. He insisted on the use of two companies of trench mortars, Basque make, 81 mm., and also on the use of two light Spanish tanks, of the type made at Trubia in the Asturias. (This was the first time that the Basques used their tanks.)

The success of the infantry attack was to depend upon a bogus display of force at the beginning, leading the enemy to divert a heavy concentration against it; this concentration to be taken in flank by a new display of force led by the tanks operating by surprise and causing panic. The Basque artillery and mortars opened up at seven-thirty, and their fire was fixed upon the centre of the main ridge, 368, and upon the forward flank of rock 365 to the south.

Two battalions moved out at eight towards this position on the Basque right, the 22nd attacking through thick wood, with their machine guns in front of them, the southern side of 365 and the grassy neck checked with pine which linked it to the main ridge; while the 35th advanced more slowly across barer country to the foot of 365 that faced inwards, where the rocks rose steeply. A concealed road running like a trench from 306 to 365 gave cover, and their fire was vigorous.

One could see movements of the enemy from the northern to the southern end of the main ridge 368. They were concentrating. Suddenly at eight-twenty the 4th battalion appeared, running behind two little tanks up the slopes of 306; the enemy here received no covering fire from 368, and took to their heels when the tanks crossed their wire. It was clear that the enemy had not thought we would use tanks on the Peña de Lemona. 365 was now assailed by machine gun fire and mortars from three sides, and was evacuated at nine-ten. The fighting and the pursuit was too close for their aviation to intervene.

GERNIKA.

[Photo: *The Times.*

The 22nd swerved right across the track of the flying garrison of 365, and lodged themselves in the pinewood square. The enemy by now could not tell who was friend or foe; and at this moment the two little tanks appeared firing ferociously on 368, with the 4th Battalion, who carried the position at nine-twenty. The action was beautifully timed and finished.

About sixty dead to artillery fire were found on the ridge, and a dazed Requete, taken prisoner, described how terrified his companions were when they saw the little tanks come up behind them. They had left six machine guns behind when they fled into the forest, piebald with pasture, that sloped back to Amorebieta. One could see the Basques in profile on the top, dancing with pleasure.

It had been great fun watching them go up to the position. Untrained troops, they advanced neither in orderly line as skirmishers nor in sections mathematically deployed. It was clear enough that the grades of sergeant and corporal were lacking in the Basque army. But they went forward with a will, and silently, and accepted orders that Cristobal telephoned very quickly; they looked pliable, steady infantry, and their officers had no difficulty in making them rise from cover under the machine guns. Then they climbed on like hundreds of enthusiastic deer-stalkers. The mortars, too, we found, had shot very true on hill 365, where there were a lot of bodies blown about behind the rocks. More and more one saw that this was a Basque war on our side, and that the friends from without, the General Staff and the allies from Santander and the Asturias, were not the elements that would ever help Vizcaya to victory.

Exception had to be made for the new General Staff, which, under General Gamir y Ulibarri, and with the pink-cheeked young Santanderino Lamas as Chief of Staff, had just arrived from Valencia. These men represented the new Popular Army formed under Prieto since the disasters which led the insurgent columns to Madrid. They were energetic and decisive.

Staff work for them was not all drinking coffee. Suddenly one began to notice that Arbex and the others were wearing uniform instead of unpressed suits, that they shaved more, and spent less time at meals, and finally that they had vanished away.

The General had decided to shift his staff from the comforts of the Carlton and settle them in a narrow street near by, which led to the river; where they had more rooms and less comfortable chairs, and he could keep them under an eye which was both paternal and strict. A fine-looking old man, he had a voice which he sometimes raised to make them jump.

Three days later the Peña de Lemona was lost again, to an enormous concentration of artillery and aviation, followed by fifteen tanks—which the Basques themselves had taught the enemy how to use in these parts. And so, it was obvious to the militia, it would be anywhere: however successfully they counter-attacked, they had not the means, neither planes, nor counter-batteries, nor anti-tank guns in open country to hold the other side.

Two days after the final loss of the Peña, Jaureghuy and I were on this front. An engagingly innocent Anarchist of the Battalion Malatesta said that we must come and see an unexploded Italian shell which had fallen there the day before. We agreed. To our utter panic and dismay the ingenuous revolutionary led us out between the lines, three hundred yards only from a machine-gun post of the enemy, in bare, open ground. Jaureghuy and I looked at each other. No, we could not show cowardice in the face of the enemy, we would have to follow. Shivering spasmodically, and sniggering, we walked up to the shell.

No one fired a shot. At that moment more than any other in a year we realised how bored were the Spanish people with the war. Except under orders they were not going to fire a single round.

XXVI

IT WAS ALWAYS SAID that the aeroplanes were coming. At the last moment they were going to save Bilbao. They never did come. But we did at least have the pleasure of meeting Letho for the first time, though his opening words were not those of welcome. Letho was a Basque, but disillusioned. He said all English, French, foreigners, journalists, etc., were swine. Then he spat, for comic effect.

His city of Bilbao, I should explain, had always lived hand to mouth for arms. The mouth was that of the Nervion, and the hand was generally Letho. This was a powerful and a daring limb. It had, quite literally, once broken out of prison; by twisting the bars far enough apart for the equally muscular body to follow.

That was in 1934. For Letho, apart from being a smuggler and an employee of the Campsa or Petroleum Import Co., was a politician with a vigorous platform. In October, 1934, as one of the livelier members of the Basque Nationalist Party, he had emptied a cinema with his single revolver, aided by his other single free fist. The movement had failed, and Letho had been jailed, and escaped . . . and gone abroad, to learn French. It was there that he learnt besides how to buy and run arms. The rebellion of 1936 found him one of the handy hardy men of the Nationalist Party, ready for any cool piece of work.

Letho's exterior, apart from a handsome, swarthy, wolf-like face, was composed almost exclusively of hair, coloured deep black. But he was not mourning for anything. Jolly Roger was written all over him, and one gained the impression that it was Jolly first and Roger afterwards. His mouth, which was always half open, exposed a set of flashing teeth; those which were not gold appeared to be canine. The lips curved up in an expression of piratical humour at either end; the sort of humour which laughs aloud when the prisoner who was to walk the plank is reprieved until to-morrow. His eyes were deep blue and lively, and ringed with black like a miner's, but from working too hard at night. A coat and shirt stood always open above the doormat which concealed his aggressive chest. It surprised me that his trousers continued to give him decent cover. Only a belt sustained them, and Letho was of the championship class whose waist is half the size of its upper story and whose hips seem to be narrower still. But there it was, they just hung on.

Letho had saved Bilbao at the end of September, 1936, when he brought into harbour the shipload of arms from Germany and Bayonne that stopped the insurgent advance at Eibar. It was risky business. In those days the *Canarias*, the *España* and the *Almirante Cervera* were all working on the coast and the Basques had only two armed trawlers. But Letho had studied the ways of the Nervion mouth (which was then unprotected by coastal batteries). Unlike more timid skippers, he avoided the danger of espionage by sending no foolish requests for berth or pilot. He slipped in at night with no other illumination but the searchlights of the warships blockading Bilbao.

And now he had come again in a vessel flying the proud flag of the Republic of Panama, with a load of fifty-five heavy Czech machine guns, 200 Czech machine gun rifles, a series of anti-aircraft guns, 10,000 Czech rifles and 20,000,000 rounds of ammunition. There was case after case besides of new German optical instruments, periscopes in field-grey as slender as reeds, range-finders great and small; what a business one can make of war, if one settles down to trade with both sides.

Everyone was very happy and struck Letho heartily on the back in the Department of Defence. A dangerous thing to do, for the return stroke of Letho made one's own effort look kittenish.

Everybody in the town knew about the arms, and spies were given information gratis at the dockyard. After all, the last ship (also Letho) had come in nearly three months back; this was news.

In the streets, on the dockyard walls there were beautiful posters warning the Bilbaino of the dangers of espionage. They showed, in the background, a landscape over which hustled in the direction of Bilbao a large ship, to be filled by the imagination of the public with every kind of lethal weapon that Bilbao needed. In the foreground on the quay sat an elderly but delighted Basque expressing his feelings upon a concertina; and behind him, an ogreish face rapaciously toothed cocked its pointed ear to eavesdrop on the old man's song. And the whole was called:

JOY IN THE PORT
BUT SILENCE
THE FASCIST IS LISTENING

The poster was universally admired, and indeed it was brimful of unambiguity. But Bilbao was still rather Spanish, and her attitude was to enjoy public exhortation to the uttermost, and to take no notice of it.

I saw the tests of the new Czech machine guns; sweet weapons, firing very fast, and new as paint. Letho for some queer reason took a liking to me and invited me to join his profession, which he said was more independent and honest than my own.

It was about now that the enemy began to shoot 320 mm. armour-piercing shells into the river at Bilbao, not far from Letho's ship. The last days of Bilbao were near. Fifty-five machine-guns! The Basques must have been ill-supplied to make a fiesta on their account. I knew one brigade in the south which till now had only three, covering a front of thirteen kilometres.

The direction of their attack was now certain. They were going to drive at the *cinturón* in force somewhere between Artebakarra, where the Bilbao road came out into the plain of Munguia, and Larrabezua, where the line turned west towards the intensive works that had been raised alongside the Nervion at El Gallo.

Deserters, who came over steadily every day in this sector, all told the same story of concentrations of infantry and guns behind Vizkargi. From this high observatory the enemy looked across our lines to the little Hermitage of San Salvador, where the right-angle of the *cinturón* followed the slope of the hill.

A penetration here, at Gastelumendi, for instance, just north of the Hermitage, would open the rear of both legs to the angle and split the *cinturón* clear away to west and north; it would be the road for the usual insurgent manœuvre, a penetration in force, followed by a broadening of the salient to maximum tension.

Their newly-placed batteries began to drop shells on the Hermitage, on Gastelumendi, on Cantoibaso, on the twin heads of Urrusti and all the way northwards along the *cinturón* ridge to Berriaga, which stood in solid mass of undergrowth and chestnut trees above the Munguia road. Their trials, which were corrected by the observation post in the ruined Ermita on Vizcargui, aimed most often at Gastelumendi.

We had a few wet days to examine the ground. Jaureghuy had long prophesied that the final offensive would break here, and Colonel Montaud, chief of the fortifications now instead of Chief of Staff, had long told the President that the *cinturón* here was greatly changed since the day when Goicoechea passed over with the plans in his pocket. We found that this was not so.

It was a fortnight since Jaureghuy had visited this area, and the improvements were not great. Then, on May 25th, he had reported:

"The principal line of resistance is solid from the coast to Artebakarra—that is, in the rear of Beldarrain's Division.

"But it is very weak south of that point. A few machine-gun nests, trenches excessively straight, an insufficiency of barbed wire. A point especially in need of installation is the mountain to the east of Gastelumendi, where no defences exist and the enemy will have a first-class front of assault."

(It was by this very point that the enemy penetrated the *cinturón* on June 12th.)

"As far as concerns the principal line of defence, refuges ought to be made for the garrison in the *contrepente* (backward slope) of the hill, and the lines of barbed wire increased. I cannot understand why, in your country, barbed wire has always to be attached to stakes of iron. Wherever there is cover in front of a position, the lower part of the trees or bushes ought to be cut clear and the trunks joined with barbed wire. This sort of work can be done effectively in daytime. It offers the great advantage that the enemy does not see the wire, and thinking that the cover is ill-defended he tries to enfiltrate through it, and falls under the fire of our machine-guns."

This passage, Ulyssean in conception, was typical of Jaureghuy.

"Reports from the battalions in occupation of the *cinturón* indicate the construction of refuges. As a matter of fact, these are refuges against the rain, not against artillery fire. The garrison refuges ought to be strongly built in *galleries*; I am sure that, given the contours of the ground, it would be possible to make such refuges with entrance on one side of the mountain and exit on the other. To do such work we have material enough."

"I suggest that all isolated farms should be organised as centres of resistance. The work is easy. Wide stretches of barbed wire, construction in the interior of the houses of protective cover for machine-guns, built in cement and supplied with a good field of fire and with refuges for the garrison. This sort of work can be done in daytime without the enemy seeing. Once the defence post is finished and the enemy bombards the house, the wreckage does nothing more than strengthen its defences.

"As it is, I find that from the point of view of the *military installation* of the *cinturón*, the most complete disorder reigns, and nothing has been organised in the way of observatories, liaison, roads, etc."

As we walked through the mud in the rain between Gastelumendi and Berriaga, we saw how little work had been done in the last fortnight.

Perhaps it was the enemy planes that had enforced this idleness. They often flew over the *cinturón* here, after long and puzzled reconnaissance over Beldarrain's front north of Munguia. The sappers, though a militarised force now, did not care to labour when they were near, so terribly did the Bilbao press paint the powers of the German aviation as it excused each sad retreat.

The only changes were two. More machine-gun nests, made by Mendigurren's brother-in-law, Gomboa, had been installed; they were of a simpler pattern than the earlier nests and their roof cement was thicker at sixty centimetres.

They were very powerfully reinforced with a new iron net frame, of which Gomboa was able to turn out five a day.

But they had obviously been placed by civilian engineers. The main fault of the *cinturón*, dating from the treachery of Goicoechea, persisted. Traced on paper by the military, it had been executed on the ground by people who knew nothing of the necessities of war.

Our new machine-gun nests could be seen miles away.

The old rectilinear trenches still existed, but certain modifications had been made in obedience to the advice of Jaureghuy. At three or four points over a front of four kilometres his typical "centres of resistance" had been constructed in advance of the main line.

These consisted of small self-concentrated trench systems, circular earth fortresses. At the rear of each there was a base redoubt, with a bombproof shelter for the garrison not yet completed. Three or four trenches ran out to right and left, where they were crossed like capital T's by two other short trenches. From the inside ends of these cross T's other communication trenches ran forward, to be crossed by the T's which formed the front line. The whole was not only surrounded, but, as it were, stitched in by barbed wire, which ran between every joint and line in the lettering. The system could be defended from every angle and lay within range of any anti-tank guns that the command might care to put in the lines above.

As we walked along the ridge from Gastelumendi northwards we saw only too few of these advance posts in the defence scheme. As for the old trenches, here and there one could hear steam compressors at work digging bomb-proof shelters, and twice we saw the sappers blowing holes with dynamite.

But of work on the *contrepente*, permitting the play of reserves under fire, there was nothing. There was no military organisation of the ground, construction of observatories, command posts, battery headquarters. All was still to do. Refuges were far too few, but the dominant fear of being seen by the aviation had laid logs across trenches, covered them with dry turf and leaves and disguised sandbags over sheets of iron.

Jaureghuy was very cross. Once more the General Staff had bluffed its way and done nothing. The linear system of defence which had failed the Basques again and again was once more to be given a chance at Gastelumendi. There was no trace of the organisation in depth that Jaureghuy and Beldarrain had enforced north of the Munguia road, and that the enemy infantry contemplated with such unwillingness.

In front of us dimly outlined in the mist across the steep valley whose bottom was spongy and brown-sparkled with wet bracken, stood the ridge of Urkulu which was now our front line—our last line before the *cinturón*. Only half a kilometre of sky wreathed grey and trembling gently with drizzle, separated the two ridges. Springing from the northward slope of Vizkargi, where we held the pass of Morga at the narrow joint of ridge and mountain, Urkulu jutted bonily parallel to the *cinturón* until it was opposite Cantoibaso: then its narrow backbone of rock, sticking like famine itself from the dry brown carcase of hillside, broke to pieces finally, to shattered pieces of rock vertebrae that tumbled into the Munguia plain. Two little hills, very low and humble now and covered with flimsy apple orchards, suggested that the dessicated body of Urkulu had once been longer by a head, whose green, gay funeral mound they had become. And behind them on the *cinturón* side, was the village of San Martin de Fika, with rich crimson rose gardens within deserted walls, and a square russet church still pointing the time, and three enormous shell-holes through the chancel scattering vestments, saintly images, gilt and purple velvet to the four winds of heaven.

It was the other side of this front line of ours that the enemy were preparing the assault upon the *cinturón*. In their high observatory up there to the right, where in this clinging weather one could no longer see the bald and poxy Ermita of Vizkargi, they were planning it all out.

We went down into the valley by a concealed road which led leisurely along its smooth green grove to the bracken at the bottom, and to Fika. Looking back at only thirty yards from the front line of the *cinturón*, we realised suddenly that we were invisible; that here was a covered approach for the enemy, ready-made and comfortable. The only place at which it could be barred was Fika itself, where all the roads joined to circumnavigate the violent steep of

Urkulu. Jaureghuy interested himself very much in the position of Fika.

We looked up at Urkulu, pinch-backed and angular above us. All the nearward side was burnt away by the German aviation; the great square patches of pine which had once clung to its sides were now dry rotten, black and grey, punctured here and there by the little silver rings where the incendiary bombs had penetrated too deep among sodden pine needles. I had been in three of these bombardments on Urkulu, where they wished to destroy the Basque reserves, not knowing, in their unteachable German way, that it was only on gala days that the Basques used reserves at all. The picture was one of terror and beauty as the enormous tongues of white smoke mouthed their way upwards at our backs, and the mysterious veil of war had risen on either side of us, shot with fire too dim to seem mischievous, too broad-sheeted not to alarm. And we coughed as the smell of flaming resin winged with ash swirled past us, and wondered if we were caught. But it died down, and nothing had happened but the toasting of a mountain-side.

Urkulu was piebald now, but the Basques still held it. Once in the hands of the insurgents, it would form an observatory far nearer and more valuable than Vizkargi, and could shelter all the troops needed for an attack upon the *cinturón*.

They would pass through at its two extremities, in the valley of San Martin de Fika and over the Pass of Morga.

Jaureghuy spent a long time here. There was a pleasant battalion of the Accion Nacionalista Vasca (non-Catholic Basque Nationalists) in position at Fika; it was enlightening to learn that their chief of Brigade had not visited his front here for three weeks. We gathered roses while sniping went on. On the high ridge behind us we could hear flattened through the mist the sound of the compressors at tardy work on the *cinturón*.

We walked back as the enemy were going to walk up to the *cinturón*. There it was at last, visible from close quarters as the covered road turned across a slope gentler than most. In the whole sweep of our sight, one "systéme Jaureghuy," two concrete machine-gun posts and the endless linear trench. Two communication ways stretched up the hill behind it, but we knew that they could feed no reserves, for the shelters where the latter were to stand by were still unfinished, perhaps only just begun.

In a flash it came to us that this was treason. Since the days of Anglada and Goicoechea, until the present organisation of the *cinturón*, the Basques had been betrayed, wilfully or technically, by the military to whom they had confided their defence.

But in the European press they were talking glibly of the Iron Ring and the Basque Maginot line. Jaureghuy had often warned the General Staff of the risk that they were running at Gastelumendi; before the position fell, on June 12th, not a single officer of the staff visited it.

The great attack came with the return of fine weather on June 11th. This was the attack that Jaureghuy had prophesied. In his view the enemy would follow the known German system—take no risks, nibble away this position and that, fight on narrow fronts, seize all possible observation points until they were about on top of their objective. Then at last they would throw their whole devastating mass of men, metal and terror into the battle, and strike home with the weight that overpowers.

Until now they had taken no risks. They had Bilbao in their power on April 28th, and again after the capture of Vizkargi, and again after the tumultuous retreat into Munguia. Yet though they had Bilbao in their hands three times, they never cared to press an advantage which, if taken in flight, would have shortened their war by nearly two months. It was the known German system, and it can have agreed but little with the finances of General Franco. It satisfied, however, the careful conspiratorial instincts of Mola, the Director-General of Security turned Director-General of Operations. A policeman born, particularly if he reaches the rank of detective, will never take a risk. He prefers to classify all the evidence first; indeed, it amuses him more than does the capture of his quarry. The feeling that everything is going well, that element is being added cleverly to element in the jig-saw puzzle, is the motive-feeling that makes him continue the game. That was Mola's attitude to the war; in spite of the massive superiority of material means to his hand, the

gendarme in him ever whispered, "Take it slowly, raze
Vizcaya to the ground bit by bit."

And now Mola was dead, crashed in the mist on the way
to Salamanca, the big body in so many mutilated pieces at
one with Sobodka, Felipe del Rio and the effete German,
and all other anonymous members of the glorious company of the carbonised. The plump-cushioned hand on the
long, over-long arm would never take up the telephone
again to dictate cipher to this garrison and that; the
heavy, ugly face, like a watchdog on guard behind the
professional spectacles, would never stoop from its height
over the map to argue the next small move with his German
and Italian staff. The uniform sashed at the waist with
the Spanish general's ribbon would never again fit a little
too tightly on his long, ungainly body whose stomach was
already beginning to drop with too much desk-work.

Strange how fate, by rule so unkind to the Basques,
carried away their conquerors before them. First Beorlegui
at San Sebastian, then Mola in front of Bilbao. But Mola
had seen his *minutiœ* of war assembled until each fitted the
other. Now it was time to strike, and hard.

I went up to Urrusti, in the *cinturón*, about nine o'clock
on June 11th. The great attack began.

The sky was full of aeroplanes. On the skyline sparkled
dozens of pieces of artillery. Flash shook away flash along
the horizon of Rigoitia and Morga, and their thunderbolts
fell upon the ridge of Urkulu just in front of us. Everything
shook.

The aeroplanes, Junker 86, Junker 52, Heinkel 111,
Dornier 17, Heinkel 51, Heinkel 45, Savoia 81, filled the
air with the celestial drill of their engines. Three by three
they passed over the ridge of Urkulu, dropping bombs and
machine-gunning, shaking, biting and torturing the earth,
the great bombers with a sad, deliberate sadism, the fighters
with more song and pleasure, like little children dancing
and shouting round the slower, more monumental displays
of a carnival procession.

On the ridge of Rigoitia and Morga the twinkle of the
guns continued, mute and fairy-like, behind the din and
torment of Urkulu.

The insurgent aviation, unopposed and careless now, did
not mind what they did. They brought out the old

Breguet bombers and put them in the hands of their Italian pilots. We were to see an incredible thing from the *cinturón*.

Fruniz was a village in their hands, some miles the other side of Urkulu, well behind their point of departure for the attack. We saw the six Breguets stoop over Fruniz, while the other bombers continued their mournful circle round them, automatically returning to tear at Urkulu.

Suddenly Fruniz was a mass of bombs. I fixed my glasses.

Men came out of Fruniz waving white sheets as the bombers returned to the target, then swerved away.

In Bilbao the motorised police intercepted a wireless message from the Fruniz commander. His troops, in reserve, had been lounging about the village in the generous sun. "Have been bombed by friendly aircraft causing many casualties. Please ask desist." Later we learned that 116 were killed in Fruniz.

Deserters described how the insurgent command attempted to avoid incidents like this, which had happened before and had, on one occasion, completely demobilised their infantry. White cloths were passed under the belt and tied to the back of the soldiers; the band of white was shaped to a point at the head of the man, broad at his behind. It was to be assumed that when he was lying on his face friendly aviation would know in which direction the enemy lay.

As it was, the German and Italian flying maps were very inadequate, and they needed help of this kind.

Big white cloths were also pegged into the ground just behind the firing-line, folded like arrows and pointing towards the enemy. The infantry were provided with a means of showing where Basque resistance was strong; they would lay a thick white cloth horizontally, T-wise, in front of the arrow. That meant "Enemy need heavy bombing here," and the aviation, it was hoped, would respond to the appeal at once.

Towards midday the enemy artillery, which had been playing up and down the ridge, began to concentrate. Their hammer-point was the southern end of the ridge, where the road climbed the Pass of Morga and lay under the machine-gun fire of Mount Vizkargi, which rose abruptly to its right.

They piled high explosive into a front of five hundred yards at this point. The firing was continuous; the Italian guns loaded and delivered eight shots a minute. The guns steamed.

Our Battalion Prieto held the pass. I had been with them twice before. They were a fine disciplined corps, who used to jump out of their trenches and fire at aeroplanes when they came to bomb. The light wire in front of their positions was chewed up in half an hour.

There was no support, no counter-battery from their own artillery. Dornier 17 and Heinkel 111 hung over our guns and silenced without bombing them. It was this that broke the hearts of the Battalion Prieto.

They stood the bombardment until the end. Then, towards two o'clock, when they had lost half their effectives, they packed up their guns and left the Pass of Morga. They were too few to defend the position against the overwhelming machine-gun fire which now descended upon it from Vizkargi, while the assault mounted the hill through pines and thick head-cover.

Many more were machine-gunned in the retreat. The Pass of Morga was in enemy hands by two o'clock.

Under a broiling sun, as the damp bracken in the valley below steamed itself dry and hard again, their artillery turned northwards along Urkulu, cracking the rocks like nuts and splintering stone knives that sang with flight through the crisp air. Their infantry turned north, still in pinewood cover.

At Bilbao the motorised police intercepted their field messages. "Have taken Pass of Morga; please order artillery move right." "Have occupied Hill 371; resistance still on Hill 370; please order artillery concentrate." "Two-forty-five. Have occupied Hill 370. Am moving right. Comandante Tutor to Chief Brigade."

The tragedy of the Basques was that they *knew* the means opposed to them; the numbers of the planes and their aerodromes, the weight of the artillery and its emplacement, the radio that worked indefatigably in German hands and speaking Spanish without code, told them at the base the hourly changes of the battle, often even the casualties of the enemy. But the Basques could do none of these things; they had no aircraft, therefore a mute artillery, radio only for Divisional Headquarters. And if they had had ten times the small arms that Letho had smuggled, they would still have been weaker than the army that opposed them.

They could only listen in Bilbao to the staccato signals of victory, while on the *cinturón* we saw the flags of scarlet and gold flutter forth along the rocks of Urkulu, which filled its windows and balconies with colour against us like crowds lining a triumph. A festal scheme along the granite hill-scarp was the lengthening wave of red and gold. Our dazed infantry stumbled back between the patches of ash and the black, broken tree trunks below.

They spread downwards to the apple orchards of Fika.

Their aviation now turned east, on to the *cinturón* itself; and to the main road that ran parallel to the *cinturón*, between the villages of Derio, Lezama, Zamudio and Larrabezua. These villages were the back areas of the positions that we had studied some days ago, from Artebakarra to Gastelumendi.

I drove down from Urrusti to Lezama, by the winding hill road, then turned south by the main road parallel at ten yards to the little railway at Larrabezua. The route was still smoking and stinking with the bombs that they had dropped; there were the hot holes of over a hundred two-hundred-pounders, but none of them had struck either system of communication. At Larrabezua, Gomez, commanding now the 1st Division, which had just lost Urkulu, was blackness and gloom dressed up in a Spanish uniform. I have never met a divisional commander more dirty, more inefficient, more pallidly loyal than this former captain of Carabineros. This was the man who had lost Gernika, Sollube and nearly Munguia; it had taken a Beldarrain to hold his ebbing line; and now the Basques' evil fortune had put him in the way of their enemy's hardest-hitting cannon and the mass of their aviation; which as we talked hopelessly, almost listlessly about the war, drummed in barbaric supremacy above us, the poor slaves of high explosive.

Gomez, with his broad *kepi* askew on black rats'-tails of hair, with his slack drooping lip, could tell me no more about the battle than I knew. So I went back to Urrusti to see the finish. We went up the road to Lezama very fast; but faster still followed the winged chariot of five German fillies of Pegasus, bombing once more the road on which we travelled. Without hitting it, again.

Five more bombers passed parallel to the west, dropping incendiaries on the thick pines which stepped the back of the *cinturón* from the valley to the top. The whole was lit with fire, acre after acre.

A single point of fire dropped from heaven like a meteor, crimson-headed and tearing a mad tail of flame behind it; and for a moment it looked as if the sky had been rent in two above the smoking *cinturón*, as the German bomber that our anti-aircraft had struck fell a red-hot stone to earth.

The men around me, forgetting danger for this same. moment, cheered and danced. "The bastard," they shouted, "he's down, and he's burnt alive."

And then a squadron of heavies passed over our heads once more flying towards Derio. At Derio the main roads between Bilbao and Larrabezua and Bilbao and Munguia crossed; so did the little railways. A superb target. They dropped their full load upon it, and you may think that I exaggerate, but the earthquake of their contact and dispersion shook the car on to the other side of the road.

They struck neither road, and neither railway.

Their bombs fell in their devastating entirety upon the cemetery of Derio, and when the picric smoke had cleared away one could see what had ghoulishly become of the walled ground, in which so many rich families were buried. Buried? No, it was resurrection day in Derio. The tombs were split asunder, exposing coffins, the coffins split asunder exposing bodies long dead and decayed; and a few rather fresher bodies were split exposing their brittle bones and their putrid inner parts, for Derio lay in a damp valley. The great burial square smelt of a macabre mixture, unknown to normal war-chemistry; old corruption and new T.N.T. Cracked colonnades, shattered angels and crosses, fell into craters from which protruded the manifold dead, layer upon layer. For this was the evening when the Basques of an older generation turned in their graves.

Their grandchildren took the bombardment of the cemetery of Derio more seriously than the loss of the line before the *cinturón*. It touched their religion deeply. It

could not have happened in any other country; but in
Bilbao the President himself sat down to write a note to
over twenty nations protesting against this criminal assault
upon the sacred dead. My own, and I am sure the German
tendency was to laugh; but in the Presidencia one had to
keep a straight face, for the faces of so many others were
rigid with sorrow and rage. Mendigurren's own eyes
flashed with horror, and he could not be prevented from
talking about the act of frightfulness until we had all gone
to bed.

All night long the fire raged along the *cinturón*. It
stood up like a stiff ragged fringe of scarlet moving only at
the tips to sense the unrelieved night sky. No stars, and
the moon was smoked out. In this chaos the incompetent
and defeated Gomez made his dispositions for the battle of
the morning. Three thousand troops were massed in the
fire behind the point of Gastelumendi, and three batteries
of our light artillery were placed upon the ridge.

By morning the great fire had slaked its dry gullet, and
was out. By morning, too, we had received documentation in Bilbao from the plane shot down the day before.
It came from the overalls of a half-carbonised, unrecognisable man, covered with blood and his body torn open like
the twice-dead of Derio by the fall from 2,000 feet. The
documents were messed with blood. Two printed slips of
paper in German, of no immediate interest, a large-scale
Michelin map of Spain to fly by, and a tin of cigarettes
bought in Vienna. He carried no passport or permit;
I fancy that the German Staff must have closed down the
travelling libraries that their airmen used to be.

All night shots were exchanged between advanced posts.
The new machine guns, olive-green hard-hitters, were
moved into the concrete emplacements at the Ermita
above Larrabezua, at Gastelumendi, Cantoibaso and
Urrusti, where the *cinturón* ridge rose to the heads that
dominated the valley between it and Urkulu. And the
other valley behind, where the lateral communications ran
which fed our front line, was filled between Lezama and
Larrabezua with wheeled transport and trains carrying
munitions and men. They passed the sad empty acres of
cement, which had been the aerodrome of Sondika, with
something very near a premonition of defeat. Then they

mounted the ridge to wait, sheltered only by the tindery pines, the issue of daylight.

On both sides of the front there must have been great tension and stress that night. Everyone knew that the morrow would decide the fate of one of the greatest cities of Spain. Our defence was very tired, very ill led, but it was willing to fight. Gomez and his officers went to bed in the early morning, to snatch a few hours' rest before the great battle opened.

XXVII

SATURDAY, JUNE 12TH: the day of the *cinturón*. A fresh-fainted sky, warming in the east. But the aeroplanes which we expected from Madrid had not come. In their place, light clouds floated by in equable movement, like boats on a calm river; like white paper boats, swimming on coloured crystal, suspended graciously above our heads.

Corman and I rose early. The talkative old porter at the Torrontegui told us that *he* knew everything; *he* knew where the enemy were, and that was pretty close. Everybody in the hotel was getting very gloomy; they were sure that Bilbao would soon be in the hands of their friends, but they would never live to see the day, because the Anarchists were going to rise and rob them and rape them and burn them and cut off essential limbs and slip dynamite in their pockets and blow what was left sky high.

My motorised police escort drove us up to the *cinturón*, at Urrusti, the northernmost point at which we expected the attack. Already at eight the ridge above the *cinturón* was plumed with gunfire, but on Urkulu opposite there was no sign of movement. Flashes showed me that they had placed four pieces of light artillery in the apple orchard on the little hill crowning Fika. They seemed to be 75's; they shot straight at us, at a range of about 1,200 yards.

On the head of Urrusti behind us, screened by a thin line of firs, we too had a battery of 75's; one of the three in line for the defence of the *cinturón*. It did not care to unmask itself.

We entered the trenches and walked along southwards towards Cantoibaso. They were lightly held. The new machine guns were only at this moment arriving in line.

Men bent double shouldered them along the trench, parts of which were still muddy after two fine days.

The motorised police stopped at the first small concrete post, and said that they would stay there. But we were keen to see the whole battle, and pressed on until we were on Cantoibaso. Shells were now passing over us frequently. The preparation of the attack was heating up, one could see the glitter of their guns now all around, from north to south across the rolling plain of Munguia, stamped by its little hamlets and brown towered churches, along the ridge of Rigoitia, on the round hills of Mendigane Meaka and Morga; and in front of us, in line from Fika to Vizkargi.

There was no need yet to take cover, as the foreground sparkled with diamonds in our eyes. The shooting was still high for the light, low for the medium artillery.

I was astonished to find not an officer in line, after walking about two thousand yards. The troops had no food; that was Gomez.

But there were plenty of steady-looking non-commissioned men, *sargentos* and *cabos*. I settled down with one of them, a young French Basque in command of a machine gun section, who in spite of a pessimism written in long italic letters on his face still maintained an authority over his men, which found expression in orders given every minute. They liked to receive this direction from above, moved about willingly with the machine gun and the ammunition, reported the enemy artillery—five guns under the apple trees on the breast-shaped hill half-left near Gamiz, three a bit left behind the little hill with pines that covers Fika. It was all very much against the tradition of Gomez, to be given instructions. They enjoyed it.

All that the Basques wanted was something to do. The long defensive war was getting on their nerves, deep though these were beneath the Basque skin.

Refuges were few along the ridge, and inadequately finished. Of the six machine gun emplacements that I passed in my walk of over a mile, two were still in their wooden frames, and only the floor had been made in cement; a third was built of logs only.

A six-inch shell would have blown all the dug-outs to pieces, except two short galleries capable of holding about one hundred men.

Yet northward of Artebakarra, and south-westward of Gastelumendi, where the *cinturón* became the property of Vidal's (the 2nd) Division, the system was complete; galleries, machine gun nests, organisation in depth, reserve refuges were all in place. The enemy must have been well-informed to attack at Gastelumendi; his aviation gave him roving eyes as well as hands.

The shells were now—it was ten o'clock—coming over faster. About thirty a minute by my watch in the sector of Cantoibaso, and speeding up every quarter of an hour. Guns came to life everywhere; it was later that we found the enemy had massed forty-five batteries against us.

The only thing to do was to take out a small edition of George Herbert and read his calm, architectonic verse. Herbert's quietism has always fascinated me. He fits verbal manœuvre to imaginative humanism with a precision befitting only a good country clergyman, and an accomplished violinist. His conceits are quaint, but they come from the heart; he compresses, but with a sensitive hand. The anagrams and puzzle poems, and the metres whose long and short lines form the contours on the page of the idea which he wishes to convey, of angels' wings or an hour-glass; these bore the ears of the impatient world, dinned so long and so unconsciously to the noise of its heavy artillery, but they're my dug-out. The neatness, the deliberate thinness of Herbert; his constant art of carelessness in language, his fall upon light phrases and linked monosyllables which almost become, but just fail to be, conversational; who ever came near them? I like everything about him; his plain, tidy dress, his innocent domestic metaphor, his parochial clarity, economy and ease. He is virtue strung on narrow but taut, tuned violin strings to spotless verse. I only wish that he had known Cromwell; then English democracy might have taken a turn for the better.

While the guns were dropping their dirt and Teutonic thunder around our trench, I selected an alcove with a head-cover of sandbags two deep, and read. It was like stripping on scorched rocks at an African lakeside and plunging into clear pebbled water without risk of *bilharzia*.

The best moral poem for bombardment is *The Church Floore:*

Mark you the floore? that square and speckled stone
  Which looks so firm and strong,
    Is Patience:
And th' other black and grave, wherewith each one
  Is checker'd all along,
    Humilitie:
The gentle rising, which on either hand
  Leads to the Quire above
    Is Confidence:
But the sweet cement, which in one sure band
  Ties the whole frame, is love
    And Charitie.
Hither sometimes sinne steals, and stains
The marbles neat and curious veins:
But all is cleansed when the marble weeps.
Sometimes Death, puffing at the doore,
Blows all the dust about the floore:
But while he thinks to spoil the room, he sweeps.
Blest be the Architect, whose art
Could build so strong in a weak heart.

And as one looked down to the tattered gardens of San Martin de Fika, where the enemy were now moving their tanks, now five, now eight, there was *"Vertue"* to give comfort:

Sweet rose, whose hue angrie and brave
  Bids the rash gazer wipe his eye:
Thy root is ever in its grave,
  And thou must die.

And the landscape, burnt by the German aviation where it should have been prettiest, was also lightly lamented:

Sweet spring, full of sweet dayes and roses,
  A box where sweets compacted lie;
My music shows ye have your closes,
  And all must die.
Only a sweet and vertuous soul
  Like season'd timber, never gives;
But though the whole world turn to coal,
  Then chiefly lives.

That, I was sure, would not apply to Gomez, round whose headquarters at Lezama the Germans were now dropping liquid thermite.

Their aviation was now out, as across the valley their tanks formed up in a square like brittle insects, jointed and snapping through hard stalks of grass, and reflecting the sun dully from ridged body-armour. The planes passed over us in their arrowhead flights, not in the religious circle that they had used yesterday, but in a narrow endless chain, turning stiffly at the end of the line and drumming back almost within brush of wings. Systematic work; there were, I think, fifty-five of them, nearly all bombers. It was midday, and the artillery had warmed up to eighty a minute. This was, until the battles of Arxanda and Brunete, the heaviest bombardment of the Civil War.

Gastelumendi, to our right, was the special target of artillery and aviation; the first attacked the line, the second mutilated our reserves under the burnt pines, behind the crest.

Their fire on Cantoibaso to the north, and on the Ermita to the south was a flickering steel curtain, to check the movement of reserves from the wings. Very German.

The planes dropped all their secondary bombs on us. They fell wide, whistling; then the ground tottered, and the trench coughed dust. Reading had become impossible, George Herbert was becoming dirty and unkempt.

I had been disturbed first from my study by the language of the militiamen as the aeroplanes approached. They became suddenly very restless and talkative, and as the giant shadows came nearer, they began to curse and swear horribly. "Excrement of God," they shouted (only the word was more agricultural than excrement), "these un-qualifiable Germans and Italians coming to pester us again. Every day, every day; and our aviation nothing but promises. Here they come, the bloody Huns, and the Italians in their second Abyssinia.

May I be forgiven for printing such unpleasant language in a book about the Basque War. But the vividness of their reaction was to me all the more extraordinary when I thought that these were Basques. The race in normal times does not swear at all, even in the mildest way; and before the offensive long notices were put up in its barracks banning blasphemy, by which it meant the mere mention of the Deity with an exclamation mark in attendance.

The young Corporal turned to me and said, "I thought it would be a short war. If I had known that it would go on so long I would never have left Bayonne. But" (he shrugged his shoulders) "we must continue to resist." Then the men all pushed back into their inadequate shelter under two feet of earth, and smoked and lay down in the half light, and in the dust film of the explosions.

I had a narrow shave. Tired of counting the planes and noting their types in the alcove, I put Herbert in my pocket and moved on. I had just passed a corner of the trench, ten yards away, when a 4-inch shell blew the little niche of sandbags to bits. It was the first direct hit on our trench that day.

The tanks on the hillock below began to move forward across the front, past Fika village into the valley between Urkulu and the *cinturón*. We had no anti-tank guns here. Corman left me to see what our artillery was doing in the firs. Just as he passed up the communication trench, one of our 75's fired three shots into a group of five tanks, stationary on the slope. What a war! Their crews jumped out and ran away.

Four minutes later their aviation was over our unmasked battery, which was sheeted in grey smoke. In ten minutes their guns were pounding at it, eight shots at a time.

Five of the crew were killed by the aviation. Corman had to lie in a shell-hole for two hours, praying that they would not use shrapnel, as the black fountains of filth spurted round him.

They had worked up now to eighty shots a minute. Our men ran up and down the trench looking for the special dynamite anti-tank grenades that Gomez ought to have sent them.

The heat and dust and smell, and too many cigarettes, made me terribly thirsty. But there was neither wine nor water to be had. The militia pointed to a puddle in an old shell-hole alongside which lay a torn sardine tin— "that's what we drink," they said. It was full of queer things, some of which floated and some of which sank, and its colour was only too recognisable, but it moistened the throat.

The tanks were manned now, and moving down the valley. We saw infantry debouch into the valley, past the tumbled northern rocks of Urkulu; and cavalry—"Moors," cried the militia, but all that I could see was men in light khaki with steel helmets, trotting on small horses along the path in the bracken, far below.

Machine guns to our right took them on, and a few rolled over; but the rest were soon lost in the covered way that Jaureghuy and I had explored a few days back.

I looked around me. No; not a single one of the "systémes Jaureghuy" constructed to meet this menace was manned. And from the pass of Morga to the right one could see tank after tank descending, followed by hundreds of men; but our artillery dared not disturb these concentrations.

Below us, a house should have been occupied opposite Fika. Two machine guns there would have dammed the river of men now flooding past Urkulu, 1,200 yards away.

Suddenly everything was in movement in front of us and around us. Their artillery was shooting faster than ever before, the planes were back again in monstrous procession, the hillside in front of Gastelumendi was wrapped in smoke, quite impenetrable smoke. One could see nothing, neither trenches nor machine gun nests nor the six double stretches of wire which had once protected it.

Tank-shells hit our parapet.

In front of us there were men and tanks running. Our machine guns opened fire, they dropped, then moved right. The shells were now falling in the trench, and to my left one exploded through one of the brushwood canopies. Two good lads had stood there firing. Both their faces were blown off, and there was nothing underneath their hair but red rags of flesh.

It was a painful thing to see. Many kinds of wound and death would not revolt me; but the human face, source of all visual charm and meaning, versatile, clever and affectionate, smiling and determined—not that—that made me feel sick. These were, one minute before, decent lads; and now they were dead, with blank red shreds of faces, moving only with blood, which pulsed out of them as their bodies still stirred gently, quite meaningless, incapable of enjoying Herbert or their Basque poets any more.

The flimsy brushwood settled on their bodies in the dirt. Shells were now falling in showers around us, and everything jumped up and down. The boys on guard in the trench were white, and their lips slack with fright. Our hole was gradually falling to pieces.

At this moment a man came running breathless along the trench from the right. He was the first officer that I had seen that day; he whispered to the corporal, "There is shooting behind us; they say that they have got in at Gastelumendi."

Everybody knew it in a minute. The corporal shouted "Silence!" and the hubbub stopped. "We must confirm it," he said, and a man went up the communication trench to the top of the ridge to inspect. He did not come back.

But by then we were assured of it. Bullets came singing through the trees on the top, taking us in reverse. They had penetrated us at Gastelumendi.

They had come by the covered way, through the shattered wire, with the tanks on either flank. They had found Gastelumendi piled thick with the dead of Vizcaya, the few machine gun nests smashed by hundred upon hundred of shells, and the linear trench fallen in and clawed to fragments over shapes in torn and motionless khaki. The whole of Gastelumendi smothered in dust and splinters of trees and metal.

Except in reference to Cantoibaso, where our machine guns sang their last song, the correspondent of the *Daily Telegraph* with the other side was right in saying that the troops of Franco were met with but a fitful fire. But what a fire they stood.

We stumbled up the hill, and when we found the trenches littered man-high with earth, we jumped out of them and walked carelessly across the open. The men pushed their berets to the back of their heads; it was very hot. There was no one to give an order to cover our right flank; and to our left, on such light wings travelled Rumour, we saw that the lines were empty already of everything except inanimate dirt. The linear system was shattered once more; but this was its fatal day.

Aeroplanes passed over us, machine-gunning, but we did not give them a damn; we were retreating. The artillery saw it and lengthened its range. We went back steadily, in little groups with their rifles dangling upside down from their shoulders through the curtain of high explosive, flopping forward when our feet felt a contact between earth and shell, till we had made the top of the brown ridge.

We passed our old battery, silenced since it hit the tanks, and with the silent dead lying face upwards in piety next the wheels. Cases of our shells untouched and the ground ripped by theirs. All the crew had gone, except for an officer and three men, who asked us why everyone was moving backward. We grinned and didn't say anything; bullets slitting through the dry bunched needles of the firs gave them their answer.

Everything was dry and dull on the tongue and in the filmy eyes, except the air itself which hurt us with its brilliant clarity. Yet one could see little detail through it, particularly to right and left; for one's head seemed to be in blinkers, and an invisible driver seemed to be turning us towards Bilbao on an easy rein. We were retreating, through dozens of shells.

There was no one who ordered us to go, and no one who stopped us. All liaison between man and man, except those that link the herd and make it follow a single direction had gone.

We were not demoralised. We were not retreating in disorder. We were not retreating in order. We were retreating.

It was some time before we rambled out of their barrage. But it did not seem to derange us. A few fell, but the rest went at a normal speed. The bombardment had so deafened and coarsened our ears that we just plodded on without caring, with flat backs.

Beyond the hill it was more quiet. My car had gone, and so had Corman. I walked down the sultry winding road into the untroubled sea of pines. The persistent aviation saw us, streamed down with its machine guns rattling at us. We sheltered behind stones, then moved on.

When the battle was far to the rear, I realised that I had a headache, sore eyes and stupid, unresponsive ears. All that I had noticed so far was the hardness of my tongue. Near Zamudio there was an officer; he did not know that the enemy had penetrated the *cinturón*.

The noise of artillery was dying away. In Zamudio I found Dominech, commander of the Brigade on Urrusti, and Larrañaga, the chief Communist political commissar attached to the Basque General Staff. They gave me an enormous quantity of wine.

They posted guards where the roads came down from the *cinturón* from Urrusti and Cantoibaso, to stop the general retreat. The Germans, tireless experimentalists, were again bombing main communications between Larrabezua and Derio. Larrañaga was going to Bilbao to report the loss of Gastelumendi and Cantoibaso, for the telephone was working badly, and he offered me a lift. I climbed in beside this gaunt, handsome young man who had once been a priest.

XXVIII

AT SIX-THIRTY THAT AFTERNOON I got out of Larrañaga's car at the Presidency portico. It was another world. The Consul and the Vice-Consul were standing on the steps in the middle of it, well dressed, peaceful and engagingly friendly. I shook my dust off upon them, and we had a long conversation. Bilbao was quite peaceful; she did not know that her *cinturón* had been pierced, then crumpled up like so much old tissue-paper. The *cinturón* was in the waste-paper basket. We went upstairs.

I was still unbelievably thirsty, and as I drank Mendigurren's sherry, sallow stuff, I thought of dust, brittle aeroplanes, tanks like crackling beetles, smart artillery and dead faces, dry bombs, tank dust and stones scattering and scratching as sharp as metal. I was in three worlds, that of the real war with its moves and counter-moves, submissive to minds, propositions, conditions, judgments, counter-judgments; in that of Mendigurren's office, with his sallow sherry, looking at his pale, thin, over-young face as he asked me, "What's happened, really, what has happened?" and in my immediate memory, which was peopled with these shining objects and the stupid, tumbled dead, and reminded me for all the world of a jackdaw's garden, full of hard, sharp things that reflect light and of the wretched dead worms and grubs and broken insects that serve him for fodder. The war was my jackdaw, playing with these elements, the hard and the breakable. I sat down in a soft chair and went to sleep.

An explosion woke me up.

The enemy were shelling the centre of Bilbao with twelve-inch armour-piercing shells. For a moment I felt excited all over again, then turned over in the chair and went to sleep.

317

Another shell fell in the Fronton Euzkalduna behind us. They must have been aiming at the Presidencia. With the dust on me still and a sour taste in my mouth of dusty sleep and sherry and an astringent heart-burn, I joined the others at the window of Mendigurren's office. Police below shouted to us to go inside. Bilbao was losing normality. The mikeletes in their scarlet berets and impeccable white gloves were shutting the iron gates of the Presidency. A whirling sound in the air, as of a stage ghost passing, and another shell fell in the house down the street.

It blew the whole house to pieces. It shook all the people in the house into irretrievable and invisible bits. They joined the house in a fine, thick dust which came floating towards us along the tramway lines. It was a dust with a body in it—nay, many bodies—and I wish Mendigurren's sherry had been the same.

Now the whole end of the street was brown and opaque and in motion. Police cars flashed below, and Red Cross cars, and journalists' cars, and all the cars of the curious were swallowed up in the murk of the dust-devil, born in this immaculate manner from the bowels of a twelve-inch shell. More shells fell, and I went to sleep again.

That night the enemy rolled up the *cinturón* towards Larrabezua, and descended over the pine-clumps and stout hills that took him to Lezama. Cristobal's Brigade went up to Urrusti and retook it miraculously; the Communist Commandant was wounded in the foot, but he recaptured the guns that I passed that afternoon in the smoke-coloured confusion. The Brigades of Dominech and Goritxu held Lezama and the line back to Erleches, to cup the wound which the enemy had made in our *cinturón*. But it bled all night, and mortars exploded dully until day-break.

It was our last night of sound sleep. The General Staff still kept a pennyworth of our confidence, and we believed that their dispositions would be carried out. Trenches and a few second-line machine-gun nests, with the steep ridge of Santa Marina, still stood between the enemy and Bilbao. Two battalions were being placed upon Santa Marina in reserve, where the long pinewoods mantled themselves this Saturday night in a dark blue sleep, as heavy as ours, and the hillside rested from the flat echo of artillery.

Jaureghuy got up quietly on Sunday morning at five-thirty. The women and some of the militia were going to mass, and there was a patter of feet under the arches of Bilbao churches; veils lay neat and virtuous on black waved hair. Through the silent town he drove up to Santa Marina along the road of the Provincial Forest Board.

He found that the militia had not occupied Santa Marina. There were no reserves, no battalions; there was not a single man there. In the valley the other side of the ridge, where the village of Lezama lay, half asleep, a crackle of machine-guns fired across each other at lazy intervals, trying here, prodding there. Occasionally the enemy artillery fired a sighting shot at the hill where he stood. In a very bad temper he came back to tousle the hair of the General Staff. Yes, something would be done about it. But the militia were slow movers, they said. Still, they would speed them up the hill to Santa Marina. In any case, Dominech and Goritxu would hold the line. The General Staff conditioned every plain statement. It is terribly hard to convince a Spaniard that he has made a mistake.

The day was turning very hot, like yesterday. The sky opened a frank blue eye upon everything, and in the middle of everything was Santa Marina, where the pine-needles were drying stiff in the heat.

At ten-thirty aeroplanes came from the south and bombed the road of the Provincial Forest Board. The long line of smoke sprouted over the hillside of Euzkadi for the hundredth time: yellow smoke, which made the sky seem hotter. I drove to Santa Marina. A little after eleven we caught up with a column of grey buses, steadying down to stop behind the summit. The drivers cursed each other in the heat behind windscreens striped with dust as they drove round new bomb-holes. The battalion stepped off slowly and stood under trees listless. Shrapnel was breaking on the other slope of the hill; women sappers in floppy overalls came down the communication trenches to rest by the roadside.

What a lovely target we were for the aviation! The

dust that we drew off the road fringed the hillside, moved with the head of the column to tell them that we were coming.

The drivers reversed slowly into half-cover in the plantations. I moved forward to get a clearer view.

It was becoming difficult to understand this battle. There were men here and there in the valley, but very few. There was no line or form in their fighting. On the low hill the other side, over Lezama, two machine-guns of theirs flickered light and fired from exposed positions on to the valley road. But our troops were invisible. To the right, near Larrabezua, rifle fire was desultory. After yesterday nobody seemed to bother much about the war.

I stood in the saddle between Santa Marina and the series of little summits which extended her system to the right and to the *cinturón*. They did not seem to be occupied.

Further down the road towards Bilbao our men could be seen moving back in disorder, like tired animals through the pines. They had not fired a shot. One could catch a glimpse of their khaki forms drifting drop-shouldered across the pine-boles, like driven buck in herds, lightening the wood as they went with pale transitory life, a sort of yellow feebleness in movement. One could curse Gomez—what chaos he had made of good, willing troops.

Pink balls of shrapnel multiplied over the forward face of Santa Marina, and dissolved in webs of pink that smoothed the upper levels of the forest. Their acute explosion came more frequently now.

A look through glasses showed that the valley was taking on form. The two machine-guns on the other side were shooting hard at Zamudio village to cover some movement of the enemy. There he was, in the open field across the road, next to Lezama. Men were running against a hedge, crossed the road crouching; they were under our fire. Once across the road they reformed, became an orderly little column; a minute square of red and yellow colour waved at their head; sixteen pack-mules followed in pairs, their troops in a long line. Little pins of men, they walked calmly behind their standard in the hot midday, through the undulating levels of our ridge, where it sloped down to the road. I lost them and found them again, nearer;

GERNIKA.

[Photo: *The Times*.

they were climbing in the pines on the hill to my right. They were bigger now, the flag broader. They advanced in order and their intention was clear — to occupy Santa Marina and clean out the whole south-eastern pocket of the *cinturón*. At the same time other detachments were spreading out over Urrusti again in the eastern *cinturón*, to Berriaga and Artebakarra. Arbex, who visited Butrón that morning, saw them swarming on the back of the *cinturón* as thick as bees. Beldarrain's division was immediately withdrawn to check their movement, as one saw them crawling north in thousands over the ridge that our useless fortifications still striped.

Suddenly troops of the enemy were visible everywhere, marching in accordance with a single plan, which was the occupation of the whole eastern and south-eastern *cinturón*.

I found that we were the last outpost of Bilbao, and withdrew behind the others. We stopped to pick rich cherries in a garden where there were bomb-holes of that morning.

As we drove behind Santa Marina we saw that the battalion transport had gone, was still going ahead in a mountain tunnel of dust. The position seemed to be deserted, as shrapnel and high explosive daubed it in a pretty impression of black and pink.

Farther north the khaki ceased to move through the slovenly pines, which now lay snapped against each other and tangled their branches in the saddest disarray. Shells had followed the withdrawal, to kill only trees.

Shells now fell on the road in front of us and struck two cars in motion, slewing them round and stopping them. We slipped past at a nervous speed. At the Presidency, in Rezola's office, the little cripple telephonist was ringing up Santa Marina observation post, which usually gave us reports of approaching planes. But to-day he could get no answer until two-thirty. Then it was a stranger's voice, and the stranger made a mistake about the little telephonist. For the stranger was a Requeté and thought that he was being called by other Requetés on his left, in newly won positions.

"Yes," he said, "we got here quite easily, without many casualties. The Italian artillery was firing better than usual and there wasn't much resistance." "Resistance!"

we laughed. Was there any left in all Bilbao? The ill-traced second line of the *cinturón* was swept away in a breath of shrapnel; the 1st Division was in scattered pieces. It was impossible to believe that Bilbao could hold out any longer. And yet she did, for Putz came that afternoon by plane and Gomez was demoted to be his Chief of Staff.

It was not the calm Bilbao of yesterday. Many that I saw that evening were secretly preparing to flee for France. Naranjo, the cynical Andalusian with a spaniel's face in the Department of War; Gerrika Echevarria, the blue-eyed, startled chief of the artillery; and all the police chiefs.

This afternoon for the first time the planes came over to machine-gun Bilbao. The long, lean bodies of Heinkel 111 turned like sharks in the lucid air over the city. As they turned or slid aslant the centre of Bilbao, they machine-gunned us cruelly. The city rattled to a metal hail from under their rigid, gliding fins.

The population spent much of the afternoon in their holes and cellars. Everybody of a sudden knew that Bilbao was falling. Towards midnight a conference was called in the President's long saloon at the Carlton Hotel. The General Gamir and his Chiefs of Section were there. Three or four of the ministers, and the other foreign advisers of the Basques, Gurieff and Jaureghuy. Glass candelabra sparkled on the gilt chairs and polished tables; all this light seemed incongruous with the spirit of the people assembled there. They were sombre men.

Aguirre asked for their views; worry had deepened the taut, limber lines of his face, and he seemed much older and paler.

First Lafuente, the former Chief of the General Staff, stated the conditions in which he found the various divisions. The 5th, on the coast, intact under Beldarrain, but necessarily withdrawing; the 1st on its right fallen into pieces— where was it? who knew?; and the 2nd, Vidal's, in order and unattacked on the right of the 1st. There were troops all the way between the 5th and the 2nd; but no liaison or grip upon them. Lafuente talked in his slow, reserved way, rather Oriental, without moving his eyes.

Aguirre asked for a decision. Could Bilbao be defended in a military sense, or could it not?

The General was doubtful. How is the artillery? they asked Gerrika-Echevarria. The chief of the artillery answered nervously, twisting a little in his chair, that of the eighty 75 mm. guns fifty had no ammunition, and the rest were served by what they made in the factories daily. The 155 mms. were better off, but they had to find new positions. He advised withdrawal.

Montaud, now head of fortifications, was asked his view. He said that he would be silent, and his thick pince-nez swallowed up his thoughts. Colonel Montaud was there in well-pressed mufti.

Arbex, sitting deep in the sofa, suddenly thrust forth a dark, excited face, and made a speech almost imploring surrender of Bilbao. What's the point of being killed here? he said. He was very emotional, poor Arbex, a bundle of nerves, always ready to drop from his lazy summer hammock of optimism to the realistic earth, from a gay and indolent mood to the very depths of depression. Ten days later he went over to the enemy. He had no principle but the beat of his pulse, which changed every minute.

Arbex had made films. His close-up of despair was most affecting. The Russian general, very calm and cool, advised the defence of Bilbao; he said that it was practicable if they had the will for it.

Jaureghuy asked if the Basques had the material. Did they expect planes, or more machine-guns?

To which Aguirre gave a loyal answer, with only a flicker of the suggestion that he had been betrayed: "We always expect planes; we have expected planes for a long time."

And Gurieff said: "For the first three weeks of the defence of Madrid we defended her with only sixteen pursuit planes; later there were thirty-two."

Other foreigners made lofty and ill-mannered speeches, urging the Basques to defend their capital to the last man. But Jaureghuy was more delicate: after all, it was not Paris, it was Bilbao that would be lost. Bilbao was not his town; it was for the Basques to decide whether they would see Bilbao destroyed or not—for she would be in ruins within three weeks. The French had seen their towns ruined—let the Basques decide for themselves. Bilbao could be defended at a cost which only the political parties could decide that they would pay. And so he threw the matter back into the hands of the Basque Government, which was the only decent thing for a foreigner to do.

Montaud broke his silence to utter the last word in the argument. He had been waiting to perorate, for, like all the old General Staff, he had played a losing game from the start. It was mediæval nonsense to talk of the defence of the river Nervion, he said. The militia were uncontrollable and the means were lacking to hold the ridge above Bilbao.

"But it's a *contrepente*," Monnier exclaimed. "Only their heavy artillery can operate." And Montaud gracefully conceded the point, and he and Monnier pretended to be enormous friends for the rest of the evening, with a politeness and wealth of phrase truly Gallic. They smiled at each other in the most engaging way.

Leizaola did not express himself. But by the interventions which he made to establish the limitations of the debate—"We want to know from you simply this (*a*) and that (*b*), not other questions"—it was evident that Leizaola was becoming the directive mind in Bilbao.

The conference broke up.

At midnight the Counsellors of the Basque Government sat down to supper with the President. Leizaola took charge.

At four in the morning they announced their decision to defend Bilbao. The civilian population would be evacuated *en masse* to the west, and meanwhile they asked the British Government to require guarantees of General Franco that he would not bomb or shell the town. They engaged themselves to evacuate in the shortest possible period of time, and invited the presence of neutral observers to control the work.

It was high time to go to bed. Jaureghuy was very pleased. "That shows spirit," he said. From now on I ceased to take my clothes off at night, though Jaureghuy said that it would smell terrible.

The British Consul took his leave of Bilbao and sailed in a destroyer next day, when the newspapers of the city mirrored the crisis by cutting their pages by half. And that half in heavy type—Backs to the Wall.

XXIX

TENSION GREW ON MONDAY. The enemy spread from Santa Marina along the ridge over Bilbao to San Roque.

The ridge was his, the *contrepente* ours. He could see the city only from Santa Marina; elsewhere the side slope of the Nervion rose to little shrugged hills, and though he held the highest points a few hundred yards to the east of them, they shouldered out his vision of Bilbao steep below. The few shrugged hills from south to north, the radio station, the Casino of Arxanda, Arxandasarri and Fuerte Vanderas, were in our hands and barred his way.

From the river the enemy was an invisible noisy thing; above one saw rare movements of men in the pines and small drooping flags of red and gold and whistling bullets. Beldarrain had pulled his division back to the northern part of the *cinturón*, from Sopelana to Artebakarra. Vidal had begun a typically incoherent withdrawal. He forgot to inform a whole brigade in the advanced position of La Cruz II; they had to insinuate themselves between two enemy columns that night and wriggle, and by a miracle they were free.

And always there were reports: "We have retaken Santa Marina. The ridge is ours. Brave Vidal . . ."

Brave Vidal. . . . That day they dropped a bomb, a hundred pounder, on the very roof of his dug-out in Galda-kano. It stood the shock: the little man was shaken up a bit, and his stomach was once more set in disorder. His troops now lay south of Santa Marina, barely clinging to the slopes that descended to the Nervion. One met stray stragglers on the Bilbao road, full of strange stories of how they were coming back with important messages, or looking for their battalions, or collecting food; deserters all in the homeward sense.

There was much talk of a counter-attack on Santa Marina. But Vidal was incapable of conducting it. A few mortars of the 2nd Division fired up the slopes. The battalions advanced raggedly, in long trails of unwillingness, up-hill through the pines. But when they came to hot, open ground the officers could not think of what next; the Divina division had given the vaguest orders. The men dribbled back down the hill to get food. They had great appetites, like all troops who are badly led and have nothing to do.

Beldarrain took his withdrawal badly. His division was fresh and well articulated; he wanted to counter-attack and restore the situation in the centre. But the General Staff were beyond thinking of counter-attacks. They insisted that he should come back.

On the left of the 1st Division, so we heard that afternoon, Putz discovered when he took over the command that the Battalion Gordexola had been left behind without orders for forty-eight hours. A whole battalion lost in front of the lines; that was Gomez. A whole battalion uninjured, unsurrounded, unattacked, unnoticed even in its isolation; that was the enemy. That was Italy and the old Spanish Army running a war against a former lieutenant of Carabineros. Tired of being forgotten, the Gordexola withdrew this afternoon from the vacuum and joined Beldarrain.

But there was hope in the air for us to catch at her. Jaureghuy went up to Begoña, the new headquarters of the 1st Division, and found a new atmosphere. A lean, restless officer was in charge, Colonel Putz. Putz —well, Putz is not a Spaniard; he is a fighting officer. News about him came through slowly: International Brigade . . . Ralph Fox's commander . . . a French municipal councillor and captain of reserve, with Great War experience . . . become a colonel in the Spanish Republican Army . . . he commanded a brigade to astonishing victory at the battle of Guadalajara.

Jaureghuy found that Putz had reconnoitred, in person, the whole of his line on Monday afternoon. He had placed the battalions, fixed the reserve points himself. This was the first time in the Basque war that we had seen a divisional commander take the risk, except for Beldarrain, the natural leader, who did it in more peaceful days. Putz had been travelling that day with bombs in his hand, trying to find the enemy machine-guns.

"All's well to-night," said Jaureghuy; "we can sleep solid. Putz will hold them; he knows his job."

Night fell, Beldarrain was ordered to withdraw again and bring his right into line with the 1st Division at Arxandasarri.

Tempers were very bad at the General Staff, for Beldarrain said that he was unwilling to do so. The old general was walking through the staff from room to room with the lurch of a fretful cockatoo, and the Russian general took the solid, well-disciplined view that orders is orders. Jaureghuy defended Beldarrain. This continual withdrawal is lunatic, he said; his division is still combative. It ought to fall on their flank; they will win. But orders is orders, said the Russian general steadily.

Yes, the staff were in a foul mood. In the past they had never seemed to mind when an order to counterattack was fumbled, or executed two days late, or disregarded wholly. But an order to retreat was a different matter, and to disobey it was rank indiscipline.

All the officers who had not seen the front for months agreed that Beldarrain must be brought to heel. (And, indeed, after the fall of Bilbao, they were able to relieve him of his Division. In the meantime he had cut up an Italian battery, taken seventy-five prisoners, destroyed two Spanish companies, protected the retreat of the 1st Division from Bilbao and blown up the bridges of the Cadagua to cover them. So the General Staff sacked him.)

One saw, in a moment of despair, how the whole system worked; how the enemy aviation and artillery had struck; how the staff had been impressed, as purely mechanical soldiers would be, by the weight of these mechanical means; morale, the breaking and the restoration of it did not interest them. They were persuaded, and they had played as losers from the very beginning. What persuaded them was the bang and crack of the machines on the other side.

So they had always retreated: orders to counter-attack had been given in an undertone, almost in the hope that they would not be heard. Lafuente had done his best, and when the new general and Lamas, his Chief of Staff, arrived, too late, they had tried to inject an offensive spirit into them. But they, too, were soon submerged in the general tide of defeatism.

The General Staff were neither class fighters, nor Basques. They were united by the ordinary ties of race, rank and education to the people against whom they were fighting, rather than to the men that they were leading. They were not traitors, but they were not enthusiasts. They had nothing to lose but, in the long run, their lives. And the long run was still long enough from Bilbao through Santander to the Asturias, with occasional midnight opportunities of catching a ship to France on the way.

They had communicated their defeatism to officers in the field. They had not relieved incompetent divisional commanders of their commands until it was too late, for the incompetent agreed with them that it was best to retreat.

And the militia, encouraged in their fears of aviation and artillery which they had never seen before, were based on Bilbao. They were not yet a full regular army. When they returned to Bilbao they scattered to their homes. There they told their families of the dangers of the front, and their families told them of the many dead in air raids along the river. All were stricken with the spirit of retreat.

Two men only held them up—Putz and Beldarrain. The half-civilian army, endowed with fine qualities of physique and combative resistance, was ruined from above by the half-willing Staff.

Their worst fears were now spreading to the whole people, and as night fell and the last aeroplane droned out of view, the population of Bilbao began its great flight to the west and to the open sea.

In a moment, with the onset of darkness, Bilbao's wide streets between banks and Government offices and high blocks of granite flats and paper-stained glass, and between the thick, dull rows of dirty sandbags, were lined with motor-lorries, dozen upon dozen of them. The pavements were packed with people, women and men holding children, or laying them down to sleep on the ground. The doorways were entangled with furniture, all butting legs and arms, which when it had struggled past hundreds of human bodies was stacked in rickety assemblies at the roadside.

Mattresses were spilled everywhere, and the streets under the still plane trees were littered with tired humanity, lolling its head on its shoulder and struggling against sleep as the lorries rolled by.

The evacuation of Bilbao had begun. From the windows one could watch, as they threaded their way through the glimmer of the night traffic like long awkward-jointed toys, trains of light artillery making for Retuerto to guard the western bank of the Nervion.

The Nervion swarmed with movement, seemed to shiver to many sirens. The whole fleet of Bilbao was being brought under steam. Orders had been issued to move every ship on the east to the western bank, there to pick up refugees for Santander and France. In rusty phalanxes of a hundred the fishing trawlers which had been brought in from San Sebastian had lain idle there for eight months, leaning against each other's sides. Now the ranks were broken and drifted fanwise, little turrets of steam shot into the sky and were lost in the darkness. A huge crowd gathered at the docks of the Altos Hornos, and Sestao and Santurce on the other side, men, women and children.

Gangways were thrown down on the destroyers *Ciscar* and *Jose Luis Diez*. In their new warpaint, they were to take women and children to France. An unstoppable mob clambered on to the destroyers, and in the middle of it were the suitcases and persons of Gerrika-Echevarria, head of the Artillery, Pikazar, head of the Motorised Police, Mendigurren, Director of Foreign Affairs, Unceta, the chief of Sanidad Militar, which was the Basque R.A.M.C., and Naranjo, the staff officer attached to the Defence Department.

The captain of the *Ciscar* found the deserters half-way, and wirelessed to Bilbao for orders. He was told to arrest them and return them. But when he arrived in a French port he was given fifteen minutes by the French authorities to disembark the whole lot, and told that if he held back any he would have to keep all.

On the decks one could, in the dark, only count hundreds of excited heads. Feet were invisible; all that one could see were heads and lips in nervous shadowy motion, explaining things. With a deckful of serried and jerking ninepins, *Ciscar* and *Jose Luis Diez* put out to sea. Water swept their sharp bows in a parabola of moonstruck light, as they went faster.

All along the riverside, for over six miles, women and children and old men were piling uncontrollably into trawlers for Santander. The night showed a moon, and the moon a restless ebb and flow of people, dressed in black, with shining hair and pale faces, and men with melancholy black berets who moved slowly over black docks and under black cranes and tips and furnaces to a riverside shuddering with motion and mirrored light.

One was struck by the solemnity of this scene, and the sad, small dignity of actors in it. It was a simple play in which they were acting, with a single motive; all would escape far from this terrible war, to food and peace at Santander. The light defiantly dancing before them on the Nervion was the light of this hope; lost and found again, lost and always to be found. But all their faces were in the shadow; they were a mass, not men; a black sea in failing movement after storm.

In the city at the bridges of the Nervion the land evacuation gathered speed. Lorries all night were rumbling through Bilbao, built high with chairs and bedsteads and sagging bundles, to which people clung and under which they cowered. The streets of Bilbao were like the lanes of a factory, with engines turning and grinding and hammering their muscles to pieces on every side. Only headlights and the street lamps were lit to illuminate this movement of an unhappy underworld. Above the blind walls of the buildings, the night seemed despite the moon to lie oppressively upon the city which we were losing.

There was a great nervousness abroad, an irresistible impulse to go to Santander. Captain Alambarri, the handsome officer on the General Staff, leant out of Rezola's office in the moonlight to look at the people who huddled and hurried below. The golden knots that dangled from his shoulder made of Alambarri a movie hero, a Douglas Fairbanks, a dark athlete rigged up in gold and khaki for some impossible romance. But the romance that he was watching was the romance of the demoralisation of a whole people, and he did not seem to understand yet that it was *his* General Staff who had made it a romance so melancholy to see. "Say what you like," he said, "*Bilbao se ha perdido—*

Bilbao is lost." He peered angrily into the dark. Militiamen from the Asturias were passing below. "Men desert-
ing," he added, with a jerk of a head to show that he was
justified. Poor, romantic, ignorant Alambarri, who had
never thought of a means to stop them.

All the time in the Plaza and the wide streets the noise
and movement went on; black shapes of men passing
before lights, lights passing more swiftly before black shapes
of tired men. Lines of bright movement round squares of
black monumental death. Evacuation and its noises, the
roar of lorries and the cry of awakened children, with the
nearer, more insistent, tones of the whisper of hundreds of
people, as one shouldered one's way through the mottled
streets.

That night the enemy aviation came out in the soft
moonlight and machine-gunned the length of the road to
Santander, flying very low. They fired tracer bullets,
which lit the lower sky with sudden strips of fire, delicate as
silk and flicked the earth to either side of the terrified
refugees. These were the whips which they had to travel
under, until they reached haven at Castro Urdiales or
Laredo or Santoña, and fell off their lorries to sleep heavily
at the roadside, all sexes and ages rolled into one common
grass bed. They were so worn out they they still went
on sleeping when the planes returned to light, with their
horrible subtle tracery, the towns where they lay before
morning broke.

And to sea, the straggling armada made for Santander
and Santoña, carrying thousands of people from Bilbao.
An enemy warship intervened to seize two; the rest bore
along by sheer swarm of numbers.

The evacuation continued every night till Friday, with
an intensity that diminished as more and more lorries
stayed behind in the west. It carried away nearly 200,000
people, over half of the swollen population of Bilbao.

It made sleep impossible. I could sleep through the
noise, but a strange inquisitive restlessness imparted by this
people kept me awake. I wondered how they got their
lorries, how they could pack their households up and be
so quickly away. I wanted to see if their terror would
spread to the army.

While I was wondering, Arbex came to the Presidencia

in panic. He entered Rezola's office, his southern face as pale as honey, and the layers of his Sicilian hair sprung up behind in straggly disorder. He talked very briskly to us to cover his fright. "I've come from the General Staff," he said, "to tell you that an Asturian Brigade has withdrawn before Asua. There is a large gap between Putz' and Beldarrain's Division just over Bilbao. The enemy is advancing with tanks down from Asua, and he can be in the city within an hour. We have telephoned for dynamite from the stores in Bilbao to blow up the bridges. They say that there is none. The only other place for dynamite is Galdakano, and it will take more than an hour to find dynamite there."

Arbex rapped this out in a hard, tense voice, like a woman giving orders. As I have said, our old General Staff was only active when it was organising a retreat. And Arbex was more than tense; he was almost off to Santander himself, so trembled his eyelids with a snakish fear. Poor Arbex, he was smoking too much. Rezola looked at him with his straight blue eyes, and jutted his chin, and curved his mouth a bit, and stood over him in a commanding way, and said, "Nonsense, there must be dynamite in Bilbao."

"There is none," said Arbex. And he was wrong; in Bilbao there were mountains of dynamite. But that short dialogue sticks in my mind, and the picture of the parties who confronted each other in Rezola's office that night. The Spaniard all nerves and the Basque a blue-eyed stubborn unbeliever. Under-morale and over-morale; they came from different worlds.

But the crisis remained. There was a gap, Arbex said that the enemy were passing through it, and they could not be stopped.

Jaureghuy volunteered to go up to the front on Arxanda and get information. He offered to take me. I always hated night manœuvres. We went up the winding road to Begoña with lights out.

Nuestra Señora de Begoña is the patron of Basque fishermen. Her church was now the headquarters of the 1st Division. Long figures in tangled khaki mantles slept at the great doorway which we entered, stumbling over them and the dark irregular steps. The men did not move.

In the church, lights of candles marked the altar far away, and a light swinging before the pulpit showed up the mysticism of the lofty roof, the rest was deep darkness. The stone floor of the nave was empty and startled us with its hard answer to our feet. Beds and mattresses and palliasses lined the aisles, and men lay in them sleeping. We passed them on tiptoe, and passed the sparkling ornaments on the altar, and the lit Cross, in a diamond of fire.

Some of the men were talking in husky voices, their elbows on the stone floor and cigarettes between their fingers. A guard with fixed bayonet stood at the door of the chapter-house, and let us pass.

Other dim lights illuminated the painted glass, under which Putz lay rolled up in his overcoat after a tiring day. The map of his sector was spreadeagled on a table at his side, a mess of red and blue chalk lines half rubbed out that dulled the light; and the red lines had moved steadily backwards and the blue forwards. A fine thin face Putz had, a neat-looking man but not a gentleman. A look of humanity between his brow and his mouth, humanity of a sort that a gentleman might be ashamed to carry. I don't know what his humble profession was before the war; but over his feet in the riding boots hung a crucifix impaled with the body of the Carpenter Christ that looked down in compassion. I am sure Putz was more elevated than a carpenter.

Grenades that he had not used that day rolled beneath the bench on which he slept. We woke up his aide, and asked him how things stood.

Things were rather bad. The Asturians had truly run, but the story of the tanks was a fiction of Arbex. A dozen tanks had appeared in Asua, the other side of the ridge northwards, but Beldarrain's men had driven them out again with a few bombs, and Asua had been re-occupied. The trouble was here, and he pointed a finger; a gap still existed to the left at Berriz and Arxandasarri; they were trying to muster two battalions to fill it.

All this in sleepy language, with much rubbing of eyes and awkward mistaken scrawling upon maps and paper. It was a gap two kilometres wide. We wiped our foreheads, and went off to look at it.

I dislike night operations, but the dim church with the

sleeping figures was soon behind us, and Jaureghuy led the way jauntily with his beret over his right ear.

There was a muffled, frowsy guard post on the way that talked to us through their blankets. After that, nothing on the road. We passed along the trenches below the skyline— light unfinished trenches of the last days behind which men huddled. All near us was dead silence; it was hard to tell whether the night sentinels were awake or asleep. In the blind distance to the eastwards there was firing, but above it we could hear our own hearts changing time. So on, under the radio station which lifted its blue bones in the moonlight, through scraggy trees to the great stucco block of the Casino, a little farther. A man stopped us. "This is the last battalion," he said, and I swore to myself that it was. Still and stiff though they seemed, they were all wide awake, and their eyes dilated in the moon like those of lemurs. They knew what danger they stood in, but they kept their ground.

We looked forward into the empty darkness. There was no noise or movement, not even the movement of wind. The stillness penetrated us; we felt more frightened than if we had heard the tanks moving there and seen their squat shoulders shining in gauche manœuvre on the near horizon. But the unknown is always more terrifying than the known, even when you know enough about it not to people it with your fears.

There were no men there, and we could hear none coming up from Bilbao below. That was enough. We listened to the firing, now distant and lame.

The firing was Beldarrain's Division, which made a brilliant sortie that night towards the old *cinturón*. On Lañamendi, the hill northwest of the *cinturón* gateway at Artebakarra, they shot up two enemy companies and took seventy-five prisoners, new Galician levies of the Regiment of Zamora. Beldarrain, good soldier, had decided to cover up the hole on his right by attacking strongly from his centre. This night he took more prisoners than did all the other divisions during two and a half months of offensive.

But we did not know that yet. A gap of two kilometres existed just above Bilbao, and the enemy could come down to the river and occupy the bridges at any moment, if he chose to launch a sudden night-attack.

It was Jaureghuy's duty to warn the Government of the danger which they incurred by remaining in Bilbao. He saw them in the early morning and described the position. They left in cars for Trucios in Western Vizcaya, where they settled in an apple orchard and a lovely scrolled caserio of stone, leaving behind a Junta de Defensa for Bilbao; which it was still possible to hold if the 1st and 2nd Divisions stood steady.

Leizaola, the Basque Nationalist Minister of Justice, Aznar the Socialist, and Astigarrabia the Communist were to rule Bilbao, with General Gamir Ulibarri to make four. Next day their curt orders were plastered in the streets.

I told the other journalists that the danger was excessively great, and persuaded Monzon the Minister of the Interior to give them a powerful automobile. Off they sped to the province of Santander, leaving me in possession of the story of the fall of Bilbao.

XXX

TUESDAY MORNING OUR LINE had seemed to stiffen. Beldarrain was solid and happy after his night's adventure; he
had proved to the General Staff what asses they had been
not to accept his plans of counter-attack earlier. Putz
argued his Asturians back into line again, part of them;
with a Basque battalion and machine guns on their
tails to keep them there. And Vidal was still at
Galdakano.

We presented a line to the enemy. That was enough
after the chaos of last night. In Bilbao I brushed my
teeth. All was going well; my mouth was foaming bravely
when the water tap failed for the final rinse and gargle.
And the lavatory plug had lost muscle, replied with a feeble
rush of wind to our cajoling. Jaureghuy, exasperated by
this underground drive upon our cleanliness, painted a
lovely military notice which he laid across the seat: "Do
not use, on pain of death."

Everything was becoming very uncomfortable. They
had bombed the water supply in the hills that morning,
and the pipe line was broken, "irreparably," said Montaud;
who always rejoiced in the gloomy view.

We went out to search for water. Quite near we found it.
An ornamental lake with a sagging fountain lay in the dip
of the public gardens between our flat and the Nervion.
A pretty lake was our discovery, laid out in a mock-lava
basin amid green grass lately mown and shrubberies opaque
enough for other purposes. In a thicket of bamboo we let
nature take that course which would have cost us our lives
at 60, Gran Via. The lake was a charming sight, in which
militiamen and young girls stooped to wash and to collect
drinking water, shave and paint lips, and pure white swans

floated with an air of effrontery, their necks smartly drilled and not a feather out of place.

From now on we washed and filled buckets in the lake every morning. It was fed with green mossy liquor from the Nervion, and women pattered backwards and forth to it all day, even when machine gun bullets were flitting through the exotic trees, whose spatulate leaves we sprinkled on the surface of each heavy bucketful, to keep them from slopping over as we marched back in triumph to the town. What water it was! Gingerly we poured it into the bath, where 50 per cent. of it solidified upon the bottom.

The planes came over again to machine-gun us, between eddies of low-flying cloud. They went all round the town, indiscriminately firing. I saw no one hit, but the tension of nerves was near breaking point. A girl collapsed in hysteria in the street below the flat; even at the artist's distance of our window it was unpleasant to see her skin go wet and pink and puffy, and her limbs jerk as the men tried to pick her up. She moaned to them "Leave me . . . leave me" from somewhere deep down, near the heart.

Montaud reported that one water system existed still. The old machinery of days before the Great War could be commissioned again, to draw water direct from the river and feed the city pipes. But, he added in a tone which may well have signified satisfaction, it would take at least eight days to grease the machinery and get it into working order. Meanwhile, he agreed, there was a certain danger of epidemic.

Montaud's conversation, so curiously insistent upon the inevitability of cause and effect, was accented by the hollow rattle of aerial machine guns over Bilbao. We noticed for the first time that our anti-aircraft, which in the past often made noises like the breach of a paper bag in the hands of an expert, had now ceased to fire. For ever. We were prone under their wings.

No water, hysteria, aeroplanes constantly over Bilbao, short papers, laconic decrees published on the walls over the name of Leizaola. These were our commonplaces now, when the enemy began the last drive which was to end in the fall of Bilbao. Finding Putz's Division a little too strong, he hammered it with high explosive all day to keep its nose to the ground, and meanwhile picked upon

Vidal for the infantry assault. Poor Vidal, he was not in a state of preparedness; he left the honour of that condition to the enemy, did self-denying Vidal. He was unwell.

They began with a barrage of artillery on the southern slopes of Santa Marina. The militia, in no liaison with headquarters, without orders from above, shifted uneasily backward. Their movement was noted by the aviation, and the fighters guided bombers to the naked strip of hillside above the Galdakano road. The scarlet flashes in the ground, the smoke curtain, the noise and the hill tumbling over each other . . . or, as the militia said, the same old story. There was no one like Putz to go among them with bombs in his hand and say, *"En avant, mes enfants, cherchez les Fascistes,"* and pat some on the back higher up and kick others on the back lower down. No, Vidal was unwell, and he was changing his headquarters. So the militia felt unwell, and in their modest way would one and all change theirs.

A few gallant machine-gunners, veterans of Irun days when shotguns were the fashion, stayed behind like sportsmen and steadied the retreat. It stopped short of the Nervion.

Vidal informed the General Staff of his predicament. And they? Why, they naturally turned to Putz, who gave them two of his best battalions, and one of the new Asturians. "Pablo" the Czech was put in charge of this covering Brigade, which was to support Vidal's retreating left in liaison with Putz's right. Tall conical Malmasin and the scraggy little hill of the Casa de Maquinas, across the Nervion, were to be its two main positions, and it was also to garrison the chimneyed industrial town of Dos Caminos in front of them. "Pablo" was given his packets of dynamite and ordered to blow up the bridges of the Nervion when the troops came across.

He never did. He was bombed severely as he moved his men into line, and he lost many to splinters, opening stomachs. Thistledown, a German *artefact*, fluttered up from Dos Caminos. Vidal's troops were now moving faster. Leap-frogged by the artillery and sprayed by the aviation, they passed across the bridges of the Nervion in bunches and made across flat country to the cover of villages and hills.

It was a rout, shameless and concerted. A real Italian

rout, each man legging it across the open to beat his neighbour. They did not suffer great injury. The list of
prisoners that the other side published next morning was a
fake list with fake numbers. But to-day we lost something
more than prisoners; we lost Bilbao itself. Vidal's 2nd
Division was shaken into dust, and it never existed as an
entity again.

As I looked from the hill of the Casa de Maquinas over
the shelving plain that skirted the Nervion, and saw the
straggling, running, hiding men in berets and steel helmets
who streamed away from the bridgeheads. I saw how one
man could win or lose a war. Two days ago it was Gomez's
battalions who were heading towards home, and Putz had
come, and encouraged them, and given an example, and
in the turnover of night to day they were fighting men
again, stubborn and steady Basques. Now it was Vidal's
turn. And Vidal's inactivity had frozen the springs of
resource in all his officers, even in Pablo. It was hard
to find one who could do his duty, or knew even where his
men had gone.

The bridges lay flat and inviting before the invader.
Our plan was to defend Bilbao on the south, as on the north,
along the Nervion; a handsome barrier. Now that plan
had gone with the wind, and with Vidal and Pablo, and
with the 2nd Division. In the last effect, Vidal and Pablo
were responsible for the fall of Bilbao.

Anybody who had a heart for war, whatever his views
on the Spanish sample, could not help feeling pity for the
Basque militia that afternoon. They were such fine fellows;
they had fought the sky so bravely. They had turned and
turned again, for nearly eighty days. They deserved better
leaders, one thought, than Colonel Vidal.

Jaureghuy visited him that night at his new headquarters
in Arrigorriaga. It was quite a little adventure. No one,
from the General Staff downwards, knew where Vidal was.
So Jaureghuy was all for finding out.

It was becoming difficult to get cars and gasoline, and we
were not able to go until night had fallen. Then at last
we made off with a full complement across the Nervion, by
the southern road which threaded narrowly between dis-
used mine mountains and behind the dark cone of Malmasin
towards Buia. He might be there.

On the road we met two battalions retiring in order, the Mateos and the Rosa Luxembourg. Our headlights lit up the great red stars on the helmets of the Communists. They had no news of Vidal; they had sent runners to different villages to find him, but there was no clue to him. They had no orders. We turned back to the Nervion, took the Galdakano road hard right, and crossed the new bridge towards Dos Caminos. We were soon stopped.

Parties of men sullenly retiring said, "It is dangerous to go farther." After the terrible bombing of the afternoon, the troops and the civilian population of Dos Caminos had panicked together. It was not certain whether the enemy had entered Dos Caminos or not; but he had crossed the Nervion.

We turned back again.

Men and civilians were drifting across the Buia road as we travelled it the second time. The militia seemed to be taking up positions, unwillingly and slowly, and very few of them, in the hills to the right. Yes, they had orders.

At Buia there was no news of Vidal. We went on; a hard, silent road of stone, with the telephone down. In the dominant shade of hills by night we felt rather nervous but we reached Arrigorriaga unchallenged. "Yes, there's a Colonel here," said a militiaman on guard, casually enough. It was Vidal, and a skeleton staff, with a map in front of them chockfull of red crosses—and erasures. Vidal must have been using the indiarubber hard all evening. But the little Colonel's hair was still smoothly oiled and plastered. What a fine moon outside, tracing the crest that we had lost with a profile line of heavy silver. I stood in the open air below it, while Jaureghuy within interrogated the chief of the 2nd Division. Vidal was explicit. The enemy was at Dos Caminos to the north, at San Miguel de Basauri in the centre, and had occupied the hill of Upo to the south; which meant that Vidal had been well beaten all along the line, and had retired without cutting a single bridge. Vidal was going to man a line like this, and his chubby finger swept over the map from red cross to red cross—hill 247, hill 200, hill 351, Malmasin, hill 200, Arbolica, San Juan de Munguia to the north-west of Miravalles. He pushed his spectacles up his forehead and peered close at the printed positions; ideal. And himself, why

he himself was going to withdraw a little to another headquarters nearer Bilbao. Jaureghuy came out into the
moonlight; he has a high complexion at the best of times,
and to-night the moon did not seem to chalk it down. He
had some horrible things to say about the 2nd Division
. . . we drove away, as we thought, back to Buia.

There were more leaderless militia on the route, in twos
and threes and bad tempers. They stopped us to ask for
their battalion headquarters, for food, for orders. We
passed on into a deserted village.

A small blue plate on a wall proclaimed San Miguel de
Basauri. If Vidal was telling the truth, we were now in
the centre of the enemy lines. So we turned about like
jack rabbits, and waited behind a wall. But there was not
a sound; the village was without people, even the dogs
had run away or been eaten up.

We had the final proof of Vidal's incompetence. His
battalions did not know where he was. The General
Staff did not know where he was. He did not know
where his battalions were. And now we had found that
he did not know where the enemy was. Anything more?

We drove back to Bilbao between laughing, protesting
and sleeping. The General Staff had already discovered
that neither Dos Caminos, nor San Miguel de Basauri,
nor Upo were occupied by the enemy. Vidal was ordered
to garrison the three points. We knew that these orders
would not be executed.

XXXI

IF UNTIL NOW WE WERE SLOW in blowing up bridges, from
Wednesday morning onward the process veered towards
the other extreme, for the Communist Party took a hand
in the business. They were justifiably annoyed by the
sluggishness of Vidal's engineers, and so they went down
river to Portugalete in the dark hours and blew up the
puente transbordador at five a.m.

It fell slap into the Nervion, leaving the left wing of
Beldarrain's Fifth Division on the right of the river mouth
without a retreat. This struck us all as a smart piece of
work.

For several days now squadrons of bombers had been
dropping their material on the *puente transbordador*. This
old-time mechanical marvel was the first thing that one
used to notice when entering the port of Bilbao. Slung
between two pairs of masts on either side of the Nervion
and suspended by wires from a lofty railroad system, the
business part of the *puente transbordador* passed rapidly
across the river with a cageful of Basques and motor-cars.
Then back again, noisily.

The planes had done it little damage. They had
ploughed up the suburbs of Portugalete (lower class)
and Las Arenas (rich) on either side, with an impartial
bomb-rack. They had killed a large number of civilians;
they had destroyed the house of the British Consul; and
they had actually, with one small projectile, jammed the
works of our show bridge. Repairs would have taken a
day, until the Communists settled the question impulsively
by blowing cage, wires and all into the Nervion.

A scarecrow wreck now blocked the harbour, and
Beldarrain perforce built two pontoon bridges out of the

iron-ore barges which lay lost in idle dirt at the quay-side, to assure his communications with the other side.

The Anarchist battalion Malatesta were posted at Portugalete to watch the other side of the harbour mouth.

A civil war broke out in Las Arenas, in the houses of the rich: a thing called the Fifth Column began to operate. Little more than a hundred young men who had evaded military service took out the red berets which they had left obscure and neat in their trouser-presses for eleven months, and, rifle in hand, ascended to the upper storeys of their elegant villas, there to discharge their pieces into the street. At the same time the Italians occupied Algorta, the next suburb to the east.

Thus rudely assaulted in the nerves, the militia withdrew from Las Arenas up-river. It was only when they had evacuated the suburb that they heard of the plot that caused their disarray. The Malatesta, who had watched everything from the beginning, sent two companies across in motor boats; they landed quickly, and pushed into Las Arenas. They blew up four houses in which arms had been abandoned, as well as a small arms' factory, and shot up anyone in a red beret whom they could see. This was the sort of fighting which they enjoyed: for two hours Las Arenas was one of the warmer corners of the world.

Their commander was the brother of the priest of Las Arenas, and the priest was, though discreet in his public professions, a Monarchist at heart, as his brother knew. So before retiring to Portugalete, his brother did a certain amount of damage to the priest's church.

I was not there, but none of these facts were withheld from me by the Basque Government, who took—as ever—a highly scientific view of the Spanish War. Carlists and Monarchists are a purely Spanish phenomenon, they said, and so is Anarchism: and Carlists who lose their faith become Anarchists immediately. And as they are Spaniards and nothing more, they fight each other: let them. Basque Nationalism, on the other hand, like Socialism and Communism, represents a world concept. One finds Nationalism everywhere; we Basques are just a phase of it. A Basque who loses his faith becomes a Socialist or a Communist. And as we are not simply Spaniards, but keep one eye ever on the outside world,

the war-fumes and the false heroism of Spain do not in-
toxicate us. We do not fight each other; we reach compromises, and in the end we will tone each other down.
So there, friend Englishman, you have the difference
between us and Spain, said Leizaola.

On the basis of this Iberian philosophy, whisps of smoke
were now issuing from the church of Las Arenas, and
Cain withdrew from Abel's altar once again to the left
back of the Nervion at Portugalete. All the fault, however,
was not on Cain's side; for priestly Abel now was sporting
a scarlet beret and a rifle with the best.

Beldarrain ordered a battalion back into Las Arenas.
One could watch it all from the other side of the river.
It was sent on a raid, like the troops who took Lañamendi
two nights before, and it was just as successful as they.

The enemy artillery was now throwing shrapnel at
Beldarrain's protective flank just south of the suburb, where
the hills that grew into the ridge of Santa Marina began.
They were sending lighter units forward, when Beldarrain's
battalion fell upon them, at the outskirts of Las Arenas.

An Italian battery of 75.27 mm. guns. Their crew
were cut down by a cross-fire as they were taking position.
There was no time to lug the guns away, but some bodies
were stripped. Documentation found upon the dead
Sergeant Pompeo Belloni, of the regular Italian artillery,
included a note-book in which the whole personnel of the
unit was inscribed.

Their work done and the enemy shaken up, the battalion
withdrew to Beldarrain's new lines, which were not disturbed again that day. Beldarrain had only undertaken
the action to cover the construction of his pontoons, which
gathered length and a super-structure of planks under the very
wings of the enemy aviation. For an untrained soldier,
Beldarrain was a marvel. He proved to the hilt what Jaureghuy always said: "Soldiering—why, it's common sense."

Yet it took something more to withdraw three lines in
three days, without at any time offering a target to the
air; and to counter-attack twice just where the enemy
was getting into touch with your lines, and break his
contact, and mystify him, and make him sit down and
puzzle out your whereabouts instead of following you and
cutting you off in small pieces. That was Beldarrain.

And Putz? He was getting the hammering of a life-time. At midday the enemy artillery settled on to his Division in real earnest.

They singled out the Casino on Arxanda and the hill of Arxandasarri for special treatment. There were bushes of smoke in the centre of the ridge over Bilbao.

Our windows rattled to their loud oratory.

Twice that afternoon the enemy attempted the frontal approach from Santo Domingo, but his artillery had frightened no one, and his infantry flattened themselves out in the pines. The First Division was holding fine. No one would have recognised in them the troops of Gomez of four days back.

There was no sound of grenades; nothing to suggest close fighting. The enemy were held and driven back to earth.

A false alarm announced thirty-two enemy tanks ap-proaching Fuerte Banderas, the northernmost point of the ridge over Bilbao. The President himself, who spent the day in Bilbao, ordered the anti-tank guns up the winding road to the top. The tanks, little crawling beetles that jerked blunt noses to right and left, stopped at the explosions, then made for home. An order had been given and obeyed quickly, and an attack had been turned to water. All was going well with the First Division.

The loss of Fuerte Banderas would be fatal to Bilbao. Her only communications were dominated by the Fort on the right bank of the Nervion. Artillery placed there could pound the two roads to Valmaseda and Santander, which rimmed the Nervion's other bank to the west, 2½ kilometres away. We had no other roads from the town but narrow tracks, which led through the fat cushion of pine-wood at our shoulders to the heights of Pastore-corta and Pagasarri, whither Vidal's Division was now retiring. We had to hold Fuerte Banderas and the sky-line to the south of it at all costs. And, indeed, we did pay the price for our short and glorious tenure of these heights. We? Not I! From this time onward it was too terrifying to climb up to them. They were crushed almost without ceasing, and slowly, by the weight of the foreign artillery. The smoke rolled away in enormous shaking plumes, dirty as sin, and obliterating in the same way the spirit of man; but there was no movement to be seen, except for the stretchers coming back and the reserves shifting inexplicably here and there to the orders of Putz.

Our artillery had spent nearly all its ammunition. Planes machine-gunned the streets again, and kept our factories from working. The enemy seemed to have an inexhaustible supply of death—shells, bombs, planes, guns; a twisted stream of fire and thunder without end. And we, nothing.

The Basque militia recognised their man in Putz, and fought on because they trusted him. They had nothing else to fight with, but a belief in their leader.

And similarly, the Second Division continued its retreat, and Vidal his approximation of his headquarters to Bilbao. Surely, and not slowly, the militia who had been driven down-hill from Santa Marina and across the valley flats, were pursued up hill that afternoon with the same nimbleness until they held the last ridge to the South-west—the great Pagasarri itself.

We lost Malmasin, the cone mountain, and the scrubby, pocked hill of the Casa de Maquinas to their artillery. The troops stood it for three hours precisely. Again and again one could see them on Malmasin, shifting back then heading forward again, while the hill spouted fire like an impertinent volcano against the milder horizon of Euzkadi. And men, hiding in every pocket of the hill of the Casa de Maquinas, pressed against banks of earth and the walls of long-dead quarries, gradually squeezing backward over the rumpled shoulder of the hill as the sun moved towards sundown, and the bullets sang closer from cover. Asturian troops: in new uniforms with smart leather equipment. But like the uncertain men of Malmasin far away—who moved in petty silhouette upon its tilted slopes, and shuddered a little to explosions— there came a moment when they held firm no longer. They had only just been able to sustain the artillery; when the enemy infantry arrived they had no more strength to fight. Leadership had failed from the top downwards. The little specks of men were no longer bold silhouettes against the gathering west; they scattered and dissolved into the hill-side, and were lost to me for ever. They came unstuck from green pockets in the earth and quarries, and soon the Casa de Maquinas was alive with little jointed men—toy Asturians—who were running away down-hill, and getting bigger as they came nearer, and bobbing out of the gorse, until they were down on the road opposite the hard red cliffs of La Peña, whose face was bleak and wrinkled as an Indian brave's, and who set a limit to their retreat with a stubborn cheek.

Malmasin was our last southern outpost before the ridge of Pastorecorta. It was our last position, really. For Pastorecorta had no road communications with Bilbao and so it was clear that the militia would not get food; and so it was clear that they would walk home when they felt hungry. That left the position of Pastorecorta clear enough.

The General Staff ordered a counter-attack on Malmasin for four o'clock the following morning, before the enemy aviation could intervene. I was with Putz that night, to watch the preparation of it. Our low stocks of shells were being jammed into the breach. From the other side of Bilbao, across the Nervion cleft, their dispatch struck in the velvet-black sky great cones of light: their arrival lit up suddenly the black counter-cone of Malmasin. It was a geometry in black and white; a nocturne which we watched from a villa garden terraced with sweet-smelling flowers—unreal shadow warfare. And behind, in the shadows of the garden, was a sweating Captain come to tell Putz that he could not make the men mount Malmasin. There were not enough officers.

The commanders of the two battalions on Malmasin and the Casa had been killed in the bombardment of the afternoon, and many officers wounded.

"But," said Putz, very gently to him, "we must re-take Malmasin; it is the key of Bilbao. We must try." Very gently, like a good nurse dealing with an excitable child, and pretending that she does not notice that it is excitable.

The captain walked off, doubtful. At four that morning he, too, was killed, and the men took his body home, quitting the attack on Malmasin.

And so, after a night of fitful lightning and sudden patterned skies, we woke for the day which was to see the last battle before Bilbao. Putz moved his headquarters to the Ministry of Agriculture at the back of the city, where he could watch his line through great airy windows. Vidal, it was rumoured, was very near the city, but nobody believed that his whereabouts were of cardinal importance.

XXXII

THESE NIGHTS THE TENSION was becoming more severe. The machine-gunning of the streets in day-time was bad enough; but now there were young men marching briskly about in threes and fours with revolvers at their sides, looking for windows from which, they said, the Fifth Column were firing on the people. And that evening the enemy began to throw shrapnel over the Nervion near our flat. It was difficult to get food cooked. Queer shapes in black, who seemed to have a prior claim to the flat, came in and sat about in chairs, and made peculiar loud-spoken plans and compacts.

Above all, one never quite knew whether one might not wake up to find that the General Staff had fled without taking farewell.

Thursday morning, however, we woke to something different: to a crack like Doomsday. At six o'clock that morning the whole ridge from Berriz to the Radio Station was a ribbon of smoke, and the building shook till our beds answered back.

Echevarria, the young Basque officer who accompanied Jaureghuy, was suddenly struck with the most gloomy forebodings. With quite unusual energy, he exclaimed: "That is the end of Bilbao." We laughed at him, and Jaureghuy told him a few stories about Verdun, and to hide my anxiety I opened one of our last tins of condensed milk. The bombardment went on with unprecedented violence.

We took out our watches and counted. Over eighty a minute, and sometimes a hundred. No intermission. No view on the ridge, but the panorama of smoke rising and being replaced without cease.

It continued for two hours. It was a prelude to the heaviest day's fighting of the Spanish war. In those two hours ten thousand shells were thrown at the Radio Station, the Casino, Arxandasarri and Berriz. They fell on four kilometres of front, and nearly all around the four main positions, which lay less than two kilometres steeply up-hill from our river-side. Nobody budged.

An infantry attack was driven back between eight and nine. There was a pause for about an hour, and then the artillery hammered the ridge again. For two more hours. It was terrible: ten thousand more shells. At midday, another infantry attack; another failure. The machine-gunners at the Radio Station sent back a genial message: "We have made mountains of corpses."

We had many dead. Reserves went up. As they moved, the enemy aviation intervened: it made fire spring wildly from the mountain-side, and choke itself in earth and ashes, under the dark scarves of pine-wood which our men were holding with an incredible courage.

Our six-inch guns battered their concentrations on San Roque and Santo Domingo. Chits came from the line for more munitions: urgent. And the carriers were off with boxes and sacks through pines muffled with smoke.

Shrapnel took sudden life and shape over the river. Metal scattered in the first streets of Bilbao. Everybody clustered in doorways with their backs to the battle. But in the line no one turned his back or budged.

Bilbao streets emptied. An anxious General Staff put its heads out of its windows to watch, incredulously. Twenty thousand shells: that was already a record for Spain. And the militia held firm: and there were more shells to come.

After midday the aeroplanes remained more or less, in permanence over the line—bombing, machine-gunning, spying every possible movement and adjustment, swooping to intervene. From the direction in which they flew away it looked as if the fighters reloaded at Sondika, our old concrete aerodrome in the valley beyond. There was every type of German and Italian plane: Junker 86, Junker 52, Heinkel 111, Heinkel 51, Heinkel 45, Savoia 81, Fiat CR 32, and two other types unrecognisable by me. And at three o'clock the artillery barrage began again:

it was break through or bust for the enemy command. They were driving their men like demons to the final decision.

The artillery barrage was more intensive and shorter than those of the morning. It seemed to concentrate on the Casino, long-swallowed in the reeking fog of war. More shrapnel spat over the city, where the Heinkel 111's returned to machine-gun us. Yet a third infantry attack; a furious stutter of automatic weapons along the ridge, rose to points of mad insistence at the Casino and yet made no impression at all, was met with equal heat.

There were many dead being carried down the mountain channels, through the vines. I could not take my eyes off the hill, shrapnel or no shrapnel. Any moment the last retreat to the river might begin; already machine-gun detachments had been installed in the warehouses. Yet there was no movement yet.

Messages came back for reinforcements. "And stop those bloody guns of yours firing on our own cars." On the right two of our 75's had joined the battle without warning.

We heard that Beldarrain had withdrawn all his men to the left bank of the Nervion, and was now at Retuerto. Impossible to leave this battle to visit him.

Our front now lay along the Nervion up to Bilbao: here it bulged eastward in a flat semi-circle which followed the ridge that we were watching: thence it crossed the Nervion to La Peña, and was merged in the helpless Division of Vidal, which was still retiring in a chaos that no man could describe.

There were many false alarms in the city; that Fuerte Banderas was taken, that Berriz was lost, that the Asturians were massing. But none were yet true. Towards six the bombers, three by three in flights which seemed to grind the guts out of the sky, passed in front of us for their last grim operation. Heavy bombs and incendiaries among the reserves, who moved convulsively over the hill.

White towers arose in Deusto across the river, climbed at a mad speed by scarlet creepers of fire. The whole orchestra of the interventionist artillery tuned in to the stroke of the celestial conductor's wand. The fourth ten thousand of the day cracked and splintered over the Radio

Station and the Casino and Arxandasarri. One seemed to
detect a new fever and fury in this shooting, and a redoubled
speed. The enemy was going to break our light trenches
at all costs before night.

I went across to the other side of the river. Bullets
flew over the ridge and past us, spinning. One could hear
grenades. Their infantry must now be very near our lines.

I sat on a pile of munition boxes, with a group of high-
spirited militiamen waiting their turn to go up.

Looking up from the bridge through the fires of Deusto
I could see the last battle rage upon Arxanda. Past me
were carried, with the fine solicitude of the people for its
own, the dead and wounded upon makeshift stretchers.
They were many. Deusto was burning fiercely, and with
her the houses on the hill where the bombs had fallen that
terrible afternoon. The houses were big villas in blocks,
of the 'twenties, timbered and plastered and capacious;
from their vulgar jaws leapt the hobgoblins of fire.

The ridge, the Casino in particular among its pine trees
and on its basis of heavy concrete, was smothered in the smoke
of the Germano-Italian artillery. For an hour one could
not count a second between the crack of the explosions. I
searched the hill closely for the sight of men retiring, but
I could see none, not one. The Casino was holding
stubbornly, though a fire raging in a building to its right
showed that the Fascists had penetrated there. They
dared not show their flag. Our incendiary mortars were
smothering them.

Our heavy guns behind Bilbao, which in the morning
had attacked the enemy concentrations upon San Roque,
were deadly silent. Above them hung like menacing
school teachers with the cane, the air fleet of Germany and
Italy. What a prize lay before their eyes! From Mount
Arraiz to the sea, and as far west as Somorrostro stretched
a landscape, patterned closely for the aviator, of iron mines,
slag heaps, tips, railways for minerals, the chimneys and
furnaces of heavy industry. All the concrete and con-
glomerate achievement of the laborious Basques, built up
after hundreds of years of careful democracy; imprinted
upon a broad pamphlet of dusty brick red, the red soil
which gives up the iron to patient effort. All to be won
so lightly by two and a half months of piracy. Raw

material! No, rather the pearls of barbaric Asia and the gold of the New World of Fascism. But to themselves the aviators said that they had come to crush the Communists in Euzkadi.

Our 75's in the Park and at the riverside could not yet answer. There were over eighty of them, but fifty had no ammunition. The Basques made, you see, the ammunition for themselves; they did not buy it from interventionist countries. Their own working class toiled in the factories to produce every day that day's cannon-fodder and to-day the bombardment and the noise were too painful; they could not work any more. They lingered in refuges.

Another squadron of bombers, invisible in the evening haze, passed in line along the ridge dropping their bombs half-way down the slope, upon our depleted reserves. As the curtain of smoke cleared upwards and dissolved in tissue, I saw a red and yellow flag hoisted in the saddle to the north of Arxanda. A sudden barrage of shrapnel, not ill laid, had driven our defenders down the slope. Their grey forms were hurrying along the gulleys, jumping quickly from stone to stone. It was 7.40 p.m.

Our 75's jerked their last shells from the riverside, where shrapnel was being laid over us a little faster now. Our seventeen machine-gun posts answered savagely from house to house over the sullen Nervion. The reserves went forward, the defence re-formed. At seven fifty-five the Fascist flag was down again and the Basques once more in place.

At eight-ten in Arxandasarri, north of the saddle and past the height of Berriz, there was a movement in the line. It flagged, grey forms ran backwards. A red and yellow banner appeared where the road, running parallel to the ridge, crossed the fading horizon. Our home-made mortars of 81, lower down, opened fire. Little balls of white sprung like mushrooms to life along the roadside, fattened outwards and seemed to wither the Fascist infantry. The flag was hauled down, the troops veered directly northwards along the road to attack Fuerte Banderas, where an Asturian Brigade quit before sundown.

At eight-thirty that evening the river valley echoed with the steady report of rifle fire. I was now behind the bridge again, waiting with the men who were to raise it at need.

ITALIAN SOLDIERS ON SANTOÑA QUAY:
AUGUST 28TH, 1937.

BASQUE MILITIA ON SANTOÑA QUAY:
ARMED GUARDS AND DISARMED TROOPS AWAITING EMBARKATION.

The troops at our side were firing up the slope, rather wildly, at the position between Berriz and Arxandasarri. The Asturians added to the din; so did the shrapnel which split over our heads.

Their commander ordered the Asturians back into the line at the bridge. A man stepped out of the ranks and shot him dead.

Troops clustered behind the first houses at the entry to Bilbao. Others were sheltered under the drawbridge. The company with which I was dug up the cobblestones of the roadway to make trenches and barricades. While they were at this work six fighting planes came over the hill and plunged full throttle at us; they were type Heinkel 51, German and slow, but carrying two machine guns which never jam.

In line, they dived upon us, firing devilish fast. But somehow, after the day's bombardment, it seemed a feeble rattle that they made. We had grown obtuse to things that would have driven us to cover before. Standing up on the hard wide road, we loosed off two hundred rifles and machine guns at them. Ah, what a memory. The mountain ridge spouting smoke like the spines of a pachyderm, fire raging across the river, everywhere the crack of artillery, the shrapnel mixed in a savage disorder with the plunging fighting planes. Evening lay over the indifferent river Nervion, and in the Park women were cowering to collect water beneath the necks of the arrogant swans. The air sang with ill-directed bullets. And what sport!

Among the airmen we picked out the brave and the cowards. There were two who dived deep at us again and again. But the others, before our fixed machine guns, fired their ammunition off along the flat and descended very little. It cheered us up to see them flattening out so early, but the brave ones were fairer game. They made the cobbles round us rattle like dice.

Deusto was blotted crimson with fire. The Asturians were still retreating. We had lost the keypoint Fuerte Banderas, where an old fort above the river provided point-blank emplacement for the enemy light artillery to batter our only roads of retreat on the western side. Fort Flags, the square brown headpiece on the hill, squat and porous with age, had to be retaken.

As night fell over the smoke and flames and unbroken row of battle, three of the flower of the Basque Nationalist infantry battalions were sent out for the final effort. The Kirikiño, the Itxas Alde, the Itxarkundia. In the history of the sacrifice of human blood for democracy, may their names live for ever! As long as laurels spring out of the generous ground, there will be leaves to crown their memory. Heroes, salute! A forlorn hope, and knowing it, they went up the line singing the solemn songs of Basque National-ism, songs like the Gaelic laments of prehistory to be accom-panied upon the bagpipes and the xistu. Their deep voices were lost in the dark.

Night and the Casino fell together, after half an hour more of intensive bombardment. Deploying out, the Basque militia went steadily up the slope. Their only arms were the rifle and the machine-gun, the hand grenade and the mortar of 81. The two latter were products of their dying city of Bilbao. With these arms alone they fought their way back into Fuerte Banderas, Berriz, Arxanda-sarri, and the Casino of Arxanda. They killed many and took prisoners and material. Their heroism and sacrifice were accompanied by the dullest and most pedestrian noises of war, the ponderous unpointed explosion of grenades and mortars, so unlike the sharp tyrannical crack of the Italo-German artillery. The Basques', you see, was not a sensational struggle. They fought in a minor key.

I went up to Begoña to talk with the armoured car men. They were tired and angry. Our own artillery had fired upon them and the infantry that afternoon in mistake for the enemy, causing heavy loss. We had been forced to withdraw to the right of the Casino in consequence, and that was the beginning of the movement which let the enemy in.

Outside, the road under the moon was sprayed with machine gun bullets, as the enemy resisted the three last battalions of Euzkadi.

They were very tired, had suffered fifty per cent. casualties. At eleven the enemy shelled and mortared the Casino again. He entered the big stucco building and its pine wood over many corpses. The other positions held. At four a.m. a final counter attack on the Casino failed. Our last line to the east in open country was pierced and we had to with-draw to the Nervion and the bridgehead of Begoña.

There was order in the streets. As the Asturians went through, the agents of Basque public order, in navy blue uniforms, silver-badged berets aslant their hard heads, patrolled Bilbao in threes with carbines slung over the shoulders. I took off my boots and coat and lay down on the mattress for a few hours rest. Difficult. Jaureghuy carefully undressed into elegant pyjamas, laughing and chatting all the time, and slept between clean sheets more soundly than I.

XXXIII

IT WAS A COOL GREY DAY, FRIDAY, when it broke. The servants had fled, and we had to do our cooking in our own cold greasy way. Jaureghuy, as a Continental, was chosen for *chef*; while I, the bonehead Englishman, was set to breaking up the drawing-room chairs for fuel. We had, besides, to prepare for evacuation, as our flat was on the extension of the Gran Via, which lay next to the riverside, now the front. As we were packing up our stocks of rice and coffee, a six-inch shell exploded on the wall behind and the house shuddered. Not an unjustifiable shell; the flat above, with a clear view over the little park, enclosed a new machine gun nest.

Below us, in the hall where lay crowded refugees, they established a forward dressing station. Muffled stretchers entered. Our silent nights in the flat were over. We sent off the baggage in the car and walked through the streets to the General Staff.

They were moving to the Civil Hospital at Basurto. Not out of Bilbao but near the door as it were. The General Staff were packing up, like us, and edging out. Typewriters, secret files of radio intercepts, declarations of prisoners, the whole information section of the Secretaria Tecnica was being jumbled into a lorry. A guard sat on top of the pile with his boots brutally pressed upon all their laboured espionage.

Gurieff, the Russian General, was there in his big grey suit, very calm, with a pipe stuck between firm lips, discussing the withdrawal with the Spaniards. Arbex was nervous and sat in a chair, looking worriedly at his feet, his spine a parabola. The maps, the flags, and the little pins had gone. All dismantled and bare.

The city remained very silent. Few people moved about; somehow the Gran Via seemed to have gained in width and length, and desolation. Over its whole spread, the city had the air of a vacant man, staring with empty starred windows in silence at nothing and ignorant of what it was waiting for; this contemplativeness without thought was only broken by stray bursts of shrapnel over our heads. The shells opened their invisible hands and scattered the city with pelting metal.

We drove down the river to see Beldarrain in his H.Q. of the 5th Division at Retuerto. He bad crossed the Nervion. Beldarrain was silent as usual, talking in mono-syllables, with difficulty distilled. As we passed in front of Fuerte Banderas we noted that the enemy had already placed a battery of 75's. They fired at our car as we drove by. Jaureghuy laughed like a child, and I must admit that I, too, was enjoying myself. It was good sport trailing one's coat in front of the Italian artillery.

Clouds plated the lower sky, and except against Vidal's Division the aviation of the enemy was inactive. Vidal was in difficulties again.

Vidal was now at Iturrigorri, and in his messages to the Staff he professed to know the positions of the various battalions at his command. But the Staff did not believe him, nor, knowing Vidal's way of staying behind the line, did Jaureghuy and I. Putz was even more convinced of Vidal's inadequacy. He sent out the 3rd Asturian Brigade to cover his right, between the abandoned mines that lay in red rust to the west of the Nervion and south of Bilbao, through heavy pine hills that clipped us in on the west to the Peak of Arraiz. An area of dense forest which spilled into downland.

The 3rd Asturian Brigade went back to the Asturias. But at this moment they were moving faster than our means of information, and for several hours we were un-conscious of the hole to the rear on our right. The Asturians exist still as a nice red line on my battered map of Bilbao, and that's the only place where I saw them bold solid.

We drove out that afternoon, after a little food and lake water, and a squeeze through the busy dressing station, to the Valmaseda road. The Italian artillery did not talk as we passed down the river, but there were several smashed cars that we had to thread our way through. They were firing up the creek of the Cadagua, though, across the girder bridges and the noiseless deserted docks of Bilbao. We turned up the creek, and came to Alonsotegui, where Pablo the Czech was trying to bolster up the other rearward cheek of Colonel Vidal.

Pablo sat in an electric power station, not distant from the wreckage of a German bombing plane. He had a staff map in front of him, on his lanky knees. A tall, thin, stiff-nosed man, Pablo, in a long khaki greatcoat which hung open around him and trailed about his knees. His uniform cap sat perfectly square upon his head and he showed us the disposition of his troops to the southward with a forefinger deformed at the tip to spade-shape.

The troops were not much good. They were the filtrations to the rear of Vidal's Division, who descended upon the road in hopes of peace in Santander. Pablo had posted a good battalion to shepherd them into the side valleys that broke in upon the road and the cleft of the Cadagua. There they were, pulling the fruit off the springy cherry trees, undusted khaki against the slim outline of Japanese green-pointed pink. Vidal had not fed them. Pablo had already reorganised others and sent them forward to occupy Arraiz and the heights of Pagasarri to the south. To the liaison officer who came in wet with heat after putting them in position, Pablo said in his slow toneless Spanish, "Thank you, camarada." We were "camaradas" too; Pablo thought he could hold the position for a day. Hill 342, Arraiz 351, Hill 357, Hill 494, Hill 681 were all in the hands of the 5th Brigade. But 691, the highest point of Pagasarri, already waved a red and yellow flag. The weaker 8th Brigade held 503 and 500, with reserves, to the south-west, and liaison was being established with Ibarrola's Third Division at Ganecogorta.

The sun came out on our last hopes for Bilbao. Above us to the south lay the hills that Pablo held. On the ridges, bare and broad-shouldered as Sussex downland, one could pick out little specks of men in movement. They looked restless; I felt that they would not stay out another day.

They were not fed. In Bilbao, with the flight of wheeled transport to Santander, the organisation of the Basque Army Service Corps was breaking down. Stocks were distributed in the city, but got no further. We left Pablo in the hard sunlight looking analytically at his distant troops, his map flopping over lanky knees.

An Asturian Brigade was debouching on the road to the west. They had abandoned the hills on Vidal's right that morning, after the enemy had fired four shells. They were quite satisfied with their battle; fierce, shaggy men, they marched off dangling on their rifles chickens taken from the farms, and their sidearms were uprooted potatoes. We went back to Bilbao, where the Junta de Defensa was in council.

As we turned the corner opposite Fuerte Banderas, the 75's opened fire. The road was an ugly pudding; broken cars, broken men lying motionless against the hillside. Little puffs of smoke. They tried to hit us, but the car was too fast; we heard the light explosions behind, and had another good laugh.

In Bilbao, Leizaola was eager to spend another day. There were war stocks to evacuate which he thought could not go out in a night—70,000 trench mortar shells, about 20,000,000 rounds of rifle ammunition, thousands of grenades; the good half of them the war production of Bilbao. We sat down to sup in the Presidency, on tinned army food, and pints of champagne. One orderly left to serve us.

It made me go a little Asturian. After supper I looted the rooms of the President, his Secretaries, and the Secretary-General of Defence. Long corridors now, vacant and dimly lit, they were a collection of polished desks, arm-chairs, carpets and cupboards without owner, name or meaning. I found two valuable photographs of the early war zone, and pocketed the President's pen and his last note pad to begin this book on.

On his balcony, where I had seen him sometimes take the salute as the Militia marched past, the twin flags of the Republic and of Euzkadi still waved, in the half-darkness, and slowly. The moonlight touched their folds with velvet. I thought how over-coloured, what a nut-milk chocolate carton was the Republican red, yellow and purple; how beautiful and fresh the apple-green cross of the Basques. No one had thought of taking them down. Underneath them rustled the trees of the Plaza, in full summer leaf, and underneath the trees rustled the paper and litter left by thousands of refugees and militiamen in passage, which sifted themselves sleepily across the dry grass. The flags moving in symbolic melancholy, the rustling trees and paper, the silent Presidency behind with solitary table lit to reflect void bottles of champagne; and outside the footfall and shuffle of the militia in the litter going to their stations at the noiseless riverside; all leave in my memory the sounds and sights, a sixth sense of dull expectancy that I think will never be deleted.

Rezola, the long figure with the square shoulders, blue eyes, jutting chin, cropped head, sat down at his desk. It seemed that he was very worried; but like Rezola always, he had to be pressed to say what was worrrying him. It came out slowly; the removal of munitions. The trains to take them had not yet arrived, and it was nearly midnight. He looked moodily out of the window. Nor were there men enough of confidence to load the trains. Rezola lost himself again in his book on the campaigns of Napoleon.

At this moment the lights went out all over Bilbao. Half-lit before, the great city was an inkpool whose sides rose in heavy black to the horizon. Luisa was suddenly at Rezola's side telephoning the power station. This was sabotage; the town must be immediately lighted up again.

Outside bare bayonets glittered in the moon. Somehow the determined voice of Basque authority, at this eleventh hour, made timid wreckers change their policies. They wanted to embarrass the Government at the power station; they knew, the whole of Bilbao knew, that her future lay on the razor's edge. But they did not dare go too far. As suddenly as they had faded into night, the streets and a few unshuttered windows lit up again.

No one but soldiers walked abroad, and they between packed barracks. The civilians who remained were keeping house, and doors were double locked. We waited a long time. The General Staff at Basurto sat down to a good dinner with Gurieff, after which they issued orders to Putz to fill the gap between the mines and Arraiz. Then they left Bilbao, the General and his Chief of Staff, who were better men than the others, travelling last. They went west.

Jaureghuy and I drove up to Putz. Four of the fast Russian

armoured cars, with the 4.7 mm. cannon aloft, stood at his door under Jean Laporte. Putz was lying on a brocaded sofa, his boots cocked up on one of the Secretary of Agriculture's finest cushions. He was, besides, eating out of a tin. He laughed at the orders of the General Staff: the Fascists are already there, he said. By now we knew that the 3rd Asturians had taken the homeward road, and in the view of Putz and Jaureghuy the evacuation could not be delayed another night. The troops at the riverside, the gallant 1st Division who were spoiling for a machine-gun battle in the town, must be withdrawn before daylight. The life of our defence in the pinewoods and Arraiz was ebbing very fast.

From the same black tapestry of the pinewoods above us we heard the blunt burst of a tank gun, like a warning noise off stage. The enemy were near. People moved slowly about Putz's headquarters as he turned over for an hour's sleep. They seemed less and less active than those that I had seen there in the morning. They drank wine out of skins, then tied papers together, then drank wine.

We took a last look from the great windows of the Agriculture building at the grave outline of Arxanda across the river—lost for good! "What a fight!" said Jaureghuy. "*Heroes!*" Then he laughed; he had a plan, he said, of remaining behind in the Presidencia and dropping a vase on the Italians as they marched in. There was a very hideous and enormous vase in the Department of Defence, and it would do Art no harm to defenestrate it, but it might do the Italians some good. We were back at the Presidencia. From this moment until I left Bilbao I hardly stopped laughing. I had unmistakably finished the last bottle of the Basque Government's champagne.

XXXIV

LEIZAOLA WAS NOW IN CHARGE of the defence of Bilbao; though he knew that the situation was desperate, he was fixed on staying another day if the troops would hold.

I asked him why. It seemed to me clear that Bilbao would have to be abandoned that night.

There were too many strange battalions in the town, he said. The trains had come, but they could not take all the stocks. And the prisoners: he was not sure whether they had all been handed over safely.

This was the first that I had heard of the prisoners. Long afterwards I asked Leizaola to explain everything. In the slow-down of the working of the central authority, only Leizaola, Rezola and Luisa seemed to be holding the Basque state in Bilbao together, and one could not ask them questions of a simply historical value now. But thus it was.

Leizaola was determined to surrender Bilbao in a civilised way. He ordered the bridges to be blown up, the war factories to be sabotaged and the mining population to be evacuated west. But he would not tolerate any arson or wanton damage, even for strategical purposes, in the greatest city of the Basques.

Bilbao is the dear, dirty "punch-bowl" of the Basque people. If it could be defended, they were willing to take their punishment. They did not mind if it sank in fire and black rubble if they could hold it; it was to save them from such hot interment that the evacuation of civilians had been carried out *en masse* since Monday.

But if Bilbao could not be held, not a sacred stone of it was to be touched.

At headquarters that afternoon Leizaola had asked for

the dispositions of the High Command for the defence of Bilbao. He found that they proposed to use certain Communist and Anarchist battalions in the town, and that preparations had been made to blow up the University opposite the Deusto drawbridge, and the old towered church of San Nicolas, opposite the bridge of the Arenal, as soon as the troops were in line on the other side of the river.

They thought that the University and the church tower would make dangerous enemy machine-gun nests.

Leizaola had other views. He wrote down his own plan of defence. Only Basque Nationalist battalions to line the river in central Bilbao. The University building to be spared, on account of the 35,000 valuable books in its library; the church similarly to be spared on account of its beauty and antiquity.

General Gamir was summoned to the Presidency, where he was obliged to agree to Leizaola's proposals. As Leizaola pointed out, the ground rose steeply behind University and church, and if they were dynamited houses unmarked behind would serve as machine-gun posts just as well as they.

Leizaola then listed the position of the Basque Nationalist battalions along the river, which from north to south swept the town of Bilbao in a quarter circle, beginning at the Deusto bridge and ending at the bridge of San Anton, rich old stone, narrow as the entry to heaven.

The Kirikiño on the left bank north-east of Deusto; the Ibaizabal at the Deusto bridge-head; the Otxandiano between the river and the Basque motorised police headquarters; the Amuartegui at the bridge of Buenos Aires.

At the old Arenal bridge and the central railway station the Itxarkundia. Right of the railway station the Itxas Alde, with the Malatu in reserve on the Gran Via. Marteatu at the next small bridge up-river, where the Nervion now flowed narrow and well-stopped at the sides by tall houses veiled by grime and night, and high clattering quays, where there seemed to be more resonant stone than water, and echoes were pistol-shots from riverside to riverside. At the San Anton bridge the battalion Bolibar. A proletarian unit was held in reserve, the U.H.P.

Two battalions, the Nationalist Gordexola and the Socialist U.G.T.8, were very tired by the fighting of

Thursday, and were sent to Barakaldo, near Beldarrain's head-quarters, to rest.

Their instructions were to destroy important machinery in the war factories at Barakaldo. But the sapping of the Gordexola began that night. The factory experts and technicians sent men among them, who said to this group and the other that it was bad to do any injury to the industrial capital of Bilbao. The Gordexola were worn out, and only waiting for conversion.

There were many groups talking among the shadowy machinery. The U.G.T. 8 were too tired to intervene.

By dawn the Gordexola had placed their own pickets on the factories of Barakaldo . . . .

Leizaola's plans were endorsed by the general. A Basque battalion supervised the removal of dynamite from the University structure.

And now Leizaola was able to carry out the proposal upon which he had set his mind some days before. As Minister of Justice as well as chief of the Defence Junta, he ordered the release of the political prisoners in the Larrinaga on the slopes of Begoña.

He was staying in Bilbao to-night in order to see that they might pass safely over the enemy lines, and that the threat to damage the city should not be carried out. I found afterwards that Leizaola had refused to leave the city until these two missions were accomplished, in spite of persistent advice from his friends to leave Bilbao, which was now almost encircled.

Somewhere in the high woods to the west of us the enemy were closing upon our commnuications without firing or resistance.

It would be difficult to exaggerate the courage and calmness of Leizaola this evening. He was not, like the rest of us, a fighting man, or a man whom risks amused. At the bottom of his heart he detested war; we liked or accepted it.

Leizaola was a lawyer of standing and integrity in Republican Spain. The dark, simple, drooping lines of his face, the skin dark and rather full about the mouth, the dark eyes wideset in a gaze of steady, mournful sincerity— everything about him was dark, unmilitary, bourgeois in the most refined and religious sense. Even his clothes were black; he always wore a dark beret.

His hair broke the line. Parted near the middle, it sprung in defiant swarthiness above the level of his crown, then lay back like a victor's wreath over his ears. It gave him the authority that more artificial constructions gave to Roman generals. He looked leonine; he dominated people.

The surrender of the prisoners was made on his order alone. Goritxu was told to arm nine guards and release all unsentenced *detenus* upon the ridge of Arxanda.

They wondered what would happen to them when they were told the doors of the Larrinaga were open. Then they headed out; I believe that Wandel, the German aviator boy, was among them. They included army officers guilty of rebellion.

There was an attempt to stop them. Leizaola went up to Putz to explain that this release was his personal order.

The prisoners moved up the winding road in the dark.

It was long before the news came back that they were safely delivered. Meanwhile Leizaola was staying to be encircled in Bilbao. He knew that if captured he would be shot, after long and painful interrogation. But he wanted to spare the prisoners the danger of remaining unguarded in a city through which armed units of their class enemies were retreating, and more than anything in the world, I think, he wished to defend the name of his dear city, Bilbao.

After all, the Basques were a small people, and they didn't have many guns or planes, and they did not receive any foreign aid, and they were terribly simple and guileless and unversed in warfare; but they had, throughout this painful civil war, held high the lantern of humanity and civilisation. They had not killed, or tortured, or in any way amused themselves at the expense of their prisoners. In the most cruel circumstances they had maintained liberty of self-expression and faith. They had scrupulously and zealously observed all the laws, written and unwritten, which enjoin on man a certain respect for his neighbour. They had made no hostages; they had responded to the inhuman methods of those who hated them by protest, nothing more. They had, as far as anyone can in war, told the truth and kept all their promises.

Now Bilbao was beaten, but the sad-faced Catholic lawyer in the thick black suit who was ruling Bilbao was determined to see his city's record clean to the finish. There he sat at the end of a telephone at the Presidency.

The lines of his face were set in a heavy calm. Not for the first time I detected in their immoveable oval symmetry a sort of nobleness, a sad strictness of character seldom to be caught in the living world. He was the finest type of Christian. Faithful to the end to his church and his social conscience, he alone can have known how hard it was to serve these two masters in Bilbao, June, 1937.

We were still discussing the plans for evacuation with Leizaola at two that morning; the hours were passing like tired and heavy militiamen on sentry-go. It was about two when the last outposts in Begoña and the old town across the river were withdrawn. The hour had come to blow up the bridges.

There was a loud shaking explosion to the front of the Presidency; that was the drawbridge. Another to the right, then rapidly two more to the right, where the Gran Via crossed the Nervion to the Arenal, to join the dusky walk by the side of the river under green copious trees that made the centre of Old Bilbao. Swelling to muscles of dynamite, the bridges fell into the river; the Nervion could not be crossed.

At the same moment all the lights in Bilbao went out together and the gas was cut off with a final spit.

Much though I liked the Basques, it was hard to swallow a final laugh. Our lion-hearted engineers, who for days had prepared the bridges against their last and final dissolution, had forgotten that the light cable and gas-pipes of Bilbao lay across one of them. Once more, and for the rest of our last night in Bilbao, the town was an ink-pool. Even the Presidency was overwhelmed. We flashed torches along the gloomy passages; the telephone no longer responded; all was dark outside except for the negro shine of the cobbles from which nailed boots knocked sparks.

Many of us were seized with panic. People ran down the Presidency stairs in the dark, stepped into their cars and drove out along the Santander road with lights dimmed or extinguished. Here at least there was moonlight, a clear view along the gleaming ribbon road, the companionship of the softly flowing river and of many other mortals also fleeing west.

I wandered alone about the streets, trying to drink in this silence and darkness. Here I was, a small fidgety animal, in a great city which was only not a desert because every corner of it echoed to the sound of my feet. But in other ways it was a desert, unpeopled except by a moonlight mirage, which on the leaves and litter of its sidewalks pretended a variety without life-blood or marrow.

At the riverside the Nationalist Militia, who were the backbone of the Basque Army, lay behind their sandbags watching and waiting. Their machine-guns pointed at the other bank. Not a shot was fired, not a movement was visible. Others lay huddled in their blankets. There were no fires to warm them. All was the same silence and darkness in which only the barrels of the machine-guns shone, and the rippling water.

Jaureghuy waited at the Presidency. He had told me before that he would not leave before Putz. "Desert a Frenchman," exclaimed Jaureghuy. "I've never run yet and I'm not running now." So he went to sleep at the Presidency, where at 4 a.m. Putz came down to establish his new headquarters.

A battalion was sent out to make sure that Mount Arraiz was ours. They arrived at five, went up the hill in open order to find the machine-guns of the enemy established on top. A runner came back to the city. The circle was very nearly closed.

The enemy now held the whole right bank of the river up to the shattered bridges. He held the whole of our rear on the left bank except for a stretch of two kilometres between Mount Arraiz and the Nervion. This gap, running along the Nervion trench, was our only exit—the railway line with its tunnels, used so often in air bombardments, and the two parallel roads to Valmaseda and Santander. Once past the shoulder of Arraiz, their ways suddenly parted, for the road to Valmaseda turned round in its tracks to follow the valley of the Cadagua south-west.

There were machine-guns on Arraiz, and across the river 75's in Fuerte Banderas. Putz began to send orders down to his battalions for the evacuation before full daylight. I felt that the time had come to say good-bye to

Bilbao. It was cold, approaching dawn, when to look at the stream of the Nervion made one shiver. It did not at this hour carry the dirty green colour of full day; it flowed past the deserted factories and foundries in relentless steel grey, making inflexibly for the sea between enemy guns.

Jaureghuy went down to the bridges to give, for Putz, the order of withdrawal. One by one the battalions were informed, but some, to whom other messengers were sent, never received the news until common report told them at daylight.

Only the Otxandiano refused to move. They said that they had heard that there was in Bilbao a battalion called the Mexico, which they believed might make trouble in the city. They would wait to see it out.

This was the same battalion that had escorted the prisoners into enemy lines from the Larrinaga prison. They had fought like lions throughout the campaign.

I walked out along the road, a long walk. When I was level with Arraiz and had passed it a little, a machine-gun opened up from the saddle of Cobetas, nearer the river. They were creeping down. So I left the road and waited for a moment in a tunnel with some militiamen. When the machine-gun stopped I abandoned my tunnel, and shunning the road, clambered over garden fences and ran past houses for about a mile until I reached safety and cover near the girder bridge of the Cadagua. The Italians in the battery across the way must have been sound asleep; they did not fire a shot at us.

Where the road turned towards Valmaseda I found a number of cars. They said that it was impassable the other side of Cobetas, but I said nonsense and persuaded an old chauffeur of mine to take me down the road. We went very fast. And sure enough the same party on the saddle of Cobetas opened fire on us as we blazed past below them on their left flank, and this time we stopped two bullets. But we were out of Bilbao.

Behind us came the wreck of the 1st Division with Putz and Jaureghuy, climbing over walls and down tunnels like a troop of monkeys. Most of the Ertzana foot and motorised police stayed in the town and surrendered.

At 11 a.m. that morning little Larrauri, Putz's Basque A.D.C., entered Bilbao in a liaison armoured car and hauled out a few hundred troops who thought that they were cut off. An hour later the enemy tanks came down to the centre of the town to reconnoitre, and found nothing.

That afternoon the Rightist minority in Bilbao tentatively opened the shutters of their windows and hung out red and yellow flags. At four a Basque tank went in, and grumbling down to the Gran Via for the last time, shot three of the flags off the balconies. The shutters were closed again.

A crowd of about two hundred in the Plaza opposite the Presidencia who were singing Fascist songs were dispersed with the tank machine-gun.

Between five and six the enemy marched into Bilbao and occupied it.

All that day I drove backwards and forwards on the roads of Valmaseda, Somorrostro and Baracaldo looking for my luggage, Putz and Jaureghuy. The first I never found, but at midday I lit on Putz and Jaureghuy, cheerful as ever, eating cold fish and drinking warm wine at Beldarrain's headquarters in the gas-mask factory of Retuerto. I was hungry, and finished both their plates and drank their dregs.

They had left Bilbao with a little more dignity than I. Their own machine-guns had compelled the enemy on Cobetas to silence before they moved, they said. Putz spoke now of enjoying two days' sleep before he saw his division again.

Outside on the roads, under a hot, open sky, there were thousand upon thousand of militiamen marching away from Bilbao. On the Valmaseda highway I counted over a division, and another division moving towards Somorrostro. Heavy lorries passed in dozens. There were great parks of cars outside the few filling stations which still had stores. The troops were walking in twos and threes. The Orden Publico of Bilbao, middle-aged men in berets and blue police uniforms, walked by slowly.

It was terribly hot and dusty. The mining villages seemed to crowd upon the roads on either side to stifle them. The roads were a fine brown curtain of dust for miles around as the men tramped along. All over the red hills of the mines to either side one could see little trails of them, moving away to the west. I thought of an

aerial bombardment; here, if ever, was the German opportunity. But the same planes that had machine-gunned the
civilian refugees five nights before did not appear to-day.
I do not put it down to deliberation; I attribute this to
the muddleheadedness of war.

As we were leaving Retuerto in the dust, past trains of
artillery and small struggling tanks slithering in the warm
tarmac of Vizcayan summer midday, two companies of a
Basque battalion came marching in, led by three superbly
handsome young men in steel helmets. I have forgotten
the battalion's name, but it belonged to Putz's division.
"Where have you come from?" we asked. "From very
far," they answered bitterly. They were angry troops.
They had been nearly caught in Bilbao. But what
astounded Jaureghuy and me was that they marched in
order and conformed to a military discipline.

It made us very sad to look at these troops, to see the
steadiness and bigness and obedience of the men in line,
and the beauty of their officers. When I say beauty I do
not mean only that they were well made and that their
features had the long Basque lines and their skins were
fresh and fair. There was more to it than that: there
was an energy in their faces and their march that meant
that they were not only cannon-fodder, rough material of
war. They were under the onset of a great emotion;
their eyes flashed anger and excitement in a wild harmony
whenever they spoke to us.

They summed up for us the fate of Bilbao, which was
the last stronghold of pure democracy in Spain. What a
fight it had put up! What a stubborn infantry it had
turned into the field! And now it had been beaten by
the combined forces of Germany, Italy and Castile, while
others, even declared allies, folded their hands to watch.
The artillery without shells, the aviation nowhere, the
General Staff at its new post in La Cubierta without telephones or communication with the fighting men. Yet here
before Jaureghuy, of Foch's General Staff, and me, who
have seen in a short life many brave men and women,
were the last defenders of Bilbao still in order, angry only
with their superiors because they had not been kept in
proper liaison. "I shall be at San Pedro de Galdames,"
said Putz, "but you should rest here for a bit."

They fell out at the roadside, and entered the glittering white courtyard of the factory to rest against sandbags. For about half an hour they kept on cursing and swearing, and making cigarettes. How hot it was in the courtyard. They turned over to sleep. Jaureghuy's darting blue eyes sparkled with a soldier's pleasure. "Marvellous," he said, "what other infantry in the world would do it?"

We drove away through Somorrostro, smashed up by bombing planes two days back. The roads under the yellow sky were still covered with dust, and the pattern of the scarf was men and more men. An epileptic whom we carried in the car to a Red Cross post slobbered a pitchy saliva over his uniform collar and shook idiotically. Where there were hedgerows or bomb-broken houses at the side of the sweltering road, men lay tumbled to sleep in hundreds in their shells of shade. It was too hot for us or the enemy to do anything. Putz fell asleep. There was no breeze from the sea as we passed, and the sea seemed as stiff and polished as the shore rocks. All the trees were dulled and dead with dust, the mine hills stood up at either side, dry points of red. The tanks made at Trubia opened their lids above and at the sides, their drivers sweated and nodded over the wheel, as they staggered behind the great retreat.

XXXV

I saw the Basques once again.

On Wednesday, August 18th, the French pilot Lebeau flew me into Santander from Biarritz. It was now a risky flight; one of the service planes had already been shot down, and a second was to fall victim to the Italian fighters in September. Plane and pilot were burnt to cinders.

The little Beechcraft skimmed over the water at only three hundred feet, the level of the filmy cloud bank, which was tattered and thin, and unsubstantial as a cobweb. We kept a sharp look-out to right and left.

We saw nothing but the headlands where I had once walked. Lequeitio, Machichaco, Jata, Plencia, the mouth of the Nervion, and the opening that led up to Somorrostro; on whose sand, which looked like pale gold as the sun sank, I had found the body of the Italian aviator Guido Piezl.

At Santander everyone was at sixes and sevens; and not the least untroubled part of Santander was the aerodrome of La Albericia. The rebel bombers had unloaded upon it with rare thoroughness a few hours before. Of five hundred missiles covering a dispersion as wide as half a mile to westward, about twenty-five had hit holes in the flying field, which the hands were languidly filling.

Lebeau took a good look at it, laughed in a French way that reminded me of Jaureghuy, shut his eyes and flew up again. On the third circle he spotted landing room, and we came down at the fourth with a lot of bumping and jumping, and a run along the ground like a snake with sunstroke. Somehow or other, we stopped without turning over. Around us at wide intervals, and untouched by the raid, stood the nine Russian Boeing monoplane fighters, type I.16. They lay there like taut grasshoppers, short stubby fuselages poised on grasshopper bow legs and wings unsheathed for flight. These were the fastest aeroplanes in Spain, capable of five hundred kilometres an hour; they had reached Santander in direct flight from Madrid after the fall of Bilbao, and their pilots were Russian, for no Spaniard was able to manage them. Del Rio, I remembered, the best pilot that Bilbao ever had, preferred to fly the slower "chato" biplane, which he said had greater stability.

We drove into Santander. What a difference from Bilbao.

For all that the world Press wrote about her at the time, Santander never was a Basque town. She was the capital of the northernmost province of Old Castile, and Basque territory ended at Castro Urdiales, fifty miles east of her. She was Spanish.

Santander and the province of wide grazing downs which led up to the Cantabrian mountain chain on her southern border were naturally of the Right and not of the Left. In the elections of February, 1936, which returned a Left Government for Spain, Santander and her hinterland voted over 60 per cent. Right.

Yet the Civil War provoked by the rebellion of the Army officers and the Right parties found her on the side of the Government. The police were loyal, and there was no garrison; therefore the Rights did not dare to move, and the usual Junta de Defensa of all the Left parties took control, as in Bilbao. But they did not benefit from the moderating influence of an organisation like the Basque Nationalists.

A vacillating governor was removed, and Señor Olazaran, a Socialist waiter, appointed in his place. The idea of a waiter ruling a Spanish county may strike the Northern mind as unusual, but in point of fact Spanish waiters are, I suppose, the most active people in the Peninsula. After all, they have to be busy and diplomatic and observant when the rest of the population is taking its coffee, which is between eleven in the morning and twelve at night.

Olazaran proved a good Governor; but he was embarrassed by a fanatical chief of police, who by now had reached the rank of Colonel Neila. In July, 1936, however, Neila was an office clerk and a leader of the Santander Socialist Party.

Neila believed in violence and terror as a method. It was he who had ordered the execution of the Santander Rights who fled at the beginning of the rebellion to the safe asylum of Bilbao, to the dark whispering corners and ever-closed bedroom doors of the Hotel Torrontegui. The Basques had quickly driven his men out, but he continued his work with system in the province of Santander.

His men took suspects for rides at night and in the early morning. The Spanish word for this activity is *paseo*—"a walk." The favourite termini of the *paseo* were the Cabo Mayor wireless station, on the promontory to the west of the Palace of Miramar, and a sequestered avenue near the village of Camargo on the Asturias road. Here Neila gave his peculiar fancy rein. Passers-by in the early days would be surprised to see tables spread with good things at the roadside, and what seemed to be honest citizens sitting in front of them, or leaning on their elbows or lying back in their chairs in attitudes of conversation. But as they drew level with the banquet, they noted that the guests were strangely motionless. They found, indeed, that they were recently dead; and they hurried on with a shiver. This was Neila's way of giving them a morning appetite; and it had one definite result, that until the moment that the defence of the city collapsed, the 5th Column did not dare come out into the streets—though they still could claim, despite his three thousand executions, a large numerical majority in Santander.

* * * * * *

When we entered Santander the game was up. The Italians, using a weight of artillery experienced by Bilbao only in the last phase, had broken through the Escudo pass in the Cantabrian mountains.

Weak and ill-organised though she was, Santander was not fated to fall to the Spanish rebels. Her conquest was due not only to the aviation and artillery of Germany and Italy, but to the predominant numbers and the over-whelming armament of the Italian infantry engaged.

Santander was not a victory for Franco; she was the last, the most barefaced triumph of the new Spanish strategy, in which the London Committee had specialised now for a year.

The troops invading Santander were three Italian Divisions of five thousand each, two Navarrese Divisions (the 60th and 61st) of the same size, two *tabors* of Moors, and eight or nine mixed squadrons of Moorish and Spanish cavalry. In other words, Mussolini's contribution to Franco's army, after a year of Non-Intervention, exceeded Franco's own.

The Italian troops, composed of the Flechas Negras (Black Arrows), Llamas Negras (Black Flames), on the 23rd of March, were endowed with the regulation armament of the Italian army. Each Bandera or Battalion of eight hundred and fifty men included one machine-gun company of twelve machine guns, and each platoon of thirty men carried two machine-gun rifles. The Division in fact developed a fire of automatic weapons incomparably stronger than anything in the Basque or the Santander armies.

Their artillery was even more formidable. Each Bandera was armed with a battery of 65 mm. light artillery, and two German anti-aircraft guns. Eighteen batteries ranging from 155 mm. (6-inch) to 75 mm. (3-inch) supported each Division, and provided an artillery orchestration twice as powerful as those behind regular divisions on manœuvres in England.

Forty-five tanks accompanied each Division, of which four-fifths were Fiat-Ansaldo two-men tanks with two machine-guns, while nine larger tanks carried a small cannon as well.

Overhead cover was not lacking. At Villarcayo, twenty miles from the front line of the Escudo, there was an aerodrome controlled by the Italians. The ground staff and the pilots were without exception Italian. Spaniards, in this great Spanish Nationalist Movement, were not encouraged to approach the Villarcayo field, on which were scattered thirty Fiat CR 32 fighting planes, almost twice the number of those at the service of Santander.

The bombers, who numbered about forty and were mostly German, were based on the aerodrome of Gamoral, three kilometres out of Burgos.

German fighting aircraft, including a fast new monoplane fighter, operated from Aguilar del Campo, behind the two Navarrese Divisions. A reserve tank park was established here, consisting of at least thirty vehicles.

And Santander; what could she range against this iron wall and steel ceiling of International Fascism? Eighteen Russian fighters; a random collection of worthless bombers, old Breguets and Potez of the once united, pre-revolutionary Spanish Air Force; and seventeen even more worthless Gourdous smuggled into Spain after the fighting began. The Gourdou is a four-year-old product of France, but when it was new it was just about as valuable as it is now. Its speciality is dive-bombing, at which it is slower than most; and as far as I could discover, it was equipped with only 100-lb. bombs. The poor old Gourdou was no death-diver; the only Disperata squadron in which she might have distinguished herself was that commanded from the rear by Sancho Panza.

The Santander army was 25,000 strong, and on her left or eastern flank lay the Basque Army, between the sea at Castro Urdiales and Valmaseda inland, another 25,000 men. It would have been possible to find, at most, two hundred foreigners among them.

If one sets these figures against the 13,000 Spaniards fighting for Franco in the Santander campaign, one can adjust to its right proportions the claim of his movement to be Spanish and National.

The Santander Army was even more feebly equipped than the Basques with automatic weapons. Their artillery, until the Basques brought their 6-inch guns from Bilbao, totalled sixty pieces, of which all except a battery of 105's (4-inch) were 75 mms. This; to cover a front of nearly one hundred miles. And the guns came from everywhere. There were little pieces called affectionately "Japoneses" because of their size and restlessness, for they jumped for joy in the air whenever they fired. There was one battery of Krupp's—the best that they had, the pride of Santander. There were Spanish Schneider of the old Spanish Army; and there were French Schneider of the Mexican Army, still marked on the breech with the Mexican eagle and struggling snake in brass. Faulty ammunition blew up two of these. Telephones and observation posts were lacking, for there was not enough wire to go round; instead, flag signals were made or runners sent with messages.

Such were the opposing forces, and such the equality of terms established by the Non-Intervention Committee. It was easy work to overrun the Santanderino lines at the Puerto de Escudo and the pass opposite Aguilar del Campo.

I have the order for artillery preparation on the Escudo for the 2nd Italian Division, Llamas Negras or, in Italian, *Fiamme Nere*. It was stripped from a dead Italian artillery officer, and is naturally written in his language. All the batteries except eight were commanded and served by Italians; even the local maps found on Spanish Staff officers in this brief campaign were of Italian make.

This order provides for an hour of slow fire on six positions along a front of half a division. There is then an interval of unrecorded length "for the intervention of the aviation." This, in my experience on the Basque front, took anything between one and three hours. The artillery then opened rapid fire for fifteen minutes, the 75's in the chorus heating up to five shots a piece a minute. After 4,505 shells and an enormous quantity of bombs had been dropped on the Santanderino line, the Italian Divisional infantry, with its 65 mm. field pieces—twenty-four in all—covering its advance, under a dozen of its fighting planes which machine-gunned the lines ahead of it at low altitude, and screened by forty-five tanks, moved slowly forward dangling its World War panoply and impedimenta of machine-guns and spades, and ambled inelegantly like the servile and impoverished peasants that they were into positions that the Santanderinos had long since vacated.

The offensive had begun four days before I arrived. By Wednesday afternoon the enemy were nearly half-way to Santander.

Posters in the town betrayed the plight in which the Santander Left found themselves. In Leizaola's view— for the Basque Minister of Justice was still in Santander— these carried the crudest political appeal ever made in Spain. Briefly they said that every good Republican citizen should denounce any defeatist or Rightist talk that he heard, and if necessary take the law into his own hands, "breaking the villain's brain with a stone."

As a Catholic Minister of Justice and Culture, Leizaola indicated the posters with the profoundest distaste. "What style," he said.

Nobody else in Santander, however, seemed to be paying the slightest attention to the notice. There were few denunciations, and the cracking of craniums could not be heard. Everybody was sauntering along the sea parade as if the front were somewhere south of Morocco. The Government had just ordered all industries and commerce not directly connected with the war to shut, so that employees might be free to construct fortifications. But somehow or other the organisation for such a heavy displacement of labour was not in the best of health and the people of Santander were enjoying a sunny holiday on the quays and the public purse; and were forgetting about the war, if indeed they had ever really believed that the stupid thing existed.

As we drove up to the white villa on Cabo Mayor that served as Presidencia to Aguirre, we saw troops of Santander marching along back from the front, with a look on their faces that showed just how prettily they knew the cards were stacked against them. Back from the front? There was no front; the army of Santander was steadily retiring without a struggle, bombed mercilessly on the open grazing ground when the mist lifted, and leaving its wounded to die in the highland waste behind it. Two days back, Ibarrola's Division from the Basque Army Corps was moved into the central front to consolidate a defence line. It resisted immovably for thirty-six hours; most of the casualties that the Italians admitted, some 1,500, fell to its fire. But the Santanderinos on either flank went home in a steady stream, in defeated khaki-bundled threes and fours across the coverless hills. And Ibarrola himself, courageous as he was, could hold no longer; the Basques had fought their last battle.

* * * * * *

The Presidencia was much calmer and more reflective, I found, than the town of Santander. Basque guards with berets watched at the four corners of its garden wall, where it stood over a little sandy cove and the blue sea. They were needed. When the Basques first came here, in June, after the fall of Bilbao, the genial Neila had bumped off the chauffeur of Ramon Aldasoro. Nobody quite knew why; the man was not even a Basque Nationalist, he was a Socialist by all accounts. But the Basques did not wait to ask questions; within two days, as almost a year before they had driven terrorism out of Vizcaya, they had killed the two policemen responsible for the death of their country-man. This display of energy and their picquet system had stopped murder in mad career.

A queer man, Neila. He flew away to France next day, and we all seemed highly relieved and gamesome to see the posteriors of him, as they passed the cockpit door on their positively last appearance in Santander.

The President was there, and Monzon, and Rezola and Basaldua, and five or six others. They were still busily working at evacuation.

They had, since the beginning of July, and in spite of all the difficulties put in their way by Britain and France, managed to get 50,000 Basque refugees out of Spain by ship.

It was pleasant to see Aguirre again. "*Saleva*," he said, laughing and clenching his fist in a comic salute. *Saleva* was a development of the proletarian greeting *salud*: it stood for *salud*—and *evacuacion*. Eguia, my first Basque friend, came up. His command had shrunk now to ten small minesweepers. The Santander Government had deprived him of his armed trawlers and replaced the Basque officers with local navigators of the Left.

The new crews that he had trained for the destroyers *Jose Luis Diez* and *Ciscar*, and who had at last cleaned the ships up and dared to put to sea, these too had been removed and the old Anarchist brothel-birds were once more in possession. The week's washing again dressed the two destroyers from stern to bows. Once indeed, when the rebel minelayer *Jupiter* appeared off the great bay of Santander, *Jose* had rushed out boldly and fired two hundred shells at her without hitting her. But Eguia, they thought, was fairer game. When the crew saw him in the street, they used to tell him that one fine day, and not so distant at that, they would settle old scores.

Next day two more Basque battalions were ordered by the General Gamir y Ulibarri to fill the gaps in the San-tander line where the enemy were marching on Torrelavega to cut Santander off from the Asturias.

For the first time the Basques refused to fight. They would not kill themselves any more doing Santander's business. They had marched far enough from their own country; they would stay where they were, on the borders of Vizcaya.

Leizaola took me in the evening to see the last peaceful evacuation that the Basques were able to make. We drove east to the bay of Santoña, closed to the north by the great peninsula of rock in whose shadow the town and port and the biggest prison in Spain, found a narrow and crowded foothold. Santoña rock was reached by a long causeway driving between well-salted hedges and over flat salt marshes; and at last we were there, followed by the sea wind.

A little ship called *Bobie* (*sic*) was anchored at the quay-side. She flew the Union Jack, a recent acquisition; for she had only been registered British a few weeks before. Her captain was a Greek, obese and damp with anxiety, who wished to be reassured at half-hourly intervals that British men-of-war would without fail protect him once he had passed the three-mile limit. Then he sat down and rested, but after thirty minutes more the old doubts would reassert their hold upon his nervous system; unlike those compatriots of his who turned down St. Paul, he was always eager both to see and to hear the same old thing.

A charming little Portuguese with literary leanings was the representative of the Control on board the *Bobie*. He was thrilled to meet for the first time the eminent Leizaola, whose books on constitutional law and Basque legal theory he so much admired. I thought that this was flattery, until the little Portuguese began quoting recognisable chunks of Leizaola; I had not realised before the very substantial reputation of my friend with the dark, grave face and the fixed, melancholy eyes. He was, of course, one of the greatest lawyers in Spain.

Here and there lamps half-lit the decks of *Bobie*, and the rough wooden ladders and trestles that led down to the hold of the tramp. They half-lit the faces, bandages, crutches, and gaps for legs and arms of the Basque soldiers who lay on the decks or down below.

There were five hundred of them. From the gaiety of their conversation and the youthfulness of the looks of those on deck one could scarcely guess that none would ever be able to fight again; that many would never be able to earn a living, or walk about any more. They were the *grands blessés* of Bilbao, the Blighty wounds of the Basques, the first five hundred of several thousand. One kept one's face in the dark shadow as one watched them drag their way along the deck to get soup and candles, matches and cigarettes, in the light of the flickering lamps. The boards where they lay were like earth sprinkled in winter with light snowdrifts, with the great white expanses of bandage that pied the ship and relieved the darkness from end to end. Below other wounded lay in crude shelves along the bottom of the ship; these were strapped in and were suffering more sharply. When they turned their hollow faces to the smoky twilight, one could see in the interplay of fire and shadow on the bone-frames of their cheeks and eyes that all their features were peaked with pain. They wanted not to be noticed, to be forgotten, and plucked their blankets uneasily over their heads.

One could smell the burnt wick as the lamps went out, like their youth, and one's eyes became accustomed to the gaunt skeleton of their hospital in the ship's hold, as hollow and dead as their future. It was a solemn and terrible cave in which we stood, banked high with wasted lives, hollow sockets of eyes that looked at us, bodies lying like corpses under blankets that could conceal their pain but not their thinness. Water from the bilge trickled under our feet as the ship slid up and down on the night tide; nobody spoke and one felt nobody wanted to.

We clambered up the ladders again. In the darkness one could see looming the shapes of buses, and dark figures carrying towards the ship bundles that, lifted over the ship's sides, turned out to be men, less the limbs that would have justified Aristotle's definition of the species. Ten Basque nurses, neatly dressed, stepped into the tramp and walked along suspended planks to the dispensary in the stern. Three doctors followed, Basques too. The *Bobie*, like all the evacuation ships since July, had been paid for and organised into a hospital by the Basques alone. Hundreds of thousands of pounds had been spent by the race on the humanitarian work that still gave them such particular pleasure.

But we saw now that one of the Captain's periods of repose was over, and I said good-bye to some of the wounded whom I recognised, who had been at my side in the Bilbao campaign. As we jumped ashore, Leizaola did an unusual thing: he pointed a moral: "You see," he said briefly, "why we Basques have always hated militarism, and the centralised Spain that glorifies it. Yet I think we fought quite well when it came to the pinch."

We drove back through the salt marshes to Santander, whose streets were crowded with thousands of refugees from her province and the Asturias, and with cattle by the hundred driven back as the army retired.

The Italians were marching steadily forward against only minor resistance. I stayed two days more, and then flew back to France.

* * * * * *

XXXVI

THE DAY I LEFT SANTANDER I saw on Rezola's table the instructions of the General Staff to evacuate all the sanitary equipment and the wounded of the XIVth (Basque) Army Corps, then stationed at Santoña Laredo and Castro Urdiales, to Ribadesella in the Asturias. This was to be the first phase of a general withdrawal from the province of Santander, for the enemy was advancing rapidly towards the coast to cut off their last exit to the west at Torrelavega.

At Santander the system was breaking up. When Captain Rodriguez de la Mata, of the *Sanidad Militar* of the Basque Army Corps, went to the city on August 24th, he found that the chief of the XVth (Santanderino) Army Corps had already fled; that there was not transport enough to evacuate the 6,000 wounded on his hands, let alone the material; and that since midday the road to Torrelavega had been under artillery fire, while the second-class road nearer the coast, through Suances, was dominated in daylight by the aviation. Nothing could be done till dark.

De la Mata returned to Santoña to see a remarkable sight.

The headquarters of *Sanidad Militar* were full of Basque doctors and orderlies, the many relics of the superb system of hospitalisation instituted long ago by the songster Unceta; every moment more came. The militia, almost all of whom until 3 p.m. were Nationalists, were walking freely through the streets: they told De la Mata that yesterday evening the Battalion Padura had occupied Santoña, and that the other Nationalist battalions had fallen back towards the coastal zone of Laredo, Colindres and Santoña in disobedience to the orders of the staff of Santander, which required a withdrawal to the Asturias.

Juan de Axuriaguera, President of the Executive Committee of the Basque Nationalist Party, had gone to arrange with General Mancini, Italian commander of the Italian division Flechas Negras, the terms of a separate peace.

An ancient Basque tradition, a bedrock principle of their democratic pacificism, was dominating the thoughts of the Basque militia.

The Basque is one of the greatest travellers in the world: he built the ships that he later navigated to the discovery of the western hemisphere, and the wealth of the Americas was much of his making. Every great city in the South American continent is stuffed with his capital; but with this love of adventure he combines a more passionate love of home. His ideal is to return to Vizcaya.

Against the Moors, the Goths, and Castile the Basque in his green mountains was a great defensive fighter. He maintained his ancient culture and his freedom from feudalism, which is the matrix of class warfare, for many centuries until this last. Because of that culture and freedom he is at heart a pacifist. At the southern boundary of Vizcaya there stood the tree Malatu, beyond which it was wrong to pass in pursuit of the defeated invader. Here was the boundary of Eden, to be feared for its flaming sword; but beyond it lived other, if lower, people, whose rights must be respected. For the freedom of the seas, and for the freedom of his own land, the Basque was prepared to fight. But it was impossible for him to be an aggressor even in the twentieth century; and in token of that one of his Nationalist battalions was called the Malatu.

By August 24th, 1937, after a year of war, the Basque fighting man had lost every square foot of his own country, except that little strip of pasture between Castro Urdiales and Santoña which had been taken from him by Castile many years before. Now he was asked to bid farewell for ever to his home; to withdraw to the wild Asturias, where feudalism had reared its most remorseless progeny; to fight not even an offensive, but a hopeless rearguard action beyond the tree Malatu. He refused to do it.

He said that he was ready to fight for his life where he was, but to retreat no more. He looked at his lovely country behind him—in ruin. Durango, Gernika, Eibar, Otxandiano, Munguia, Mugika, Elgeta, Markina, Bolibar,

Il Popolo d'Italia

Fondatore: BENITO MUSSOLINI

MILANO · Anno XXIV · Via Armaldo Mussolini, 10

N. 240 · Domenica 29 Agosto 1937-XV E. F.

Cent. 30

IN ESTREMO ORIENTE

La lotta divampa

a Sciangai e nelle risaicacie

Una nota di protesta trasmessa dall'Inghilterra al Giappone

DOPO LA SEDAN DEL MARXISMO

Santander liberata dal giogo rosso

inneggia all'Italia e al Duce

Le vittoriose truppe legionarie

passate in rassegna dal gen. Davila

I generali italiani che hanno condotto in Ispagna le truppe legionarie alla vittoria

ETTORE BASTICO
Comandante di Corpo d'Armata

ANNIBALE BERGONZOLI
« Barba Elettrica »

LUIGI FRUSCI
Comandante delle Fiamme Nere

ALESSANDRO BISCACCIANTI
Capoide generale della Milizia

ATTILIO TERUZZI
Ispettore delle Camicie Nere

ITALY ACCLAIMS HER TROOPS AND GENERAL OFFICERS.

Arbacegui and Guerrikaiz; Cortezubi, Ceanuri, Dima, Villaro, Yurre, Castillo y Eleijabeitia, Amorebieta, Lemona, Fika, Rigoitia, Galdakano—these villages were all destroyed, totally or in part, by the German bombers. Mola and his allies had conscientiously carried out their promise to raze Vizcaya. At the thought of it the homesick Basque was struck with an over-mastering melancholy; the means of the other side and his own sufferings were too great, and he could do no more.

And now the Italians of Llamas Negras occupied Torrelavega, cutting off the Asturian retreat which the Basques refused to take. Aguirre entered his plane to France and left the villa over the sandy cove. The General Staff, the wireless, the political Left of Santander had already gone. There was wild firing in the streets of the city. Old Pursey trained a crew of thirteen British, French, German and Spanish subjects, including Miss Caton, of the "Save the Children Fund," with unequal oars, to row into the Bay of Biscay and the mist until fortune put them in the track of a British destroyer. They passed many empty boats, floating oars and helpless refugees; in the great mass evacuation of Santander to the open sea there must have been many hundreds drowned, and the crew of thirteen owed it to their destiny and to Pursey, immortal gossip and navigator, that they did not swell the number in the Biscay fog.

And Eguia, the big-headed Anglicised captain of the port of Bilbao, who had constantly and correctly informed the Royal Navy of the conditions in Basque territorial waters—how did he escape? Well, Eguia, he appointed himself admiral commanding the Biscay fleet, which had dwindled, for the Santanderinos had deprived him of his old fighters, the *bous*, the armed trawlers. But Eguia still administered ten of the mine-sweepers that had kept Bilbao territorial waters clean. They were unarmed, and Santander was, as the English said, *blockaded*. But Eguia put on his admiral's hat, which was a dusty old Basque beret, and slipped his best seafaring mackintosh over his blue suit, and assumed his tie and telescope and walked down with the crews and his department most nautically to the ten sweepers. Machine-guns for infighting were hoisted aboard. Then to the signal of Admiral Eguia, which was a broad Basque grin, the last of the invincible armadas swept through the blockade to France without loss or scratch.

My friend Rezola and the rest of his Defence Department were sent to Santoña with their archives; they were told that British ships would call to take them off to France, meanwhile they were to supervise the surrender of the Basque Army.

Once all these people were in Santoña they found that they could not, if they wished, get out again, either by sea or by land, back to Santander. The Basque Nationalist battalions and Executive Committee had formed a Junta de Defensa for the capitulation, and closed the port and all the roads with machine-guns.

The terms reached between Juan de Axuriaguera, head of the Party, and his lieutenant, Artetxe, with General Mancini, were as follows:

> *On the part of the Basque troops:*
> I. *To lay down their arms in order and surrender their material to the Italian legionary forces, who should occupy the region of Santoña without resistance.*
> II. *To maintain public order in the zone that they occupied.*
> III. *To assure the life and liberty of the political hostages in the prisons of Laredo and Santoña.*
>
> *On the part of the Italian forces:*
> I. *To guarantee the lives of all Basque combatants.*
> II. *To guarantee the lives and authorise the departure abroad of all Basque political personalities and functionaries at present in the territory of Santoña and Santander.*
> III. *To consider Basque combatants subject to this capitulation free of all obligation to take part in the civil war.*
> IV. *To assure that the Basque population loyal to the Provisional Government of Euzkadi should not be persecuted.*

On these conditions the Basques, who are not a Machiavellian people, were prepared one and all to lay down their arms to the Italian division, Flechas Negras, and thank God that the war was over. The flag of Euzkadi was raised at Laredo and Santoña, for in the interval before surrender the Basques had declared themselves free of both Spains.

They had surrendered to the Italians because it was Italy that had beaten them, not Franco. And now the political leaders and functionaries, like Rezola, were waiting for the ships that would take them to France.

They gathered in the Town Hall of Santoña under the great rock bronzed by the heat which makes of the port a northern Gibraltar. The deep bay, puddling on the flanks to salt marshes and stemmed by dykes, stretched away to the south till it reached the sands of Laredo and Colindres. An August sun on its closed and level waters polished them to sparkle like a chromium floor. So they waited there, under the Basque flag, for the 24th and 25th August, shading their eyes against the violent light and doing nothing. They waited for the Italians.

The second day, Wednesday, August 25th, the Gudaris began to show their discontent. Some said that they did not trust the Italians and that they were afraid that they might be forced to fight for Franco; others came into the Town Hall to magnify their own political importance, claiming not ingenuously equal rights of evacuation with the leaders. A large number took the obstructive position that if they were not evacuated, nobody else would be. In the afternoon the port filled up with small trawlers and fishing smacks and there were a few brief hours of optimism in which the Basques of Santoña believed that there might be room for all. All tried to fit in, without any control, embarking even with their rifles and machine-guns; but when the ships were settling in the water there were still Basque troops on the quay, and more coming; and there were still a number of officers and *politicos* in the different barracks. The ships lay there all night without permission to leave the harbour. There was no hurry; the Italians were trusted by the Junta de Defensa.

As it grew dark they saw across the great bay, where the road from Bilbao twisted down the hillside, a long convoy of lorries with all their lights ablaze, stiffly moving towards the sea. The Italians were entering Laredo.

An Italian lieutenant-colonel preceded the troops in the side-car of a motor-cycle, and as soon as they had occupied the Plaza the terms of the Basque surrender were publicly read and affixed under the Italian flag. One Basque less simple than the others felt that, for all the flag print and words, it would be better to remove to Santoña, which was not yet occupied by the foreigner; with a few others who were not to be so lucky as he, Captain Juan Marcaide Pildain went down to Laredo beach and rowed a boat across to Santoña under the moon.

Thursday, the 26th, had hardly broken when the Gudaris had to move again. On orders from the Junta de Defensa, who still showed confidence in the promise of Mancini, the fishing-boats and trawlers drew up to the quay again and disembarked their loads. The troops were ordered to their barracks and mostly disarmed. It was known that the Italians would enter in the afternoon and would regulate the new embarkation, with proper lists which the Basque Staff began to draw up in the Town Hall.

It was towards five o'clock when the Italians entered Santoña, a battalion of Flechas Negras with a battery of ultra-light artillery (65 mm.) and a few ragged Spanish troops from Extremadura inadequately equipped. In a few minutes the balconies were full of hangings and flags in the colours of the monarchy, and the streets of Fascist cries and songs, particularly sustained by feminine voices. The Basque infantry let the procession pass without a salute or gesture in the street. Those who could not hide their feelings went indoors. The Italian Colonel Fergosi took over the administration of Santoña from the Basque Junta de Defensa; the Basques had carried out their clauses in the agreement to the letter, laying down arms, surrendering their material and prisoners and maintaining public order in their zone.

At this solemn moment in the history of the Basques two small British ships entered Santoña Bay. *Bobie* led the way and *Seven Seas Spray* followed. They had been sent from Bayonne to evacuate the Basque *responsables* in accordance with the Mancini Agreement. *Bobie* was in charge of a charming Frenchman, M. Georges Dupuy, who once ran arms to the Boers from Madagascar. I leave him to tell his own story.

"*It was at 4 p.m. on Thursday,*" he writes, "*and we were before Santoña. In our natural uncertainty with regard to the events in that town, we moved somewhat prudently towards the port. At 4.20 a little tug passed the point. A flag flew at its*

*bows, but because of the light we took some time to identify it;
at last we were able to assure ourselves that it was the flag of Euzkadi.
At that we made rapidly for the harbour and cast anchor.*

"*The harbour was most animated. A large number of fishing-
boats were lying in the anchorage, full of people. The 'Gazteiz'*"
—a small armed trawler—"*and two or three other small vessels
were there also, and crowded. On the quay there was a mass of
people throwing all their arms in heaps—rifles, revolvers, machine-
guns, cartridge belts, everything. Armed men, Basques, guarded
the quay and its surroundings. Troops in fair order were coming
along the roads which opened on the port, then disarmed and
dispersed.*

"*I went ashore with the captain of 'Gazteiz.' In the town
great animation, flags, banners, draperies in the colours of Franco,
fluttering everywhere. Almost all the women were sporting Fascist
ribbons and emblems. On two of the squares Italian soldiers were
sitting and singing, their arms piled and unguarded.*

"*I went to the Town Hall, which was surrounded by a crowd
of Basques without arms. Inside, the stairs and corridors were
packed with people, and I had great difficulty pushing my way into
the room where the leaders were. This room had also been invaded
by the crowd, and there were wounded almost everywhere. An open
door at the other end showed another room full of wounded.*"

"*I asked for M. Axuriaguera whom I had been recommended to
see before anyone else, and learned that he was at Vitoria and was
expected back at any moment.*"

Dupuy was then fully informed of the conditions of
surrender. He asked for instructions about the embarkation of the militia, and was told that they were waiting for
news. Though he advised them to act quickly, and send
the fishing boats away that night, nothing was done, and
the only orders which he received, and carried out, were to
move the archives and the radio equipment aboard *Bobie*.

"*On my way back I noted nothing unusual. The streets and
the quays were crowded, but order reigned. The Italians did not
seem any more aggressive than before, and there was no blue Falangist
uniform to be seen. At ten and about midnight, still no news.*

"*At six next morning, August 27th, I returned to the Town
Hall, and found Italians there as well as Basques. The leaders
did not seem to have the same control over their men's movements as
yesterday. No news of M. Axuriaguera. The Town Hall was
surrounded by Italian soldiers.*

"*At the same time, the Basques began to mass on the quay, in good order, waiting for the embarkation. At nine I received the order to begin to embark all those in possession of a special ticket issued by the leaders, or a passport of the Government of Euzkadi. The officer-observer of the Non-Intervention Committee on 'Bobie,' M. Costa e Silva, examined the papers with me and the work went on in a businesslike way on both ships, 'Bobie' and 'Seven Seas Spray.'*

"*At ten o'clock an officer in the uniform of the Italian army, but a Spaniard, and carrying the Falangist badge, came and gave me the order to interrupt the embarkation, and wait for new orders. I asked him who had told him to do so, and he said Colonel Fergosi, commanding Santoña.*

"*I stopped, and at this moment—about ten-fifteen—sections of Italian soldiers appeared on the quay, closed around the crowd of Basques who were waiting to board us, placed four machine guns in excellently chosen positions and set a guard on 'Bobie's' gangway, composed of a dozen men and a non-commissioned officer. All communication between ship and shore was forbidden.*

"*Italians piled the material abandoned by the Basques in lorries. I saw quite a column of gudaris, disarmed, going along the Laredo road, and also lorries, all of which carried the Italian flag.*

"*At two that afternoon Silva and I, escorted by four Italian soldiers, visited Colonel Fergosi at the Town Hall. None of the Basque leaders was there now, and it was occupied by Italians entirely.*

"*Colonel Fergosi told me that he had received formal orders from the Generalissimo—Franco—that no one, Basque or foreign, was to leave Santoña. I drew his attention to the fact that all the Basques on the two ships were now under the protection of the British flag and that if no more Basques could come on board I could nevertheless leave with those there already—and 'Seven Seas Spray' too. His answer was definite. 'No one is allowed to leave Santoña, and the 'Almirante Cervera,' which is outside, is already so informed.' Silva also insisted, but to no effect. We were separated, and our papers verified. (Their treatment of me having nothing to do with the point at issue, I pass over in silence the petty incidents which followed until nine o'clock that night.)*

"*I returned to the ship at nine. The same Spanish officer ordered all the passengers to leave 'Bobie.' All was done in an orderly way and the ship was then searched from top to bottom by this person and four other Falangist officers. Next, the identity of 'Bobie's' crew was verified and their papers examined word by wearisome word by the Falangists, particularly those of the two engineer officers (both Basques) and my own. At last, at midnight, the Falangist officer and his acolytes departed after strictly forbidding all communication with the shore.*

"*Saturday; and as daylight began to show, I saw the men who had been disembarked that evening walking along the road to Laredo. There were others on lorries which carried the Italian flag, that went away by another road. I do not know where.*

"*Then other Basques I saw were coming down to the quay to mass there; the Italian guard was commanded by Lieutenant-Colonel Farina. And there were Colonels Fergosi and Piesch, the latter in charge of concentration camps.*

"*Two groups formed on the quay; on one side the Basques who had fought in the war and been disarmed, on the other the political leaders. I was allowed to communicate with them, and learned:*

"(*i*)   *That there was no news of M. Axuriaguera, who ought to have left Vitoria the evening before;*

"(*ii*) *That there was some hope that the negotiations now in progress would end in an order for all to go aboard. I was asked to delay our departure as long as possible for this reason.*

"*In truth, confidence and hope reigned in Santoña . . . at least among the leaders.*

"*At the same time, I received the order to disembark the archives and the radio. I resisted as long as I could, but without success in spite of the ardour and ingenuity of my arguments. The disembarkation had to be made and was completed by ten-thirty.*

"*All this time I was in conversation with Colonels Piesch and Farina. The latter in a frank moment expressed all his bitterness, and said how angered he was to see all that was going on. 'It is disgraceful,' says Farina, 'to see that an Italian General cannot keep the promise which he has given (sic)' and 'there is no case in all history of such a thing happening.' Colonel Piesch added words of assent.*

"*Towards eleven, Colonel Farina told 'Bobie to make out to anchor and await orders, and 'Seven Seas Spray' to lay on to the quay and disembark the people aboard.*

"*Before 'Bobie' left the quay I saw Colonel Fergosi and asked him in the presence of Colonel Farina if the Basques were really prisoners of the Italian Army, and only of the Italian Army. He assured me that such was the case, and that it was not in the intention of General Mancini to deliver the Basques, whoever they were, to the Falangists. I thanked him for this assurance, and expressed a fervent hope that the promise would be kept.*

"At the last moment I shook hands with the leaders and asked them if they had any message for the Presidencia; *unfortunately their optimism was still too strong for them to think of anything to send. They only asked me to stay as long as possible at Santoña, in hope that the conversations would reach a successful conclusion.*

"At mid-day we were settled at our anchorage. We could see the Laredo road, and columns of men upon it, every now and again groups of lorries with the Italian flag.

"At 9 *p.m. an Italian officer, accompanied by four Falangists, themselves officers, came aboard to give us the order to leave. Another search of the ship, and at* 10 *p.m. she was head on to the open sea . . .. The rest of the night passed without incident, except for the appearance on deck of six men who had hidden in the machinery.* We were in Bayonne next morning at nine-fifty."*

And that was the end of the Basques, and Dupuy's history.

* * * * * *

So the oldest democracy in Europe passed under the yoke, and was taken away in Roman lorries to captivity; the Basques were cheated by a nation of whose history in the breaking of promises they ought, perhaps, to have been aware. Fascist Italy had, after all, dishonoured her signature to many agreements and treaties in the two years preceding the surrender of the Basques; but to none with such speed, and without even an attempt to discredit the other party. On one day, General Mancini had signed a peace settlement; three days later, when the Basques had fulfilled their obligations and the Italians had occupied Santoña so peacefully that they could pile arms and sing, Colonels Piesch and Farina were excusing the breach of the agreement by references to the Italian past, which could bear the tone but not the limelight of melodrama. "Never in history," indeed. What of the free surrender followed by execution of the sons of Ras Kassa? What of the Treaty of friendship between Italy and Ethiopia of 1928?

The functionaries, including the keen-eyed and jut-chinned Rezola, were put in a concentration camp at Santoña instead of being allowed to leave for France. It

---

* Including De la Mata and Captain Marcaide Pildain.

would be idle to defend Mancini on the grounds that he yielded to *force majeure*. The whole world knew now that it was not Franco but the Italians who led the partnership; for not only her enemies but Italy herself alleged it. On August 27th, when the Italians made their triumphal entry not only into Santoña, but Santander, the Italian Press claimed the victory as their own. A fourth Italian Division, the Littoria, had been called into the field; and Signor Mussolini himself sent telegrams of congratulation to the ten generals of the Italian Regular Army and Blackshirt Militia who had enabled Franco to win this victory after ten days' campaigning—Bergonzoli, Biscaccianti, Bastico, Perti, Frusci, Roatta, Piazzoni, Francisci, Velarda, Manca (but not to Mancini, the commander of Flechas Negras).

Neither the official character nor the value of Italian intervention was longer denied. To the embarrassment of Franco, it was boasted.

Mancini, therefore, if he had wished to do so, could have seen that his promises were kept. But he did not care to take the trouble. In a few weeks, his Division had moved with the rest of the Italians to the Aragon front, where the crucial battle of the war was to be fought. He did not even leave the Basques under an Italian guard; contrary to the engagement taken to Dupuy by Colonel Fergosi, they were surrendered to Spaniards.

By the third week of October it was known that six hundred of the men whom the Italians had promised to send to France had already been condemned to death. Fourteen had been executed (two from each party forming the Popular Front) by October 21st; and as I write these words the promise of mass murder, of which this was in modern diplomatic terminology a token, is being fully carried out. On people, be it noted, who had neither murdered, robbed nor burnt, but maintained order and released their political prisoners without injury; including spies like Schneider whom any other régime would have shot and men who sat on the very courts-martial that now sent them to the wall. A Spanish gentleman when he is roused can be an animal merely, without gratitude, pity, mercy, or even man's first differentiation from the beasts, which is the refinement of memory.

Of the leaders, several disappeared; including Rezola,

my friend of the *Presidencia* and of Truende, who had led the charge after the bolting Italians, who had crossed himself before coffee in the line and gone on drinking calmly as the planes flew over bombing. His long, powerful frame, firm face and grim blue eyes, his steady voice are fixed in my sense-history for ever. How often did I sit next to him at lunch and supper in the Carlton, and we talked frankly of each retreat, each small recovery; how he towered over Arbex, and over Unceta at the piano, the medical officer who had ordered him to set an example of cleanliness to the militia by shaving his hair—and he did. His calm study of Napoleon on Bilbao's last night, the slow, half-embarrassed laugh on that stubborn mouth of his the evening that he came back with his Italian booty—how could we forget them? A rock of bronze, Rezola, an indomitable, unfrightenable man. His was the perfect type of fraternity, stubbornness, seriousness and humanity to which all Basques were an unselfconscious approximation. And now he was seen no more; and the Basques, his people, were traded into captivity.

At Bilbao the usual reign of judicial murder had been inaugurated over the civilian population too in the military courts, death sentences upon fantastic charges were passed every day. The brutal spirit of tyranny which, even at moments of great crisis, in the hard weeks after the air-raid and prison massacre of January 4th, 1937, the Basques had never wished to impose; the cruel suppression of political enemies which the Basques had spared all members of the Right; these were Basque commonplaces now. An innkeeper at Pedernales of my acquaintance was sentenced to the supreme penalty "for giving meals to Basque Nationalists," priests for preaching sermons or saying masses for the militia at the front; an ill old lady of Mundaka whom I knew, a most virtuous old Catholic who had run all the church charities of the village and was indeed rather reactionary at her unpolitical heart, was sent to the common prison for six years because her son had been a civil servant of Aguirre's Government. All these cases were published in the *Gaceta del Norte*, the Fascist paper now established in Bilbao; the conquerors did not think these sentences barbarous but natural, and worthy of the world's attention. The word humanity, the idea that women should not be kept as political prisoners, the not so very civilised theory that people are not necessarily punished for the behaviour of their relatives, these were things that meant less than nothing to the men for whom Germany and Italy had gained the victory. For the first time in the history of the world the rule of blood and the class war were set up in Vizcaya.

It is my belief, and history will show, that this oppression will not last for ever. Centuries of struggle, the five wild oceans of adventure have made of the Basque a man with infinite reserves of strength, and silence. His shoulders are free under any régime; his classless moral state is not written in constitutions but in history and pre-history, not defended by arms but by an immovable consciousness of its superiority to all others. Because he has never been a slave or villein, the Basque is better than his neighbour, and he knows it.

He is proud, too, of the year in which he governed himself; of how he kept order and the true church's peace, gave freedom to all consciences, fed the poor, cured the wounded, ran all the services of a government without a single quarrel, either between executive and people or between the widely divergent theorists in his executive. Alone in all Spain he showed that he was fit to rule; where others murdered and butchered, terrorised the working class and sold their country to foreigners, the Basque bound together his little nation in strong bands of human solidarity, as strong as the sides of his great steel trawlers. His was a real People's Front, without any dark motive of policy to form it. Its roots were very deep, and its lineage very old, but its leaves are full of a greenness and virtue that are renewed every year; they gather everlasting life and health from the health of the classless society, and they stand unshaken in the fire and the explosions to give shade to future law-givers who are the people's choice. Their symbol, and their history, is Gernika's Tree.

INDEX